Kamal Salhi (ed.)

French in and out of France

Language Policies, Intercultural Antagonisms and Dialogue

PETER LANG

Oxford · Bern · Berlin · Bruxelles · Frankfurt a.M. · New York · Wien

Bibliographic information published by Die Deutsche Bibliothek
Die Deutsche Bibliothek lists this publication in the Deutsche
Nationalbibliografie; detailed bibliographic data is available in the
Internet at ‹http://dnb.ddb.de›.

British Library and Library of Congress Cataloguing-in-Publication Data:
A catalogue record for this book is available from *The British Library*,
Great Britain, and from *The Library of Congress*, USA

ISSN 1422-9005
ISBN 3-906768-47-3
US-ISBN 0-8204-5859-7

© Peter Lang AG, European Academic Publishers, Bern 2002
Hochfeldstrasse 32, Postfach 746, CH-3000 Bern 9, Switzerland
info@peterlang.com, www.peterlang.com, www.peterlang.net

Printed in Germany

French in and out of France

Modern French Identities

Edited by Peter Collier

Volume 18

PETER LANG

Oxford · Bern · Berlin · Bruxelles · Frankfurt a.M. · New York · Wien

Contents

Acknowledgements

This work is the product of several years of fruitful research as well as two years of co-ordination and academic stress and, often, overwhelming professional demands. Many people throughout these years bore with me and yet always responded promptly and efficiently to my endless queries; to the contributors I owe a great deal.

I should like to thank the following colleagues for the advisory role they played during the preparation of this volume.

Dr Farida Abu-Haidar   (University of Oxford)
Mrs Marie-Anne Hintze   (University of Leeds)
Professor Anne Judge   (University of Surrey)
Professor Rachel Killick   (University of Leeds)

Finally, I am grateful to Elizabeth Kapff, the copy-editor, for her insightful comments on the manuscript and for the attention received from Dr Peter Collier, the Editor of the series, *Modern French Identities* at Peter Lang.

Kamal Salhi

Introduction: French Within and Without France

The studies of language issues within and beyond France collected in this book are the result of a long collaborative research project carried out between fellow scholars working in British, Irish, French and Australian universities. These qualitative and quantitative studies have been guided by recent developments in policies and attitudes with regard to the situation of French and the languages with which it coexists in Europe, Africa, the Americas, Australia and the Middle East. The work collected here is representative only of the French language and its effects in the world, and the geographical coverage has no claims to exhaustiveness. The theme of the volume is dictated very largely by the nature of this particular area of language study and the attempts that have been made to steer developments in the recent history of the French language, either in terms of policy, social attitudes, literary and cultural work or of conflicts centred on language issues. The various chapters are therefore intended to constitute a coherent pattern of distinct but closely related elements. They concentrate primarily on three European countries: France, Switzerland and Belgium; three North African countries: Morocco, Algeria and Tunisia; the countries of West and Southern Africa; three Middle Eastern countries: Syria, Egypt and Lebanon; the Americas; and Australia.

The first two chapters of this book set the cultural, political and linguistic parameters of the areas under discussion. They elucidate the concept of *la francophonie* and examine France's approach to linguistic policymaking.

The last three decades have seen changes in all these countries in their educational, political, and cultural systems, and in the introduction of new legislation. Many of these developments have affected the use of various languages in education and institutions, and ultimately the very role of French and other languages in the societies and regions concerned. Not all of the language issues dealt with here, however, are confined to policy and planning. Indeed, some of the issues discussed would have arisen even if there had been agreement, resulting from either consensus or political diktat, on the language or languages to be used and taught in each country. Planning for the role of different languages in a given society or nation, and the planning or development of the forms of languages that will best satisfy this role, are often inextricably inter- twined, and both the forms and the functions of various languages must be considered in the formulation of language policy. Only when the implementation stage has been reached can the role and the form of a given language be successfully disassociated from one another. Educa- tion, for example, is often affected by issues that have more to do with social, economic, political, cultural, and religious questions of a general nature than with education as such. During the last three decades the situation of French in these countries has been affected by many different policies and attitudes, official and unofficial, and responses and reactions have come from various parts of the public, organisations and individuals concerned. Some of these policies have been tried and found wanting.

La francophonie appears to be the term most frequently used to refer to the nations, provinces, regions and communities where French is spoken. *Francité* is another term used to describe the heterogeneous group of traits characteristic of French civilisation, and can also refer to the latter's intellectual and cultural qualities, expressible perhaps as 'l'âme de la francophonie'.[1] *Francophonie* and *francité* are now being associated with, or even replaced by, ethnicity in theoretical studies with an emphasis on 'the French ethnic community where French is the mother tongue of the population; primarily associated with Europe and Canada.'[2] An ethnic group is a people of common genetic origin, so that this definition is used to distinguish those communities who are not only Francophone but also genetically related to the French, as in Canada and Europe, as distinct from those Francophone communities whose links are historical, linguistic and cultural, but not genetic, as in Africa, the Indian Ocean or the Caribbean.

1   Cf. Xavier Deniau, *La Francophonie, Que sais-je?* (Paris: Presses Universitaires de France, 1983).

2   Colin Old, *Quebec Relations with Francophonie, a Political Geographic Perspec- tive*, Carleton Geography Discussion Papers, 1 (Ottawa: Carleton University, 1984), p. iii.

In linguistic practice this book also explores how, regardless of their high sounding egalitarian motto, French governments have crafted a very unequal hierarchy of ethnolinguistic privileges. This hierarchy has ranked nationalities of some Francophone countries or regions into developmental categories, roughly corresponding to a people, a nationality or a nation. Each of these formal groups has had to be content with a specific degree of cultural autonomy, depending on its assigned attributes of 'civilisation'. French has remained the prestige language of the majority of *la francophonie*. This hierarchisation has institutionalised the post-Independence governments' wavering and local commitment to the development of native, non-French languages, and, in formal and legal terms, their explicit and universal commitment to the status and prestige of French. It represents these governments' wish to develop a complex system of rules within which national representatives might develop their own literary languages, yet appreciate the enduring civic value of French. It also represents a central piece of evidence in recent debates about the character of post-colonial national policies. Were they basically egalitarian and pluralistic? Or were they hierarchical and unitary? No doubt they were a combination of both, a combination structured nonetheless by the imperative need for state order and central power.

This ethnolinguistic hierarchy goes some way to show that language policy and reform have been of no less strategic value to post-colonial Francophones than the definition of ethnic groupings or the demarcation of national territorial borders. Language has been even more important as a territory of the mind, the most primordial source of communal identity, and thereby a powerful means by which to define the peripheries and govern them. For most of the Francophone world, language has a purely instrumental value. The French-language hierarchy transformed the Marxian logic of history, in post-Independence Africa for example, into the post-colonial structure of nationality. The hierarchy translated the horizontal progress of people through time into the vertical relationships of people in space. When it ranked the Francophone nationalities as civilised or primitive, it locked them into both historical logic and spatial structure, and therefore into positions of dominance or submission.

One might theorise about an ascending scale of freedom, by which French-speaking people, during the last 30 or 40 years, have used distinct levels of speech such as meaningful sounds and forms, as well as combined meanings, not only to communicate but also to express themselves more creatively. But what may be true for language in the abstract is not necessarily true for language in society. When faced with language planning and politics, the ascending scale of freedom is turned on its head. Clear concepts suddenly give way to difficult choices. The self-evident forms and meanings of language give way to political conflict and cultural antagonism. Language planners and linguists are confronted by the demands of the governments for political control, but also face the newly articulated rights and freedoms of the national identities – who presume to know better what to do with the sounds and signs of their peoples' languages. When the post-colonial governments, especially in North and Sub-Saharan Africa, set in motion a pattern of native language recognition, they admitted their dependence on national leaders of cultural and ethnic movements to help implement cultural and language reforms. Like the linguists with their various theories, ethnic leaders have their own agendas in mind with regard to the creation of national language cultures. Their challenge is to establish a group identity in which both intellectuals and illiterates could recognise themselves.

In much of the recent linguistic scholarship of the Francophones, the meaning of language is reducible to its unproblematic and verifiable component parts. Language reform and policy and the creation of national literary cultures always depend on the technical acts of linguists to ensure effective systems. However, as the chapters of this book show, their success depend perhaps even more on the broader political and social, and often radical changes within which they operate. In public forums as well as in private communication language has remained a very creative and problematic means of expression, open to several layers of political, scholarly and national complexity. Once written down and learned by people already sharing a common homeland, kinship, ethnic background or religion, language becomes a powerful means of self-representation and a symbol of national consciousness. The theories and methods that are designed for practice are thus often rent apart by its windstorm. Language construction becomes charged with all the hopes, fears, and passions of the post-colonial era. The struggle to build a language community, like the struggle to build a common political culture, is weighed down by the competition of group interests and by chronic backwardness. As millions of men, women and children have become the focus of education efforts, language planners and national representatives have tried to achieve, in a few years of often centralised planning, that which had taken centuries of evolution in parts of Europe. The difficulties of creating a 'common speech' and establishing dialogue between sections of the French-speaking populations were compounded by the scores of languages of the African countries, most of which are much less developed than French for purposes of national communication.

The language issue also dominates Quebec's social and political life. The sometimes uneasy coexistence of French and English, which has dominated social transactions for decades, often makes the headlines. On the French-speaking side, the concept of Quebec as a 'French society' is predominant among people mostly of French origin, but also from other backgrounds, and concerns the majority of Quebecers. This view is strongly supported by language legislation. The English-speaking section of the population, which includes Canadians of English origin and immigrants from elsewhere in the world, tends to have reservations about language legislation promoting French and argues for official bilingualism. Language policy and bilingualism in Canada, in general, continue to be controversial issues and sometimes generate heated debate. Although Canada's Francophone provinces have remained relatively stable, there remains a gap between the opinions and attitudes of French-speakers and English-speakers with regard to language policies that have been designed to make the provinces more bilingual. Over the last three decades successive Quebec governments have made commitments to the promotion of a distinctively 'French society' through language policy, while protecting the historic rights of the province's English-speaking minority and maintaining good relations with English-speaking Canada and the United States. If it is true that the only politics available to a society are those of its geography, then the policies of Quebec and New Brunswick will tend to be aimed at enabling relatively small areas in completely, or nearly completely, English-speaking North America to remain essentially French in their culture and outlook. This means enabling the populations of these provinces to use French in all walks of life and, indeed, ensuring that all residents in these areas, whatever their origins, adopt French as a common language, a unifying factor in social transactions of all kinds that supports ideological and political efforts to create cohesion.

It can be argued that the main concern of most Francophones in North America – and Europe – is to ensure equality of access to services in their own language. This is why they support plurality and decentralisation, which should assure Francophones of receiving services without being subject to delay or waiting for translations to be made. The 1977 Quebec charter of the French language, for example, imposes French as the language of the workplace and thus makes it obligatory for employers to use French in communications sent to their personnel. Also, any company employing 50 or more persons in Quebec must undertake measures leading to a certificate of 'Francisation' confirming that the company applies the different provisions of the Charter and has implemented the general use of French in its Quebec operations. Under the Charter, Quebec consumers have the right to be informed and assisted in French by businesses, public signs have to be in French, and commercial literature and similar publications for circulation in Quebec must be in French. Although the Charter has been amended several times, relaxing or reinforcing the implementation of particular *francisation* measures, bilingualism is generally accepted. In Quebec French is imposed as a norm in schools, subject to limited exceptions. There is universal access to French public education, while English education is freely available in the public system at the university and college levels, and to a more limited extent at the primary level. Residents from other countries and Canadian citizens may also enrol their children in English-speaking private schools or partly state-subsidised schools, many of which teach in both English and French.

A major characteristic of most Francophone societies that have emerged as independent entities is that although they constitute 'states' they have not yet become 'nations', that although their members share a common division of political labour, to a significant degree they have not developed a feeling of mutual identification, of belonging together as a group, that although they form a 'political community' they do not have a sense of community. The lack of a deeper sense of a 'Francophone community' on a society-wide basis arises from the fact that intense loyalties based on vertical divisions such as race, religion and language, have not been domesticated, moderated or subordinated to a larger national and regional loyalty. Such vertical divisions have implications different from those stemming from horizontal divisions such as class, occupation or vocation within an overriding society-wide loyalty. In the event of alienation, horizontal divisions may constitute a threat to incumbent governments and, in extreme cases, the constitutional framework, but vertical divisions are likely to threaten the very existence of the state or political community, as is evident in the case of many North and Sub-Saharan African countries, and to a certain extent Canada.

Although this pattern of incongruence between state and nation, between political community and sense of community, has diverged radically from the situation in most Western European countries, it parallels, in large measure, their historical experience. In most of these countries, too, the state has preceded the nation. Typically many different cultural and linguistic groups were brought together, through force and diplomacy, under a common ruler. Over a period of several centuries, such groups, within the womb of a single state, finally emerged into a nation. In this long process of nation-building, war and resource mobilisation for war played a very significant role. On the contrary, not all African post-Independence states, for example, have succeeded in welding their constituent groups into a single nation and, when confronted with internal or external crises, have themselves collapsed as a result of the pressure from such groups, as is the case of Algeria, Congo/Zaire, Ivory Coast and other African countries. There is no empirical evidence from history that a sense of community must precede the formation of a political community.

A political community has in most cases preceded the emergence and growth of a sense of community, although the original political community itself was either the result of conquest, the consequence of the convergence of certain instrumental purposes or an historical accident. Therefore, the problem of the political survival of the new post-colonial states is an especially acute one, for the hallmark of such states is an ineffective sense of community in a setting of the greatest stress. This sense of community has derived from opposition to colonial rule, but with the achievement of independence this source has in many cases ceased to be a potent factor in the creation of political unity. These states are confronted by a series of crises in political development; crises that arise as traditional societies undergo modernisation. Moreover, this integration crisis is often aggravated by, and at the same time a reflection of, a crisis in communication. At all times, language is one of the most important tools of communication and is in itself an expression in short-hand of cultural differences. Cultural differentiation finds its immediate manifestation in controversy over the role of different languages in education and administration. The social mobilisation of different cultural groups, not possessing French as a common language in this instance, but nonetheless highly relevant politically, makes both political management and nation-building very difficult. This is so because the capacity to communicate across regional and national groupings and between élite and mass is at the heart of the post-colonial political process and the cohesion of nations.

Regarding the significance of communication in nation-building, one could, however, reject the traditional concept of the nation as a group possessing some common objective characteristics, such as language or history. In reality many nations are not possessed of any of these characteristics. French is spoken in various independent 'nations', whereas within France, there is French but also, for example, Basque, Breton, Catalan and the German dialect of Alsace. In Switzerland, four different languages are spoken, the dominant one being German. At the same time, German is the language not only of Germany but of Austria and Luxembourg. Therefore, one should rather consider the question of nationality in this case and provide a functional definition, distinguishing sharply between society and community. In this view society would be a group of individuals made interdependent by the division of labour, the production and distribution of goods and services, whereas a community would consist of people who have learned to communicate with each other and to understand each other for purposes well beyond the mere interchange of services. It is nonetheless communicative effectiveness that is of fundamental importance, for this is what allows members of the nation to feel their commonality. In the end it is always through the symbols of language that intercultural communication takes place. Although it is not imperative that a nation should consist of a single language group, it is essential that at least the politically relevant strata of the political community, which may belong to different language groups, are able to communicate with each other through some common linguistic instrument.

In looking at each country considered in this book, one is impressed by the large-scale governmental efforts aimed at promoting language policies designed to equip the population for internal, national or regional communication. Various sectors of national life affected by language planning are the administration and institutions, and the educational and media systems. In the administrative and institutional spheres there are the questions of official languages and minority languages. In the other sectors there is the question of what language or languages should serve; and at what stages of education, for example, as the medium of instruction, languages should be made the subject of study and communication. These aspects are obviously closely interrelated. A language such as French, Arabic or English, that has been made an official language, regardless of any direct intervention in the educational system, comes to occupy an important part in school and university curricula as well in political life. Explorations into the official status and the nature of prospects for official status, of French and the languages within which it coexists may provide, in this book, a highly valuable guide to future individual monographic studies.

Within this outlook, attention is also paid in this volume to the Australian experience. The case of Australia could provide an illuminating example for policymakers in the English-speaking world, particularly Britain, where decisions on languages in education are currently under discussion. Many of the assumptions on which Australian policy is based have become commonplace among specialists in language development, but questions about the translation of these objectives into practice remain to be answered. Multilingualism, pluralism and multiculturalism are facts of Australian life and represent resources for language policy and cultural developments.

Above and beyond their contributions to furthering our knowledge of the sociolinguistic situation in a large part of the Francophone world, Australia and the nationalism about which we have hitherto been woefully ignorant, the studies by the contributors of this book aim to provide examples of the type of interdisciplinary and multi-level inquiries in which the field of languages and cultures stands in need. The data and material they examine and analyse are language-related and linguistic, historical and cultural, social and demographic, educational and legal, sporadic and chronological. The questions that they seek to answer via this material are both synchronic and diachronic, theoretical and applied, descriptive and predictive.

GABRIELLE PARKER

The Fifth Republic and the Francophone Project

The launch of the Francophone Project and the establishment of the Fifth Republic did not coincide exactly. The Fourth Republic invested in the promotion of French language, and its successor pursued largely the same policy and collected the dividends. Both the word, and the notion of, *francophonie* re-emerged in 1962, four years after the foundation of the Republic[1] and long after the word was originally coined at the end of the nineteenth century. Language policy was elaborated over the years, and adapted to international circumstances and the particular approach taken by each successive President. In the course of time structures were developed to provide the framework for, and means to implement, these policies. The Secrétariat d'État chargé de la Francophonie, for instance, was only created in 1986.

Continuity and a large measure of consensus have been the hallmarks of French language policy. France's linguistic and cultural policies are subsets of the country's foreign policy. The French language is perceived as the symbol of French identity. In consequence, to promote the language is to promote France and French interests; to protect the language is to protect French interests; to protect French interests is to protect the language: 'La défense de la langue française est devenue, au fil du temps, un enjeu identitaire largement consensuel.'[2]

There has been continuity in two specific areas throughout the four decades of the Fifth Republic: the political consensus regarding the understanding that the extension of the country's influence and prestige depended on the medium of language; and the fact that French foreign policy and international relations were inextricably entwined with France's

---

1   See, inter alia: Xavier Deniau, *La Francophonie* (Paris: PUF, 1983, 1995), p. 3; Michel Tétu, *Qu'est-ce que la Francophonie?* (Vanves: Hachette, 1997), p. 17.

2   Jean-Michel Djian, *La Politique culturelle* (Brussels: Le Monde-Éditions, 1996), p. 40.

external cultural project. Language is not an independent entity. The linguistic dimension requires its own specific foreign policy, which is a necessary condition of its *rayonnement*, or influence, and necessary in order to avoid it becoming weakened. The status of French in international organisations is seen as an index for the language's health, and action can be taken on the basis of these indices to improve the situation or halt any decline.[3]

The choice of any specific period for detailed scrutiny is bound to be arbitrary, but the Fifth Republic has been especially active in the field of language policy.[4] It has also been responsible for the addition of a fourth attribute of the nation to the text of the Constitution first drafted in 1946: apart from the national emblem, the national anthem and the national motto, this now specifies the national language as well: 'La langue de la République est le français.'[5] However, an attempt on the part of the Sénat in 1996 to introduce a clause relating to *francophonie*[6] was opposed by the Minister of Justice, M. Toubon, on the grounds that statements of this kind properly belonged to French foreign policy and could not be the concern of the Constitution.

The introductory paragraphs of *Le projet culturel extérieur de la France* – originally part of the Socialist government's manifesto and adopted by the Assemblée nationale in 1983 – highlighted the continuity of linguistic policy a quarter of a century after the inception of the Fifth Republic. They stressed the innovative and original project that defined

3   Jean-Marie Pontier, *Droit de la langue française* (Paris: Dalloz, 1997), p. 26.
4   Pontier (pp. 5–11) surveys language legislation from the *Ancien Régime* to the present. Following Francis I and Villers-Cotterêts (Ordonnance sur le fait de justice, 1539), and the series of laws inspired by the Revolution passed under the first two Republics, no laws relating to language were enacted until 1975, when the Loi Bas-Lauriol was adopted. This was supplanted by Loi 94-665 of 4 August 1994, also known as the 'Loi Toubon', after Jacques Toubon, the Minister of Justice at this time.
5   Art. 2, French Constitution, 1992. Pontier (p. 20 and pp. 35–6) notes that this form of words was chosen by the Sénat to replace the original draft, 'le français est la langue de la République', in order to take account of the fact that French is no longer solely the language of France.
6   According to Pontier (p. 36), the proposed clause read: 'La République participe au développement de la solidarité et de la coopération entre les États et les peuples ayant le français en partage.'

a foreign *cultural* policy, ensuring that it was underpinned by appropriate administrative structures and financial support, and boasting of the unmatched resources invested in sustaining the project.

The text also recognised General de Gaulle's pioneering and inspiring role in this field, and set it in context: the aim was to reinstate France's global status and influence, which had been weakened by the Second World War. Both language and culture were explicitly identified as the joint means to this end. The country's overall prestige depended on their expansion and the extension of their influence. The education of local élites in French educational establishments was seen as a means to this end, as were scientific and technical co-operation, which was intended to assist the promotion of France as a country with a modern image and generate external trade. Development aid was associated with the defence of strategic interests and the protection of supply channels. This was to be secured via bilateral agreements, which were to guarantee that French would be taught and used as a medium of instruction. In the first instance, this applied to emerging nations, and for the most part aid was 'réservée aux nouveaux États issus de notre empire colonial et placés dans notre sphère d'influence'.[7] However, it also came to be extended to other parts of the world, Latin America in particular, in order to facilitate international co-operation outside the superpowers' spheres of influence in regions unaffected by the Cold War.[8]

Francophonie

It was not by coincidence that this term was adopted at the same time as Algerian independence in 1962: Algeria's move to independence was the last of a series that started in 1954 and heralded the demise of France's empire. Nevertheless, the collective psyche was not yet entirely ready to accept that French colonial influence was dead, to be replaced by the hay concept of *la Francophonie*. As Tétu relates in his history of the

7 Ministère des relations extérieures, *Le Projet culturel extérieur de la France* (Paris: La Documentation française, 1984), p. 9.
8 Ministère des relations extérieures, p. 9.

term,[9] the French were slow to adopt it. Indeed, it still does not raise much passion, as the current Ministre délégué auprès du ministre des Affaires étrangères, chargé de la Francophonie, Charles Josselin, readily admits.[10] The term is defined in several different ways,[11] which tend to blur in the minds and utterances both of ordinary users and of politicians.

French supporters and historians of *la Francophonie*, like to credit non-metropolitan French politicians with the initiative.[12] Dominique Gallet claims that for some 20 years Presidents Léopold Sédar Senghor, Habib Bourguiba, Hamani Diori and Prince Norodom Sihanouk persistently and vainly asked France to establish a community of French-speaking states. Gallet interprets de Gaulle's muted response as caution: immediately after a number of African countries had obtained their independence, prudence required that this 'necessary' undertaking should not be compromised by suspicions of neo-colonialism. However, in his view, de Gaulle's caution with regard to the establishment of formal institutions was balanced by his decisive influence on the French-speaking movement, 'conçu comme un instrument du droit des peuples à disposer d'eux-mêmes et du refus de l'hégémonie américaine'.[13] The first Francophone meeting took place in 1969 in Niamey: de Gaulle sent Malraux as his representative.

9   Tétu, pp. 16–19.

10   Ch. Josselin, *'Discours introductif' au dîner-débat du cercle Richelieu Senghor*, 4 November 1997. Text provided by the Ministère des Affaires étrangères.

11   See Deniau, pp. 15–24, and Tétu, p. 14: *la francophonie* refers to people who use French habitually as their language of communication; *la Francophonie* refers to the official body or bodies that bring together governments, countries and organisations that use French to communicate; *l'espace francophone* does not refer so much to a linguistic or geographical space as to the realm of culture. Tétu describes *l'espace francophone* as the least defined ('la plus floue'), but most productive ('la plus féconde') of these terms. Maurice Druon, Secrétaire perpétuel de l'Académie française, does not appear to be concerned whether these words are capitalised or not, but adds a fourth definition, adding a spiritual dimension to the word: 'un sens spirituel et mystique [...] le sentiment d'appartenir à une même communauté'.

12   Cf. in particular, Deniau, pp. 9–12; also Dominique Gallet, *Pour une ambition francophone. Le désir et l'indifférence* (Paris: L'Harmattan, 1995).

13   Gallet, p. 7. Deniau (p. 54) also notes de Gaulle's 'discrétion' with regard to *la Francophonie*.

The result of this first meeting was the creation of the Agence de la coopération culturelle et technique (ACTT) at Niamey (Niger) in March 1970, bringing together 21 countries. A plethora of institutions and organisations were to follow over the years. However, the birth of *la Francophonie* is frequently dated from that of its first institution, which was to be renamed the Agence de la Francophonie in 1998, by which time it represented 49 nations.

Philippe Rossillon lists the Francophone institutions in his *Atlas de la langue française*, published in 1995. He gives full credit to de Gaulle for agreeing to Rossillon's proposals in 1965 – from the broad lines of linguistic policy to the appropriate inter-ministerial organisations to be charged with defining this policy: 'Ce fut le Haut Comité créé par le décret du 31 mars 1966 et rattaché au Premier Ministre qui était alors Georges Pompidou.'[14]

Rossillon became its first *rapporteur général*. His contribution to the cause of *la Francophonie* was indeed acknowledged in the obituaries published after his death in September 1997, and in particular in the *Hommage* written by Jean-Marc Léger: 'il n'est pas excessif de dire qu'il en a été l'un des prophètes et l'un des principaux artisans.'[15]

In the conceptual history of *la Francophonie*, de Gaulle's speeches in Pnom-Penh and Montreal are seen as defining moments in the shaping of this concept. In connection with the latter event, Gallet quotes Jean de Broglie, who wrote in 1967 of the 'Vive le Québec libre!' episode that it gave French diplomacy a new dimension: that of *francophonie*.[16]

It is the very fact that language and culture go hand in hand that is both meant to serve the Francophone project and that arouses suspicions of neo-colonialism. This 'neo-colonialism' relates to old ambitions, as Churchill foresaw: 'the empires of the future are the empires of the

---

14   Philippe Rossillon (ed.), *Atlas de la langue française* (Paris: Bordas, 1995), p. 18.
15   Jean-Michel Léger, 'Hommage à Philippe Rossillon', *AFI* (*Année francophone internationale*) (Quebec: 1998), p. 297.
16   Gallet, p. 78. See also Tétu, pp. 240–]2, where De Broglie's article in *Le Monde* of 5–6 November 1967 is quoted. De Broglie interprets de Gaulle's initiative in the following terms: 'Il faut le dire ouvertement. La francophonie sera finalement politique, ou elle ne sera pas. [...] Mais par-delà, le sens politique de cette affaire a bien été de donner une dimension nouvelle à la diplomatie française: celle de la *francophonie*' (de Broglie's emphasis).

mind.'[17] Austin and Panter-Brick have traced the evolution of the concept
from a strategy of resistance to Anglo-Saxon hegemony that led to the
creation of a fortress-like structure to shelter French-speaking countries
under the protection of the French flag, to the adoption of a network
strategy.[18] This strategy is based on the development and exploitation of
a multiplicity of networks, including alliances between countries with a
similar stake in fighting cultural monopolies. The Francophone community that this has created is one that welcomes linguistic and cultural
diversity. Austin and Panter-Brick also trace the resolution of political
obstacles, such as the official representation of French-speaking minorities within larger states (e.g. in Canada, Belgium and Switzerland) as
well as countries with mainly French-speaking populations. This problem
was resolved by the agreement that government ministers should be
present at intergovernmental summits, allowing both central and regional administrations to be represented. The first Francophone summit at
which regional governments participated was held in 1986 in Paris.[19] It
left unresolved the issue of representation for Francophone minorities
within larger countries that do not belong to *la Francophonie*, such as
the populations of the Val d'Aoste, Louisiana, New England or Pondi-
cherry, in contrast to countries such as Romania, Moldavia, Bulgaria or
Egypt, where French is not particularly widely used as a medium of
communication.

Histories of French cultural diplomacy since 1945 have been published by a number of authors and bodies. More specifically, *Une politique pour le français*, published in 1996 by the Ministère des affaires
étrangères, traces '50 ans d'action linguistique'.[20] Although it is a useful

17   In Alistair Pennycook, *The Cultural Politics of English as an International Lan-
     guage* (London: Longman, 1994), p. 131.
18   Dennis Austin and Keith Panter-Brick, 'Le Post-Colonialisme', in Françoise de la
     Serre, Jacques Leruez and Helen Wallace (eds), *Les Politiques étrangères de la
     France et de la Grande-Bretagne depuis 1945. L'inévitable ajustement* (Oxford
     and Paris: Presses de la Fondation des Sciences Politiques and Berg, 1996), pp.
     165–85.
19   On the relationships between Paris, Quebec and Ottawa, and the negotiations at
     this time, see Tétu (pp. 237–42) for an account of the final compromise on rep-
     resentation.
20   Ministère des Affaires étrangères, *Une politique pour le français* (Paris: La Docu-
     mentation française, 1996).

reference work, it is expository, rather than analytical, in nature. A year earlier the authors of a survey of French foreign policy since 1945, both former senior figures in the French diplomatic service, described the vision that has informed foreign policy since 1945 as a strong idea buttressed by a strong political vision. They acknowledged that those who set it in place were worried by two distinct concerns: how to compensate for the loss of Empire, and how to make up for the loosening of the close ties that once bound the former Empire to France. The best response, it was felt at the time, was to increase the power of attraction held by France's cultural and technological significance. It was deemed paramount that France should continue to exercise global influence and extend that influence to newly founded states. New and different methods had to be found to do this, in particular by meeting the needs of developing countries. Turning to Europe, which was then still in the process of defining and shaping itself, the authors see France as seeking to exercise intellectual leadership – including technical and scientific leadership – as a means of preserving its original identity. This notion implied that France was *destined* – a Gaullist concept – to be a leader of other nations. It also implied that being led, influenced rather than influencing, necessarily entails alterity and induces an alteration of personality and loss of identity.

Policy Tools

L.-J. Calvet has traced the history of French linguistic policy as a specific aspect of French general cultural foreign policy.[21] According to Calvet, 'C'est avec la Révolution que débute une action culturelle et linguistique de la France.' However, this action relied on private initiatives supported by various ministries (such as the Ministère des Affaires étrangères, or the Ministère des colonies). It was not until 1909 that the Ministère des Affaires étrangères introduced a service 'des écoles et des oeuvres françaises'. As Calvet explains, France's approach to cultural matters in

21   Ministère des Affaires étrangères, *Histoire de la diplomatie culturelle des origines à 1995* (Paris: La Documentation française, 1995), pp. 92–3.

foreign policy was shaped during the Second World War. In 1941 de
Gaulle created the *commissariats*, the precursors of ministries. The 'commissariat aux Affaires étrangères' was divided into a 'direction des affaires politiques' and a 'service des affaires administratives et consulaires
et des oeuvres françaises à l'étranger',[22] which became the Direction
générale des relations culturelles et de oeuvres françaises à l'étranger
after the liberation of France, and has continued to exist to the present
under various names.[23]

A number of different tools are used to support these policies.
Firstly, there is the organisation's infrastructure: the network of personnel
within and outside France whose training and functions are focused on
the promotion of French language and culture, including the teaching of
both. Secondly, there are various institutions, including the legislative
framework, the different ministries and their varying remits within France
and world-wide. Policy is maintained by concerted planning and the
allocation of financial resources for implementation. Finally, policy is
also informed by academic research, scholarship and know-how.

There has been investment in personnel, institutions, planning and
policy under all five Presidents, always in the spirit of the initiatives
taken by de Gaulle in London during the Second World War and at the
time of the Liberation.

The first decade after the Liberation saw the establishment of the
institutions, networks and tools with which France's foreign policy objectives could be pursued. The Direction générale des relations culturelles et des oeuvres françaises à l'étranger within the Ministère des
affaires étrangères was founded by decree on 13 April 1945.[24] It was to
put in place a network of attachés culturels, French schools abroad,
Instituts français, teachers on secondment from the Ministry of Education, a system of *lecteurs* and *lectrices* assigned to foreign universities,
and opportunities for foreign learners and future teachers of French to
immerse themselves in French language and culture at the CIEP (Centre
international d'études pédagogiques) in Sèvres. The mission of the Direction – under its various guises – has not only been to promote French

22   *Journal officiel de la France libre*, 14 October 1941, quoted in Louis-Jean Calvet,
     Les Politiques linguistiques (Paris: PUF, 1996), p. 100.
23   Calvet, pp. 99–111.
24   Calvet, p. 100.

culture, but to do so via the medium of language. This mission, as Calvet notes, eventually came to encompass the promotion of science and technology, again through the medium of the French language, an aim that implies a substantial investment of resources in the teaching of French. According to Calvet, France sends more teachers abroad than any other country: 'sa politique culturelle extérieure est avant tout une politique de diffusion de la langue française.'[25] The high levels of investment in personnel continue, but there has been a shift from the linguistic to the cultural front. The mission of French *centres culturels* across the world is fourfold: to promote the French language; to disseminate information about France; to promote French cultural products; and to foster dialogue and exchanges between the host culture and French culture.

In 1956 the Direction générale des relations culturelles became the Direction générale des affaires culturelles et techniques, its change of name reflecting an intention to integrate technical co-operation into the ministry's area of responsibility. Between 1956 and 1958 administrative responsibility for French teachers on assignment in Morocco, Tunisia, Laos, Cambodia and Vietnam switched from the Ministère des Affaires étrangères to the Ministère pour la Coopération. As of 1966, this was also to apply to those working in Algeria.[26]

There was steady growth from 1959 to 1969 on the basis of two consecutive five-year plans, which increased the resources devoted to external cultural policy. These plans provided for the consolidation of work in traditional areas of influence, as well as co-operation with, and aid to, newly independent countries.

This was also the *décennie Malraux*, a period marked by continuity of vision, ambition and confident dynamism, as well as an unprecedented shared sense of mission regarding cultural matters, in which language played a key role. Yet, paradoxically, the establishment of the ministry was the result of a combination of circumstances, rather than deliberate political thinking.[27] De Gaulle was not sure what to do with Malraux and the newly created ministry, and Malraux himself was equally unsure about its role. He was also rather unworldly and never fought successfully

---

25   Calvet, p. 99.
26   Ministère des affaires étrangères, *Une politique pour le français*, p. 31.
27   Djian, p. 69.

for the budgetary resources required to implement his policies.[28] Another paradox that casts doubt on the notion that such policies were planned, explicit and deliberate is highlighted by Roche and Pigniau in their 'histories' of cultural diplomacy: Couve de Murville, another long-standing figure in the de Gaulle administration who served as Ministre des Affaires étrangères between 1959 and 1968, dedicated half of the ministry's budget to Affaires culturelles et techniques throughout his time in office, yet hardly mentioned the subject in his memoirs.[29]

In 1969 science and technology were added to the responsibilities of the Direction générale. There was a shift in focus and priorities: on the one hand, young French people were encouraged to travel and work abroad in order to promote French culture, technology and know-how around the world; on the other, the teaching of French was now to be less reliant on French teachers working abroad and more on a network of *assistants pédagogiques* and advisers.[30] During Pompidou's presidency a number of institutions were created with the aim of defending the French language, such as the *commissions de terminologie* in a number of ministries. France also took steps to secure the status of French in European institutions.[31] Ten per cent of all teachers employed by the national education system were posted abroad.[32]

During Giscard d'Estaing's presidency, when the budget allocated to the promotion of French abroad dwindled, the *Rapport Rigaud (Les Relations culturelles extérieures)* of 1979 reaffirmed the commitment to co-operation and exchanges, albeit with reduced resources. Giscard's presidency is not regarded by commentators in the field to be one of the high points of French foreign policy (the ministry itself was downgraded in its governmental status), at least in terms of cultural work and language promotion. Gallet highlights two instances that support this judgement: the newly elected President responding to questions from the international media in English and, the disappointment of Cajuns from Louisi-

28   Djian, pp. 69–72.
29   Ministère des affaires étrangères, *Histoire de la diplomatie culturelle des origines à 1995*, pp. 104–5.
30   Ministère des affaires étrangères, *Une politique pour le français*.
31   See Deniau; and Gallet, pp. 9–10.
32   Ministère des affaires étrangères, *Histoire de la diplomatie culturelle des origines à 1995*, p. 104.

ana who had gone to great trouble to go and hear 'the French President' on a visit to their country, only to find him addressing his audience in English.[33]

The election of President Mitterrand in 1981 and subsequent changes in personnel did not, in fact, constitute a break with tradition in this domain of foreign policy. Rather, there was a return to earlier policies:

> La mise en oeuvre d'une politique de la langue française à l'étranger est l'une des constantes de notre action culturelle extérieure et elle figure au tout premier rang de ses priorités.

New structures were established to underpin this approach:

> La création, récemment annoncée, d'un Haut Conseil de la francophonie, d'un Haut Commisssariat de la langue française ainsi que d'un comité consultatif, traduit sur le plan de nos institutions la volonté du Gouvernement de relancer cette politique de la langue et de resserrer les liens unissant les différentes communautés francophones.[34]

The new policies were intended to implement the recommendations of the 1979 Rigaud report, with regard to exchanges, for instance. They focused on radio and television projects: Radio France Internationale was involved in the 1982–7 five-year plan, and the first TV5 programme (in association with Belgian and Swiss networks) was broadcast in January 1984. As well as continuing Pompidou's work with the creation of organisations dedicated to the study and defence of the language within France (such as the Délégation générale à la langue française), Mitterrand was also concerned with the wider world of *la Francophonie*, partly thanks to the influence of his old African friends, Senghor and Houphouët-Boigny.[35] The creation of the Haut Conseil de la Francophonie and Francophone summits were his initiatives, and Gaullists tend to attribute Mitterrand's work in the Francophone movement to his Gaullist leanings.

1984 also saw the creation of a Direction du français. This development was part of a policy intended to be 'offensive', 'visant à valoriser

33   Gallet, p. 10.
34   Ministère des relations extérieures, p. 27.
35   Gallet, pp. 29–30; *AFI*, pp. 259–60.

l'image de la France et du français, à agir sur les motivations des publics étrangers et à mobiliser les médias'.[36] *Assistants linguistiques* were replaced by *attachés linguistiques*, and there were reductions in the number of personnel teaching French abroad. The central government sought to exploit the success of devolution by involving the regions in national efforts to promote French abroad: the 'Français 2001' project was designed to initiate, and contribute to, international initiatives and partnerships at regional level. This period saw the use of marketing ideas and techniques for the promotion of French, a development in keeping with the increasing commodification of culture.

The Secrétariat d'État à la Francophonie was created in 1986, the year of the first summit of heads of state and government of French-speaking countries in Paris. The ambitions of the late 1980s rested on audiovisual policies, new technologies and co-operation in matters of education – with a focus on the teaching of French. These developments brought together several ministries in a first attempt to address the diversity and multiplicity of agencies involved in an issue that required careful co-ordination. The fall of the Berlin Wall in 1989, and subsequent developments in Central and Eastern Europe diverted interest and resources to that area for a while: former partnerships and old alliances were revived (Prague, Bucharest, Moscow) and France joined the scramble of Western states and organisations (Germany, the UK through The British Council, the United States) trying to fill the gap left by the collapse of Soviet influence.

In 1994 yet another reshuffle assigned cultural, scientific and technical relations to the Direction générale, thus bringing together linguistic and cultural policymaking. Further rationalisation in the summer of 1998 added co-operation to its responsibilities.

It should come as no surprise that Jacques Chirac has maintained the traditional approach. Annual Francophone events celebrating *la francophonie* have also been introduced under his Presidency. During the second set of celebrations in 1997, *Le Pèlerin Magazine* interviewed Margie Surdre, then Secrétaire d'État à la Francophonie. In an introductory paragraph headed '*La langue de chez nous*', the magazine described the context within which the interview was conducted:

36   Ministère des Affaires étrangères, *Une politique pour le français*, p. 35.

Le président Chirac veut faire de la langue française un outil de conquête pour permettre à la France d'accroître son rayonnement dans le monde, à la fois sur le plan culturel et économique. Plus de 200 millions d'hommes et de femmes parlent, à travers les cinq continents, la langue de chez nous.[37]

Simultaneously, though, the President expressed a veiled concern that *la Francophonie* did not stir sufficient commitment and enthusiasm among his compatriots: 'L'intérêt que suscite notre langue est très grand, même si les Français n'en ont pas toujours conscience. C'est pourquoi la francophonie reste une grande cause nationale.'[38]

French Interests

French interests include managing the decline of French power and influence, as discussed above, a desire to maintain France's position in the world order, the promotion of trade and investment and the perceived need to contain, or balance, the influence of the world's two superpowers. France's image abroad is paramount: political influence and commercial success are based on the country's prestige. Not only has the evolution of linguistic policy reflected the temperament and priorities of individual Presidents, whose concerns are major factors in policymaking, it has also been led by the development of French interests.

Throughout the history of French policy, from the *mission civilisatrice*, which implied that there could be no reciprocity and that the more 'advanced' nation was bestowing the benefits of its progress on the less privileged one, to co-operation, the common thread remains the control of resources and raw materials, the domination of trade routes and the containment of the inevitable processes of 'globalisation'.

France's former colonial power and influence has been replaced with a two-track approach. The first element in this approach is aid to

37   Gérard Bardy, ' "La langue française est un vrai outil de conquête". Une interview de Margie Surdre, secrétaire d'État à la Francophonie', *Le Pèlerin Magazine*, 5964, 21 March 1997, pp. 26–7. 'La langue de chez nous' is the title of a song by Yves Duteil. The song includes the line 'C'est une belle langue à qui sait la défendre.'

38   Bardy, p. 26.

Third World countries and the promotion of the French language. According to Raoul Girardet, French aid and co-operation policy 'recouvre les mêmes élans désintéressés et la même sincérité dans la générosité' as the colonial ideal. This idealistic view is characterised by the same understanding of relationships between cultures, and the same self-satisfied, complacent confidence in the superiority of Western models that once inspired the dynamic imperial expansion of the European powers' empires, justifying their actions with moral certainties.[39] The second element is the defence of French as an international language: the use of French and the adoption of French ways of thinking are indicative of France's *rayonnement*, and the nation's self-respect is at stake. Furthermore, the general use of French is perceived as the sole protection available to countries whose cultural identities are threatened by the global hegemony of the English language.[40]

This is a matter in which logic – or is it *bonne foi*? – seems to desert French officials: the hegemony of English is a cause of cultural alienation, while French provides a shield for speakers of other languages, protecting them against the erosion of cultural identity caused by the widespread use of English.

France's main concern is to gain political allies and thereby increase its influence on the world stage. The construction of alliances with French-speaking countries began in the 1940s: Africa had been 'France in exile' during the Second World War, and African alliances had been vital.

Diplomacy always serves national interests: if the French language is inextricably linked to diplomacy and international relations, the promotion of French becomes an essential component of diplomatic activity. Moreover, Gaullist notions, such as *grandeur* and position or *rang*, as in *retrouver son rang*, depend on the range and scope of the country's influence.

Conversely, the national interests of different countries may coincide. Language may provide a basis for solidarity between countries whose concerns might otherwise seem rather different. For instance, in Africa, aid and co-operation based on the notion of *la francophonie* have

39   Austin and Panter-Brick, p. 173.
40   Austin and Panter-Brick, p. 173.

been extended beyond France's former possessions to three former Belgian colonies (Zaire, Ruanda and Burundi), three former Portuguese colonies (Angola, Cap Verde and Mozambique), one former Spanish colony (Spanish Guinea) and three former British colonies (Mauritius, the Seychelles and Gambia), as well as Liberia.

Given the importance attached to the status of French as an official working language in international organisations, it is essential to ensure that as many Francophone states as possible are active in international bodies. The hope is that this will create a virtuous circle, ensuring that Francophone countries' interests coincide with those of France and that they vote in support of French positions in such fora.

The role of the cultural industries in the French economy is considerable. According to the French Ministère des Affaires étrangères, this sector provides 300,000 jobs, and the combined turnover of the publishing, graphic arts, television, music and cinema industries is estimated at approximately FF 170 billion.[41] Hence the grateful acknowledgements of the support provided by Francophone countries during the GATT negotiations that saw the recognition of *l'exception culturelle*, a concerted effort that has been quoted as an example of Francophone solidarity. Depending on whether habitual or occasional speakers are included, the number of people who speak French is calculated to be between 150 million and 400 million. However, these figures are not the whole story. As Surdre explains:

> Mais les 49 pays de la francophonie représentent un poids politique de plus de 400 millions d'habitants. Ce qui est très important, comme nous avons pu le constater lorsque la France a défendu 'l'exception culturelle' lors des négociations du Gatt, il y a trois ans.[42]

It is this *poids politique* that brings the Francophone project full circle. Brand image is not a uniquely French concern: similar preoccupations prompted Dr Nick Tate, the British Government's chief adviser on the school curriculum to underline the importance of establishing 'the authority of British English' when he addressed a conference on the teaching

41   Data provided by the Direction de la Communication et de l'Information (DCI), published in literature available from French embassies.
42   Cf. *Le Pèlerin Magazine*, p. 26.

of English in the European Union. According to a newspaper report of
his views,

> There was no need for those teaching English as a foreign language to take into
> account different versions of British English: 'Learners of English as a foreign
> language need a version that most people can understand. The language spoken
> by sub-groups within the UK or the USA does not provide this. Standard-British
> English does.'[43]

Linguistic Research and Development

There is a dimension of the Francophone project that concerns linguists
in particular: linguistic research and its applications. While de Gaulle
was already preoccupied with maintaining the status of French and its
promotion during the Second World War, Churchill and Roosevelt were
taking a close interest in BASIC English (the acronym stood for British
American Scientific International Commercial), which had been developed in 1930 by the Cambridge philosopher C. K. Ogden.[44]

Besides its systems, structures and manpower, *'Maison France'*
soon developed what could be described as its own R&D department,
which underpinned the promotion of the language. It was during the first
decade following the war that the rapid spread of English prompted the
development of teaching manuals and methodologies: this was the decade
of the 'Mauger'[45] and the drafting of *français fondamental* (1954). It
should be noted that US and French interest in, and awareness of, the

43 'English teachers urged to promote British English', *The Independent*, 3, 434, 22
    October 1997.
44 Pennycook, pp. 129–30. Pennycook quotes a letter from Churchill to the Secretary
    of the War Cabinet: 'I am very interested in the question of Basic English. The
    widespread use of this would be a gain to us far more durable and fruitful than the
    annexation of great provinces. It would also fit in with my ideas of closer union
    with the United States by making it even more worth while to belong to the
    English-speaking club.'
45 G. Mauger, *Cours de langue et de civilisation françaises* (Paris: Alliance fran-
    çaise/Hachette, 1950).

need to invest in linguistic research was simultaneous; the thinking was the same on both sides of the Atlantic, even though the funding available from public or private sources was not comparable.[46]

In 1951 the École normale supérieure at Saint-Cloud was charged with developing a simplified grammar and new pedagogic approaches to the teaching of French as a foreign language.[47] Similarly, the work of CREDIF (Centre de recherche pour l'enseignement et la diffusion du français, founded in 1950) supported and sustained the developments in French language policy that marked the early period of the Fifth Republic and especially the years 1959–69. The first issue of *Le français dans le monde* was published on 1 May 1961. A number of centres for research in applied linguistics were created outside the university network: BEL, the Bureau d'enseignement et de liaison (which later became BELC, the Bureau d'étude des langues et cultures) in 1959, and CALB, CRUEF, CAVILAM and CRAPEL at Besançon, Bordeaux, Vichy and Nancy respectively. These agencies were seen by the ministry as active partners in the implementation and execution of official policy. Their work supported the 900,000 teachers of French abroad. The raising of consciousness brought about by these developments bore fruit with the foundation of the Association des universités partiellement ou entièrement de langue française (AUPELF) in 1961 and the Fédération internationale des professeurs de français (FIF) in 1969. The Haut Comité de la langue fran-

46 See Pennycook, pp. 133–4: 'An important reason for the quick growth and consolidation of applied linguistics after the war was Defence Department spending and, later, money from the new National Defence Education Act of 1958, a response to a crisis in US confidence after the 1957 USSR launching of Sputnik. [...] As Mortimer Graves, the Executive Secretary of the American Council of Learned Societies, a major source of research funding, stated in 1950: "Ideological World War III has started [...]. In this war for men's minds, obviously the big guns of our armament is competence in languages and linguistics."' This candid statement can be contrasted and compared with the article by Daniel Coste, 'Recherche universitaire et enseignement du français langue étrangère. A propos d'une rencontre de 1961', *Langue française*, February 1998, p. 92. In relation to linguistic 'investment' in research on language-teaching, Coste notes that this is 'investissement à forte rentabilité, puisque sont ainsi obtenus les moyens de mener à bien des descriptions et d'introduire massivement la discipline dans la formation (ou du moins dans le perfectionnement professionnel) des enseignants.'
47 Ministère des affaires étrangères, *Une politique pour le français*, pp. 29–37.

çaise was established in 1966.[48] Research in linguistics continued to respond to developments during the Pompidou era. This period saw the development of French for specific purposes and the publication of *Le français scientifique et technique* in 1971. Research into teaching methods also continued throughout the rest of the decade, with *Niveau seuil* appearing in 1977.

French as a foreign language entered university programmes in 1983. Louis Porcher's work to make the academic world accept the discipline deserves to be acknowledged here.[49] His own accounts afford a glimpse of rivalries and territorial disputes between the ministries of Education and Foreign Affairs. New university programmes were introduced in FLE (*le français langue étrangère*), from undergraduate courses to postgraduate research degrees, all recognised with university degrees and diplomas. Two new qualifications designed to assess the competence of non-first-language learners were introduced in 1985, the Diplôme d'études de langue française (DELF) and the Diplôme approfondi de langue française (DALF). The recognition of the academic legitimacy of this field of research may be seen as its full coming of age. However, with the benefit of hindsight, the conclusion of the process of normalisa-

---

48   Ministère des affaires étrangères, *Une politique pour le français*, pp. 31–2.
49   Louis Porcher, *Le français langue étrangère* (Paris: Hachette, 1995), p. 7. 'Le général de Gaulle, durant la seconde guerre mondiale, avait perçu que les langues et les cultures constituaient des biens identitaires, patrimoniaux, et qu'elles faisaient partie de la puissance d'un pays. […] C'est pourquoi, dès son retour sur le territoire français, de Gaulle instaure, au sein du ministère des Affaires étrangères, une direction générale des Affaires culturelles, chargée de prendre en main la diffusion planétaire de la langue et de la culture françaises. Culture et langue sont bien plus que des biens patrimoniaux, ce sont aussi des biens de rayonnement, des moyens de répandre l'esprit national sur l'ensemble de la Terre.' The tone is reminiscent of the didactic commentators who flourished during the Third Republic. In a footnote to his article on the teaching of, and research into, French, Daniel Coste (p. 83) records that: 'l'expression "français langue étrangère" (entre guillemets et avec virgule) se voit consacrée une première fois dans un numéro de la revue *Les Cahiers pédagogiques* que dirige André Reboulet en 1957. Elle s'installe ensuite plus avant, avec la création de la revue *Le français dans le monde* et le développement du CREDIF et du BEL. Peu à peu, elle perd virgule et guillemets, se sigle F.L.E., voire FLE.'

tion – or outsourcing? – probably also marked the beginning of the end for specialist research centres such as the CREDIF.

Shifts in French interests were paralleled by shifts in the content of the French Studies programmes designed by French bodies for use abroad. Research on the evolution of teaching materials and teaching media, methods, concepts and syllabus content would no doubt yield interesting insights, for developments in this area do not merely reflect evolution in educational theory, but also reflect changes in the cultural and political climate, as well as changes in the type of audience targeted.

This aspect of the Francophone project brings us back to the *interests* discussed above. The preoccupation with methodology and the production of teaching materials seems to indicate a desire to *control*. A significant cultural industry engaged in the teaching of French as a foreign language (the sale of books, tapes and other materials, examination fees and the export of personnel) represents a major source of revenue. Also at stake is the control of content, the quality of the product being promoted and the image(s) conveyed. The TEFL approach has served as model, and other Western European states have followed it in trying to control the delivery and provision of language teaching, as well as the commodity itself. This is rationalised *post hoc* in terms of 'immersion', and, with the blessing of educational theory, the main driving force is economic and 'quality' control. To a certain extent, this is a response to the pervasive tide of cultural products, artefacts and media output from the USA and other English-speaking countries, an apparently unstoppable flow of cultural imperialism. France's attempts to maintain its grip on the language spoken within *la Francophonie* have alienated both Quebecers and Walloons at times, in particular with regard to the application of findings on gender-marked occupational titles.[50]

---

50   See, for instance, the correspondence between Maurice Druon, Secrétaire perpétuel de l'Académie française, and his counterpart at the Académie royale de langue et de littérature françaises de Belgique, Jean Tordeur, quoted by Druon himself in Maurice Druon, *Lettre aux Français sur leur langue et leur âme* (Paris: Julliard, 1994), pp. 91–5.

The State of la Francophonie

After some 40 years of concerted action, the institution of *la Franco-phonie* has 49 members who subscribe to a loose definition of what *la Francophonie* means as a community of nations 'ayant en partage la langue française'. The number of speakers of French is steadily decreasing, both in absolute numbers and as a proportion of the global population. Yet its geographic spread is impressive: French continues to be spoken on all of the world's five continents and not a few scattered islands. The number of learners has increased, although their relative proportion is going down: 7% of school children around the world were learning French in 1984, 6% in 1994.[51] This modest change hides great disparities: numbers have gone down significantly in North Africa and the Middle East, and there has been a steady, if still small, decline in Latin America, while numbers remain healthy in Western Europe.

Thanks to the vigilance and combative approach of successive French governments, French remains an official language and a working language of most international organisations. The number of positions filled by French-speakers in international organisations is estimated at 13,000, approximately 12% of total staffing.[52] However, at the UN French tends only to be used in translation: just 20% of the documents produced are originally drafted in French.[53] In her official report on the state of *la Francophonie*, Yvette Roudy notes that in 1986 70% of primary documents published by the European Commission were in French, while ten years later this proportion had fallen to 38.5%.[54]

As Roudy also points out, demography is not on the side of French: 60% of French-speakers live in Western Europe, the geographical region with the slowest-growing populations in the world. The second difficulty she identifies is the failure of one aspect of external policy discussed earlier: the decision taken in the 1980s to withdraw French teachers from host countries in order to support and train local teachers:

51   Yvette Roudy, *La francophonie: de la culture à la politique*, Rapport d'Information 390 (Paris: Assemblée Nationale, October 1997), p. 8.
52   Pontier, p. 26.
53   Pontier, pp. 17ff.
54   Roudy, p. 8.

Cette volonté de mettre fin à une politique assimilée à un assistanat est explicable. Il n'en demeure pas moins que les relais locaux ne se mettent pas nécessairement en place de façon satisfaisante, ni même durable.[55]

Finally, the third weakness highlighted by Roudy is the fact that, outside France French is nearly always a minority language in the countries in which it is spoken.

Roudy defines *la Francophonie* as united by 'l'amour commun d'une même langue d'origine, d'une culture partagée'.[56] This definition is somewhat tempered by her own analysis of the membership of the organisation, in which she admits that the definition of the community as one of countries 'ayant en partage la langue française' needs 'd'être d'interprétation souple'.[57] She gives her own explanations for the success of *la Francophonie* as an institution: the intensive, high profile coverage of its events, which affords a platform to member states that would otherwise remain ignored by the world's media; the development of new roles that provide existing members with proof of the organisation's vitality and success; and, finally, the vital support *la Francophonie* provides for the poorer countries through its aid programmes.

Roudy's report notes the progress made by the Francophone institutions and the strengthening of their core political commitment, welcoming both developments. However, she also allows herself to speculate on the concrete benefits of both for the states that make up *la Francophonie*.

Moreover, Roudy raises the important, if paradoxical, question of the place and weight of language in *la Francophonie* as currently constituted, pointing out that the status of French is questionable in the new, extended community, containing as it does countries such as Moldavia and Bulgaria, and noting in passing that the Hanoi summit necessitated the emergency teaching of elementary French to 2000 people in order to ensure a minimum communicative capacity in French on the part of the personnel who welcomed the delegates, a sign that French is not flourishing in the region. She concludes her report with a number of proposals

55   Roudy, p. 9.
56   Roudy, p. 7.
57   Roudy, p. 12.

intended to strengthen *la Francophonie*.[58] Her first four proposals were aimed at consolidating and rationalising its organisation and policies. Similar goals lay behind her fifth proposal, which, however, also sought to reinstate an emphasis on the linguistic dimension *and* the values the language is deemed to carry within it, 'droits de l'homme, démocratie et développement'.[59] Furthermore, all official events should be conducted in French. Finally, the fact that French has often become a minority language can be a political asset, especially in areas that have grown sensitive to the encroachments of Anglo-Saxon culture, such as Latin America. In the Europe context, Roudy also revived the proposal made by Michel Rocard (although she does not acknowledge his contribution) when he was Prime Minister, that the European Union adopt a policy of 'langues parentes':

> Il y aura, après l'élargissement de l'Union européenne, trois grandes aires linguis-tiques en son sein (langues latines, germaniques, slaves). Le plurilinguisme pour-rait passer par l'apprentissage obligatoire de deux langues étrangères relevant d'un groupe linguistique autre que celui de sa langue maternelle. Un Anglais apprendrait par exemple le français et le polonais; un Allemand, le français et le tchèque.[60]

On-line learning and related developments in distance teaching add to the threats posed by globalisation: the Web favours US universities and the further spread of the English language.

A full reckoning of the returns on decades of consistent investment in, and concerted action on, the Francophone Project is almost impos-sible, since it is so difficult to measure either the outlay or its outcomes. For instance, *la Francophonie* is increasingly dominated by networks: official, private, diplomatic, commercial, formal, informal and virtual. *L'action linguistique* has also made language a significant sector of the economy, helping to develop and sustain the media and communications industries, giving impetus to electronic developments and investment on

58 Roudy, p. 17ff. The five proposals are: 'rationaliser les structures françaises char-gées de la francophonie'; 'améliorer la gestion des actions'; 'rendre plus efficace notre coopération bilatérale'; 'développer une stratégie francophone offensive'; 'manifester un véritable engagement politique en faveur de la francophonie, de la défense de la langue française.'
59 Roudy, p. 26.
60 Roudy, p. 28.

the World Wide Web, and encouraging creativity and invention. Bilateral and multilateral agreements have boosted local economies and development while benefiting trade at home. From Yaounde to Lomé, *la Francophonie* has helped to protect and support emerging economies, and provided a platform for the production of ideas and intellectual exchange. Humanitarian organisations and aid have become key strands in the complex system *la Francophonie* weaves across the world. This complexity is also a feature of the community's less positive aspects: from its networks of corruption, political intrigues and unprincipled interventions to the burdens of debt and expectations imposed on emerging nations. The ethical dimension of *l'action linguistique* is frequently ignored completely.

Is France a member of *la Francophonie*? Michel Tétu points out that, in contrast with the Commonwealth, whose permanent Head is the Queen, making Great Britain *prima inter pares*, the leadership of *la Francophonie* is held by the head of state who hosted the most recent summit, who is then replaced by the head of the state where the next summit is held. There is a tension between this worthy commitment to equality between nations and the purpose of the Francophone project from its inception as a vehicle for the promotion of France's influence in world politics. France needs the weight of the Francophone world's backing, but also needs to protect its own *image de marque*, which is intimately associated with its language and culture. The conservatism that opposes the moves made in Quebec and Belgium to permit feminine forms of terms referring to professions, for instance, is no doubt genuine. However, Maurice Druon and the Académie do not appear to have enjoyed much success in their dispute with their counterparts in Montreal and Brussels. France and *la Francophonie* have to live with these contradictions.

ANNE JUDGE

Contemporary Issues in French Linguistic Policies

France is a country with a long history marked by violent upheavals and turbulence, and yet with a remarkable degree of underlying continuity. This history has been typified by evolution rather than revolution. Thus, the roots of many of today's linguistic ideals, policies and antagonisms may be traced back to the Middle Ages and the 'Ancien Régime'. It is true that during the 1789 Revolution they took on a new meaning, a new dynamism and a new purpose, but they remained intrinsically true to tradition. It is only in very recent years that completely different forces have come to the fore, clashing with traditional policies and attitudes. It is unclear at present whether these forces will be dominant in the future, but they have, so far, led to major debates in which the very foundations of the state have been re-examined.

Some of these forces work within the state and have brought about the centralisation of the state and standardisation of the language. There are also forces external to the state, principally the European Union, which is able to limit France's power to legislate on language issues, and the Council of Europe, which is influential, though its decisions are not binding. At the same time, since these external forces have liberated many previously repressed internal forces, the attitudes of some French people are changing to the point that questions are being asked that might one day affect the very existence of the state. Hence the changes in government policy that have been made in order to achieve some form of consensus and prevent the nation splitting.

In other words, linguistic policy is an area in which France can no longer function without taking account of views that differ from the traditional attitude, a situation that represents a very new departure.

Forces within France

Centralisation of the French State

All major debates in France tend to gravitate around key words. Such a debate took place in the spring and summer of 1999, when France signed, but failed to ratify, the Charter for Regional or Minority Languages drawn up by the Council of Europe. The word most often bandied around in this context was 'Jacobinism', sometimes followed by its opposites, 'Girondism', 'regionalism' and even 'communitarianism'. The meaning of the first term is clear, while the meaning of the three other words is open to various interpretations. This is particularly true of 'communitarianism', which may be used either as a simple adjective to refer to matters related to the European Community – in which case it is not controversial in any way – or to refer to a very different ideal, that of a Europe of regions, in which there would be no nation states, in which case it is dynamite. It is only used with the latter meaning in this chapter.

Today, Jacobinism is sometimes seen in positive terms, sometimes in negative terms, but hardly ever in neutral terms. It is only recently, however, that the concept has become a political issue. The Jacobins were members of a French revolutionary political club established in Paris in 1789. They took power in 1793 – having eliminated the Girondins – and had a lasting influence on the nation as a whole. Despite the bloodshed that marred their regime, they symbolise an extreme form of democracy based on absolute equality. Nevertheless, some of their views may also be seen as the natural development of a much older movement that led France to be transformed gradually from a territorially small entity surrounded by often, unruly provinces into a highly centralised nation state. The main pillar of the state before the 1789 Revolution had been the king, who ruled by divine right. Once the king had been disposed of – beheaded by the Jacobins – new foundations had to be found for the new fledgling nation state. The Jacobins played a major role in this respect.

After 1789, France gradually became 'unified'. It was unified religiously in the sense that the state no longer recognised a faith. Its status as a secular state became a religion in itself, though this 'religion' has recently been questioned, as is discussed below in the context of the 'affaire des foulards'.

It became unified as a territory, the old provinces with their strong regional identities having been replaced by the neutral, innocuous 'départements', which were directly responsible to central government. In short, the nation became 'une et indivisible', and this was to be one of the main stumbling blocks preventing the ratification of the Charter for Regional or Minority Languages in the summer of 1999.

France also acquired the unified legal and administrative system embodied in the Napoleonic Codes. Previously, there had been many different systems functioning in different parts of the kingdom. Indeed, Voltaire used to complain that, when travelling through France, one changed legal systems more often than one changed post-horses. However, although different forms of customary law were applied in France until the 1789 Revolution, the law was already unified linguistically. Very early on, and little by little, legal matters came to be dealt with in French rather than Latin, at least in everyday life.[1] Thus, wills and deeds, originally in Latin, had, by the middle of the thirteenth century, begun to be drawn up in French, a practice which had become frequent by the beginning of the fourteenth century. Since there was a degree of uncertainty as to the content of the customary law systems, they came to be recorded in 'coutumiers', sometimes in Latin, but more often in French for the convenience of litigants with no knowledge of Latin. They followed the Latin style, but usually in a simpler form. Documents issued by the Chancellerie Royale were often in French, because France's kings were either not too well versed in Latin or simply preferred French. This led eventually to the adoption of French as the sole official language of law and administration (Ordonnance de Villers-Cotterêts of 1539).[2]

The style of French used by lawyers in the earliest French legal documents was famous for its conciseness, simplicity and sophistication. It was originally seen as a model for all, but then fell into disrepute, to

1 Canon law continued to be in Latin, while legal works, which had traditionally been in Latin, began to be written in French in the sixteenth century.
2 For further detail, see A. Judge, 'A Planned Language?', in C. Sanders (ed.), *French Today: Language in its Social Context* (Cambridge: Cambridge University Press, 1993), pp. 7–26.

the point of being banned from polite society by Malherbe (1555–1628) for having become a jargon incomprehensible to the layman. Efforts were made, however, to correct this tendency during the eighteenth century. The aim was to avoid linguistic confusion by defining the meaning of words and creating new ones, and to encourage writing of classical clarity. The Napoleonic Codes were thus organised in a clear and intelligible manner, and French legal language has, to this day, been regularly updated when it was felt it had become too archaic. This ideal of clarity is embodied in the Déclaration des Droits de l'Homme et du Citoyen and the Napoleonic Codes, though not all texts meet such exacting standards.[3] The importance attributed to French as the common language of the land is therefore due, at least in part, to its having been shaped to make it into as effective a tool of communication as possible, one that could replace Latin, and this was widely recognised to be the case across Europe.

Thus it was that the French language itself became a 'pillar' of the aristocratic, bourgeois state at an early date. As such, it tended to exclude the powerless. After the Revolution, the aim was to make it a pillar of an all-inclusive state, since the Revolutionaries considered it impossible to create a nation of citizens equal before the law if those citizens could neither understand the law nor communicate with one another in speech and in writing. As a result, they decided to impose French on the whole nation:

> Cette entreprise, qui ne fut pleinement exécutée chez aucun peuple, est digne du peuple français, qui centralise toutes les branches de l'organisation sociale et qui doit être jaloux de consacrer au plus tôt, dans une République une et indivisible, l'usage unique et invariable de la langue de la liberté.[4]

A lack of financial resources, Napoleon's rise to power and the First Restoration delayed the implementation of the various decisions

---

3   The language used in administrative texts, in particular, retained a plethora of archaic phrases, such as 'le dit', 'lequel', 'sur ce', etc. Only gradually were the ideals of intelligibility and simplicity put into practice.

4   Quoted in M. Certeau, D. Julia and J. Revel, 'Le rapport Grégoire' in *Une politique de la langue, la Révolution française et les patois* (Paris: Gallimard, 1976), p. 302.

that had been taken with the aim of making French the common language of the nation. This did not stop French becoming – and remaining – one of the most important symbols of unity and equality in the country. Indeed, the French language came to be seen as one of the most stable foundations of the State: there were several restorations of the monarchy, each time bringing Catholicism back as a state religion, but neither the language nor the newly unified legal system, nor the principle of territorial unity ('la France une et indivisible') were ever challenged again, until very recently, at least. Today the French language is still claimed to be the 'cement' that helps immigrants settle in their host country. It is seen as a tool of assimilation that promotes integration and equality.

Now, however, cracks are beginning to appear in the edifice, though the edifice itself is probably not at risk. The Jacobins saw the nation state as unified by its confinement within a defined territory. This is no longer quite the case because of the legacy of the French colonial empire. On the one hand, the DOM-TOMs have their own nationalist movements, which reject France and French; on the other hand, some 51 countries, many with a history of French colonialism, have recently established the Organisation internationale de la Francophonie, which is rather similar to the British Commonwealth and has a high profile General Secretary in Boutros Boutros-Ghali. The fact that all these countries are united by a common allegiance to the French language has blurred the Jacobin vision of the language as being exclusive to France. Indeed, according to the report presented to the French Parliament by the Délégation générale à la langue française (DGLF)[5] in 1999, 'le français est la langue d'unité nationale' within France and 'le ciment de la francophonie' as well as being 'une grande langue de communication internationale'.[6]

The Revolutionaries' fiercely held attitude towards religion, which was that it should be a personal matter that should not intrude into the public domain, is also under threat nowadays, as is shown by the 'affaire des foulards', which opened the door to 'unostentatious' signs of reli-

---

5   The DGLF co-ordinates linguistic initiatives between the various ministries.
6   'Rapport au Parlement sur l'application de la loi du 4 août 1994 relative à l'emploi de la langue française', 1999, p. 4.

gion.[7] Finally, the campaigns in France over the last few years to push
the government to sign the Charter for Regional or Minority Languages
show that there are still minority languages to contend with.

The Position of France's Regional Languages

France's regional languages were supposed to disappear, but have refused
to go away, despite the efforts made not only by the Jacobins, but also by
all who have followed them in government. This policy seems to have
been supported by many speakers of regional languages, who (like the
Jacobins) saw them as impediments to social mobility and therefore to
equality of opportunity. 'Délivrez-nous de nos patois,' was a frequently
heard cry, according to the Abbé Grégoire's survey of languages spoken
in France (the survey was begun in 1790 and the report completed by
1794). However, the move towards a common language and the destruction of the regional languages from 1793 onwards was motivated not
only by the desire for equality and the fact that French had been more
consciously refined than any of the other languages spoken in the country.
It was also driven by political factors, as is clear from the frequently
quoted Barère report drawn up in the name of the Comité de Salut Public
in 1794:

> Le fédéralisme et la superstition parlent bas-breton; l'émigration et la haine de la
> République parlent allemand; la contre-révolution parle l'italien, et le fanatisme
> parle le basque. Cassons ces instruments de dommage et d'erreur.[8]

7   The 'affaire des foulards' goes back to 1989, when three girls at a junior school in
     Creil were suspended for wearing headscarves, symbols of their Muslim faith.
     This brought into question the whole principle of the secular state, in which signs
     of religious affiliation are seen as divisive, particularly in schools. When François
     Bayrou was Minister for Education he issued a 'circulaire' stating that all ostenta-
     tious signs of religious affiliation were forbidden. The problem is how to define
     'ostentatious'. Furthermore, the judgement given by the Conseil d'État in 1992
     gave a new, pluralist meaning to the concept of the secular state since it allowed
     public expressions of faith hitherto restricted to the private sphere. The issue is
     still a problem and the debate continues as to whether the secular principle should
     be enforced on all or give way to the concept of a multicultural France in the name
     of freedom of expression.
8   Quoted in Certeau, Julia and Revel, p. 295.

There are many similar passages in the Barère report, which analyses these languages and the dangers their speakers were perceived to present for the fledgling Republic. The following passage deals with the Corsican problem (author's italics):

> Un autre département mérite d'attirer vos regards: c'est le département de Corse. Amis ardents de la liberté, quand *un perfide Paoli et des administrateurs fédéralistes ligués avec des prêtres ne les égarent pas,* les Corses sont des citoyens français; mais, depuis quatre ans de révolution, ils ignorent nos lois, ils ne connaissent pas les événements et les crises de notre liberté. Trop voisins de l'Italie, que pouvaient-ils en recevoir? Des prêtres, des indulgences, des Adresses séditieuses, des mouvements fanatiques. *Pascal Paoli,* Anglais par reconnaissance, dissimulé par habitude, faible par son âge, Italien par principe, sacerdotal par besoin, *se sert puissamment de la langue italienne pour pervertir l'esprit public, pour égarer le peuple,* pour grossir son parti; il se sert surtout de l'ignorance des habitants de Corse, *qui ne soupçonnent pas même l'existence des lois françaises, parce qu'elles sont dans une langue qu'ils n'entendent pas. Il est vrai qu'on traduit depuis quelques mois notre législation en italien; mais ne vaut-il pas mieux y établir des instituteurs de notre langue que des traducteurs dans une langue qu'ils n'entendent pas.*[9]

To this day, it is widely assumed that the overwhelming majority of Corsicans wish to remain French (various polls seem to prove this), and that the Corsican language is linked with separatist policies (the main demands of the Corsican nationalists is for the compulsory teaching of Corsican in all schools, and for recognition of Corsican citizenship[10]).

Grégoire and Barère made similar points about other regional languages, and it is again easy to find rather similar views in today's press, albeit in a watered-down form. No less a person than President Pompidou echoed Grégoire when he stated: 'Il n'y a pas de place pour les langues minoritaires dans une France destinée à marquer l'Europe de son sceau.'[11] Such comments have become rare, at least in such a form, since the Charter became a subject of debate during the spring and summer of 1999. Since then the Jacobins have been on the defensive, and their confidence in the future of what, to them, is one of the fundamentals of the

9   Certeau, Julia and Revel, p. 294.
10 See article by Jean-Guy Talamoni in *Le Monde*, 1 January 2000.
11 Quoted in R. Wardaugh, *Languages in Competition* (Oxford: Blackwell, 1987), p. 118.

French regime, i.e. the use of a single common language, has been seriously eroded. It is even possible to detect a mood of panic among those who fear that two centuries of hard work could be foolishly destroyed.

Another factor that militates against the regional or minority languages is the widely held belief that French is a means of assimilating immigrants, with citizens, new and old, enjoying equal status through their common language. Thus Toubon, when Minister for Culture and Francophone Affairs, referred to the importance of the French language to immigrants in the following terms:

> la langue française est pour eux [les Français de fraîche date] leur premier capital, le signe de leur dignité, le passeur de l'intégration, le diapason d'une culture universelle, le partage d'un patrimoine commun, une part du rêve français.[12]

Efforts to achieve equality through linguistic uniformity (mainly through compulsory education and military service), fear of any form of separatism that could lead to what has sometimes been referred to as the 'balkanisation' of France and the need to integrate immigrants have all militated against the survival of the regional languages. To quote from a linguistic survey conducted by INSEE/INED and published in December 1993 in *Population et sociétés*, this move towards linguistic uniformity has been variously described as 'the linguistic unification of France', 'the collapse of the regional languages', 'the move to French' and 'the domination of French'. It explains why Haritschelhar, in an article contrasting the linguistic rights of the Spanish and French Basques, wrote in 1994:

> Il faudra une importante évolution des mentalités pour que le gouvernement français accepte de signer la Charte européenne des langues régionales ou minoritaires [...] Il est évident que la patrie des droits de l'Homme n'est pas la patrie des droits linguistiques.[13]

And yet the Charter was signed on 7 May 1999, though it is not being ratified (see S. Judge: Language as a Human Right). This at least shows that mentalities have changed. The extent to which they have

12   *Le Monde*, 4 August 1994, p. 16.
13   Haritschelhar, 'Les langues régionales et l'Europe', *Revue internationale d'éducation*, 3, September 1994, p. 92.

changed among ordinary people, as against politicians, is shown by the results of a survey organised by IFOP on 6–7 April 2000 for the Alsatian-Moselle Frankish section of the European Bureau for Lesser Used Languages (EBLUL). When respondents were asked whether or not they favoured the ratification of the Charter for Regional or Minority Languages, 82% were in favour, of whom 27% were strongly in favour and 55% more or less in favour; 11% were opposed to the ratification of the Charter, of whom 6% were strongly opposed; and 1% of respondents had no opinion on the subject. When asked whether they favoured the modification of the French Constitution in order to make ratification possible, 79% were in favour, of whom 22% were strongly in favour and 57% more or less in favour; 11% were opposed to this step, of whom 8% were strongly opposed. 2% of respondents were classified as 'don't knows'.[14] These figures were presented on 15 April 2000 at a meeting organised by UNESCO that brought together over 400 representatives of the various languages spoken in France.

The unexpected renaissance of the regional languages was encouraged by the EU, mainly at the initiation of the European Parliament and the Council of Europe. These bodies are currently the main champions of Europe's regional or minority languages. The French government was pressurised by campaigners in France and by these bodies into signing the Charter for Regional or Minority Languages on 7 May 1999. The Conseil constitutionnel, however, declared the Charter to be partially incompatible with the Constitution on 15 June 1999, ruling that the Constitution would need to be amended before the Charter could be ratified. As many people from all parts of the political spectrum are violently opposed to ratification, the debate has raged ever since. It is worth noting that the terms 'Regional or Minority Languages' only applied at this stage to indigenous languages, and did not refer to languages such as Arabic or Berber, the 'other languages' most widely spoken in France today.

14   'Sondatge: majoritat per la Carta europèa e per la modificacion de la constitucion', *Setmana, Setmanèr Occitan d'Informacion*, 253, 20–26 April 2000.

New Legislation Enforcing the Use of French

The defence or undermining of regional or minority languages is not the only linguistic problem the French have had to contend with. Another is the threat of English. There are two aspects to this threat: the success of English in supplanting French as the language of international diplomacy and the increasing dominance of English in science, medicine, technology and financial matters.

In the 1980s the use of English in international diplomacy led to a belated strengthening of links between France and her ex-colonies, as well as other Francophone countries. France had originally ignored the creation of the Communauté francophone in the 1960s, and the community's most important institution, the Agence de coopération culturelle et technique (1970), because they had been created primarily at the instigation of the new leaders of France's former colonies[15]. But these countries were then joined by other Francophone countries and regions, such as Belgium and Quebec and 20 years later, President Mitterrand enthusiastically embraced the concept of 'la Francophonie', establishing the Haut Conseil de la Francophonie in 1984. Apart from a genuine belief in 'la Francophonie', it suited his political agenda, enabling him to function in a world-wide network of links between countries that, without necessarily being 'Francophone', are committed to the cause of French. All the bodies involved in 'la Francophonie' were eventually brought together under one umbrella organisation with the establishment of the Organisation internationale de la Francophonie. It is seen by all concerned as an important tool for linguistic propagation and protectionism[16], and an argument against ratifying the Charter for Regional or Minority Languages.

The second cause for concern, the increasing role played by English in metropolitan France, has led over the years to the creation of a number

---

15   De Gaulle was particularly worried that if France took an active role in such a creation, this would be seen as colonialism in disguise and would eventually lead to its demise, as happened to the short-lived Communauté française, founded in 1958.

16   For further details see A. Judge, 'Voices and Policies', in K. Salhi (ed.), *Francophone Voices* (Exeter: Elm Bank Publications, 1999), pp. 1–26.

of bodies with a prescriptive and protectionist role. These are at present the Conseil supérieur de la langue française and the Délégation générale à la langue française et aux langues de France (DGLFLF),[17] and a terminological commission for each ministry to develop new French words, so making it possible to avoid excessive borrowing from English. Some of these commissions seek to achieve greater linguistic unity and coherence throughout the Francophone world by including representatives from other 'Francophone' countries. Their decisions as to what is terminologically acceptable are disseminated to all official organisations in France and to the members of the Organisation internationale de la Francophonie.

The increasing domination of English has also led to direct legislation. The Loi Bas-Lauriol of 1975[18] marked the beginning of the linguistic debate so characteristic of France today by establishing the principle of the use of French in France. Its aim was to protect French citizens by providing for clear terminology and giving them the right to be informed in their mother tongue. The law refers to three domains in which French was to become compulsory: in commercial contexts and advertising (which proved to be the most problematic) in order to protect consumers; in contracts of employment in order to protect the employee; and in the context of information given to consumers either by private firms or public bodies, usually in the form of leaflets. It also stipulated that the new terminology drawn up by the terminological commissions would be compulsory in all government documents and contracts, in the education system and in all other state institutions. The rule was that where a French term existed, it had to be used. Non-compliance by companies was punishable by a fine. The actual implementation of the law was dependent

17 The first body to deal with linguistic matters was the Haut comité pour la défense et l'expansion de la langue française, founded in 1966. It became the Haut Comité de la langue française in 1973 and was replaced by two bodies, the Comité consultatif de la langue française and the Commissariat général à la langue française, in 1984. These, in turn, became the Conseil supérieur de la langue française and the Délégation générale à la langue française in 1989. The latter became the Délégation générale à la langue française et aux langues de France in 2001. These terminological changes reflect changes in orientation and brief.

18 No. 75-1349, 31 December 1975. The version of the law finally implemented was less rigid than the draft presented to the Assemblée nationale in May 1973, which was felt to contravene EC law.

on various governmental bodies, such as the Direction de la consom-
mation et de la répression des fraudes, but they brought very few prosecu-
tions and, generally speaking, the law was felt to be all bark and no bite.

Subsequently, in 1992, in response to fears about further encroachments on national sovereignty with the signing of the Maastricht Treaty,
the Constitution was changed to make French the official language of the
Republic. This had, of course, long been the case, but previously it had
not been felt necessary to include a statement to that effect in the Constitution, possibly so as not to offend the speakers of regional languages.

Finally, 1994 saw the adoption of the Loi Toubon.[19] Like the Loi
Bas-Lauriol, it sought to protect French consumers, but more effectively.
Clearly, many headings would be the same, such as the obligatory use of
French in advertisements, contracts of employment, the dissemination
of information to the general public, etc. However, by 1994 many people's
outlook had changed and the attempt to ban foreign words from publicity
materials and the media was considered by some to be neither useful nor
realistic. The law was ridiculed in much of the press, with journalists
imagining themselves imprisoned for using an English word. Indeed,
certain aspects of the law pertaining to the use of language in the private
sphere were even declared unconstitutional by the Conseil constitutionnel[20] (namely that it was not possible for the law to be enforced in
private communications between individuals on account of the principle
of freedom of speech, that the enforcement of specific terminology was
not applicable to radio and television broadcasts, and that languages other
than French could continue to be used at meetings, conferences, etc.
provided that interpretation into French was provided). This law created
some rather paradoxical situations, in that a term of foreign origin could
be forbidden in the context of communication between an official body
and an individual, but could be used in a radio programme.

The changes demanded by the Conseil constitutionnel removed
some of the law's bite, but more legislation was to follow, further defining
– and usually narrowing – the scope of the law: the 'décret' of 3 March
1995[21] that defined possible infractions of the law punishable by sanc-

19   Loi no. 94-665, 4 August 1994 (JO, 5 August 1994).
20   Décision no. 94-345 DC of 29 July 1994.
21   Décret No.95-240 (JO, 3 March 1995).

tions, i.e. fines; the 'arrêté' of 2 May 1995 that specified which associations for the defence of the French language (there are over 200 in France) would be allowed to take transgressors to court; and the 'circulaire' of 19 March 1996 that restricted the scope of the law, bringing it into line with EC labelling regulations and other European legislation.

Whereas the Loi Bas-Lauriol of 1975 and the constitutional change in 1992 were passed without too much comment, the Loi Toubon became a *cause célèbre*. This was a result of changes in the political climate, with linguists and non-linguists no longer seeing French as a fortress capable of being defended by protectionist linguistic policies. A survey conducted by SOFRES in 1994 showed that, although 97% of the population were proud of their language, only 70% were proud of its international status. Only 39% felt that defending French against outside forces was an important issue for the government, 51% thought it important but not excessively so, and 9% thought it was not an important issue. As regards the use of foreign words, 30% thought they were useful, 19% thought they were amusing and 41% thought they were modern. Very few disapproved.

External Forces: The Impact of the EU[22] and the Council of Europe

The Direct Impact of the European Parliament and the Council of Europe

The promotion by the Council of Europe, in conjunction with the European Parliament (EP), of regional or minority languages, although not enforceable by law, has had a major impact, bringing about something of a renaissance for some of the languages involved. Together, these institutions are able to boast of many achievements, one of the most

---

22　There is often confusion between the terms EC (European Community) and EU (European Union). The EC is a legal entity whereas the EU is a political entity, but nowadays these terms are frequently used interchangeably, which can be very confusing. The terms are used here in accordance with this distinction.

important being the drafting of the Charter for Regional or Minority Languages. The Charter is significant not only on account of its benefits for lesser used languages, but also in drawing attention to their very existence and their importance.

The Charter for Regional or Minority Languages, although promulgated by the Council of Europe, derives in part from initiatives taken by the European Parliament during the late 1970s and the 1980s. Numerous resolutions called for concrete measures to save the Community's endangered languages and for action to support the Council of Europe's efforts to draw up a Charter for Regional or Minority Languages. In turn, this led to the establishment of the European Bureau for Lesser Used Languages (EBLUL) by the EC in 1982. An official budget to support minority languages and cultures was set up by the Commission in 1983, and since then the European Commission budget has subsidised many projects in the minority linguistic communities of Europe.

However, on 12 May 1998 a decision of the European Court of Justice (ECJ) declared that it was illegal for the Commission and the European Parliament to maintain a budget for which there was no legal basis, and funding was to be discontinued. Following this, on 22 September 1998, at the annual conference of EBLUL, Mr Fronia, representing the Commission, read out a speech by Édith Cresson, then European Commissioner for Research, Innovation, Education, Training and Youth, in which she promised to establish a legal basis for the funding of regional and minority languages. The principle of helping regional languages and cultures was clearly too well entrenched for it to be ditched on the grounds of legal niceties.[23]

---

23   On 25 October 2001, the European Parliament's Budget Committee adopted a proposal from the Committee for Culture, Youth and Media to introduce a new budget line B3 – 1007. Parliament provisionally reserved 1 million euros for 'Preparatory Actions concerning the Promotion and Safeguarding of Regional and Minority Languages, Dialects and Cultures'. Projects with the aim of preserving or protecting a regional or minority languages, dialects or cultures seen as an integral part of the European cultural heritage will be considered eligible for support. It is now up to the Commission to resolve any legal problems that might arise from this. (See Contact Bulletin, March 2002).

The Indirect Impact of the EU on French Linguistic Legislation[24]

It was never expected that the EEC should play a role in the language issue. The EEC was always intended to be a multilingual community following the precedent of the European Coal and Steel Community (ECSC). The ECSC was created in 1951 with French as its official language, but by 1953 its *Official Journal* was being published in the four languages then represented in the ECSC: French, Italian, German and Dutch. Today the EC has 11 official languages: Danish, Dutch, Finnish, French, English, German, Greek, Italian, Portuguese, Spanish and Swedish. Two Treaty languages have also been adopted: Irish in 1972 and Luxembourgish in 1984, when it became an official language of Luxembourg.

Each member state is free to choose its official language, a situation that may lead to problems in a multilingual state. For example, in Spain Castilian is the official language, though three regional languages have official status within the geographical regions in which they are spoken: Catalan, Basque and Galician. The MEPs of these regions – in particular Catalonia – frequently press for some recognition of their language by the European Parliament. The same demands are made by representatives of the French regional languages.

The EC still adheres in theory to the principle of multilingualism. Suggestions that the Community should adopt one of its official languages as the official language of the Community are resisted – particularly by France, for the likely winner would be English, and all the other official languages would become *de facto* regional or minority languages. This would also give Great Britain an unfair advantage in economic terms. There have, therefore, been suggestions that an artificial language – Esperanto is the front runner – should be made the official language, but such proposals seem to infuriate many, and this is not generally regarded as a serious possibility. Meanwhile, in practice, some languages are more equal than others. Thus, in most institutions French and English

---

24   See A. Judge and S. Judge, 'The Impact of European Linguistic Policies on French', in D. Marley, M.-A. Hintze and G. Parker (eds), *Linguistic Identities and Policies in France and the French-speaking World* (London: AFLS and CILT, 1998), pp. 292–317.

are the dominant languages, but there are signs that Germany wants German to be placed on an equal footing with English and French.[25] French and English are also the dominant languages of the European Court of Justice (ECJ), even where the dispute involves parties from other Member States whose official languages are neither French nor English.

Recently, certain languages have been designated as working languages for particular institutions. The Community Trade Marks Office, created in 1993, accepts initial applications in all official languages, but subsequent dealings are restricted to five working languages: English, French, German, Italian and Spanish. In *Christine Kik v. Le Conseil de l'Union Européenne et la Commission de la CE*,[26] a Dutch lawyer unsuccessfully contested the refusal to allow the use of Dutch.

At present, France is fearful that French might be gradually, 'pragmatically' replaced by English as a working language. It is certainly the case that the Directorate Generals that deal with financial and economic matters already use English more than French. This fear has been reinforced by a new decision of the Council of Europe, in which English and French are equal working languages: whereas in the past the European Court of Human Rights gave its decisions in both French and English, it now only has to give them in one or the other of these languages, a move that has led to an increase in the use of English.

Apart from the principle of multilingualism, the European Community's approach to linguistic policy is purely pragmatic. It is not concerned with regional or minority languages, and its only concern is that *national linguistic restrictions must not frustrate the fundamental freedoms of the Community* enshrined in the EC Treaty 1957 and implemented by delegated legislation.[27] It is in this respect that French linguistic legislation could be seen to infringe Community law. The following

---

25   See, among others, *The Guardian*, 2 July 1999.
26   Case T-107/94 [1995] 2 CMLR 857. CMLR refers to the *Common Market Law Reports*.
27   Under Article 249, the EP can make regulations and issue directives jointly with the Council and the Commission. Regulations are binding in their entirety and directly applicable in all member states. Directives bind the member states to which they are addressed as to what must be achieved, but each member state chooses the form and method of their implementation by national legislation.

cases either refer to France or another Member State, and constitute precedents that France has to take into account.

Articles 49–55[28] of the EC Treaty prohibit restrictions on freedom to provide services within the Community in respect of nationals of Member States. Thus, in *The Commission v. The French Republic*, *The Commission v. the Hellenic Republic* and *The Commission v. The Italian Republic* (1989) (three nearly identical cases decided on the same day),[29] national regulations requiring tourist guides for visitors from other Member States to have a national diploma obtainable only after a course of study in the country and requiring linguistic competence in French, Greek or Italian were held to be discriminatory. This precedent was later followed in *The Commission v. Spain* (1994).[30]

Articles 28 and 29 prohibit quantitative restrictions and all measures having an equivalent effect on the movement of goods between member states. In respect of these, Directive 79/112 concerns the labelling, packaging and marketing of foodstuffs. Article 14 of the Directive allows member states to restrict the sale of foodstuffs only if the labelling details are not in a language that is 'easily comprehensible to the buyer'. To comply with this Directive, Belgium promulgated a law ('le Décret Royal du 13 novembre 1986') that specified that labelling had to be in the language of the region where the product was to be sold. In the 'Peeters Decision' (1993),[31] the defendant was prosecuted for selling mineral water in the Flemish-speaking part of Belgium in bottles labelled only in French and German. The European Court of Justice decided that these labels could easily be understood by buyers and that the Belgian law was contrary to European law and inapplicable. The aim of the Directive was to ensure the free movement of goods and also the protection of the consumer, and the Belgian law was considered to have gone beyond

28   The Treaty of Amsterdam amended the EC Treaty 1957 with effect from 1 May
     1999. The article numbers in this chapter reflect those changes.
29   *The Commission v. The French Republic*, Case 154/87 [1994] 3 CMLR 500, *The
     Commission v. The Hellenic Republic* and *The Commission v. The Italian Republic*,
     Case 198/89 and Case 180/89 [1994] 3 CMLR 500.
30   *The Commission v. The Republic of Spain*, Case C-375/92 [1994] 3 CMLR 500.
31   *Groupement des producteurs, importateurs et agents généraux d'eaux minérales
     étrangères (PIAGEME) v. Peeters*, Case C-369/89 [1993] 3 CMLR 725.

these aims. This is a precedent that French policy-makers need to keep in mind.

Following this decision, on 10 November 1993 the European Commission published a Communication[32] on linguistic policy and consumer protection, which recognises that, on the question of languages, competence resides with the member states. This is in keeping with the principle of subsidiarity enshrined in the Maastricht Treaty, but it also drew attention to the confusion relating to existing regulations, which vary according to the nature of the product. In consequence, a second Communication, which attempted to establish guidelines concerning Article 14 in the light of the Peeters Decision,[33] was published on the same day. Two possible situations were identified, depending on whether the goods imported from one Member State to another were being put on sale with or without any alteration to the product's packaging. The Commission limited the operation of Article 14, which allows member states to restrict the sale of foodstuffs only if their labelling is not in a language easily comprehensible to the buyer, to cases in which the packaging is not altered. In other words, this article does not apply where the packaging is altered, in which case France can insist on the labelling being in French.

Following the publication of these Communications, the French government requested that the notion of an 'easily comprehensible language' be abandoned in favour of a formula that would be less ambiguous and 'plus respectueuse des souverainetés linguistiques'. This approach reflected a general, mistaken perception in France that 'easily comprehensible language' referred to English, which was certainly not the intention. Nevertheless, this illustrates France's nervousness in relation to moves by the EU on the language issue.

Restrictions on the 'shape, size, weight, composition, presentation or identification' of a product may also be contrary to Community law, even though they are applicable to both domestic and imported products, if they effectively bar imports or make them more difficult or more costly to market than equivalent domestic products. The *Cassis de Dijon Case*[34]

32   COM (93) 456 final.
33   COM (93) 532 final.
34   The popular name for *Rewe-Zentral AG v Bundesmonopolverwaltung fur Brant-wein*, Case C-120/78 [1979] ECR 649.

concerned a German restriction on the marketing of fruit liqueurs with an alcoholic content of less than 25%, which prevented the import of the French liqueur 'Cassis de Dijon'. The European Court of Justice held the German regulation to be illegal. In the *Clinique Case*,[35] a German law relating to misleading advertising prevented Estée Lauder from using the trade name 'Clinique' on packaging and in advertising, since the name had medical associations for German consumers. The European Court of Justice held that the fact that this entailed extra costs for the producers affected free trade, and that the law was excessively restrictive and inapplicable. Again, this is a precedent that limits France's freedom to legislate in linguistic matters.

Language laws aimed at protecting a national language may also fall within the scope of Article 28. Thus, the legality of Articles 2, 3 and 4 of the Loi Toubon could be questioned.[36] These articles require the use of French for (i) all sales descriptions, presentations, terms of supply and invoices in respect of the sale of any good or service; (ii) any advertisement, whether written, oral or audio-visual for any goods or service; (iii) any slogan or product description registered with a trade mark; (iv) any poster to be displayed in a public place.

There are exceptions where foreign words that are easily understandable describe a well-known product.[37] There is also an exception where the foreign-language text is accompanied by a French translation, which must be as 'readable', 'audible' or 'intelligible' as the foreign-language version. In relation to the packaging, labelling and advertising of products imported from other member states, this could entail the imposition of extra costs, which constitutes a restriction on free import. Where the labelling of foodstuffs is concerned, the French have to take the Labelling Directive into consideration in the light of the Peeters

---

35   Case C - 315/92 [1994] ECR 1 - 317.
36   N. McCarthy and H. Mercer, 'Language as a Barrier to Trade: The Loi Toubon', 5 ECLR (1996), pp. 308–14.
37   In some cases, French linguistic decisions may appear strange in these matters. Thus, in 1984 a court in Versailles decided that 'pizza', 'sandwich' and 'hot dog' were commonly understood by the French, whereas 'cheeseburger' and 'hamburger' were not! Cour d'appel de Versailles, 24 June 1984.

Decision, which clearly limits the scope of the law. The French law may
also infringe the Community Trade Mark Regulation 40/94 of 20 December 1993, since it could hinder a pan-European marketing strategy (e.g.
Audi's 'Vorsprung durch Technik' or Nike's 'Just do it').

All these restrictions probably explain the 'Circulaire' of 19 March
1996,[38] which allows the use of foreign expressions, without a translation,
in the use of packaging and labelling, if they are felt to be common
knowledge. The examples given are 'for example', 'made in', 'copyright'
and 'on/off'. Where advertisements are concerned, they may include
extracts from original works in a foreign language. The Loi Toubon does
not apply to trademarks made up of one or several foreign words, though
it does apply to any accompanying text, in an advertisement for example.
Although this 'circulaire' appears to weaken the Loi Toubon, it makes
its application more realistic by making it more sensible.

The Debate about the Charter: Questioning the Foundations of the State[39]

The Modern Descendants of the Jacobins and Girondins

The Toubon debate revealed a much more relaxed attitude towards language issues than had previously been the case, although commitment to
French as the national language had in no way been eroded. Then came
the signing of the Charter, which sparked off a debate about a variety of
old, deeply held beliefs, with the terms 'Jacobins' and 'Girondins' re-
emerging in the process. Nowadays the Jacobins stand for a strong cen-

---

38   Published in *Les brèves*, 5, 1996; and in the *Journal officiel*, 20 March 1996.
39   An earlier form of this section appeared as A. Judge and S. Judge, 'Linguistic
     Policies in France and Contemporary Issues: The Signing of the Charter for Re-
     gional or Minority Languages', *International Journal of Francophone Studies*,
     vol. 3, 2, 2000, pp. 106–27.

tralised state,[40] while the Girondins stand for a less rigid, decentralised form of government.[41] These are emotive terms reflecting the passions stirred by the current debate. Thus, G. Dupoac'h, in *Libération*, explaining why nobody in authority had foreseen the importance of the Celtic revival, refers to their lack of imagination and 'une sclérose jacobine'.[42] E. Aeschmann, in another issue, refers to 'le girondisme':

Il (Jospin) a mis en place le CAPES de corse, a approuvé l'idée du 'peuple corse' inscrit dans le projet Joxe en 1991[43] et n'ignore pas qu'un peu de *girondisme* peut contribuer à moderniser son image.[44]

The Jacobins are supposed to be against the Charter (but there are important exceptions), whereas the Girondins are in favour.

These terms have sometimes been updated in the press. 'Jacobin' has been replaced by 'souverainiste', which refers to those who put the unity of the nation above all else, as in 'Souverainistes: la guerre des tranchées' or 'les ardeurs des "souverainistes"'[45]. 'Intégriste' is also used in this context, as in 'L'intégrisme français dit "jacobin" et, en réalité historique, se trouve légitimé par le Conseil constitutionnel.'[46] 'Girondisme' is a more difficult term to replace, because the Girondins were not

---

40 Originally 'Jacobins' were members of a French political club established in 1789 in Paris. The name derives from the fact that they met in the old monastery of the Jacobins, who were Dominican friars. Their aim was to maintain and propagate the principles of democracy and absolute equality. They also stood for a unified, centralised government in a unified, centralised state. The principle of France as *une et indivisible* goes back to them.

41 The 'Girondins' derive their name from the fact that many of them came from the Gironde area around Bordeaux. They were moderate Republicans who sat in the French Assembly between 1791 and 1793. They opposed the worst excesses of the Revolution and objected to the political domination of France by Paris. Military disaster in 1793 brought about their downfall (21 were guillotined).

42 G. Dupoac'h, *Libération*, 6 August 1999.

43 Later held to be unconstitutional, see chapter by S. Judge in this volume.

44 E. Aeschmann, *Libération,* 5 July 1999, p. 2.

45 'Souverainistes: la guerre des tranchées': front page of *Libération*, 25 June 1999; 'les ardeurs des "souverainistes" du MDC (Mouvement des Citoyens)': *Le Monde*, 24 June 1999.

46 H. Giordan and R. Lafont, *Libération*, 12 July 1999.

long in power and their position is less well understood. The terms
'communautaristes' (communitarians)[47] and 'régionalistes' are also used
in opposition to 'jacobin' or 'souverainiste'. According to regionalists, it
is possible for a state to allow the regions their own identity in terms of
institutions and culture without endangering cohesion. For example,
Daniel Cohn-Bendit advocates the application of the principle of subsidiarity to the relationship between the state and its regions. The 'communautaristes', however, want a Europe of regions that ignores the concept
of nation state. According to a detractor:

> Ceux qui brandissent l'étendard de la sauvegarde des langues minoritaires défen-
> dent, qui l'autonomie, qui l'indépendance, qui l'Europe des régions. Nous ne
> voulons pas que la République soit remise en question par une 'Europe sans
> drapeaux'.[48]

Though there are many 'regionalists' in France, there are very few 'communitarians', a word used mainly to describe Corsican, Basque and
Breton separatists, and some extreme right-wing politicians. It is felt to
be contrary to the French tradition. Thus, politicians as different as Cohn-
Bendit (French Green Party) and Henri Guaino (a traditional republican
sociologist) both reject communitarianism in favour of the concept of
the Republic as a melting pot. At a public debate, Guaino, representing
the Jacobin stand, stated (author's italics):

> *dans la République, tout se joue sur la capacité à assimiler, à travers l'école,
> l'emploi, la citoyenneté, ceux qui viennent de l'extérieur.* Le problème de l'im-
> migration ne se joue pas sur la frontière mais dans le creuset. Et le principe de
> la République comme creuset s'oppose absolument au communautarisme et au
> différentialisme. Si on opte pour le droit à la différence, pour la discrimination
> positive, pour l'organisation en communautés solidaires et repliées sur elles-
> mêmes, alors, de fait, c'est sur la frontière que se joue le problème de l'im-
> migration: dans ce cas, en effet, la croissance continue de communautés dont le
> système de valeurs est en décalage par rapport au système central de valeurs de la
> société pose des problèmes insolubles. *Il y a donc un vrai choix entre le creuset,
> l'assimilation, la citoyenneté, l'unité, l'indivisibilité comme principes d'une polit-*

47   An ambiguous term, since lawyers also use it with a quite different meaning, i.e.
     as an adjective relating to the European Community.
48   G. Sarre, *Le Monde*, 25 June 1999.

> *ique républicaine et le différentialisme qui fonde une autre politique, entre le modèle unitaire français et le modèle communautaire américain.*[49]

To which Cohn-Bendit answered:

> je ne suis, enfin, pas plus favorable que vous au communautarisme.[...] Il faut que la France accepte le métissage des communautés qui la composent sans nier leurs personnalités propres, afin d'accélérer leur fusion consciente.[50]

Since 'communitarianism' implies a tribal approach, with language seen as a means of exclusion, it is regarded negatively by almost all French politicians. The main conflict therefore takes place between sovereignists and regionalists, with regionalism being sometimes seen in institutional terms, sometimes in terms of cultural identity and sometimes in terms of minorities. The opponents of the Charter are normally sovereignists, and, as such, they usually have nationalist views and links with conservative politics, though some conservative politicians, such as François Bayrou, are in favour of the Charter. Similarly, not all left-wing politicians support regionalism and the Charter. Reactions on this issue thus cut across the political divide, bringing about a *rapprochement* between the left and right.

Opponents of the Charter

The *rapprochement* of left and right goes back to disagreements over the Maastricht Treaty (1992), at which time politicians like Jean-Pierre Chevènement (then Socialist), Philippe Séguin (RPR) and Charles Pasqua (then RPR, but now head of his own party, the RPF) all discovered they had at least one thing in common: they were all against a federal EU. As a result, Chevènement left the Socialist Party to found the Mouvement des Citoyens (MDC), whose spokesman is Georges Sarre (MP for Paris) and whose aim is to fight for the traditional Jacobin values of the French Republic. Since these are common to many from the traditional left and

---

49   D. Cohn-Bendit and J. Guaino, *La France est-elle soluble dans l'Europe, Le débat enfin!* (Paris: Gallimard, 1999), pp. 38–9.
50   Cohn-Bendit and Guaino, p. 39.

the traditional right, the movement has attracted people from both sides who believe that the principles at stake are more important than party politics. This does not, however, prevent them from also being members of their respective political parties, since the MDC is essentially a movement rather than a party.

The MDC stands for a Gaullist, i.e. nationalist, view of the French Republic dominated by a strong state. This is perfectly compatible with socialism in that it permits state interference in economic matters. The Marc Bloch Foundation, created in 1998, is devoted to the study and advancement of such a concept of National-Republicanism, and brings out publications on the subject. One of its leading philosophers is Régis Debray. The Marc Bloch Foundation is essentially against the kind of Europe set out in the Maastricht and Amsterdam Treaties. It is against *la pensée unique*, i.e. globalisation, which stops European countries, and France in particular, finding solutions to their own problems, which then remain unsolved and continue to fester. They feel that lawyers and bankers have far too much power for the democratic process to take place, and believe that the European edifice is terribly fragile. This is reflected in the title of Cohn-Bendit and Guaino publication quoted above, *'La France est-elle soluble dans l'Europe? Le débat enfin!'* They see the rise of the French National Front as an alarming sign of the fragility of the French Republic and French democracy. The foundation is intended to bring together intellectuals, political parties, unions and associations of all kinds that wish to resist this trend and develop alternative policies. They do not reject the concept of a united Europe, but do not want a federal state. Georges Sarre therefore considers that signing a document such as the Charter is a dangerous step. He fears it could become a political tool used by movements fighting for regional autonomy, which could destabilise the country. It could also be used by unscrupulous politicians against the will of the silent majority. Such a misuse of the Charter is sometimes referred to as a 'dérapage', suggesting that the nation could 'slide out of control'. The concept is clearly described by Régis Debray, in a book in which he defines the Republic as a compromise between the sword and the rule of law (author's italics):

> Arbitrer par la loi et non soumettre par la guerre est ce qui distingue le droit républicain du droit impérial. Mais pour faire appliquer la loi, nationale et internationale, il faut se doter des moyens de la guerre – une armée et une police.

Lesquelles, par nature et définition, fonctionnent à la violence. *Le glaive peut ainsi à tout moment se retourner contre le code. Ce qui fait déraper la République vers l'Empire – et ses colonies – n'est donc pas extérieur à la République.*[51]

Such a *dérapage* could lead to the creation of a Europe of the regions and the disintegration of the French State. Chevènement and others, such as Debray, call this the 'Balkanisation' of France.[52]

Sarre is not, however, opposed to the principle of safeguarding the future of regional languages as part of the national French heritage (although he thinks this is largely nostalgic) since he is not against the general use of regional languages and their teaching in schools. He has also pointed out that some countries that have signed the Charter, such as Croatia, practise linguistic discrimination (incorrectly declaring Serb to be a 'separate' language from Croatian in order to aggravate the divisions between ethnic groups in Croatia). Other countries that have not signed the Charter, such as Italy, the UK[53] and Belgium, are cited as examples of countries where linguistic minorities are respected. He also feels that the Charter would be unhelpful as far as the Organisation internationale de la Francophonie is concerned.

On a more philosophical level, Sarre has been accused of being a disciple of the Abbé Grégoire, whose linguistic survey of France led to the declaration of war against the regional languages in the name of equality and national unity, and formed the basis of the Jacobin position. Sarre does not see this as an insult. On the contrary, he points out that it was the Abbé who granted citizenship to the Jews and who freed the slaves in the colonies. If the Third Republic continued to attack regional languages, he argues, it was because the enemies of the Republic (the monarchists) were manipulating regionalism as a means of returning to power. According to Sarre, these enemies of the French state still exist, and ratifying the Charter would be a step towards a communitarian model. This would be contrary to the French Republican tradition, which is founded on the principle of citizenship (*la citoyenneté*) and not on the

51   R. Debray, *Le code et le glaive* (Paris: Albin Michel/Fondation Marc Bloch, 1999), pp. 54–5.
52   Debray, p. 29.
53   The UK has, however, now both signed and ratified the Charter. Italy has signed but not yet ratified it.

principle of diverse ethnic identities: 'ils défont la République et nuisent
à l'intégration des Français d'origine étrangère, *laquelle ne peut passer
que par le français*'.[54]

The fact that, constitutionally, no distinctions may be made on the
grounds of origin, race or religion is clearly more important than party
politics for politicians such as Chevènement and Sarre. Their views in
this respect are similar to those expressed by members of other parties,
such as the RPR, who are also against the Charter. This does not automatically imply a negative attitude towards regional languages. In its
journal, *La Lettre de la Nation* (9 July 1999), the RPR expressed its
attachment to regional culture, but not to the point of endangering the
fundamental principles upon which the nation is founded. They are firmly
in favour of Chirac's suggestion that a *loi-programme* is all that is needed
to improve the development of the regional or minority languages. This
approach is popular with large sections of the French public.

Supporters of the Charter

The Charter's supporters maintain that its opponents have not always
read it properly. For instance, Béatrice Vallaeys wrote in *Libération* of
those who 'fantasise' about the Charter leading to different languages
being used in all contexts throughout the country. She pointed out that
the articles for which France has signed up relate only to education,
culture and the media, and that French remained the sole official language. In no context would it be possible to address an administrative or
judicial body in anything but French, either orally or in writing. Nor will
social security leaflets be published in any language but French. She
stressed the symbolic nature of the Charter and the fact that its main
advantage was to officially recognise the existence of regional and minority languages.[55]

This contradicts people like Mireille Grandval[56] who stated that, if
France ratifies the Charter, the most important legislation and all health

54   *Libération*, 22 June 1999, p. 6.
55   *Libération*, 25 June 1999.
56   *Libération*, 5 July 1999.

and safety notices would have to be translated into the regional or minority languages. She saw this as a waste of money since, with the exception of Alsatian, Corsican and maybe Basque, these languages are no longer transmitted naturally from parent to child. Josselin de Rohan, a descendant of the Dukes of Brittany, in spite of his stated pride in his Breton identity, also claimed that the Charter would involve the translation of the laws of the country into all the minority languages and the use of these languages in all aspects of public life. As a senator and Président du Conseil régional de Bretagne, his critics thought that he should have read the articles to which France had signed up more carefully.[57]

The truth of the matter is that neither of the two opinions quoted above are accurate. The facts as they stand are that, on ratification, states must sign up for at least one paragraph or sub-paragraph from Articles 9, 10 and 13, which relate to judicial authorities, administrative authorities and public services, and economic and social life. In respect of judicial authorities, France had agreed to make the most important national statutory texts available in the regional or minority languages designated at the time of ratification. Nobody knows quite how many languages this would involve since this would only have been stated at the time of ratification. Indeed, Bernard Cerquiglini's report, which was drawn up specifically to establish how many regional or minority languages existed in France and the DOM-TOMs, came up with the rather amazing figure of 75, over 55 of which are spoken in the DOM-TOMs. This still left far more than the traditional 6 or 7 regional languages of France, since it included non-territorial languages such as a form of Dialectal Arabic spoken only in France, and Berber, which is not officially recognised by any state, to mention the two most widely spoken examples.[58] This clearly marks the first step towards recognising such languages, and as such is very important.

Not all these languages would need to be treated alike, however, even were the Charter to be ratified. It allows a distinction to be made

---

57   *Le Figaro*, 24 August 1999.
58   For further details, see A. Judge and S. Judge, 'Linguistic Policies in France and Contemporary Issues: The Signing of the Charter for Regional or Minority Languages', *International Journal of Francophone Studies*, vol. 333, 2, 2000, pp. 106–27.

between those languages that would be simply given Part II protection and those that are to be positively promoted by the specific measures contained in Part III. On ratification of the Charter, all regional and minority languages falling within the definition of the Charter come under Part II, but those under Part III have to be listed. It is not clear whether languages such as the Dialectal Arabic spoken in France and Berber would be included, nor which of the languages spoken in the DOM-TOMs would also benefit from the Charter. Since the Loi Toubon is not applicable to the TOMs, it could be argued that the Charter need not apply to them either. It may, however, be seen as more politically correct to include them – although not necessarily all of them – given the demands expressed regularly for autonomy or even independence in some of these territories. As matters stand, the figure of 75 languages seems to amount to scaremongering, since the author of this report is not only an excellent linguist, but also a well-known Jacobin. In more general terms, the importance of ratification depends to a large degree on this unknown factor, which has not really surfaced in the press, and to which there is at present no answer.

Apart from accusing opponents to the Charter of having misread it, there are other more positive arguments put forward by its defenders. One such argument is that the independent schools functioning in regional languages are, in fact, secular, democratic and tolerant. They are not restricted to 'locals', and certainly do not promote ideas about 'racial purity'. Their ethos emphasises that loss of a language – any language – is loss of a world-view, and that a bilingual education is a personal enrichment that makes for understanding and tolerance. Against the view that bilingualism means a 'communitarian' vision of France, they cite the example of General de Gaulle, the modern father of sovereignism, who made a speech partly in Breton when campaigning for regionalisation. Bilingualism, they claim, also helps children to learn other languages.

The movement in favour of ratification of the Charter is greatly helped by a fashion for regional culture in certain areas – and *vice versa*. Regional cultures are even seen as giving economic advantages in terms of tourism, etc., to the extent that some politicians have felt a need to change tack. This is what Josselin de Rohan did in view of the success enjoyed by Jean-Yves Cozan, the member of parliament for Finistère who favours Breton autonomy, and the fact that the Breton self-rule movement has two seats in the Conseil régional de Bretagne. Moreover, other important politicians, such as Jean-Yves Le Drian, the member of parliament for Lorient, and Bernard Poignant, the mayor of Quimper, and many other personalities in Brittany are also in favour of the Charter. As a result, de Rohan started arguing that there should be better funding for Breton and defended the foundation of a bilingual Diwan secondary school in Carhaix, moves that could seem somewhat opportunistic. All this explains why one journalist referred to politicians who were 'Breton in Brittany, but no longer in Paris', and another to the 'rapid conversion syndrome'.[59]

Surprisingly, the Charter's supporters are not all regionalists. For example, Claude Sicre, one of the two members of the Occitanist Rap group Fabulos Trobadors has stated that he is anti-regionalist. In an interview in *Libération*,[60] Sicre maintained that the debate should be about cultural decentralisation, i.e. 'cultural democracy', which would lead to 'cultural plurality'. A few weeks later *Libération* carried a number of articles on Breton identity on account of the numerous Breton festivals taking place at that time. The main message was that there was no conflict in being both French and Breton, since these identities function at different levels. The old right-wing link between territory and language has clearly been abandoned. What is still being debated is whether it is necessary to learn Breton in order to defend its culture. This is seen as essential by some people, while others, citing the 'Irishness' of the English used by Irish writers of English, maintain that culture is more than a language.

Many people are exasperated by the whole debate, which they see as an artificial problem. For example, *Libération* printed another article alongside the one by Georges Sarre with the title 'The Republic will be multicultural', in which Norbert Rouland argued that the Conseil constitutionnel was out of touch, since French society had increasingly evolved towards a certain kind of multiculturalism, whether the French liked it or not.[61] He argued that multiculturalism can coexist with the

59   Pierre-Henri Allain, *Libération,* 6 August 1999.
60   *Libération,* 13 July 1999.
61   *Libération,* 22 June 1999.

nation state as long as it is not synonymous with communitarianism. He also pointed out that the 1992 Conseil d'État judgement in the 'affaire des foulards' gave a new pluralistic meaning to the concept of the secular state since it allowed the public expression of faith (in this case Islam), something that had hitherto been restricted to the private sphere.

The intense opposition to the ratification of the Charter from the sovereignists has forced its supporters to campaign more actively. For example, José Rossi (Démocratie libérale) suggested that MPs should initiate constitutional reform, since this was allowed by the Constitution. As a result, Démocratie libérale has put forward a draft bill including the same provisions as Jospin's text. The Conseil régional d'Alsace and the Conseil régional des Pyrénées, of which François Bayrou is the Président, passed a motion in favour of the Charter. Nine socialist parliamentarians declared that they too intended to put forward a bill aimed at changing the Constitution. And 25 right-wing members of parliament in the DL, UDF and RPR signed a document in support of the regional languages 'sans défaire la France', i.e. without destroying the Republic:

> Il y a aujourd'hui dans notre pays un clivage fondamental entre ceux qui restent repliés frileusement sur un esprit jacobin centralisateur et réducteur et ceux, de plus en plus nombreux, qui choisissent une France moderne ouverte à la diversité et à la liberté.[62]

This does not, however, mean abandoning the basic principles of national unity: 'Creating a Europe of regions without destroying France: that is the fascinating task at hand.' It is interesting that this attitude is adopted by centrist and conservative MPs as well as some socialists.

The Aftermath of the Debate: Present-day Policies

France is, on the surface, a volatile country and great debates (and revolutions) usually fizzle out, but not without leaving some permanent changes, usually of a rather minor nature. But it is a succession of these

62   *Le Monde*, 25 June 1999.

minor changes that have defined the evolution of the country. They usually concern the nation as a whole, in that they figure largely in all the media and are much discussed at a personal level. They are in themselves a factor of unity and show democracy functioning at the popular level. It would therefore be a mistake to underrate their importance. Thus it is possible to distinguish France after May 1968 from France before May 1968: there were no fundamental changes, and yet nothing was the same. Similarly, the perennial debates on spelling reform appear to have amounted to very little, since the last 'law' on the subject became 'optional' (!); nevertheless, the debate led to a far less prescriptive attitude, at least in practice. And, surprisingly, according to the Délégation générale à la langue française (DGLF), the Loi Toubon has been a success in spite of the ridicule heaped on it at the time of its promulgation (see Part I of the *Rapport au Parlement sur l'application de la loi du 4 août 1994 relative à l'emploi de la langue française*). So, has anything changed since the debate on the Charter fizzled out in the late summer of 1999?

As far as EBLUL is concerned, ratification of the Charter would have been a great event, but the mere signing of the Charter was an achievement in itself. EBLUL is happy that the debate has given the regional and minority languages such a high profile and is satisfied that France will in effect implement the Charter provisions by way of internal legislation.[63]

This satisfaction is fully justified, for there are important signs of an increased awareness of the value and cultural importance of minority languages in France. To some extent this predates the controversy and merely reflects the pressures to sign the Charter. In 1998 the Minister for Culture and Communication, Catherine Trautmann, asked the DGLF to set up an 'observatory of linguistic usages' to study not only French in all its various forms, but also all the other languages spoken on French territory (including the DOM-TOMs) and the educational consequences of their interaction. This was to further the development of new linguistic policies. Thus, for the first time non-indigenous minority languages were

---

63   Personal communication to S. Judge by Dónal Ó Riagáin.

recognised as part of the French heritage, a point that was highlighted during the 'debate'[64].

The aim of the DGLF's 1999 report was to give a full account of the state of French in the nation and the success or otherwise of the Loi Toubon in ensuring that both French and official terminology are used as required by the law. This tends to be judged in terms of how many lawsuits have been conducted, by whom and what fines have been paid. But the report goes much further than these questions, since it also gives an account of all governmental linguistic policies and expresses opinions as to how they should be developed. Not surprisingly, the DGLF report shows these policies in the best light possible. It is interesting to note, in this respect, how the Loi Toubon is presented, five years after it was debated and ridiculed. The new approach is to punish only where advice and encouragement have not worked. This represents a major shift in style compared to traditional Jacobin methods, although the underlying aims are still the same.

The report starts by listing the cases in which the use of French and approved terminology are compulsory. It refers to the fact that radio and television stations have been 'asked' to promote the use of official terminology and the concept of 'la Francophonie'. It broadens the problem to the need for public-sector services to set a good example, not only by using French and official terminology, but also by promoting multilingualism in their dealings with foreigners. For example, their websites are supposed to be in French and two other languages (presumably to combat the predominance of English). The report reiterates the principle that all children should learn two foreign languages at school; it also contains a section on the new Linguistic Observatories and the regional languages.

More specifically, as far as the Internet is concerned, the report states that although France was late in grasping the potential of the Internet, it is now developing a strong on-line presence. The need now is

---

64   François Bayrou stated at one point (author's italics), "Les langues de nos régions, le basque, le breton, le béarnais, l'occitan, le corse, le gascon, l'alsacien, *le créole* ont le droit à l'existence. C'est le même combat que la défense du français contre l'anglais.' Quoted in *Le Monde*, 19 June 1999. Others have made similar comments, referring mainly to Arabic and Berber.

to mobilise the private sector in this field, which means giving financial help. Grants are being awarded to the press to create Web sites in French and other languages. Similarly, the cinema industry is being given funds both to help produce films in French and to help adapt French multimedia packages into other languages. It is a surprise, however, to read in Décret no. 90-66 of 17 January 1990 on the cinema and audio-visual industries that 'French works' include either works in French or in a regional language of France. The same provision applies to songs: the law demands that 40% of all songs on the radio should be in 'French', which includes regional languages).

The government also wishes all information useful to its citizens and those of the Francophone countries to be free on the Internet. Using 'la Francophonie' to increase the size of the French network is clearly of major importance. Quebec is mentioned specifically in this context. In other words, exemplary conduct on the part of official bodies and generous funding are the carrots used to enforce the law. Another section deals with 'l'enrichissement de la langue française' i.e. increasing its vocabulary and bringing about terminological standardisation within the Francophone world, an example of which is the 'feminisation' of words referring to professions, again a subject of much debate in the past. The report quotes the Prime Minister as saying that the government was not able to impose the new terminology, but wished to set a good example.

Under 'sensibilisation' reference is made to the success of the 'Le français comme on l'aime' week (Le français comme on l'aime: la semaine de la langue française et de la francophonie, 12–21 March 1999) and the 'Journée internationale de la francophonie', which takes place every year on 20 March. These are intended to be 'fun' events that make both French and French linguistic policies attractive. Some of the work carried out by the DGLF also comes under this heading, principally the numerous booklets and leaflets given out to the general public on all kinds of linguistic topics ('La langue française dans le monde', 'Le français et l'internet', 'La maîtrise du français et le lien social', to mention but a few). The aim is to combat the feeling that French is in decline. Interestingly, there is now a booklet on 'La valorisation des langues régionales', and free information on 'the 75 languages of France' is promised in the near future.

The final section of the report deals with the Observatoire des pratiques linguistiques and the 'valorisation' of the regional languages. The 'Observatory' does not, in fact, carry out research itself, but is responsible for selecting and funding research projects. The DGLF was given a budget for these activities in 1999. The budget finances two types of projects: those dealing with research into languages are funded centrally, while those intended to encourage a variety of cultural activities and publications are funded at a regional level. The funds come from the Directions régionales des affaires culturelles (the DRACs), which were created during 1974–5 and now equal the Conseils régionaux in number (22). The total budget for 1999 was FF 1,200,000 (about £120,000). This was not a large amount, but it was a start. Projects that received grants included: support for Corsican on television (FF 70,000), assistance for the publication of stories in Kanak (FF 60,000) and a project to record Occitan digitally (FF 50,000).

The Observatoire des pratiques linguistiques has ushered in a new interest in non-prescriptive descriptions of French (particularly in urban dialects) that marks another new departure from tradition. This move was signalled by the Prime Minister, Lionel Jospin, when he inaugurated the new Conseil supérieur de la langue française on 16 November 1999. In the *Lettre d'information* (11 February 2000) of the Ministry for Culture and Communication, he is quoted as stating that he wanted the French language to open up to modernisation. He also stated his intention to implement fully the 39 articles of the Charter to which France had become committed by signing the Charter.

The Ministry of Education has, in the past, seemed less concerned with the problem, but a small project started in September 2000 was meant to collect information on the teaching of regional languages in the primary sector in terms of the numbers of children involved, hours of teaching and the methods used. Since the aim is to find out what is actually happening on the ground, only Basque, Breton, Corsican, the German dialects of Alsace and the Moselle area, Occitan and Gallo are relevant to the project. Corsican is seen as a special case, since Corsica has a separate status embodied by the 'Collectivité territoriale de Corse', which funds the teaching of Corsican in schools through a mixture of local taxes and state subsidies. Moreover, Jack Lang, while Minster for Education, spoke on a number of occasions in support of the regional languages, and his intention to implement the Charter, despite the fact France had not ratified it. A 'circulaire' was sent in 2001 to all 'recteurs d'académies'[65] asking for a 'Conseil académique des langues et cultures' to be created in each of the 'académies'. Some have so far refused. He has also encouraged the training of teachers of these languages.

At a non-state level, the most obvious sign of progress for the regional languages was been the opening on 1 May 1999 of a new Breton Language Bureau in Carhaix (Office de la langue bretonne), the aim of which is to collect data, coordinate terminology and improve co-ordination between the different bodies working to support Breton. It also monitors sociological changes in Breton language use and conducts sociolinguistic surveys. Regionalists hope that other linguistic communities in France will set up similar bodies, which exist elsewhere in the EU. It may be worrying for the sovereignists, however, that this new body should be seen as the first step towards the creation of a language planning policy in Brittany.

More negatively, the Ministry for Culture does not give any specific help to cultural activities in regional languages, which have to compete against works in the French language for funds. The report states that French works do not get preferential treatment, but this is unlikely to be the case, if only because of the much smaller number of people working in the regional languages. But, the report does make the point that it would be a good thing if the Ministry were to set up funds specifically for cultural activities in the regional languages. To date, only the 'collectivités territoriales', such as those of Corsica, Brittany and Languedoc-Roussillon, have spent money on these matters, but this expenditure comes from their normal budgets. Mention is made in the report of the presence of the regional languages on radio and television, but the figures given in terms of hours per week are pathetically low (85 hours in Breton for the whole of 1999 on France 3, the station that shows programmes in regional languages, with even less for all the other languages). Only in the DOM-TOMs is there much broadcasting in regional languages (59 hours per week in French Polynesia). Education in the regional languages is on the increase, but mainly thanks to the efforts of the private sector.

65   France is divided into regional 'académies' that are responsible for educational provision.

There is next to no help for publications in the regional or minority languages. Moreover the proposed integration of Diwan Breton-language schools has been suspended, the draft agreement signed by Jack Lang, the French Minister for Education and Andrew Lincoln, president of the Breton language Diwan schools in May 2001 having been annulled by the Conseil d'État in October 2001.

However, it is also true that there is now a permanent representative for the regional languages at the DGLF, which is a remarkable sign of progress and that the DGLF was renamed 'la Délégation générale à la langue française et aux langues de France' in October 2001. The main outstanding problem is a tendency, particularly since the debate on the Charter, to see these languages in terms of France's 'heritage', i.e. as worthy of conservation rather than development.

Conclusion

This chapter began with the question of whether France was going to change its approach to linguistic policymaking. The signs suggest this is indeed happening, though the pace of change is very slow. It would seem that, as passions die down and the nation gets excited about other matters, there will be a gradual process as measures are taken that may in themselves be insignificant, but ultimately will amount to a real change of direction.

There are a number of factors that suggest this is likely to be the case:

(i)   Numerous cracks have appeared in the system as the very foundations of the state are questioned: the 'invisibility of religion', the *unicity* of the country – as against its unity – and demands from both territorial and non-territorial users of minority languages for the right to use their own languages.
(ii) The development of the Organisation internationale de la Francophonie: although it reinforces the status of French, it also opens the door to different kinds of French and different practices. Instead of

being regarded as the only possible model, other varieties are now taken into account, resulting in a far more descriptive approach to the study of the language.

(iii) The rejection of what were seen as the excesses of the Loi Toubon led to changes in legislation in order to adapt to the present climate, for which it was not suited in its original form. The implementation of the law is now based on seeking to attract and convince doubters rather than punish them. This is a major departure from the prescriptive Jacobin approaches of the past.[66]

(iv) The signing of the Charter for Regional or Minority Languages, which marked the recognition of their existence; and, in the wake of the Cerquiglini report, the recognition that languages such as Dialectal Arabic and Berber are also acknowledged to be 'minority languages' worthy of protection.

(v) The government's repeated commitment to the implementation of the 39 articles, despite failure to ratify the Charter.

(vi) The recognition, following the publication of the Cerquiglini report, of more minority languages than was ever thought possible. This is particularly important for the langues d'oïl.

It is true that, at present, there is more talk of conservation than revitalisation, but some see this as a first step. Nevertheless, it could be a dangerous step: not only are the Jacobins opposed to the formal ratification of the Charter, but many people who wish to see the regional and minority languages protected are against it too. On the whole, they would prefer conservation, 'folklorisation' even, to revitalisation or the continued use of immigrant languages in education and culture in the interests of a more gradual and harmonious integration than that afforded by a violent plastering of French as the 'cement of the nation'.

Real revitalisation of the regional and minority languages is feared because of the fundamental dangers that might be posed by a 'dérapage',

---

66 Prime examples include the (in)famous notice found at many schools: 'il est interdit de cracher et de parler Breton' and the policy of 'le signe', under which any pupil who was caught speaking a language other than French had to carry a sign proclaiming this misdemeanour, which was then passed on to the next child to infringe the rules. This went on in some schools until the end of the Second World War.

which could see the break-up of a country built on the principle of equality rather than freedom. Opposition to ratification is sometimes seen as a 'Jacobin' position in the best sense of the word, but the factors listed above point to the decline of the Jacobin approach in the narrow and purely historical sense of the word.

STEPHEN JUDGE

Language as a Human Right: A Legal Problem for France

An important contemporary issue in terms of language policy is the legal status of regional and minority languages in relation to a country's official language(s). Since the continued existence of these languages is often threatened, it is often argued that linguistic minorities should be protected and their languages promoted on the grounds of cultural diversity. However, the protection of linguistic minorities can also be seen as a threat to national stability in that it can encourage ideas about self-determination. In addition, the recognition and protection of linguistic minorities is sometimes seen as contrary to the principle of the equality of individuals before the law. This chapter is concerned with describing and analysing the history of the protection afforded to linguistic minorities internationally and within Europe, and the extent to which they can be said to have the right to claim protection for their language and their right to use it in the private and the public sphere as a legally enforceable human right.

This chapter also examines the problems that the French state has with regard to the recognition of linguistic minority rights with specific reference to the Council of Europe's Charter for Regional or Minority Languages, which the French signed in May 1999, but which was declared incapable of ratification in June 1999 due to its partial incompatibility with the French Constitution.

The Nature of Human Rights

While there is widespread acceptance of the importance of human rights in international structures, there is considerable confusion as to their precise nature and role in international law.[1] The Western view of international human rights has tended to emphasise the basic civil and political rights of *individuals*, which limit the power of government over the governed. These rights include the right to the protection of the law, the rights to freedom of expression, assembly and religion, and the right to political participation in the process of government. In the nineteenth century state sovereignty and domestic jurisdiction reigned supreme, and there were few issues that were considered to be of international concern. All matters that would be regarded as human rights issues were universally regarded as within the sphere of national jurisdiction. Thus, the protection afforded by rights such as Habeas Corpus in Britain, the Bill of Rights in the USA and the Déclaration des droits de l'homme in France, were national in their scope.

Movements towards the development of internationally recognised human rights began in the twentieth century following the two World Wars. The first important step came with the establishment of the League of Nations in 1919. The impact of the Second World War on the development of human rights law was immense, with the United Nations replacing the League of Nations in 1945.

In respect of international law, there are some basic principles that must be understood before considering the nature of human rights and their protection. Human rights are a matter of international law because they do not depend upon the nationality of the person, and the protection of these rights is not limited to the jurisdiction of any one state. However, their enforcement can be through the agency of national courts. In practice, however, much of the international rights law operates beyond national legal systems, since most alleged breaches will be by states acting against the rights of their citizens or persons within their jurisdiction. The traditional international law of state-based jurisdictional exclusivity must therefore give way to a realisation that the rights of humans matter more than the rights of states.[2]

The basic rule of traditional international law is that no state has the right to encroach upon the preserve of another state's internal affairs.

1   Malcolm N. Shaw, *International Law*, 4th edn (Cambridge: Cambridge University Press, 1997), p. 196.
2   Martin Dixon and Robert McCorquodale, *Cases and Materials on International Law*, 3rd edn (London: Blackstone Press, 2000), p. 184.

This is based on the principle of the equality and sovereignty of states and is reflected in Article 2 (7)[3] of the UN Charter. In the human rights field, however, states may no longer plead this rule as a bar to international concern and consideration of human rights situations.[4] Furthermore, this first rule gives rise to the principle that states must be permitted to solve their internal problems in accordance with their own constitutional procedures before there can be recourse to international mechanisms. In consequence, the requirement that petitioners must exhaust their domestic remedies before resorting to international mechanisms appears in all international and regional human rights instruments.[5]

Prevention of Discrimination and Protection of Minorities

The extension of human rights protection to the issue of linguistic minorities raises a number of problems. Essentially, the international treaties and other instruments that protect human rights are concerned with ensuring the equality of *individuals* before the law, securing freedom from discrimination. The issue of giving guarantees of special protection to ethnic, religious or linguistic minorities is something that may be seen to contradict notions of equal treatment before the law, and there is therefore a dichotomy between individual human rights and the special protection of minorities. The protection of minorities is

> the protection of non-dominant groups which, while wishing in general for equality of treatment with the majority, wish for a measure of *differential treatment* in order to preserve the basic characteristics which [...] distinguish them from the majority of the population.'[6]

3   'Nothing contained in the present Charter shall authorize the UN to intervene in matters which are essentially within the domestic jurisdiction of any State [...]'
4   Dixon and McCorquodale, no. 2, p. 202.
5   E.g. Article 41 (c) of the International Covenant on Civil and Political Rights; Article 26 of the European Convention on Human Rights and Fundamental Freedoms (ECHR).
6   Warwick McKean, *Equality and Discrimination under International Law* (Oxford: Clarendon Press, 1983), p. 82.

The special protection of minorities may also be regarded as a significant threat to the sovereign state since it can be seen as threatening to national unity. Approaches to this issue have changed considerably between 1919 and the present day.

Immediately after the First World War, following the collapse of the German, Ottoman, Russian and Austro-Hungarian Empires and the rise of a number of independent nation states in Eastern and Central Europe, the League of Nations sought to protect those groups to whom sovereignty and statehood could not be guaranteed. Persons belonging to racial, religious or linguistic minorities were to be given the same treatment, and the same civil and political rights as other nationals in the state in question. Article 22 of the Covenant of the League set up the mandate system for peoples in the colonies of the German and Ottoman empires under which the mandatory power was required to guarantee freedom of conscience and religion, and Article 23 provided for the just treatment of these peoples. The 1919 peace agreements with Eastern European and Balkan states included provisions relating to the protection of minorities. The League of Nations supervised these provisions, and there was a right of petition to the League of Nations. These schemes for protection did not work well for a variety of reasons.

After the Second World War, the focus shifted to the international protection of universal individual human rights. It was not until the adoption of the International Covenant on Civil and Political Rights in 1966 that the question of minority rights came back onto the international agenda and then only in the form of the modest and rather negative provisions of Article 27 (see below).

The International Protection of Linguistic Minorities

The international treaties and instruments relating to human rights contain numerous references to the fact that individuals should not be discriminated against on the grounds of their language. Article 1 of the United Nations Charter sets out the purposes of the United Nations, including the aim:

> To achieve international co-operation in solving international problems of an economic, cultural or humanitarian character, and in promoting and encouraging respect for human rights and for fundamental freedoms for all without distinction as to race, sex, language, or religion.

Article 55 sets out what the UN is intended to promote 'in the interests of creating conditions of stability [...] necessary for peaceful and friendly relations among nations'. This includes 'universal respect for, and observance of, human rights and fundamental freedoms for all without distinction as to race, sex, language, or religion'.

The General Assembly of the United Nations adopted the Universal Declaration of Human Rights on 10 November 1948.[7] In drawing up the Declaration, the Sub-Commission on Human Rights agreed that its two tasks were the prevention of discrimination and the protection of minorities. In respect of minorities, the characteristics meriting protection were race, religion and language, but, in order to qualify for protection, a minority had to owe undivided allegiance to the government of the state in which it lived and its members had to be nationals of that state. The Commission on Human Rights approved the Sub-Commission's text on the prevention of discrimination, but no decision was reached on the protection of minorities. The fundamental difference between the two was, however, identified. Discrimination implied any act or conduct that denied to certain individuals equality of treatment with other individuals because they belonged to a particular social group, whereas the protection of a minority requires positive action in favour of that minority in order to achieve real equality before the law.

The Declaration was intended to lead to a single treaty protecting all human rights within a short space of time. In fact, it took 20 years for the drafting to be completed and, in the event, two treaties called 'Covenants' were created dealing with different rights. These are the International Covenant on Civil and Political Rights (ICCPR) 1966[8] and the International Covenant on Economic, Social and Cultural Rights (ICESCR) 1966.[9]

7   General Assembly Resolution 217A (III).
8   999 UNTS 171, UKTS (1977) 6, Cmnd 6702. The ICCPR entered into force on 23 March 1976 and had been ratified by 199 states as of November 1999.
9   993 UNTS 3. The ICESCR entered into force on 3 January 1976 and had been ratified by 142 states as of November 1999.

Article 26 of the ICCPR concerns freedom from discrimination and states that,

> All persons are equal before the law and are entitled without any discrimination to the equal protection of the law. In this respect, the law shall prohibit any discrimination and guarantee to all persons equal and effective protection against discrimination on any ground such as race, colour, sex, language, religion, political or other opinion, national or social origin, property, birth or other status.

The protection of minorities is only mentioned in Article 27, which is the only article that could form the basis for the protection of linguistic minorities. This article is worded as follows (author's italics):

> In those States in which ethnic, religious or *linguistic minorities* exist, persons belonging to such minorities *shall not be denied the right*, in community with the other members of their group, to enjoy their own culture, to profess and practise their own religion, or *to use their own language*.[10]

This is not very far reaching since it does not specify the contexts in which the language can be used. Furthermore, actual protection is only offered to '*persons belonging to such minorities* [...] in community with the other members of their group' rather than to the *minority group* as such. There is also no definition of the concept of minorities.

Attempts to define minorities have focused on their numerical inferiority and non-dominant position, the existence of certain objective features differentiating them from the majority population and the subjective wish of the minority to preserve those characteristics. The UN Human Rights Committee adopted a General Comment on Article 27 in 1994.[11] This distinguished between the *rights of minorities and the right of self-determination* on the one hand, and the *right to equality and non-discrimination* on the other. The Comment emphasised that the rights

---

10   The text differs from that proposed by the Sub-Commission in 1950 (UN doc. E/ CN.4/358,22): 'Persons belonging to ethnic, religious, or linguistic minorities shall not be denied the right [...]' The wording was changed as a concession to states who claimed that no minorities existed within their territories.

11   General Comment no. 23, HRI/GEN/1/Rev.1, p. 38.

founded in Article 27 did not prejudice the sovereignty and territorial integrity of states. The Committee also stressed that minorities need not be nationals or even permanent residents, but that migrant workers and even visitors might be protected. The Committee also pointed out that Article 27 required positive measures of protection from the state or other persons within the state.

Article 27 has now been supplemented by the Declaration of the Rights of Persons belonging to National or Ethnic, Religious and Linguistic Minorities 1992.[12] Article 1 is worded as follows (author's italics):

> States shall protect the existence and the national or ethnic, cultural, religious *and linguistic identity of minorities* within their respective territories and shall encourage conditions for the promotion of that identity.

Article 2 provides for the right of such minorities '*to use their own language, in private and in public*, freely and without interference or any form of discrimination'. According to Article 3, states are also required to 'take appropriate measures so that, wherever possible, persons belonging to minorities may have adequate opportunities to learn their mother tongue or to have instruction in the mother tongue,' while Article 4 requires states to 'take measures in the field of education, in order to encourage knowledge of the history, traditions, language and culture of the minorities existing within their territory'.

In June 1993, following a UN World Conference on Human Rights in which all states participated, the Vienna Declaration[13] was agreed by consensus. The Declaration was a reaffirmation of the commitment made by all states to fulfil their obligations to promote universal respect for, and observance and protection of, all human rights and fundamental freedoms for all in accordance with the UN Charter and other international human rights instruments, in particular the ICCPR and the ICESCR.

12   Resolution 47/135.
13   32 ILM 1661 (1993).

Language as a Human Right and the Council of Europe

In addition to international protection for human rights, there are three regions where human rights treaties have been ratified: Europe, the Americas and Africa. This chapter only discusses the situation in Europe.

The European Convention for the Protection of Human Rights and Fundamental Freedoms (ECHR) was signed in Rome on 4 November 1950 and entered into force on 3 September 1953. It established one of the most successful systems of international law for the protection of human rights. The ECHR was drafted during 1949 and 1950, and there are now a number of Protocols that have supplemented the original Convention. All states joining the Council of Europe are required to ratify the Convention.

In addition to the Convention, the Council of Europe has recently promulgated two further Conventions relevant to the issue of linguistic minority rights. These are the European Charter for Regional or Minority Languages 1992 and the Framework Convention for the Protection of National Minorities 1994. The Charter for Regional or Minority Languages 1992 relates exclusively to the promotion of autochthonous regional or minority languages, whereas the Framework Convention for the Protection of National Minorities 1994 includes provisions relating to the linguistic rights of 'national minorities'.

The European Convention on Human Rights and Fundamental Freedoms (ECHR)

The ECHR is enforced by a permanent Court of Human Rights based in Strasbourg. However, in 'monist' states, such as France, the Convention became part of national law on ratification, and its provisions can therefore be enforced in the domestic courts. The UK has now passed the Human Rights Act 1998 and the Convention became enforceable through the country's national courts as of 2 October 2000.[14]

---

14   This legislation has been incorporated into Scottish Law since devolution.

The Convention and subsequent Protocols protect a number of human rights but exclude protection for linguistic minorities, which was felt to be too explosive an issue to be included in a document that required the unanimous approval of its signatories. Linguistic minorities have, nonetheless, sought protection against linguistic discrimination under Article 14, which ensures non-discrimination. They have also sought to use Article 2 of the First Protocol, which ensures access to education in the minority language. One problem relating to the anti-discrimination provisions under Article 14 is that the article does not give a limitless right to protection against discrimination of the kind given by Article 2(1) of the International Covenant on Civil and Political Rights. It merely provides for absence of discrimination in the application of the other substantive rights recognised in the Convention:

> The enjoyment of the rights and freedoms set forth in this Convention shall be secured without discrimination on any ground such as sex, race, colour, language, religion, political or other opinion, national or social origin, association with a national minority, property, birth or other status.

The inadequacy of these articles as tools for the protection of linguistic minorities was established in the *Affaire Linguistique Belge*,[15] in which the claimants argued unsuccessfully that obliging a child to attend a school that used a language other than his or her mother tongue constituted discrimination and a denial of the right to education. The decision settled two issues. Firstly, the Court of Human Rights recognised a distinction between legal and illegal discrimination. Discrimination could be legal if (i) the discrimination had a legitimate purpose, and (ii) the discrimination practised was proportional to the purpose. The Court found that the discrimination operated by Belgium was legal and proportionate in respect of the linguistic policies of the state, which it supported. The Court also stated that the right to education would be meaningless without recognition of the right to an education in the national language or one of the national languages of the country. However, it also stated that the Convention did not oblige a state to finance or to subsidise a specific form of education. Thus, if a state decides that it cannot afford

15   A 6 (1968).

to establish education in a particular language, nothing under Article 2 obliges it to do so.

The European Charter for Regional or Minority Languages 1992

Although promulgated by the Council of Europe, the Charter derives in part from initiatives taken by the European Parliament (EP) during the late 1970s and the 1980s. In 1979 and 1980 the EP passed several motions demanding protection for regional and minority languages and cultures. The First Arté Resolution 1981 resulted in the creation of the European Bureau for Lesser Used Languages (EBLUL) in 1982. The Second Arté Resolution 1983 led to an 'official' budget to support Community languages and cultures.[16] The 1987 Kuijpers Resolution demanded concrete measures to save and promote regional languages and cultures, and support for the Council of Europe's proposed Charter for Regional or Minority Languages.

The Charter can be traced back to the public debate on regional and minority languages held at the Palais de l'Europe in 1984, when the Standing Conference of Local and Regional Authorities of Europe established a Committee of Experts to prepare a draft European Charter for Regional or Minority Languages. The Committee included two members of the EBLUL Council, and EBLUL's Secretary General, Dónal Ó Riagáin, was consulted on the final draft. The Charter was adopted by the Standing Conference in March 1988 and was received favourably by the Parliamentary Assembly of the Council of Europe in October 1988. An expert *ad hoc* committee (CAHLR), set up to advise on the form to be accorded to the document, reported in April 1992. In June 1992 the Committee of Ministers of the Council of Europe voted to accord the Charter the legal form of a Convention. Only France, the UK, Cyprus and Turkey abstained and Greece voted against. The Convention was open for signature on 5 November 1992 and required ratification by five member states of the Council of Europe. It had been ratified by eight countries, Croatia, Finland, Germany, Hungary, Liechtenstein, The Netherlands, Norway and Switzerland, by 2 November 1999, and came

16   For details of this budget see the chapter in this publication by Anne Judge.

into force in these countries on 1 March 1998 (1 April 1998 in Switzerland and 1 January 1999 in Germany). Twelve other countries, Azerbaijan, Cyprus, the Czech Republic, France, Iceland, Italy, Luxembourg, Malta, Romania, Russia, 'the former Yugoslav Republic of Macedonia' and Ukraine, have signed the convention but not yet ratified it.[17] Sixteen countries have signed and ratified the Charter: Armenia, Austria, Croatia, Denmark, Finland, Germany, Hungary, Liechtenstein, The Netherlands, Norway, Slovakia, Slovenia, Spain, Sweden, Switzerland and the UK.[18] Ratification is a prerequisite for the accession to the European Union of all new members.

In principle, the Charter is far reaching. Part I deals with generalities, including a definition of the term 'regional or minority languages', while Part II sets out the principles and aims that each contracting party must accept in their entirety in respect of all regional or minority languages spoken within the state. The most important part of the Charter is Part III, which contains measures to promote the use of a specific number of regional or minority languages that have been identified by the state as falling within the protection of Part III at the time of ratification. These deal with the status of each regional or minority language in a number of areas: education (Article 8), justice (Article 9), public services (Article 10), the media (Article 11), cultural activities and facilities, including libraries, museums, archives, theatre, literary and cinematographic output (Article 12), and economic and social life (Article 13). States must agree to apply a minimum of 35 paragraphs or sub-paragraphs of Part III to each language designated for Part III recognition by the state on ratification, with at least three chosen from each of Articles 8 and 12 (education and cultural activities), and one from each of Articles 9, 10, 11 and 13 (justice, public services, the media, and economic and social life). Part IV is concerned with the enforcement of the Charter.

Enforcement of the Charter is monitored by the parties presenting periodic reports to the Secretary General of the Council – one in the first year after ratification and then at three-yearly intervals (Article 15 [1]). These reports are to be made public (Article 15 [2]). These reports are

17   The treaty can be signed by member states of the Council of Europe and non-member states.
18   As at 3 May 2002. Source: Treaty Office on http://conventions.coe.int.

examined by a Committee of Experts constituted in accordance with
Article 17 (Article 16 [1]). National bodies and associations may make
representations to the Committee (Article 16 [2]). The Committee then
prepares a report for the Committee of Ministers incorporating the state's
report and any representations received (Article 16 [3]). The Secretary
General of the Council of Europe delivers a detailed report to the Parliamentary Assembly on the Charter's application every two years (Article
16 [5]).

The languages protected by the Charter are identified in Article 1,
which defines the term 'regional or minority languages' as

> languages that are (i) traditionally used within a given territory of a State by nation-
> als of that State who form a group numerically smaller than the rest of the State's
> population, and (ii) different from the official language(s) of that State; it does not
> include either dialects of the official languages of the State or the languages of
> migrants. (Article 1 [a])

The 'territory in which the regional or minority language is used' means
'the geographical area in which the said language is the mode of expression of a number of people justifying the adoption of the various protective and promotional measures provided for in this Charter' (Article 1
[b]). The Charter also covers 'non-territorial languages', which are defined as

> languages used by nationals of the State which differ from the language or lan-
> guages used by the rest of the State's population but which, although traditionally
> used within the territory of the State, cannot be identified with a particular area
> thereof. (Article 1 [c])

The Charter aims to protect the indigenous minority languages of the
state but not the languages of migrants. These are covered by the Framework Convention for the Protection of National Minorities.

A weakness of the Charter – one that makes it easier for states to
ratify it – is that it allows states to choose the degree to which they will
recognise the designated regional or minority language under each heading. This allows for the possibility of full and equal status in all fields or
mere tolerance.

The Framework Convention for the Protection of National Minorities

The Vienna Summit of the Member States of the Council of Europe resulted in the Vienna Declaration, which includes the statement:

> States should create the conditions necessary for persons belonging to national minorities to develop their culture, while preserving their religion, traditions and customs. These persons must be able to use their language both in private and in public and should be able to use it, under certain conditions, in their relations with the public authorities.

This Declaration was supported by the European Commission, which was represented in Vienna, and led to the Framework Convention for the Protection of National Minorities 1994. This was signed by all member countries except France, Belgium and Greece. The Convention has been ratified by the requisite number of member states (12) and entered into force in those states on 1 February 1998. This document is primarily made up of recommendations only. The Convention had been ratified by 24 states (including seven EU member states) by 31 December 1999.

The aim of the Convention is stated in Article 1:

> The protection of national minorities and the rights and freedoms of persons belonging to these minorities are an integral part of the international protection of the rights of man and, as such, are within the domain of international co-operation.

The Convention has 32 articles and covers a range of extremely diverse questions, such as resistance to assimilation, legal equality, the right of peaceful assembly, media access to minority groups, participation in cultural, social and economic life, and cross-border contacts and co-operation. Articles 9–14 deal with language and culture. In this respect, the Convention recognises the right to freedom of expression in a minority language by national minorities (Article 9); the freedom to use the minority language in private and public, orally and in writing (Article 10); the right to the use of name and surname in the minority language and the right to display signs in the minority language (Article 11); the obligation of the state to foster knowledge of the culture, history, language and religion of national minorities (Article 12); a recognition

of the right to private educational establishments (without financial obligation on the part of the state) (Article 13); the right to learn minority
languages and the right to be taught the minority language or receive
instruction in this language, subject to sufficient demand (Article 14).

The Convention fails to define the term 'national minority'. An
explanatory document states that,

> For certain persons the term only applies to historical national minorities. For
> others, it encompasses historically multinational minority groups, Gypsies or Jews
> for example, and regional minorities. Whereas for others the term should also
> include new minority groups, such as migrant workers and refugees.

The failure to give a legal definition of national minorities gives
this Convention almost limitless scope. The French government has not
expressed an intention to sign and ratify this Convention and, indeed, it
is difficult to see how the Convention could be compatible with the
French Constitution, since it rejects the constitutional aim of assimilating
minority groups into the French melting pot, 'le creuset français' (see
the later discussion on the incompatibility of the Charter for Regional or
Minority Languages).

Linguistic Minority Rights Under the European Conventions

The issue of the establishment of new legal rights for linguistic minorities
arises as a result of the fourth paragraph of the Preamble to the Charter
for Regional or Minority Languages. This states that,

> [...] the right to use a regional or minority language in private and public life is an
> inalienable right conforming to the principles embodied in the United Nations
> International Covenant on Civil and Political Rights and according to the spirit of
> the Council of Europe Convention for the Protection of Human Rights and Funda-
> mental Freedoms (ECHR).

The preamble to the Framework Convention for the Protection of
National Minorities 1994 makes similar references to the ECHR, and to
the conventions and declarations of the United Nations. The justification
for the existence of these conventions therefore derives from perceived
notions of existing rights for linguistic minorities.

At present, the conventions have no force in law. However, the Parliamentary Assembly of the Council of Europe[19] has declared its intention to complement these two conventions

> with an additional protocol to the European Convention on Human Rights setting out clearly defined rights which individuals may invoke before independent judiciary organs.

Over the long term, therefore, the intention is that the rights of linguistic minorities should receive judicial protection along with the other human rights.

The Council of Europe clearly regards these two charters as complementary and has been reported as having expressed the wish that there should be close co-operation between the two committees charged with ensuring the implementation of the undertakings made by the signatories to the two conventions.[20] This would tend to reinforce the move towards the recognition of linguistic minorities and action to protect their rights.

France's Traditional Approach to Linguistic Minorities

France has a long history of linguistic intervention.[21] Most of this intervention has pursued the aim of ensuring the supremacy of French as against the regional or minority languages. The most famous example of such legislation is the Ordonnance de Villers-Cotterêts 1539, which decreed that all business, administrative or judicial, would henceforth be conducted in French. The French Academy, founded in 1635, laid down prescriptive policies with the intention of moulding French into a perfect tool of communication for all registers.

19   Recommendation 1285 of the 1996 Ordinary Session, Paragraph 10.
20   Note by Jean-Manuel Larralde, Le Dalloz (1999), no. 39, p. 598 at p. 601.
21   A. Judge, 'French: a Planned Language?', in C. Sanders (ed.), *French Today: Language in its Social Context* (Cambridge: Cambridge University Press, 1993), pp. 7–26.

The report drawn up after the French Revolution by the Abbé Grégoire (1794) revealed that French was only the exclusive language in 15 *départements* out of a total of 83.[22] The report also showed that only 6 million of the population could speak some French, and only 3 million could speak the language properly, though fewer still actually did so. There were more than 6 million, mainly rural citizens who could not understand French at all. The Abbé Grégoire estimated that well over half the population spoke a language other than French as their mother tongue. The result of this was a drive by the Convention[23] to appoint French language teachers in every commune[24] and commission a new school grammar. French was to be the language of all municipal councils. These decisions were only implemented much later,[25] but French became – and remains – one of the most important symbols of the French nation state, the 'cement' of the nation.[26]

Since the 1950s, a series of legislative instruments that directly or indirectly addressed the issue of the regional languages have gradually relaxed the restrictions on their teaching and their use in various contexts. The Loi Deixonne of 1951[27] was the first to permit reference to, and some teaching of, local languages and dialects. Primary teachers could teach the local language for one hour per week and devote a further hour to local culture and literature. This was purely optional, however, and initially the law only applied to four languages: Breton, Basque, Catalan and Occitan. German was added to this list the following year, but Alsatian was only added in 1988, along with Gallo. Corsican was added by

22   The *départements* are administrative units established in 1790 by the revolutionary Assemblée constituante.
23   The Convention succeeded the Assemblée nationale and governed the country from 1792 to 1795.
24   An administrative unit similar to the English 'parish'.
25   Guizot organised the primary school system in 1832, but primary education did not become compulsory until the 1880s.
26   'Depuis l'ordonnance de Villers-Cotterêts de 1539 – qui dispose que la justice est rendue en français – et la création de l'Académie française en 1635 – qui a donné à notre langue un gardien – la langue française, *ciment de l'unité nationale et élément fondamental de notre patrimoine,* a fait l'objet de politiques publiques' (in the context of the debate about the *loi Toubon*) (author's italics). Ministère de la culture et de la francophonie, NOR: MCCX9400007L.
27   No. 51-46 of 11 January 1951.

decree in 1974.[28] This law strengthened the position of the regional languages to which it applied and encouraged other groups to fight for recognition. The languages of the DOM-TOMs were added later.[29]

In 1975 Article 12 of the Loi Haby of 1975[30] permitted the optional teaching of regional languages at all levels and made provision for the infrastructure required in order to teach regional languages. The 'Savary circulaires'[31] refer to a teaching programme for regional languages and cultures, and the absence of any list of languages meant that all France's minority languages were covered, including the langues d'oïl. A number of arrêtés followed relating to secondary education programmes for Basque, Breton, Catalan, Corsican, Occitan (and its dialects), Gallo, the regional languages in Alsace and Tahiti,[32] and Melanesian.[33] Several arrêtés led to the establishment in 1991 of a CAPES – a national teacher-training qualification – for teachers of these languages.[34] An *arrêté* of 1994[35] allowed year 3 children in bilingual secondary schools (aged around 15) to sit their history and geography examinations in a regional language. Moreover, in 1990, a convention[36] was drawn up by Lionel Jospin, then the socialist Minister of Education, recognising the validity of teaching regional languages and providing funds for specialist teachers in the nursery and primary sector.

François Bayrou, the Minister of Education in 1995, drew up the Circulaire Bayrou,[37] which stressed the state's commitment to an essential

28 Décret no. 74-33 of 16 January 1974.
29 Décret no. 81-553 of 12 May 1981 added Tahitian; Loi no. 84-747 of 2 August 1984 covered the languages of Guadeloupe, French Guyana, Martinique and Reunion, and Loi no. 88-1028 of 20 October 1992 covered those of New Caledonia.
30 No. 75-620 of 11 July 1975, named after the then Ministre de l'Éducation, René Haby.
31 No. 82-261 of 21 June 1982 and no. 83-547 of 30 December 1983.
32 15 April 1988 and 17 September 1991.
33 20 October 1992.
34 *Arrêtés* of 30 April 1991, 29 May 1996 and 4 September 1997.
35 23 June 1994.
36 A *convention* is an agreement drawn up between two legal persons, in this case the Ministry of Education and local administrations and associations. *Conventions* are presumably seen as important only at a local level, since they are not listed in the Bulletin officiel de l'éducation nationale.
37 No 95-86 of 26 June 1995.

part of France's heritage through the transmission of regional languages and cultures.

Article 5 of a law dating from 1982[38] on audio-visual communication placed a duty on public-service radio and television stations to maintain the presence of regional languages and cultures. This encouraged the regionalisation of the media to the benefit of Breton, Occitan, Basque, Catalan, Corsican and Alsatian, which all obtained a few hours of exposure each week. The development of private radio stations has also led to the establishment of minority programmes, including some directed at linguistic minorities. Furthermore, the 'Loi Carignon'[39] stipulated that 40% of the songs on French radio should be in French. However, in a letter,[40] the Conseil supérieur de l'audiovisuelle[41] (CSA) defined 'a song in French' as including 'a song in French *or in a regional language of France*' (author's italics).

The other main area of legislation relating to language has had the aim of protecting French against the encroachment of English. This has led to the creation of a number of bodies with a prescriptive, protectionist role: the Conseil supérieur de la langue française, the Délégation générale à la langue française,[42] and a terminological commission for each ministry charged with developing new French words to prevent excessive borrowing from English. Some of these commissions include representatives from other 'Francophone' countries. Their decisions as to what is terminologically acceptable are disseminated to all official organisations.

The best-known laws in this respect are essentially prescriptive. The Loi Bas-Lauriol of 1975[43] and the Loi Toubon of 1994[44] relate solely to the defence of French. The only reference to France's regional languages in the Loi Toubon is a statement in Article 21 that it is not intended to be detrimental to them.

38   No. 82-652 of 29 July 1982.
39   No. 94-88 of 1 February 1994.
40   No. 88 of January 1997.
41   A public organisation that monitors quotas, carries out surveys and handles complaints.
42   This was renamed the Délégation générale à la langue française et aux langues de France in October 2001.
43   No. 75-1349 of 31 December 1975.
44   No. 94-312 of 4 August 1994.

The French government's previous freedom to legislate to protect and promote French against English is now restricted by external factors.[45]

The Signing by France of the Charter for Regional or Minority Languages

The signing of the Charter for Regional or Minority Languages on 7 May 1999 came as a surprise to most French people. It was, in fact, the result of a great deal of lobbying of the French Parliament by supporters of the country's regional or minority languages. Also, in the spring of 1998 there were a number of large demonstrations in Bayonne, Rennes and Strasbourg demanding more aid for regional languages.

The sequence of events that led up to the signing of the Charter by France can be broken down into a number of stages. On 29 May 1996 Jacques Chirac, the President of the Republic, expressed his approval in principle for the signing of the Charter at a dinner given by Bernard Poignant, the socialist mayor of Quimper. On 24 September 1996 the Conseil d'État,[46] having been asked to consider the constitutionality of this step by the then Prime Minister, Alain Juppé, stated that it was incompatible with the Constitution.[47] Without disputing the Charter's aim of protecting historic regional or minority languages in Europe, and while admitting that, subject to certain precautions, most of the measures in Articles 8, 11 and 12 could be implemented without any constitutional objection, the Conseil d'État considered that the obligations under Articles 9 and 10 could not be fulfilled without conflict with Article 2 Paragraph 1 of the Constitution, which states that 'The language of the Republic is French'. In respect of the measures contained in Article 9 relating to the judicial system, the Conseil d'État had already declared

---

45 See the chapter in this volume by A. Judge for a full discussion of this topic.
46 The Conseil d'État, first created in 1799, advises the government in administrative and judicial matters. It also acts as the Court of Appeal for administrative matters.
47 Opinion no. 359461 of 24 September 1996, *Rapport public annuel*, p. 303.

that the use of a language other than French in court was contrary to the general principles of legal procedure.[48] This requirement, they decided, had now been elevated to the level of a constitutional issue by virtue of the change made to the Constitution in 1992.[49] In respect of the provisions concerning administrative matters and public services in Article 10, the Conseil d'État considered that the state could not comply with its Charter obligations by simply choosing some marginal provisions relating to the use of regional or minority languages in an auxiliary capacity, since this would not be consistent with the state's obligations under Part II to promote the use of these languages in public and private life.

On 1 July 1998 the Prime Minister, Lionel Jospin, was presented with the Péry-Poignant Report, which argued that France's regional languages were part of the national heritage and advocated the ratification of the Charter subject to clarification of its constitutionality. On 6 October 1998 Guy Carcassonne, the professor of constitutional law at the University of Paris X-Nanterre, was asked to report on the constitutionality of the Charter and concluded that France could accept 52 of the Charter commitments without any problem. He recommended, however, an interpretative declaration accompanying the Charter to clarify its scope.

On 6 May 1999, faced with the contradictory advice of the Conseil d'État and Guy Carcassonne, Jacques Chirac decided that the promise made by the Prime Minister to sign the Charter could be honoured, and Pierre Moscovici, the Minister of European Affairs, signed the Charter in Budapest on 7 May 1999. On 20 May 1999 Jacques Chirac referred the Charter to the Conseil constitutionnel[50] for a final decision on its constitutionality.

A number of precautions were taken in respect of the signing of the Charter that were inspired by the decision of the Conseil constitutionnel a short while earlier concerning the use of Tahitian and the other Polynesian languages.[51] These precautions were not negligible. On the one

---

48 CE. Sect. 22 November 1985, Quillevère, AJDA (1985), p. 751.
49 Loi constitutionnelle no. 92-554 of 25 June 1992.
50 One of the main roles of the Conseil constitutionnel is to examine the constitutionality of new laws when they are drafted or before they are promulgated.
51 Décision no. 96-373 DC 9 April 1996, Loi organique portant statut d'autonomie de la Polynésie française. Rec. p. 43, cons. 90 to 94.

hand, the 39 paragraphs or sub-paragraphs of Part III to which France subscribed were very near the minimum requirement of 35. Most of them related to the areas that posed the least likelihood of conflict with Article 2 of the Constitution: teaching, media and cultural facilities. As regards the more problematic areas of 'public' usage, a single measure, the minimum allowed for in the Charter, was chosen in respect of justice, and the choice fell on the requirements that were least problematic in their scope. Moreover, the signing of the Charter was accompanied by an interpretative declaration on France's constitutional concerns that echoed the terms of the decision about the Statut de Polynésie.[52]

In addition to this, on 7 May 1999 a report was published by Bernard Cerquiglini, the head of the Institut National de la Langue Française. This report had been commissioned by the Ministry of Education, Research and Technology and the Ministry of Culture and Communication. It identified 75 different regional or minority languages in use within French territory, including the overseas departments and territories. Within France itself the report identified 25 languages, including: Alsatian, Basque, Breton, Catalan, Corsican, Flemish, Franco-provençal, Occitan, the langues d'oïl, Berber, Dialectal Arabic, Yiddish, Romany and Western Armenian.

Finally, on 15 June 1999 the Conseil constitutionnel[53] decided that some aspects of the Charter were incompatible with Articles 1 and 2 of the Constitution. Subsequently, on 23 June 1999, Lionel Jospin suggested a constitutional amendment that would enable France to ratify the Charter. The President of the Republic declared that he would not personally order the revision requested by the Prime Minister. On 5 July 1999 the President stated that there was no need for the Charter, since most of what had been signed up for was already in place in France. He suggested that it would be simpler for Prime Minister Jospin to draw up a 'loi-programme pour le développement des langues régionales' to put the Charter commitments into effect.

---

52 Décision no. 96-373 DC 9 April 1996.
53 Décision no. 99-412 DC, JO 18 June 1999, p. 8964 (http://www.legifrance. gouv.fr./).

The Legal Basis for the Declaration of Incompatibility

An examination of the reasons why the Charter was found to be incompatible with the French Constitution must begin with an examination of the Charter itself. The originality of the Charter lies in the fact that states can choose to respect only one part of the provisions of the Charter. This is clarified by Article 2, which is entitled 'Undertakings' and is set out in two parts: 1– 'Each party undertakes to apply the provisions of Part II to all the regional or minority languages spoken within its territory and complying with the definition in Article 1'; and 2 – 'In respect of each language specified at the time of ratification, acceptance or approval, in accordance with Article 3, each party undertakes to apply a minimum of thirty-five paragraphs or sub-paragraphs chosen from among the provisions of Part III of the Charter, including at least three chosen from each of the Articles 8 and 12 and one from each of Articles 9, 10, 11, and 13.' In consequence, states choosing to sign the Charter must subject themselves to the whole of its 'objectives and principles' as set out in Part II and then choose to implement at least 35 measures of the total of 98 measures in respect of any languages that it chooses to designate in accordance with Part III. The state is not obliged to both sign and designate; it may simply sign.

The main constitutional problem raised by the Charter for the French is that it has the effect of creating specific rights in favour of 'groups of speakers', both in the private and public domain. This is the essential problem, since France does not recognise the existence of groups within the state. This includes ethnic, religious and linguistic groups, and any other minority. This is a result of the constitutional principle of equality set out in the first article of the 1958 Constitution. This has been the French position since the 1789 Revolution and is justified by the fact that the state guarantees the equality of all citizens, and not the equality of groups of citizens identified according to various criteria. The ultimate aim is assimilation and integration into the French melting-pot, 'le creuset français'.

This fundamental constitutional principle was recognised by the Conseil d'État on 24 September 1996 when it stated that the Charter was incompatible with the Constitution. According to Ferdinand Mélin-Soucramanien, Professor at the Université Montesquieu-Bordeaux IV,[54] this fact was also clearly acknowledged by Guy Carcassonne in his report published in September 1997. Although he found that the Charter was not incompatible with the Constitution, this decision relied very much on the attribution of an extremely limited interpretation of 'groups' being entitled to linguistic rights. This is why he states specifically that 'the aim of the Charter is to protect the languages and not, necessarily, to confer inalienable rights on their speakers.' This is also why he suggests that the Charter should only be signed in conjunction with an interpretative declaration, which would restrict the scope of the definition of these groups.

This is apparent from the text of the first paragraph of the interpretative declaration:

> Insofar as the Charter does not aim at recognising and protecting minorities, but only at promoting the European linguistic heritage and in so far as the term 'groups using languages' does not mean to confer collective rights on those groups, the Government of the French Republic interprets the Charter to be compatible with the Preamble of the French Constitution, which guarantees the equality of all citizens before the law and recognises only the French people, comprising all citizens without any distinction as to origin, race or religion.

The need for this interpretative declaration arose because the Charter drastically restricts the extent to which states can make reservations excluding them from the application of one or more of the Charter provisions when they sign the Charter. This is a result of Article 21 Paragraph 1, which only allows states to make reservations to Paragraphs 2 to 5 of Article 7. Generally, whenever France has signed an international treaty in which one or more articles has the effect of recognising the existence of ethnic, religious or linguistic minorities, it has always been subject to the following reservation: 'the government of the Republic declares, taking account of article 1 of the Constitution of the French Republic, that article [...] does not apply in respect of the Republic.' This was the solution adopted for Article 27 of the United Nations International Covenant on Civil and Political Rights when it was adopted by France on 19 December 1966 (see above) and again for Article 30 of the Inter-

---

54   'La République contre Babel', *Revue du Droit Public*, 1, 1999, pp. 985.

national Convention on the Rights of Children, which contained an almost identical Article in respect of minority groups, when it was adopted on 26 January 1990. Whenever a state wishes 'to exclude or to modify the legal effect of certain Treaty provisions in their application to the State' this must be done by way of a reservation that is defined by Article 2-1 d of the Vienna Convention on Treaties. It is not possible to achieve the same effect by using an interpretative declaration that can only set out the sense and the scope that a state intends to give to the treaty in its domestic interpretation for the national courts.

For this reason, the Conseil constitutionnel decided that the interpretative declaration formulated by France 'had no other legal force than to constitute a supporting instrument in connection with the treaty and, in the event of any litigation, helping with its interpretation.' It therefore concluded that the issue of the constitutionality of the Charter should be considered 'independently of this declaration'.[55]

In considering the constitutionality of the Charter, the Conseil constitutionnel found that the Charter was incompatible with the principles of the indivisibility of the Republic, equality before the law and the unicity of the French people. It also found that the Charter was contrary to the principle that French is the language of the Republic.

In respect of the first objection, having cited Article 1 of the Constitution, the Conseil constitutionnel stated that 'the principle of the unicity of the French people, of which no group can claim the right to exercise national sovereignty, had a constitutional worth.'[56] The Conseil then stated that, 'these fundamental principles prevent the recognition of the collective rights of any group whatsoever, identified by their place of origin, their culture, language or beliefs.'[57]

Given this premise, it was predictable that the Conseil should declare the stipulations set out in Paragraph 4 of the Preamble, Article 1 (a) and (b) of Part 1, and Article 7, Paragraphs 1 and 4 of Part II Paragraph 4 because they confer 'specific rights to "groups" of speakers of regional

---

55   Cons. 4. Judgments of the court are given in paragraphs beginning with the words 'Considérant que...' These paragraphs are normally identified by their number as 'Cons. 1', etc.
56   Cons. 5.
57   Cons. 6.

or minority languages in "territories" within which these languages are practised'.[58]

The crucial part of the Preamble is the fourth paragraph, which maintains that

> the right to use a regional or minority language in private and public life is an inalienable right conforming to the principles embodied in the United Nations International Covenant on Civil and Political Rights and according to the spirit of the Council of Europe Convention for the Protection of Human Rights and Fundamental Values.

Although the preamble has no binding force in itself, it has some legal value in that it is a guide to the interpretation of the Charter. In interpreting the substantive terms of the Charter, a national judge will abide by the spirit of the Preamble. Thus, if one of the statements of the Preamble conflicts with a constitutional principle, it puts the whole of the Charter into question.

Article 1 (a) defines regional and minority languages as languages 'traditionally used within a given territory of a State *by nationals of that State who form a group* (author's italics) numerically smaller than the rest of the State's population' and 'different from the official language(s) of that State,' excluding 'dialects of the official language(s) of the State or the languages of migrants.' Article 1 (b) defines the territory in which the regional or minority language is used as 'the geographical area in which the said language is the mode of expression of a number of people justifying the adoption of various protective and promotional measures'.

Article 7 is a statement of the objectives and principles underlying the policies, legislation and practice of the parties to the Charter. Paragraphs 1–4 contain statements of principle in respect of regional or minority languages that are territorially linked. Paragraph 5 states that parties will undertake to extend the same principles to non-territorial languages, but in a flexible manner. There are particular concerns about Article 7, Paragraph 1 (b) regarding 'the respect of the geographical area of each regional or minority language in order to ensure that existing or new administrative divisions do not constitute an obstacle to the promotion of the regional or minority language in question,' while Article 7, Paragraph 1 (d) concerns 'the facilitation and/or encouragement of the

58   Cons. 10.

use of the regional or minority languages, in speech and writing, in public and private life'.

Article 7, Paragraph 4 states that the parties 'shall take into consideration the needs and wishes expressed by the groups which use such languages' and that the parties 'are encouraged to establish bodies, if necessary, for [this] purpose'.

The decision of the Conseil constitutionnel is entirely consistent with earlier precedents. The Conseil constitutionnel has invariably declared that any form of discrimination in respect of minorities, whether based upon origin, race, religion, beliefs or sex, is incompatible with the constitution.[59] In its decision on the 'Statut de la Corse',[60] the Conseil constitutionnel declared the first article, which recognised the existence of a 'peuple corse, composante du peuple français', to be unconstitutional because the Constitution 'only knew of the French people, composed of all French citizens without distinction of origin, race or religion'.[61] A more recent decision on equality of access to electoral lists for women was also declared unconstitutional since it favoured minority groups.[62]

In respect of the principle that French is the language of the Republic, the Conseil constitutionnel found that Article 7 Paragraph 1 (d) was contrary to Article 2 of the Constitution because one of the objects and principles of the signatory states was to be 'the facilitation and/or the encouragement of the use of regional or minority languages, in speech and in writing, in public and private life'.[63]

59   'Quotas par Sexe', 18 November 1982, Décision no. 82-146 DC, préc., cons. 7.
     'Statut du territoire de Polynésie française', Décision no. 84-177 DC, RJC, 1-194,
     cons. 7. 'Statut du territoire de Nouvelle-Calédonie', Décision no. 84-178 DC,
     RJC, 1-195, cons. 8. 'Évolution de la Nouvelle-Calédonie', Décision no. 85-196
     DC, RJC, 10234, cons. 16. 'Statut de la Corse', Décision no. 91-290 DC, RJC, 1-
     438, cons. 14.
60   Décision no. 91-290.
61   Décision no. 91-290, cons. 13.
62   Décision no. 2000-429 DC, 30 May 2000; Loi tendant à favoriser l'égal accés des
     femmes et des hommes aux mandats électoraux et fonctions électives.
63   In connection with Article 7 1 (d), the interpretative declaration states that the
     French Government understands Article 7, paragraph 1 (d) to be the statement of
     a principle that is not contrary to Article 2 of the French Constitution. This para-
     graph concerns the right to use a regional or minority language without, however,
     undermining the principle that the country's official language is French.

In this respect, the Conseil constitutionnel also declared that Article 2 of the Constitution took precedence over Article 11 of the Declaration of the Rights of Man. It declared that, even though Article 11 of the Declaration of the Rights of Man of 1789 implied the right of the citizen to speak, write or print in the language of his or her choice, this provision of the Charter was contrary to Article 2, Paragraph 1 of the Constitution, which was changed in 1992 to read 'The language of the Republic is French,' in so far as the Charter tends 'to recognise a right to practise a language other than French not only in the private sphere but also in the public sphere, which, under the Charter, includes the legal system, administrative authorities and public services'.[64]

This would be counter to the principle accepted since the Ordonnance de Villers-Cotterêts of 1535, according to which French is the sole language used in legal and administrative business. This has always meant that a petition drafted in a regional language is not admissible in an administrative court[65] or a civil court.[66] For the same reason, letters must be addressed in French and not in a regional language.[67]

However, this rule is not absolute. In connection with the Loi Toubon, a decision in 1994[68] censured the obligatory use of French official terminology in certain situations, such as radio and television communications, whether private or public.[69] The same position applies in private communication between individuals,[70] and in respect of teachers and researchers.[71] The court also held that the stipulation that French should be used at meetings, conferences, etc. could be satisfied if the organisers provided interpretation into French as an alternative.[72]

---

64 Cons. 11.
65 Association de défense et de promotion des langues de France, req. 52379; CE, 10 June 1991, *Kerrain*, req. 99608.
66 Cass. civ., 17 February 1981, cited by D. Latournerie, 'Le droit de la langue française', *EDCE*, 36, 1984–1985, p. 103; Cass. crim., 4 March 1986, Turkson, Bull. crim., p. 214, cited by R. Debbasch, 'La reconnaissance constitutionnelle de la langue française', *RFDC*, 11, p. 457.
67 CE, 15 April 1992, D. Le Duigou, 1992, note R. Debbasch.
68 Décision no. 94-345 DC, RJC, 1-595.
69 Cons. 9.
70 Cons. 10.
71 Cons. 24.
72 Cons. 7.

Flexibility can also be seen in the decision 'Autonomie de la Polynésie française'.[73] This ruled on the interpretation of the first paragraph of Article 115, which read: 'Le français étant la langue officielle, la langue tahitienne et les autres langues polynésiennes peuvent être utilisées.' This was interpreted as requiring the use of French 'by public bodies and private persons in the exercise of a public service mission, as well as consumers in their relations with the administration and the public services'. The decision nevertheless allowed the use of Tahitian and other languages in audiovisual communication, even within the public sphere,[74] and in higher education and research.[75] It was also permissible for languages other than French to be used in teaching at the pre-school, primary and secondary levels, provided that their use was not obligatory.[76]

Jean-Éric Schoettl, a Conseiller d'État, also gives as an exception a scenario in which a member of the public and a public official use a regional language to carry out a public function where they are both familiar with the language and choose to use it. What is contrary to Article 2 of the Constitution is any notion that persons have the right to use a language other than French in the public sphere.[77]

With regard to Part III, none of the 39 measures to which France had agreed posed any constitutional problem. Most of the 39 measures related to non-contentious areas. Thus, France agreed to 11 paragraphs in Article 8 (education), nine in Article 11 (media), eight in Article 12 (cultural activities and facilities) and two in Article 14 (transfrontier exchanges). The position adopted was less generous in respect of the 'difficult' articles. Article 9 (justice) posed the most problems. It is not surprising, therefore, that France only agreed to one of the 15 measures in this article, Article 9 (3), which was to 'make available in the regional or minority languages the most important national statutory texts and those relating particularly to users of these languages, unless they are otherwise provided'. In this connection, Paragraph 4 of the interpretative declaration stated,

---

73   Décision no. 96-373 DC, RJC, 1-660.
74   Cons. 9.
75   Cons. 20 to 24.
76   Cons. 92.
77   Décisions du Conseil constitutionnel 'Langue française', in *L'Actualité juridique – Droit administratif*, 20 July/20 August 1999, p. 573.

> The Government of the Republic interprets article 9 (3) as not being inconsistent with the fact that only the official version in the French language, of the texts which are translated into the regional or minority languages, shall alone have legal value and can be used by public authorities as well as by the public in their relations with the administration and the public service.

Since the legal requirement to use French in the public sphere already allows the use of translations,[78] Article 9 (3) cannot be considered incompatible with the Constitution.

France agreed to three out of a total of 21 measures in Article 10 in respect of administrative authorities and public services: 10 (2) (c), (d) and (g). The wording of these provisions is as follows:

> In respect of the local and regional authorities on whose territory the number of residents who are users of regional or minority languages is such as to justify the measures specified below, the Parties undertake to allow and/or encourage: (c) the publication by regional authorities of their official documents also in the relevant regional or minority languages; (d) the publication by local authorities of their official documents also in the relevant regional or minority languages; and (g) the use or adoption, if necessary in conjunction with the name in the official language(s), of traditional and correct forms of place-names in regional or minority languages.

France agreed to five measures out of the nine contained in Article 13 (economic and social life). The first three, Article 1 (b), (c) and (d) related to 'eliminating, prohibiting or opposing practices tending to discourage the use of the regional or minority languages in documents relating to economic or social life'. Since these activities are outside the public sphere, far from being contrary to the Constitution, they enhance the freedom of communication provided for in Article 11 of the Declaration of the Rights of Man of 1789. The two other measures, Article 2 (b) and (c), place a duty on the state 'in the economic and social sectors directly under their control (public sector), [to] organise activities to promote the use of regional or minority languages,' and to

> ensure that social care facilities such as hospitals, retirement homes and hostels offer the possibility of receiving and treating in their own language persons using

78   Décision no. 94-345 DC, cons. 7.

a regional or minority language who are in need of care on grounds of ill-health, old age or for other reasons.

Neither of these undertakings poses a constitutional problem.

Thus, the undertakings in Part II are unconstitutional, and those to which France has agreed in Part III are pointless, since they have for the most part already been implemented without any need to ratify the Charter.

Ferdinand Mélin-Soucramanien[79] also draws attention to the nature of the judgment returned by the Conseil constitutionnel. He points out that the decision of the Conseil constitutionnel was based on the notion of the 'unicity' of the French nation rather than the more usual 'unity'. He remarks that the notion of unicity had been used previously in a decision in 1991,[80] but that this could simply have been the court replicating the arguments of the claimants in that case. The second use of the principle removes this doubt, since the court used the phrase twice in the course of its judgment.[81] He reflects on whether there is any difference of meaning between the two terms, which are generally considered to be synonymous, and concludes that unity reflects simply the notion that the state is united, whereas unicity expresses an intrinsic quality of something that can never be divided into its constituent parts.[82] He also notes that, for the first time, the first article of the decision does not use the standard formula 'The authorisation to ratify the treaty [...] demands a revision of the Constitution.' The statement used was simply 'The European Charter for Regional or Minority Languages contains clauses which are contrary to the Constitution.' This may reflect the fact that, in respect of the 39 specific undertakings in Part III, the court found that none of them were contrary to the Constitution and that, 'the majority limited themselves to recognised practices which were already in operation in favour of the regional languages.' The Conseil constitutionnel implied that there was no need for a revision of the Constitution, and that the way ahead for the regional languages was for France to proceed by way of domestic legislation.

---

79   F. Mélin-Soucramanien, 'La République contre Babel', *Revue du Droit Public*, 1, 1999, p. 999.
80   Décision no. 91-290 DC, 'Statut de la Corse'.
81   Cons. 5 and 10.
82   Mélin-Soucramanien, p. 996.

Language as a Human Right and the European Community

As has already been stated, the EC has been a major influence on the promotion of minority and regional languages and cultures, largely through initiatives taken by the European Parliament. These have resulted in the establishment of the European Bureau for Lesser Used Languages (EBLUL) and generous funding for the promotion of regional or minority languages throughout Europe. In addition to this, there have been numerous initiatives on regional or minority languages, including research into the numbers of people speaking these languages, the promotion of cultural events and funding for translations into these languages.[83]

The EC Commission's general stance on linguistic policy[84] is that, under the principle of subsidiarity, language is the responsibility of the member states. Concerns only arise when national linguistic restrictions restrict the fundamental freedoms of the Community.[85]

The choice of official language is a decision for the member state, a position that may create problems in a multilingual state. For example, in Spain, Castilian is the official language, though three regional languages have official status within the geographical regions in which they are spoken: Catalan, Basque and Galician. The MEPs of these regions, in particular those from Catalonia, frequently press for some recognition of their language by the European Parliament (EP).

There has been one attempt by a linguistic minority to use EC law to claim the right to use a minority language on the basis of legislation

---

83 A. Judge and S. Judge, 'The Impact of European Linguistic Policies on French', in Dawn Marley, Marie-Anne Hintze and Gabrielle Parker (eds), *Linguistic Identities and Policies in France and the French-speaking World* (London: AFLS and CILT, 1998), pp. 292–317.

84 There is often confusion between the EC and the EU. The EC is a legal entity whereas the EU is a political entity. The EC, the European Coal and Steel Community (ECSC) and the European Atomic Energy Community (Euratom) together form one of the three pillars of the EU. The others are intergovernmental organisations whose decisions are made by co-ordinated or joint action of the member states. They are the Common Foreign Security Policy (CFSP) and Cooperation in Justice and Home Affairs (CJHA).

85 See the chapter in this volume by A. Judge.

ensuring the right of establishment under Articles 39–42[86] of the EC Treaty of 1957. In *Camille Petit v. L'Office National de Retraite (1991)*,[87] M. Petit, a Francophone Belgian national who had lived all his life in Belgium filed a document in a legal action in French rather than Flemish, as required by the language laws of the region in which he lived. He sought to justify his position under Regulation 1408/71 (updated by Regulation 2001/83), Article 2 of which prohibits national authorities, institutions and courts from refusing to accept documents in the official language of another member state. The ECJ held that the Article in question only applied to nationals of one member state who had established themselves permanently in another member state.

Another decision of the European Court of Justice that is of some significance for linguistic minority rights concerned the transliteration of names and surnames of persons from a member state with a different alphabet. This is usually done so as to convey the closest possible approximation to the correct pronunciation to a native speaker of the target language. The International Organisation for Standardisation (ISO) has produced a system for the transliteration of Greek names valid in all countries using the Roman alphabet. The use of this system is required by Article 3 of the Convention on the Representation of Names and Surnames in Registers of Civil Status.[88] This article was held to conflict with EC regulations in the decision *Christos Konstantinidis v. Stadt Altensteig Standesamt and another*.[89] In this case, the transliteration of the claimant's marriage certificate and his birth certificate were inconsistent. He therefore applied to change his marriage certificate from 'Christos KonstADinidis' to 'Christos KonstANTinidis', which more accurately reflected the correct pronunciation of his name. Unfortunately, as a result, Mr. Konstantinidis's first name was rendered as 'Hréstos' instead of 'Christos', which he claimed was misleading for his clientele. The ECJ held that the obligation to have his name transliterated in a way that

86   The article numbers cited here reflect the changes in numbering following the Treaty of Amsterdam.
87   Case C-168/91 [1993] 1 CMLR 476.
88   Convention no. 14 of the International Commission on Civil Status of 13 September 1973 [1976], BGBl. 1473. The Convention exists only in a French version.
89   Case C - 168/91 [1993] 3 CMLR 401.

modified and distorted its pronunciation and caused confusion among his clientele was contrary to his right of establishment under Article 43 of the EC Treaty. The court also stated that

> if the ISO system is used [...] in any other Member State, many Greek names [...] will be written in a way that gives a highly misleading impression of their true pronunciation.

Conclusion

Although the protection of minorities, including linguistic minorities, has generally been given less priority than the protection of the individual, international and European initiatives are clearly moving towards the protection of minorities being given a higher profile. In addition, from an earlier restrictive definition of minorities as nationals of the state in question, the most recent international and European statements point towards a widening of the definition to include migrant workers and even visitors. This is clearly implied by the International Covenants promulgated by the UN and Declarations and General Comments relating to them.

The position of the Council of Europe, encouraged by the European Community, also indicates a future in which linguistic minorities, whether indigenous or otherwise, will be recognised as having legally enforceable rights to use their languages in private and public. It is striking that these rights are justified in the relevant Conventions as merely being a statement of an already existing *status quo*.

Warwick McKean cites a statement by Professor Kunz, who wondered whether there might not be 'fashions in international law just as there are in neckties'. At the end of the First World War

> international protection of minorities was the great fashion; treaties in abundance, conferences, League of Nations activities, and enormous literature. Recently this fashion has become almost obsolete.[90]

90   Case C - 168/91 [1993] 3 CMLR 401, note 6, p. 12.

This was written in 1982. It seems as though the protection of minorities may be coming back into fashion.

This whole development presents a major problem for the French, who will probably be forced to rethink the whole basis of their constitutional refusal to recognise minorities.[91] Whether such a fundamental change to the essentially Jacobin French Constitution, moving it towards a more Girondin stance, can be undertaken without major upheaval is another matter. Will the Constitution allow the French to resolve the dichotomy between the equality of the citizen before the law and the protection of minorities? And, if so, will this be a good thing for the unity of France? Does the statement by Léopold Sédar Senghor in 1958 still hold true: 'la République ne peut être à la fois une et indivisible et multiple et divisible'?

---

91 In November 2001, the Committee on Economic, Social and Cultural Rights of the UN High Commission for Human Rights suggested that France should 'review its position with regard to minorities by ensuring that minority groups have the right to exist and be protected as such in the State party [...] withdraw it reservation with regard to Article 27 of the International Covenant on Civil and Political Rights, and [...] ratify the Council of Europe's Framework Convention on the Protection of National Minorities, as well as the European Charter for Regional or Minority Languages.' Reported 'contact bulletin', vol. 18. No. 1 at p. 5.

NIGEL ARMSTRONG AND MIKAËL JAMIN

Le français des banlieues: Uniformity and Discontinuity in the French of the Hexagone

The French language in the *hexagone* is interesting to the sociolinguist on account of the paradoxes it presents. This introductory section will discuss these from a threefold perspective. The chapter will then go on to describe some changes that may be in progress in the speech of *banlieue* French speakers, and concludes with a consideration of the relation between these changes and the relative uniformity of 'mainstream' French.

Firstly, French shows a particularly wide gulf between the standard and non-standard varieties of the language, wider perhaps than in other comparable (i.e. standardised Western) languages. Moreover, this gulf is more apparent on certain linguistic levels than others. As is conventional, the linguistic levels of analysis used in this chapter are lexis, grammar and pronunciation. Variation between the standard and non-standard varieties is of course apparent in French at all linguistic levels, but as Lodge suggests in the course of a discussion of whether contemporary French may be characterised by a form of diglossia, 'it is probably in the lexicon that style-shifting in French is indicated most obviously.'[1] In one sense, this is unsurprising, since the lexical level is characterised by the greatest degree of salience. Nevertheless, French seems distinctive on account of the rather large number of the pairs of lexical doublets or alternants that speakers have available. One example from this lexical set is the pair *voiture* (standard) and *bagnole* (non-standard), both of which have the equivalent reference 'car', but each of which conveys different connotative or associative meaning.

In contrast with this perhaps quasi-diglossic state, a second distinctive feature that appears to characterise 'standard' French, a term that refers to the set of varieties distributed north of the Garonne and the

---

1   R. A. Lodge, *French: From Dialect to Standard* (London: Routledge, 1993), p. 256.

Massif Central, excluding peripheral areas such as western Brittany and Alsace where there is influence from non-Romance languages, is the rather high degree of uniformity in pronunciation. For the sake of brevity, these varieties will be termed '*oïl* French'. In particular, there now exists a certain amount of empirical evidence to suggest that phonological variation in *oïl* French may be distinctive in lacking any significant regional component.[2]

The results of the perceptual study reported by Armstrong and Boughton suggested that a sample of *oïl* French speaker-listeners from Rennes were able to identify with quite a high degree of success the social class of the members of a different sample of speakers from Nancy on the basis of their speech, but were much less successful in identifying accurately any regional elements. Leaving aside the question of the extent to which the Rennes informant sample exploited clues in syntax and lexis, as well as on other linguistic levels when formulating their judgements of social class, this result supports the findings of several researchers who have reported sociolinguistic variation in *oïl* pronunciation of segments that are also rather clearly marked in French orthography, principally schwa and the liquid consonants /l/ and /r/.[3] These findings may reflect the fact that variable deletion of these segments is undoubtedly socially diagnostic, and at the same time that perhaps rather little else is exploited in the French phonemic inventory to signal social identity. The relative absence of regional localisation in socially diagnostic *oïl* French is suggested further by the fact that similar findings have been reported for these French variables in fairly widely separated locations in the *oïl* region.[4]

---

2   N. Armstrong and Z. Boughton, 'Identification and Evaluation Responses to a French Accent: Some Results and Issues of Methodology', *Revue Parole*, 1997, 5/6, pp. 27–60.

3   N. Armstrong, 'Deletion of French /l/: Linguistic, Social and Stylistic Factors', *Journal of French Language Studies*, 1996, 6 (1), pp. 1–21; W. Ashby, 'Français du Canada/français de France: divergence et convergence', *French Review*, 1988, 6 (5), pp. 693–702; B. Laks, 'Contribution empirique à l'analyse socio-différen-tielle de la chute de /r/ dans les groupes consonantiques finales', *Langue Française*, 1977, 34, pp. 109–25.

4   N. Armstrong (Lorraine); W. Ashby (Tours); B. Laks (Paris).

Thirdly, there is a rather wide degree of impressionistic agreement that 'hyperstyle' variation is now the normal situation in *oïl* French. Convincing arguments have been put forward that hyperstyle variation, the sociolinguistic pattern in which variation along the stylistic or 'intraspeaker' dimension exceeds that observed along the social-group or 'interspeaker' axes (social class, age, sex) is an aberrant pattern of variation.[5] However, observations endorsing the prevalence of hyperstyle variation in French can be found in the writings of several distinguished scholars of French sociolinguistics; for instance, Gadet expresses her view of the matter in the following terms:

> Je ferai l'hypothèse que le français, après avoir connu une période où l'axe décisif est diatopique (XIXe siècle), puis une phase de saillance diastratique correspondant à l'urbanisation (époque de fortes distorsions entre 'langues de classes', qui correspond aussi à la francisation radicale), serait actuellement dans un primat du diaphasique.[6]

Gadet's terms 'diatopique', 'diastratique' and diaphasique' correspond to 'regional/geographical', 'interspeaker/social-group' and 'intraspeaker/ style'. Sanders represents a similar perspective:

> A major difference between English and French is the way in which spoken French has come to diverge from written French. Related to this – though not identical with it – is the distinction between 'informal' and 'formal' usage, which is much greater in French than it is in British English.[7]

A comparable view has been expressed orally to one of the authors of this chapter by another distinguished French scholar of linguistics in relation to *ne* deletion, which in this scholar's opinion has intraspeaker value but not interspeaker value (Yaguello, personal communication). Views such as these, expressed by distinguished linguists who are also

5   A. Bell, 'Language Style as Audience Design', *Language in Society*, 1984, 13, pp. 145–204.

6   F. Gadet, 'Cette dimension de variation que l'on ne sait nommer', *Sociolinguistica*, 1998, 12, pp. 53–71.

7   C. Sanders, 'Sociosituational Variation', in C. Sanders (ed.), *French Today: Language in its Social Context* (Cambridge: Cambridge University Press, 1993), p. 27.

native French speakers, seem worthy of serious consideration. Insuffici-
ent empirical data is available to endorse these views with any degree of
certainty, but we discuss briefly here the conditions necessary for a
'primat du diaphasique'.

There appear to be three principal issues involved. The first relates
to the supposedly large degree of divergence between spoken and written
French, as expressed by Sanders above. If this situation does obtain, it is
relatively straightforward to hypothesise why speakers in the experimental conditions of the type set up in sociolinguistic interviews would
show the high degrees of convergence that are necessary to produce
hyperstyle variation. The second issue relates to the social conditions
necessary to bring about a high degree of linguistic conformity, both in
scripted and unscripted formal speech styles, on the part of a large proportion of the population. The third issue, the spontaneous hyperstyle shift
between unscripted styles, is rather more difficult to explain, but an
attempt will be made to do so below. Firstly however, the two factors
inducing speakers to show high degrees of convergence in the scripted
styles elicited by sociolinguists are as follows:

(i)   It would be necessary for many, if not most, French pronunciation
      variables to derive their socio-stylistic value from their transparent
      representation in spelling. This would entail a ready recoverability
      of the standard variants in reading passages and word lists that
      would induce speakers to realise them in these styles. This appears
      to be true generally of French phonological variables, and naturally
      applies also to items of morpho-syntax such as *ne*. The opposite
      case is the English vocalic variable exemplified by Norwich (a:). In
      cases such as these, the relation of the variants to the spelling is
      more opaque, with less stylistic variation as a consequence.[8]

(ii) The condition formulated in (i) is necessary but not sufficient to
      bring about hyperstyle variation. The high degree of convergence
      found among all speaker groups in formal styles necessary for the
      hyperstyle effect implies that the influence of conservative written
      forms should have been successfully imposed upon virtually all

8   J. K. Chambers and P. Trudgill, *Dialectology* (Cambridge: Cambridge University
     Press, 1998), p. 71.

speakers, such that high degrees of convergence are produced in formal styles. What are relevant here are the highly formal and normative methods that are still used to teach the French language in France. To this factor we may add the training that French school pupils receive in the recitation of verse. Chambers and Trudgill explain the rationale for eliciting formal speech through word-list styles from the perspective of self-monitoring: 'reading out one word at a time is a much simpler task than coping with a passage of connected prose, and informants are therefore correspondingly more able to direct even more attention to their speech, rather than to what they are reading.'[9] A further explanatory factor that relates directly to hyperstyle variation in French is that different norms apply across different styles of reading. Therefore the response of French informants to a word-list style may well be influenced by the rules of verse speaking, which broadly require the realisation of all orthographic schwas in all contexts except the pre-vocalic when reciting poetry. French school-pupils are of course taught to recite poetry according to these rules. Thus we can postulate that French speakers have available at least two reading-style norms: (non-elevated) connected prose, and verse.

Evidence that the vast majority of French speakers are affected by these linguistic pressures is of course recalcitrant to rigorous quantification, but it is no doubt significant that several authors have expended a good deal of polemic in criticising the highly normative methods used in French schools to teach the French language.[10] These authors assert that these methods put a premium on rote learning and imitation of the linguistic model that the teacher provides, and of course a discount on the child's capacity for individual expression. The title of Dannequin's book and article, *Les enfants bâillonnés*, provides eloquent testimony of her view of the strongly repressive tendency of these methods. Dannequin's opinion is of course debatable, but certain of the facts she alleges are indis-

---

9   Chambers and Trudgill, *Dialectology*, p. 80.
10   C. Dannequin, *Les enfants bâillonnés* (Paris: CEDIL, 1977); C. Dannequin, 'Les enfants bâillonnés (Gagged Children): the Teaching of French as Mother Tongue in Elementary School', *Language and Education*, 1988, 1, pp. 15–31; C. Duneton, *A hurler le soir au fond des colleges* (Paris: Seuil, 1984).

putable. For example, she mentions the very early age at which French children begin to come into contact with the normative institutional approach to language: from two to three years of age at the *école maternelle*. In addition to this factor, it may be mentioned that normative linguistic pressures are exerted, at least in principle, upon all French school pupils, in contrast to the UK situation where traditional methods of teaching English grammar are largely confined to the small fee-paying school sector, which represents less than 10% of pupils. Furthermore, the post-16 staying-on rate in France is higher than in the UK, and French is compulsory for all pupils who take either the academically oriented *baccalauréat* or more vocational qualifications such as the *Brevet d'études professionnelles*. It seems likely that all of these factors contribute in some measure to condition (ii) set out above.

(iii) Another issue that it is necessary to consider here is the language associated with the conservative written norm and its production in spontaneous, i.e. non-scripted, formal styles. Essentially the same remarks as made above apply in this connection. What seems necessary for the hyperstyle effect to be widespread in formal spontaneous styles is that all, or a preponderant majority of, French speakers should be subject to the association between spoken and written French as it affects their ability to style-shift in formal situations. To reiterate, this seems to be the principal necessary condition, whatever the precise way in which this association may be activated in psychosocial terms. As mentioned previously, it appears that many French phonological variables are of the type that can be internalised by reference to written norms, rather than by prolonged immersion in a highly exclusive socio-cultural environment. In addition to the Norwich (a:) variable already discussed, we may note the UK English example of the type of variable exemplified by the vowels distributed in lexical splits found in pairs such as 'putt' and 'put', which are differentiated in southern standard English by two distinct back vowels, respectively [ʌ] and [ʊ], the distribution of which is not reliably marked in the orthography. Words such as these are notorious shibboleths in English, but French examples depending on transparent vocalic or consonantal pairs (as opposed to more complex areas such as variable liaison, where morphology and syntax are also involved) come less easily to hand. The inference is that the standard phonology is more widely and readily available to a substantial majority of French speakers compared to what obtains in the UK; further that this greater availability depends partly on the more transparent relation between French phonological variables and their representation in spelling, and partly on the intensive promotion of the conservative written variety in the French school system.

Discontinuity in French: The Case of the banlieues

The previous section suggested that *oïl* French is unusual in several respects: firstly by virtue of its relative uniformity in pronunciation, combined secondly with an unusually large gulf between formal and informal styles, both in speech and writing. The third, rather distinctive aspect of French, related to the relative absence of variation observable, is the relatively small number of changes in progress, especially in the pronunciation system. Space is lacking for an exhaustive examination of these here, but we may mention briefly the following: the progressive loss of variable liaison; fronting of [ɔ] in the direction of [ɔ̃], [œ] or [ø]; variation between nasal vowel phonemes; and insertion of schwa word-finally (so-called 'schwa-tagging').[11] The relatively small volume of research on variation and change in *oïl* French reflects perhaps the lesser sociolinguistic importance of the pronunciation level, as suggested above. In any event this situation contrasts rather sharply with what obtains in comparable languages such as English, where processes of variation and

11   A. Smith, 'French Variable Liaison: A Proposed Simplification', *Francophonie*, 1998, 17, pp. 11–14; M. Landick, 'The Mid-vowels in Figures: Hard Facts', *French Review*, 1995, 69 (1), pp. 88–103; A. B. Hansen, *Les voyelles nasales du français parisien moderne. Aspects linguistiques, sociolinguistiques et perceptuels des changements en cours* (Copenhagen: Museum Tusculanum, 1998); A. B. Hansen, 'Le nouveau [«] prépausal dans le français parlé à Paris', in J. Perrot (ed.), *Polyphonie pour Iván Fónagy: mélanges offerts en hommage à Iván Fónagy par un groupe de disciples, collègues et admirateurs* (Paris: L'Harmattan, 1997), pp. 173–98.

change in phonology are salient and serve to mark social-group differences quite sharply.[12]

An important exception in the French situation is represented by what is happening in the *banlieues* surrounding many cities.[13] Ethnic-group differences expressed in language are of course also salient in other countries, but France seems to provide an especially marked case of ethnic differences reflected in linguistic differences. If we consider linguistic differentiation from the viewpoint of variation and change, it seems that, according to the linguistic level and indeed the type of linguistic variable concerned, certain variables found in the *banlieues* are encountering resistance as they come into contact with the French mainstream system. The following sections discuss the distinctiveness of the French *banlieue*, concentrating subsequently on the Paris situation and outlining some linguistic changes in progress there that appear to be diverging sharply from *oïl* French.

The French *banlieue*: Historical Overview

The contemporary French *banlieue* was essentially created as a result of three historical phenomena: rural exodus, the Industrial Revolution and the development of transport in the nineteenth and twentieth centuries. Until recently, the 3,000 *banlieue* towns continued to show rapid demographic growth, with an increase of 7% between 1982 and 1992. In 1996 they represented a population of 18.2 million inhabitants and covered 6% of metropolitan French territory.[14] The reasons underlying the grow-

12 For a recent overview see P. Foulkes and G. J. Docherty (eds), *Urban Voices: Accent Studies in the British Isles* (London: Arnold, 1999).

13 It is more accurate denotationally to use the term *grands ensembles* ('high-rise estates') to refer to the districts of interest here. This is because within the general term *banlieue* there exists a distinction between *petite* and *grande banlieue*, which is discussed below. However, the term *banlieue* is preferred in this chapter on account of its general currency and its use in phrases such as *accent de banlieue*, *langage de banlieue*, etc.

14 H. Vieillard-Baron, *Les banlieues* (Paris: Flammarion, 1996), p. 65.

ing size of the *banlieues* are essentially the higher birth and immigration rates in peripheries than in town centres. Nevertheless, and notwithstanding a movement of industry towards the peripheries, the unemployment rate is generally greater in the *banlieues* than nationally. Young people constitute a major proportion of the suburban population with the under-25 group varying between 25% and 50% of residents in these areas. With regard to non-Parisian populations, concentrations of 70% young people are found in some *banlieues*, while in certain suburban schools, 95% of the pupils are of non-metropolitan origin. Alongside these high concentrations of immigrant populations, there are considerable regional differences in non-metropolitan densities. Immigrant populations are mainly concentrated in the Rhônes-Alpes and the Ile-de-France regions, where they make up more than 13% of the population in some areas, while in other regions (e.g. Brittany) less than 2.5% of the population is made up of these groups.

The Paris banlieue

The term *banlieue* is often associated with the French capital, probably owing to the fact that its suburban expansion started earlier than in other cities and has been on a larger scale.[15] In 1990, 40% of French *banlieusards* lived in the Paris *banlieue*, representing a population of seven million. From a historical viewpoint, migration to the *banlieue* and especially to the south and west of Paris from the end of the seventeenth century on was dominated by the aristocracy, who were fleeing the noise and commotion of the court in search of a calmer, rural pace of life. Living in the *banlieue* was then seen as a luxury generally enjoyed by the upper classes. With the advent of the Industrial Revolution, a large-scale rural exodus took place and the migrant populations settled in the north and north-east of the capital, where industry had begun to develop. Large working-class areas were formed around factories, as in Saint-Denis, which was the largest such settlement by 1891. The industrial

---

15   D. Pinson, *Des Banlieues et des villes: dérive et eurocompétition*, Collection Portes Ouvertes (Paris: Editions Ouvrières, 1992), pp. 72–3.

role played by the northern *banlieues* was reinforced during the First World War, as a major part of the French arms factories and heavy industry were based in the area. At the end of the nineteenth century and the start of the twentieth century three different types of *banlieues* could be distinguished across the geography of Paris:

(1) the working-class suburbs of the north and north-east;
(2) the middle-class quarters of the west and south-west (essentially consisting of the aristocracy and people with private incomes);
(3) the farming suburban areas of the south and south-east.

This threefold distribution in the Paris Region still applies today to some extent. The northern parts of Paris, including its *banlieue*, remain poorer and more industrial. By contrast, the economy of the *département des Hauts-de-Seine* is larger than that of Greece. As regards the population in the South of Paris, half of all French industrial researchers work in the Yvette valley. Apart from this large socio-economic difference within its geography, the sheer size of the Paris region is significant: the area produces 30% of France's GNP. The major economic influence of the French capital is probably due to the large degree of centralisation characteristic of France. It has been argued that this phenomenon has been aggravated in the last 150 years by various state policies intended to establish central control over Paris without allowing the provincial cities to develop accordingly.[16] The detail of these policies is beyond the scope of the present chapter, but it will be suggested below that the high degree of political and administrative centralisation could well have had sociolinguistic consequences.

The Modern French banlieue

In 1934 Le Corbusier wrote in the *Charte d'Athènes* that the *banlieue*

> est le symbole à la fois du déchet et de la tentative. C'est une sorte d'écume battant les murs de la ville. Au cours des dix-neuvième et vingtième siècles, cette écume est devenue marée, puis inondation.

16   B. Marchand, *Paris, histoire d'une ville: XIXe–XXe siècles* (Paris: Seuil, 1993), pp. 379–400.

This demographic growth of Paris and its outskirts, a result of the massive rural exodus of the nineteenth century, was greatly reinforced by a considerable baby boom and the arrival of non-metropolitan immigrants after the Second World War. The problems caused were dramatically aggravated by the fact that earlier governments had not considered the increasing need for housing as a priority, and therefore fell critically behind in this area. The consequence of this 'demographic flood' was the development of shanty-towns in the suburbs of Paris. In 1966 120 shanty-towns with a combined population of 50,000 still surrounded the Paris Region.[17]

In response to this, rapid action was taken to make housing a national priority with the creation of ZUPs (*Zones à Urbaniser en Priorité*) in 1958. Mass production methods were adopted to optimise productivity: immense residential areas were built on this basis.[18] The housing effort became so intensive that the amount of land taken up by urban areas increased from 7% in 1954 to 14% in 1975. This reflects developments during the *grands ensembles* period, to which can be attributed the modern face of the French *banlieues*. Unfortunately, this architectural mass production led to a standardisation of the shape and size of the French suburbs. The design of a whole *grand ensemble* project was usually assigned to a single architect, who would impose his vision without any preliminary consultation with the local authorities. The architects' primary aim was simply to provide accommodation, so facilities for socialising and community activities were sparsely planned and remained artificial. Public transport was also neglected, or limited to what was provided for commuting purposes. As a result, a large number of the *grands ensembles* have been classified as *zones sensibles* since the early 1980s. The social trauma caused by ZUP developments in some suburban towns can be illustrated by the example of Grigny (south of Paris), where the population increased from 1,700 inhabitants in 1967 to 25,600 in 1975. The emergence of *grands ensembles* was accompanied by a loss of landmarks and historical associations for both the local and migrant populations, and added to the social tensions caused by the economic

---

17   Pinson, *Des Banlieues et des villes: dérive et eurocompétition*, p. 52.
18   J. Menanteau, *Les banlieues* (Paris: Le Monde/Marabout, 1994), p. 55.

recession. The very nature of this suburban architecture acts as an isolating influence on whole communities who do not relate to the concept of a town, but to that of a *quartier*.

French *banlieues* are therefore very different from the suburbs of the USA or Great Britain. The differences clearly result from historical influences acting on the urban development of these countries. France is highly centralised, and the attraction exerted by Paris has shaped the structure and size of the city and its outskirts. As in any large urban centre in the world, there are important socio-economic differences between the different suburbs of Paris, but, in broad terms, their historical development is unique.

Hasty solutions adopted to cope with a major housing shortage after the Second World War prompted the emergence of the *grands ensembles*. This revolution in town planning has had important socio-economic consequences for French *banlieusards*, especially in Paris, where they were built on a the largest scale. When they were first built, it was hoped that the *grands ensembles* would represent an improvement in modernity and comfort. Twenty per cent of their population was middle-class in the post-war years. However, as families from different backgrounds and with different ways of life gathered in the same areas, collective life soon lost its appeal. Those who could afford to leave moved out into individual houses in the *grande banlieue* and were replaced in the 1960s and 1970s by a population of non-metropolitan immigrants (for the most part from the Maghreb and sub-Saharan Africa), who were attracted by lower rents in these areas.

Some 15 years later, the size of immigrant households being generally larger, the population of young people in the *banlieues* is on average proportionally greater than other age groups. Youth unemployment in the *banlieues* is higher than the national average (18.8% in the *banlieues*, compared with 9% nationally for the youngest age group in 1990). Crime rates are also proportionally higher, aggravated by the lower educational standards that result from language problems and a lesser degree of parental competence in the supervision of school work. Crime, the lack of educational infrastructure and unemployment have prompted the emergence of a street culture that appears to be associated with the development of new sociolinguistically significant features, some of which we discuss below.

Banlieues and Social Marking

Two broad types of *banlieues* can be distinguished: *petite* and *grande banlieues*. The *grande banlieue* shows similarities with the American conception of a middle-class residential area. The desire for a slower and more rural pace of life as well as the rise in city-centre property prices are factors influencing this 'peri-urbanisation'. The *petites banlieues*, the zones directly in contact with the city centres, were originally distinct villages or towns that have been assimilated by the progressive development of the larger conurbations. The population of the *petite banlieue* generally consists of the lower classes. Similarities with the American inner cities can be found in a high rate of unemployment, a concentration of ethnic minorities and low-quality housing stock. The contemporary connotation of the term *banlieue*, which now evokes social malaise of the kind associated with the socio-economic phenomena discussed above, is relatively recent and is illustrated in cinema by the change in the artistic treatment of French suburban life.[19] The close-knit working-class communities of the period from the 1930s to the 1950s, depicted in films such as Duvivier's *La Belle Equipe* (1936) and Renoir's *Partie de Campagne* (1936), contrast sharply with Kassovitz's focus on drugs and violence, and the general impression of entrapment in *La Haine* (1990). With the beginning of the end of the 'Trente Glorieuses' in the late 1970s and the ensuing economic recession, the *banlieues*, until then symbol of economic growth and modernity, became what Vieillard-Baron has called an 'antimodèle'.[20]

Some scholars have argued that the press has been instrumental in the development of the social marking of the *banlieue*.[21] In their depiction of 'suburban' life, journalists, politicians and other writers project social myths and fears through their use of images and metaphors. The use of analogy here is particularly powerful: linguistic devices perpetrating the myth of the savage, of entrapment, of decay and illness introduce new

19   See Vieillard-Baron, *Les banlieues*, pp. 56–7.
20   Vieillard-Baron, *Les banlieues*, p. 75.
21   C. Bachmann and L. Basier, *Mise en image d'une banlieue ordinaire* (Paris: Syros, 1989).

negative symbolisms that confirm outsiders in their social assumptions. Therefore both press and 'outsider' share responsibility for the negative marking of the banlieue, since its journalistic depiction merely confirms the outsiders in their biased pre-conceptualisation of life in the *cités*. This stigma is, once socially established, internalised by the inhabitants of the *banlieue* themselves. Two complementary attitudes have been identified among the inhabitants of the *4000 grands ensembles*, the districts of interest here, when dealing with this social marking.[22] The first approach involves rejecting the image attached to the *grands ensembles* by accusing the public of being influenced by inaccurate stereotypes. The second is to adopt a distancing attitude through the use of humour or sarcasm to neutralise the stigmata, for instance by calling the housing estate *les 4000 poubelles*. Owing to its organisation in series of blocks forming districts (*quartiers*) that are separated by the main routes of communication, the feeling of entrapment in the *4000* is considerable. Furthermore, the absence of the street as a social space is inadequately replaced by other public spaces, such as staircases and the entrances of buildings. This generates a lack of distinction between private and public territories, and a feeling of imprisonment, a typical feature of what has been called *la sarcellite* (the jocular term derives from the well-known *banlieue* Sarcelles and depends for its humorous effect on an evocation of *cellulite*). Lepoutre argues that suburban unhappiness is created by the failure of public spaces to generate intermediary social contacts, that is links that are intermediate in a scale between family ties and secondary, anonymous contacts.[23]

Bachmann and Basier add that this lack of distinction between private and public space, and the absence of social contact between generations are causes of tensions between the older and younger populations.[24] The proportion of young people is larger than any other age group in the *grands ensembles*, and this accentuates social tension between generations, if there is a perception on the part of older inhabitants that a high proportion of young people equates with a less secure environment.

22   D. Lepoutre, *Coeur de banlieue: codes, rites et langages* (Paris: Editions Odile Jacob, 1997), p. 39.
23   Lepoutre, *Coeur de banlieue: codes, rites et langages*, p. 31.
24   Bachmann and Basier, *Mise en image d'une banlieue ordinaire*, pp. 99–100.

Furthermore, the younger population is consistently exposed to the older, as the sole meeting places available for the youngsters are at the bases of the blocks and in the squares. Hence the creation of social myths in which youth is identified with criminality.

A consequence of the enclosure within the *grands ensembles* is the youngsters' symbolic construction of territory on a *quartier* basis. Not only does the *quartier*, representing a series of blocks or towers, refer to the area in which someone lives, it also defines who they are. The notion of belonging to the *4000 Nord*, the *4000 Sud* or *Barbusse* is of tremendous importance for the young people there, who reconstruct the toponymy according to the place they wish to belong to or view themselves in symbolically. The *Quartiers Nord* of Paris and its *banlieue* are often considered the toughest, and this is an important covert prestige feature of street culture. These districts also are the subject of French rap songs and evoke similarities with the tough districts of New York, such as Harlem, The Bronx and Brooklyn. The territorial identification in terms of *quartier* entails social marking that separates blocks or areas. Bachmann and Basier[25] state that, for certain inhabitants, 'to change block often represents a change of life': territories are so isolated that myths about certain buildings are created and a hierarchy instituted between them. Some *4000* inhabitants are convinced that crime is higher in certain blocks or towers, or sometimes assume that their building is worse than another in this regard.

For the younger generation, the *quartier* or *cité* is a territory that has to be defended against intruders from other districts or buildings. As shown in the creation of their own toponymy, the *quartier* represents the centre of a mentally constructed world where anything situated outside this centre is considered peripheral. This centre-periphery construction defines young people's social space, and its protection provides them with a sense of a peer community. The importance of street culture in the French *grands ensembles* is therefore paramount and essentially concerns young people aged from ten to 16.[26] Lepoutre explains that this is an age range during which children gain access to a certain independence from parental supervision. This autonomy is granted at a time when the adult

---

25   Bachmann and Basier, *Mise en image d'une banlieue ordinaire*, p. 46.
26   Lepoutre, *Coeur de banlieue: codes, rites et langages*, pp. 22–4.

perspective of a working life still has no significant influence. The development of an overall conceptualisation of society and the desire to find a place within it seem to be located at the end of adolescence.

Therefore, just as no human community can function without the basis of a system of shared values or attitudes, street culture provides the young population with a common vision of the world, based on close-knit social networks and a strong sense of belonging to a *cité* or *quartier*.[27] The French hip-hop culture described by Bazin, Bachmann and Basier, and Cannon among others, has been embraced by the young population of the *banlieues*.[28] Its values, defending multiculturalism, denouncing the moral contradictions of society and offering a street-based approach to art (e.g. graffiti, breakdance), are closely related to the teenage experience of the *grand ensemble*. In consequence, street culture and the myth of the *quartiers Nord* all participate in creating a covertly prestigious image of *banlieue* life. The fact of adolescents often underlining their origin in the *4000* as a sign of toughness is a recurrent illustration of this tendency.[29] A similar attitude was reported to the fieldworker (Jamin) by young informants in Fontenay-sous-Bois who avoided a fight when on holiday in a French provincial region simply by stating that they came from the *banlieue parisienne*.

Sociolinguistic Implications of Social Marking in the *banlieue*

The creation by French suburban youth of a socially marked street-culture has been accompanied by the development of culturally recognisable speech features. Conein and Gadet suggest that stress and intonation

---

27   Lepoutre, *Coeur de banlieue: codes, rites et langages*, p. 20.
28   H. Bazin, *La culture hip-hop* (Paris: Desclée de Brouwer, 1995); B. Bachmann and L. Basier, 'Junior s'entraîne très fort, ou le smurf comme mobilisation symbolique', *Langage et Société*, 1985, 34, pp. 57–68; S. Cannon, 'Panama City Rapping: B-Boys in the Banlieues and Beyond', in A. G. Hargreaves and M. McKinney (eds), *Post-Colonial Cultures in France* (London: Routledge, 1997), pp. 150–66.
29   Bachmann and Basier, *Mise en image d'une banlieue ordinaire*, p. 65.

features are the elements that distinguish *le français des banlieues* from *le français populaire*, but public attention also focuses upon *verlan* and other types of slang, extended use of relativiser *que* compared with the standard language and certain features of pronunciation discussed below.[30]

The relative size of the younger age group in the *banlieues* goes some way towards explaining the extent of the phenomenon. It has of course been shown in many linguistic studies that the development of vernacular features is at its highest in adolescent years and that the vernacular reinforces in-group membership and identity.[31] In terms of social networks, the density and multiplexity of ties within the enclosed environment of the *cités* explain the maintenance of this *banlieue* vernacular, for it has been shown that dense and multiplex social networks act as norm-enforcement mechanisms on every type of social behaviour, including of course linguistic.[32]

The covert prestige associated with suburban life and perpetuated through hip-hop culture can plausibly be assumed as making certain features of suburban vernacular attractive to young mainstream speakers of French. Moreover, the fact that *grands ensembles* such as the *4000* are located in the vicinity of Paris, where the French media are based, facilitates the dissemination of *banlieue* culture to all social classes and regions. Adapting the argument of Milroy and Milroy, we can suggest that the media, in the case of the *banlieue* vernacular, act as a weak tie promoting linguistic changes from one social network to another, at least at the lexical level.[33] In addition, face-to-face contacts exist between speakers of *banlieue* vernacular and those of mainstream French in the sense that the Champs-Elysées, the Gare du Nord and Les Halles are favoured by young *banlieusards*, who travel to these areas of Paris be-

30 B. Conein and F. Gadet, 'Français populaire? Français des banlieues?', in F. Aitsiselmi (ed.), *Black, Blanc, Beur: Youth Language and Identity in France* (Bradford: Interface, 2000), pp. 39–49.

31 S. Romaine, *The Language of Children and Adolescents* (Oxford: Blackwell, 1984), p. 10.

32 L. Milroy, *Language and Social Networks* (Oxford: Blackwell, 1987).

33 J. Milroy and L. Milroy, 'Social Network and Social Class: Toward an Integrated Sociolinguistic Model', *Language in Society*, 1992, 21, pp. 1–26.

cause they offer services (fast-food, sportswear shops, clubs and cinemas), adapted to their tastes and needs.[34] These contacts are of course additional to those created institutionally, most notably at school.

The following subsection describes briefly the research site, La Courneuve, from which the results presented in the rest of this chapter derive.

The Research Site

La Courneuve is situated about five kilometres north of Paris in the *département* of Seine-Saint-Denis. This *département* experienced the intensive industrialisation of the late-nineteenth and early-twentieth centuries, as well as the *grands ensembles* policies of the 1950s and 1960s discussed above. More recently, the town of Saint-Denis was chosen as the site for the building of the *Stade de France* for the 1998 football World Cup. This event has been beneficial for the *département* and especially for Saint-Denis, with the building of new rail lines and a new station linking the town to Paris. *France 98* also accelerated the renovation of the Saint-Denis town centre. Although renovation programmes have also been implemented in La Courneuve, Saint-Denis is perceived as a richer rival or a better place, according to some of the informants interviewed for the study in question. Bachmann and Basier argue that La Courneuve is challenged economically by its neighbouring towns for reasons connected with urban development. Its town centre cannot compete with the attraction of other towns because it is divided into heterogeneous quarters facing opposite directions.[35] This distribution has sociological consequences, which we discuss below.

Demography of La Courneuve

La Courneuve is a suburban town of some 35,000 inhabitants with a high proportion of young people; 63.7% of the population is under 40, 41% under 25. The number of immigrants is also considerable, at 25.3%

---

34   Lepoutre, *Coeur de banlieue: codes, rites et langages*, p. 60.
35   Bachmann and Basier, *Mise en image d'une banlieue ordinaire*, pp. 129–30.

of the total population. The majority of these immigrants do not originate from the European Union. Industry is still one of the most important employers, with 43.9% of the working population in 1990. The town's principal economic activities are heavy industry, services, commerce and transport. The unemployment rate in 1990 was higher than the national average (10.8%) at 16.7%. Unemployment also affects more women than men (19.6% against 14.4%). The young age group has the highest unemployment with a rate of 30.1%.

Housing in La Courneuve consists predominantly of flats (10,000 flats compared to 1,538 individual houses or bungalows). In conseqence, 87% of the population live in flats, 8,000 of which are council-owned (all the figures given are taken from the 1990 census). Only 27% of the inhabitants of La Courneuve own their homes, 69% rent their accommodation and 4% do not have to pay any rent for socio-economic reasons. The town is often associated with the *grands ensembles* of the *4000 logements*; whose population represents about 42% of the inhabitants of La Courneuve. This housing development, typical of the ZUP era, is often used in the press as a national symbol for the social difficulties typical of the *banlieues* and for the dilapidated state into which buildings in the *banlieues* often fall.[36] Built in the early 1960s, the *4000* in fact contains 3,600 accommodation units out of the 4,100 planned. Eighty per cent of its households have a gross annual income of less than FF 100,000 and 44% earn below FF 50,000. The vast majority (82.4%) of the *4000* inhabitants are junior non-manual and manual workers who represent 28.1% of the total population of La Courneuve.

Fieldwork Methodology

The fieldwork for the study reported in this chapter was carried out in 1998. It has been reported in the literature that random samples are difficult to obtain from speakers in France, owing to a high rate of refusals

36   Bachmann and Basier, *Mise en image d'une banlieue ordinaire*, p. 14; D. Lepoutre, *Coeur de banlieue: codes, rites et langages*, p. 37.

for interviews.[37] As the fieldwork was to take place over a short period of time (two months), it was decided to proceed with the collection of a judgement sample. The informants were approached through local societies and clubs, which provided locations where intermediaries were available to facilitate contacts. Moreover, as a large part of the sample were minors, it was judged prudent to work with official institutions of this kind and to conduct the recording of the younger age group under their aegis.

The *Service Jeunesse* of La Courneuve was the principal point of contact for the research. The *Service Jeunesse* provides adolescents aged between 12 and 17 with a range of cultural and sports activities, aiming to educate and socialise them. Holidays to French provincial locations or abroad are also offered, as well as homework tuition at night during the school year. The advantage of working with the *Service Jeunesse* was that it offered access to four different *maisons de quartier* (Youth Clubs) distributed within the *4000 Nord*, the town centre, and the *4000 Sud*. This made it possible to include a relatively large variety and range of young people in the study sample. Nevertheless, since a sole researcher was to carry out all the recordings, it was decided with the team director firstly to base the fieldwork in one of the youth clubs: the *Club Beaufils*, situated in *ensemble B* of the *4000 Sud*.

Beaufils was ideal for the fieldwork, as its facilities included a large common room, in which most of the socialising took place, and three smaller and more intimate rooms in which it was easy to record in reasonably good acoustic conditions. In early August 1998, when all the potential informants at the club were interviewed, it was decided to try to circulate between at least three clubs, targeting informants according to which sample cells needed to be filled (see Table 1). *Beaufils* was still kept as the main base, while the *Club Edgard Quinet* (town centre) and the *Maison Pour Tous Guy Moquet* (*4000 Nord*) were used as sites for recordings that had previously been arranged with informants. The fact that each club was in a different part of La Courneuve was interesting in terms of correlations between speech and housing type, since more indi-

---

37   A. B. Coveney, *Variability in Spoken French: A Sociolinguistic Study of Interrogation and Negation* (Exeter: Elm Bank, 1996), p. 5; M. Lennig, *Acoustic Measurement of Linguistic Change: The Modern Parisian Vowel System*, unpublished PhD thesis, University of Pennsylvania, 1978, pp. 9–10.

		Younger males	Older males	Younger females	Older females
	BAF	1	0	3	0
MC	NAF	1	3	2	0
	MF	0	2	1	4
	BAF	4	4	5	0
WC	NAF	4	3	4	2
	MF	4	3	4	3

Key: BAF = Black African French; NAF = North African French; MF = Metropolitan French; MC = middle class; WC = working class

Table 1:   Size and structure of the La Courneuve speaker sample.

vidual houses could be found in the town-centre than in the *4000 grand ensemble*. The sociolinguistic interest of such a correlation is that housing type might be expected to play a role in determining speakers' social networks.

One of the main advantages of the youth-club structure was that the adolescents were grouped in two age ranges, 12–14 and 15–17. This made it possible to sample fairly homogeneous age groups. Furthermore, as certain youth leaders were allocated to supervise either the older group or the younger group, participating in the activities of both groups made it easier for the fieldworker to familiarise each member of the team with his presence and project.

The Corpus

The speaker sample was controlled using four variables: sex, social class, ethnicity and age. These variables made it possible to measure the variation of linguistic patterns across groups of speakers sharing differing combinations of these characteristics. Many sociolinguistic studies have now observed a tendency on the part of females and the higher classes to adopt more standardised linguistic forms, especially in formal situations, such as interviews.[38] It is also generally accepted that adolescent speech is more closely associated with the vernacular language than adult.[39]

38   L. Milroy, *Observing and Analysing Natural Language* (Oxford: Blackwell, 1987), pp. 95–6.
39   Romaine, *The Language of Children and Adolescents*, p. 104.

The Age Variable

It was decided to distinguish two main age groups: a younger group, aged between 15 and 25, and an older group between 30 and 50. This rather narrow gap between the age groups was thought to be large enough to show age-related linguistic variation because it was felt that the adoption of suburban features decreased sharply or even stopped when a speaker adopted a working lifestyle or rejected the street culture. Coveney used a similar age classification, based on that of Thibault.[40] Within the five age groups considered, Thibault divided her younger informants into two groups, distinguishing *les jeunes* (15–23) from *les jeunes adultes* (24–35). The criterion for this distinction was speakers' access to professional life or marriage. Coveney states that 'there are grounds to believe that both marriage and employment have a significant effect on the individual's social network pattern, and consequently on their linguistic behaviour also.'[41] Furthermore, Lepoutre argues that the rejection of street culture occurs between the ages of 16 and 25, and corresponds to the time when young people project themselves onto a wider social canvas and accept the prospect of a working future.[42] This consequently promotes the adoption of a different lifestyle that shares similarities with that of the middle class.

Thus, the non-standard suburban variety was judged by the field researcher to be incompatible with integration into the working environment. Twenty-five years therefore seemed to be a reasonable age limit for most speakers to accede to working life, while 30 was felt to be an age when speakers were more likely to have adopted and accepted this sort of lifestyle. A larger generational gap could conceal the key age range during which the potential dropping of suburban features might be occurring. We hypothesised that a narrower gap between the two age

40   P. Thibault, *Equivalence et Grammaticalisation*, unpublished PhD thesis, Université de Montréal, 1983 (cited in Coveney, *Variability in Spoken French: A Sociolinguistic Study of Interrogation and Negation*).

41   Coveney, *Variability in Spoken French: A Sociolinguistic Study of Interrogation and Negation*, p. 21.

42   Lepoutre, *Coeur de banlieue: codes, rites et langages*, p. 24.

groups, as selected here, would have the potential to reveal more precisely at what age any change might be taking place.

Ethnicity Variable

The general impression received in La Courneuve during the pilot study fieldwork on the issue of ethnicity was that the features of *banlieue* vernacular were largely shared by informants from all ethnic origins, so long as the age of the speaker was approximately between 10 and 25. The majority of these features could not be allocated to any specific ethnic group, contrasting with the case of African American Vernacular English (AAVE).[43] Interestingly, Great Britain shows similarities with the United States: although they are competent English speakers, the use of Creole by young British-born Black speakers in the West Midlands has been analysed as a 'positive assertion of their black identity and a rejection of the negative connotations placed on Black language by the dominant White society'.[44] This seems to contrast with the French model of *banlieue* vernacular, although Arabic dialects were used to some extent by North African youngsters in interactions among themselves.

Nevertheless, this issue was taken into account in the fieldwork, for the original hypothesis was that *banlieue* vernacular was the result of a merger of *titi parisien*, the working-class vernacular of 1930s Paris with certain features of North African French, commonly known as the *pied noir* accent.[45] The two dialects are thought to have come in contact during the periods of large-scale immigration in the 1950s and 1960s as immigrants from the Maghreb settled in the capital. The hypothesis is that the *beur* population (the French-born children of North African immigrants) adopted features from both dialects and created what now constitutes the present suburban dialect. The research issue of interest here relates

43   P. Trudgill, *Sociolinguistics*, 3rd edn (Harmondsworth: Penguin, 1995), pp. 49–61.
44   V. Edwards, 'Patois and the Politics of Process: Black English in British Class-rooms', in N. Coupland and A. Jaworski (eds), *Sociolinguistics: A Reader and Coursebook* (Basingstoke: Macmillan, 1997), pp. 408–15.
45   P. Merle, *Argot, verlan et tchatches* (Paris: Editions Milan, 1997).

to whether both the native French and immigrant populations are adopting this variety. The long-term object of the present study is the investigation of this question. Table 1 shows the speaker sample recorded in La Courneuve during the summer of 1998.

Fifty-five speakers were selected according to age, sex, class and ethnic origin. Owing to time constraints on the fieldwork, not all cells were filled. The sample was therefore unsuccessful in collecting the minimum of four informants per cell that is generally considered to be required for statistical regularity in sociolinguistic studies.[46] In particular, the sample generally lacks older informants, females and especially females of immigrant origins. This is probably due to the fact that the latter are difficult to make contact with, as cultural traditions confine them to the home.[47] Meetings with strangers, especially young white males such as the fieldworker, are often taboo and thus avoided. The sample also generally lacks middle-class speakers, especially older ones; this was considered a minor failure, since *banlieue* vernacular is essentially a young working-class phenomenon. Furthermore, it would always be possible to go back to La Courneuve in order to collect more recordings of this group, taking into consideration that, since the majority of the middle-class population can afford to go on holiday, further fieldwork should not be conducted during the summer.

Nevertheless, the sample of the younger age group, which was the most important for the study and the most difficult to collect, was considered satisfactory in relation to these extra-linguistic variables. Furthermore, if the variable of ethnicity is not taken into account, the La Courneuve sample seemed relatively satisfactory, except for representative young middle-class males, as Table 2 shows.

The Speech Styles Elicited

Following many sociolinguistic studies, three speech styles were elicited, in descending order of formality: Word List Style, Reading Passage Style, and Casual Style, abbreviated as WLS, RPS and CS. Labov first devel-

46   Milroy, *Observing and Analysing Natural Language*, pp. 21–2.
47   P. Milburn, 'Les problèmes des jeunes dans le grand ensemble de La Courneuve en vue d'actions de prévention', Rapport 2. Association RESSCOM, Conseil général de Seine-Saint-Denis, Aide Sociale à l'Enfance, 1992.

	YM	OM	YF	OF
MC	2	5	6	4
WC	12	10	9	5

Key: YM = younger male; OM = older male; YF = younger female; OF = older female; MC = middle class; WC = working class.

Table 2:   Structure and size of the La Courneuve speaker sample excluding the ethnicity variable.

oped a methodology for observing variation in style (ranging from formal to informal) according to the degree of attention speakers pay to their speech.[48] During the interview, the reading passages were read first, followed by the word lists. This was designed to enhance formal style by ensuring that informants paid a maximum of attention to their speech. The rest of the interview was dedicated to an informal discussion to collect a sample of more casual speech. The rationale motivating the elicitation of several speech styles is that linguistic changes in progress are often observable through steep patterns of stylistic variation, caused by an awareness of the disapproval which the innovating variants attract. Steep patterns of differentiation along the other social dimensions (age, sex, social class) can also be interpreted as indicating linguistic change in progress, especially when these are found in association with stylistic variation. One such pattern from the La Courneuve speaker sample below is examined below.

The Linguistic Variables

As mentioned above, the *banlieue* vernacular phonological system seems to have absorbed features of *titi parisien*, the working-class French spoken in Paris in the first half of the twentieth century and new patterns borrowed from *pied noir* French.

---

48   W. Labov, *Sociolinguistic Patterns* (Philadelphia: University of Pennsylvania Press, 1972), pp. 70–109.

Given the relative stability of the French consonantal system, it was postulated at the design stage of the research project that any innovations would be located in the vocalic system:

- /ɑ/ for standard /a/ in all linguistic contexts, e.g.: *la table* [lɑtɑb], [sɛgʀɑv] *c'est grave*;
- raising of /ɔ/ towards /o/, e.g.: [lɑmoʁ] *la mort*, [lɑpolis] *la police*;
- closing of /ɛ/ to /e/ before an uvular approximant in final position, e.g.: [tɑmeʁ] *ta mère*, [ʃɥiveʁ] *j'suis vert*;[49]
- raising and lengthening of /oe/ towards /ø/ before /ʀ/, e.g.: [ʒepøːʁ] *j'ai peur.*

However, after listening to tapes made during a pilot study, two striking features were apparent in the consonantal system: the development of a glottalised realisation of /ʀ/ that appears to have received rather little attention:

- /ʀʔ/ in final position: [tɑmeʁʔ] *ta mère*;

and the affrication of velar and dental plosives in certain environments:

- [ʒvødʒiːkʃəː] *j'veux dire...que...*; [tʃydi] *tu dis?*

The *banlieue* system also has non-standard linguistic features noted as characteristic of informal French, such as deletion of /l/, /r/ and schwa. An example of variable realisation of affrication in the La Courneuve speaker sample will now be examined.

Variable Affrication in La Courneuve

Table 3 shows some preliminary results from the La Courneuve study. Social-class results have not yet been analysed for this variable. The

---

49 F. Gadet, 'Des fortifs aux técis: persistances et discontinuités dans la langue populaire', in D. Marley, M.-A. Hintze and G. Parker (eds), *Linguistic Identities and Policies in France and the French-speaking World* (London: AFLS/CILT, 1998), p 19; M. Lennig, *Acoustic Measurement of Linguistic Change: The Modern Parisian Vowel System*, p. 79.

	Casual style		RPS + WLS	
	(*N*)	%	(*N*)	%
Males 15–25	1369	22.5	111	17.3
Females 15–25	387	13.4	26	8.3
Males 30–50	18	0.6	1	0.2
Females 30–50	52	1.4	1	0.2

Table 3: Total numbers (*N*) and percentage realisation rates for /ʃ/ in all possible linguistic contexts, i.e. post-dental and post-velar plosives not followed by a consonant.

display reveals a quite striking pattern of age- and sex-related differentiation that shows young males especially using affrication after /t/ and /k/. Differentiation between the younger and older age groups is dramatic for both sexes, and appears to justify the decision to distinguish between people under and over the age of 30 in the speaker sample. Variation across the scripted and unscripted speech styles is sharper for the younger females than the younger males, a result that recalls many examples in the literature that show the greater stylistic sensitivity of females and their tendency to avoid vernacular forms. Affrication in La Courneuve is clearly a feature used by young speakers, but these results taken alone do not of course justify any assertions regarding the spread of the feature into the wider La Courneuve community. Affrication after /t/ and /k/ is a feature that has been associated with the Paris vernacular for several centuries as well as being a well-attested historical phenomenon.[50] It may be that this feature is currently widespread in the wider Paris WC community, but few other recent results or comments, other than those made by Rosset, which are in any event anecdotal, appear to be available.

In the La Courneuve speaker sample, palatalisation and affrication were observed in the following phonetic contexts:

- for velar plosives, before /a, ɑ, i, ɛ, ə, y, œ, ø/ and all nasal vowels, usually in initial but also in final positions: [kʃi] *qui*; [dɔ̃kʃ] *donc*;
- for dental plosives, before /i, y, w/ only, as in: [tʃydzi] *tu dis?*; [tʃwa] *toi*.

50   T. Rosset, *Les origines de la prononciation moderne* (Paris: Armand Colin, 1911), p. 314; G. Price, *The French Language* (London: Grant & Cutler, 1984), pp. 49–50.

This distribution is unusual because affrication is generally reported as occurring in a way that seems phonetically motivated. For instance, Rosset reports affrication of /g/ before front vowels, where the back–front sequence motivates affrication or palatalisation of the velar consonant in anticipation of the front vowel. However, affrication seems to be spreading to other contexts in the speech of the young La Courneuve speakers. The phenomenon in word-final position, as in [dɔkʃ] *donc*, is commented on by Léon in the following terms: 'on en trouve des exemples [of palatalisation] dans les sketches du comédien Coluche, qui palatalisait *même en finale*' (emphasis added).[51] Léon's phrasing seems to confirm the stigmatised nature of this word-final feature in mainstream French.

The next section discusses the linguistic-social factors influencing any possible spread of the vernacular features described above into mainstream French from the point of view of the 'uniformity and discontinuity' referred to in the title of this chapter.

Concluding Remarks

At the beginning of this chapter reference was made to some of the paradoxical characteristics of standard or *oïl* French. These can be taken as stemming essentially from the intense processes of standardisation to which the language has been subject for at least 200 years. As Judge remarks, 'France is famous for the degree of state interference in linguistic matters.'[52] The extent to which this planned interference has been successful in suppressing variation in French is another matter; but the resistance to linguistic innovation among certain conservative and influential sections of the French population, as well as among speakers generally, is undeniable. From this viewpoint it is interesting to speculate on the fate of the innovating variants described above. We can suggest a

51   P. Léon, *Précis de phonostylistique* (Paris: Nathan, 1993), p. 204.
52   A. Judge, 'French: a Planned Language?', in Sanders, *French Today: Language in its Social Context*, p. 7.

tentative distinction, on the one hand between 'strong' or 'marked' *ban-lieue* variants such as glottalised /ʀ/ and /e/ and /o/ found in closed syllables; and on the other, affricated stops and back /ɑ/, which appear to be distributed variably in mainstream French but are found at higher levels of use in *banlieue* French.

Intuitively, it seems plausible that variants that are perceived as running counter to the phonemic structure of French, such as /e/ and /o/ in closed syllables, or those which appear more marginal in the French sound system such as glottalised /ʀ/, will encounter resistance if encountered by mainstream French speakers. No figures are yet available from the La Courneuve corpus to confirm this categorisation, but impressionistically, glottalised /ʀ/ appears to be found in small numbers in the corpus and is confined to speakers of Maghrebian origin. It is unclear whether the word-final glottalised /ʀ/ sequence is an Arabic transfer. In any event, Malécot reports utterance-final glottal stops in a corpus of Parisian French after consonants and vowels.[53] He remarks: 'It [the utterance-final glottal stop] serves mainly to announce or mark an emphasis in the following utterance or in the preceding words.' This seems to be its function in sequences such as *ta mère*.

By contrast, the treatment of affricated stops and back /ɑ/ characteristic of *banlieue* French may be adopted by young *Français(es) de souche*, if certain aspects of the covert prestige attaching to the *banlieues* are sufficiently attractive. As suggested above, it appears that speakers adopt variants and use them in a more intensive way, if these variants are felt to be part of the pronunciation system. This is because pronunciation seems to be perceived as a more intimate and structural level of language, in contrast to lexis, for example, where there is a history of the ready (if ephemeral) adoption into mainstream French of some lexical items from the *verlan* of the *banlieues*.

The extent to which this resistance to the adoption of more 'exotic' pronunciation features is more characteristic of French than other comparable languages remains unclear. No recent examples of English borrowing of foreign pronunciation features come readily to mind, but the adoption by young southern English speakers of the invariant tag 'innit' is a striking example of an exogenous linguistic item that is closer to the

53   A. Malécot, 'The Glottal Stop in French', *Phonetica*, 1975, 31, pp. 51–63.

grammatical level than the lexical.[54] The closest French equivalent is to be found in prosody: as mentioned above, Conein and Gadet suggest that stress and intonation features are the innovative elements that distinguish *le français des banlieues* from *le français populaire*.[55] What remains to determine is the use of these new features by the different ethnic groups in the *banlieues*. More quantitative evidence is required to determine whether the very sharp discontinuity between *banlieue* and mainstream French constitutes a further example of *l'exception française*.

54   G. Andersen, 'The Use and Development of Invariant Tags in London Teenage Speech', paper presented at the First UK Language Variation Workshop, University of Reading, UK, April 1997.
55   Conein and Gadet, 'Français populaire? Français des banlieues?', pp. 41–2.

KAMAL SALHI AND HENRI JEANJEAN

France and her Linguistic Minorities: A Case of 'Domestic Colonialism' in Occitania

Linguistic and cultural matters have always been high on the list of priorities for French governments. As Minister for Foreign Affairs, Alain Juppé remarked that 'la diplomatie culturelle constitue une dimension essentielle de notre politique étrangère et, d'une certaine façon, est la marque de sa singularité.'[1] At the 1995 Francophone summit held in Cotonou, Jacques Chirac, the French President asserted that 'la langue étant l'expression d'un peuple, il fallait tout faire pour conserver les langues.'[2] The campaigners who denounce the growing use of English in international forums, on the Internet or in French public life, and organise themselves to defend the French language claim that their actions are motivated by a concern for linguistic pluralism. However, it is necessary to understand these campaigns in their historical context: for centuries French language policies have been framed with the purpose of wiping out minority languages in the country. The current concern about the French language may be seen as a response to the threats that are thought to be posed by two relatively recent political developments: the decentralisation of France and the creation of the European Union. Both appear to offer opportunities for action to strengthen regional languages and encourage the resolve of those who, like the Occitanists,[3] have been working to keep their culture alive for over a century. The focus in this chapter is on Occitan.

1   'Los francofònes en dangièr a l'ONU', *La Setmana*, 4, 8 June 1995.
2   'Chirac sauvador de las lengas', *La Setmana*, 30, 14 December 1995.
3   Militants fighting for the survival of the Occitan language and culture.

Organising the Defence of the French Language

The decline of French as a world language is not a new phenomenon. In 1958 the situation was felt to be so alarming that an organisation, Défense de la Langue Française, was formed with the following objectives:

- assurer la sauvegarde des qualités qui ont longtemps valu au français la précellence au sein des langues européennes, en s'opposant en particulier à l'invasion incontrôlée, et partant nuisible, des vocables étrangers.
- l'adapter aux exigences de la vie moderne, notamment par un enrichissement lexical permanent.
- Œuvrer à son rayonnement dans le monde.[4]

Declarations signed by 1,100 figures from across the political spectrum were published in *Le Monde* on 11 July and 1 December 1992 entitled 'Appel à une Europe multilingue'. They denounced 'ces quelques "décideurs" qui se sont mis en tête de faire renoncer la France à sa propre langue et de la faire parler en anglais, ou plutôt américain.'[5] In the name of a people's right to self-determination, particularly as far as their culture and language were concerned, they urged the French President to take action that would increase the amount of French-language material in information sources, the broadcast media, cinema and sound and visual recordings in France and the rest of the world.

The organisations Futur de la Langue Française and Défense de la Langue Française are both members of an umbrella group founded in 1994, Droit de Comprendre.[6] The functions of this group include: the

4   Défense de la Langue Française, languefr@micronet.fr.
5   Avenir de la langue française, languefr@micronet.fr.
6   'Nos moyens:
- ressources financières: outre les cotisations symboliques des adhérents directs, le Droit de comprendre est financé par ses associations membres sur la base de 0,5% de leurs ressources, ainsi que par une subvention de la Délégation générale à la langue française.
- les adhérents: les adhérents, directs ou représentants des associations membres, se réunissent régulièrement pour examiner les divers cas signalés.
- les bénévoles: nous bénéficions du concours de juristes sympathisants que nous consultons sur l'opportunité d'engager des actions contentieuses.
- une organisation: nous bénéficions de l'équipement bureautique d'une des associations membres et d'un secrétariat.'
More information is available on the website: http://persoweb.francenet.fr/~languefr/

co-ordination of the action taken by all organisations working for the development of the French-speaking world; and the provision of support for all initiatives intended to strengthen the influence of the French language and maintain the citizen's linguistic rights within the framework of current legislation at the national level and within European institutions.

In 1995 another association was established within the United Nations agencies to counter the tendency for the importance of French to diminish within the United Nations system. The number of French translators had gone down from 22 to 12 in 15 years. The members of this association blamed the United States, whom they accused of 'threatening the UN's multilingualism'.[7] The dangers faced by the French language were also at the heart of the 'Francophone Week' organised from 18 to 24 March 1996.[8] The newsletter of the Conseil Supérieur de la Délégation Générale à la Langue Française[9] set out the objectives of the week, which were, firstly, to underline that the promotion of French went hand in hand with a recognition of the need for linguistic pluralism and openness to others by showing respect for their languages and cultures; and, secondly, to reaffirm the French policy of support for multilingualism in international organisations, which was intended to protect cultural diversity in a world rapidly becoming more and more homogeneous as a result of the increasing globalisation. The newsletter underlined, again, the role of France, '[qui] a pris tant d'initiatives pour favoriser le pluralisme linguistique à l'intérieur de l'Union Européenne,' citing as an example the Loi Toubon passed in 1994.[10] This legislation on the protection of the French language was widely regarded as a weapon that could be used to counter the growing influence of English in French public life, in particular in the cinema, music and broadcasting. In this context,

> la programmation doit spécialement viser à améliorer les moyens de connaissance et de défense de la langue française tout en illustrant l'expression de la francophonie dans le monde.

7 'Los francofònes en dangièr a l'ONU', *La Setmana*, 4, 28 March 1996.
8 'La setmana de la francofonia', *La Setmana*, 45, 28 March 1996.
9 N84 du 1er trimestre 1996, quoted in *La Setmana*, 45.
10 Loi no. 94-88 of 1 February 1994, *Journal Officiel de la République Française*, 2 February 1994, amending Loi no. 86-1067 of 30 September 1986 relating to freedom of communication.

Article 12 stipulated that the proportion of musical works written or performed by French-speaking artists had to reach a minimum of 40% of broadcast time by 1 January 1996, half of which had to be accounted for by new performers or new recordings. In spite of all the initial denials, this law has increasingly come to be seen to be a continuation of the centuries-old tradition of centralist language policy aimed at suppressing the minority languages of France, an approach dating back to the fifteenth century. This law has been implemented fully by all the governments that have come into power since it was adopted.

Linguistic Hegemony

Claude de Seyssel, an adviser to Louis XII, was the first person to articulate this policy. He advised his sovereign to follow the example set by the Romans, for whom political, economic and cultural forms of colonisation were all complementary. The Romans

> n'ont trouvé de moyens plus sûrs de rendre leur domination éternelle que de magnifier, enrichir et sublimer leur langue latine [...] et de la communiquer aux pays et provinces et peuples par eux conquis.[11]

There have always been politicians prepared to impose a common language in the hope that this will encourage the spread of uniform cultural values among populations that are not always easy to control.

The first text to translate this concept into legislation, the Ordonnance de Villers-Cotterêts, dates back to 1539. In 1490 the first French law dealing with the language problem asked lawyers to use the vernacular instead of Latin. As it was not observed, it had to be re-enacted in 1510 and 1532, with one small change: lawyers and administrators were asked to write in French, while any other languages should only be used as a last resort. The Ordonnance de Villers-Cotterêts imposed French as the only official language of the kingdom. At the beginning of the sixteenth century the États provinciaux and the États particuliers were still in existence. On the one hand, the États provinciaux were the fiscal agents

11   'Langue française et néo-jacobinisme', *Libération*, 4 August 1992.

of royal power – determining the level of taxation and organising its collection – while, on the other, they were also engaged in a struggle to maintain the exemptions and freedoms that they enjoyed in the 'country'. The Ordonnance de Villers-Cotterêts is just one of the elements of a whole series of laws and actions that were part of a project begun at the end of the Middle Ages that organised the kingdom around a sole, centralised power. Between 1515 and 1559 Francis I and Henry II reinforced this policy of integration, which was later continued by Henry III, then Louis XIII and Richelieu. The process, or rather processes, of integration, took place in several overlapping phases: the creation of a network of institutions that directly represented royal power at the same time as the provincial and regional assemblies found themselves losing their traditional rights. City councils also faced a similar erosion of their powers and freedoms. It took more than two centuries of government action to defeat the resistance of the rural districts of the Midi. In 1537 and 1545 the Édit de Moulins and the Édit de La Fère are examples of attacks by the monarch on consular jurisdictions. The Ordonnance de Villers-Cotterêts is just one part of a larger process of political centralisation.

At the time, when the concept of nationalism and the belief in primacy of the nation state were first being put forward in a number of European countries, the idea of French's superiority over all other languages was developed by Henri Estienne in his book *De la précellence du langage français*,[12] which was published in 1579. From the middle of the seventeenth century, the annexation of newly conquered provinces would be followed by the publication of an edict proclaiming French as the sole official language. The aim was not to impose French on the local population with the intention of educating them, as there was no state education provision at this time,[13] but to unify the local élites, who, cut off from their roots in the culture and society around them, would identify with the French state and serve it with greater loyalty. Language therefore became, *de facto*, an instrument of social discrimination: social superiority and linguistic superiority were merged as symbols of power and allegiance to the centre.

12   '*Of the Pre-eminence of the French Language*'.
13   There was one exception: when it was annexed in 1620, Béarn had, for religious reasons, a well established schooling policy.

In contrast to this, the proponents of the French Revolution claimed that its roots were among the people. In setting about the task of organising a new social and political order, the revolutionaries were confronted with the necessity of politically educating the masses.[14] At first, Republican decrees were translated into the various regional languages (Breton, Occitan, etc.). Soon, though, the victory of the centralist Montagnards over the federalist Girondins led to a change of attitude. The revolutionary leaders began to argue that French was the only language capable of disseminating revolutionary ideas and that all 'foreign' languages were inevitably the carriers of reactionary and counter-revolutionary ideologies. The government's first attacks were directed against the languages unrelated to French (Breton, Basque, German and Corsican). Later, a decree of 8 Pluviôse of Year 2 banned the use of any language other than French in all dealings, including private business.

On the basis of his vast survey, Abbé Grégoire wrote to the Convention, presenting a 'Rapport sur la nécessité et les moyens d'anéantir les patois et d'universaliser l'usage de la langue française'.[15] A reading of this report and of the questionnaire sent out prior to its drafting, illuminate the ideology underlying Revolutionary language policy.

Grégoire's questionnaire revealed his prejudices against the various languages spoken in France, which are referred to as 'patois', a word that has had a pejorative meaning since it first came into use during the eighth century. The rural populations speaking 'patois' are deemed to belong to a culture inferior to that of those who speak standard French.[16] Two questions defined most clearly the objective in view: What would be the religious and political significance of the complete destruction of these dialects? And how could this be achieved?[17]

---

14   A more detailed study of the linguistic policies of the Revolution can be found in
     M. de Certeau, D. Julia and J. Revel, *Une politique de la langue* (Paris: Gallimard,
     1975).
15   De Certeau, Julia and Revel.
16   P. Robert, *Dictionnaire de la langue française* (Paris: SNL, 1973).
17   It can be argued that many people did look favourably on the imposition of French.
     However, at this time they only represented part of the bourgeoisie. The notion
     that French is good for social promotion did not gain general currency until after
     the First World War.

Grégoire was a priest from a bourgeois family in Lorraine and constitutional bishop of Blois. He despised regional languages and dialects, and had all the prejudices of his class.[18] His correspondents all belonged to the same social group, which wanted to prevent the lower classes, the peasants and workers, from gaining any hold over power. In a centralised system of government and administration, the lower classes who did not speak standard French would be excluded from the democratic process. The assertion of their linguistic superiority helped the bourgeoisie to maintain their political ascendancy.

Arguments put forward by the Jacobins between 1790 and 1794 in a number of reports presented to the various assemblies formed the basis of the compulsory primary education policy of the Third Republic.[19] Free compulsory schooling may be regarded as the product of egalitarian sentiments, and the social mobility made possible by education is an undeniable reality – though it is often overstated. However, the main reason for the increasing speed with which French spread in the 1880s was the fact that the country suddenly needed vast numbers of workers with a minimum of education. The industrial revolution, the increased importance of bureaucratic systems and the administration of the new colonies created many new posts requiring some degree of literacy from the staff filling them. Compulsory education was also a way of forcibly gallicising communities who may not have been considered as entirely reliable by the government. Following the defeat of 1870 and the ensuing loss of Alsace-Lorraine to Prussia, the ideology of French nationalism was going through a process of redefinition. There may well have been alarm at the fact that some regions had only recently been incorporated into France,[20] and that French-speakers were a minority not just in these areas, but also in parts of the country that had been conquered some 500 years previously, such as the parts of Occitania annexed after the end of the Crusade against the Albigensians.

18   The education of the lower classes is a way of imposing the ideology of the ruling class. A language conveys ways of thinking. If people integrate into the *status quo*, the hierarchical order, they are less likely to resist it.

19   Talleyrand, Condorcet, Romme, Lakanal, Daunou, Sieyès, Le Pelletier and Bouquier made various proposals; cf. L.-H. Parias (ed.), *Histoire Générale de l'Enseignement et de l'Éducation en France*, vol. III (Nelle Librairie de France, 1981).

20   Nice and Savoy were only incorporated into France in 1860.

A number of texts have guided the course of policy since the Second World War. The first was the law proposed by Joseph Deixonne, the Deputy for Tarn, that was promulgated on 11 January 1951, the only text that the French Parliament had had to debate. The Loi Haby of 1976 expanded its scope without modifying its structure. The Loi Jospin of 10 July 1989 made it possible for the teaching of regional languages and cultures to be included in the syllabuses of schools within the national education system. Many circulars have also been issued. Three were particularly important and wide-ranging in their effects: the two circulars issued by Alain Savary, 'L'enseignement des cultures et langues région-ales dans le service public de l'Éducation Nationale' (21 June 1982) and 'Texte d'orientation sur l'enseignement des cultures et langues région-ales' (30 December 1983), and the circular issued by François Bayrou 'Enseignement des langues et cultures régionales' (7 April 1995). The backgrounds of Joseph Deixonne, René Haby, Alain Savary, Lionel Jos-pin and François Bayrou, illuminate the geography of these ministerial texts. Of the five ministers, four represented areas in the south west of France, Occitanie, Tarn, Haute-Garonne and Pyrénées-Atlantiques, while René Haby was not an elected member of parliament when his law was enacted. In addition to these legislative instruments, there is an impressive series of proposed laws that have been deposited with the Bureau des Assemblées since the Second World War. There are dozens of them, but none of them has ever been discussed. The problem is that there are a number of groups bitterly opposed to the teaching of regional languages within the national education administration – at all levels – and in the teachers' unions that have succeeded in obstructing progress until recent years. The laws put in place show that, although some figures have been sensitive to the regionalists' arguments, the political and administrative classes as a whole have been bitterly opposed to them.

The last chapter in the decline of France's regional languages came in the 1950s and 1960s, a period that saw a number of factors coming together. Firstly, technological progress in agriculture led to large-scale population movements from the countryside to the cities, cutting off a large proportion of the population from their sociolinguistic roots. The modernisation of agriculture was accompanied by the disappearance of numerous traditional work practices based on mutual aid inside com-munities and social relationships within which communication was largely conducted in regional languages and dialects. At the same time, the introduction of television, which was strictly controlled by the state, completed the process by firmly establishing a situation of diglossia: regional languages came increasingly to be viewed as inferior by those who spoke them. To some extent, in France it was not only a question of High and Low variants. The education system used various means to instil a sentiment of shame in those speaking regional languages and this is still present today. In spite of all of this, regional languages and minority languages survived and resisted the measures taken against them by successive governments. This modern resistance can be traced back to the nineteenth century.

The Early Occitan Resistance

The nineteenth century saw a renewed interest in the Troubadours and their chivalric, Christian poetry, which was read across Europe. Indeed, as Mme de Staël notes, the very word 'Romantic' denoted Provençal poetry when it was introduced into German.[21] Classicism claimed to derive from realistic rationalism; the Romantics, by contrast, sought out forms of escapism, both spatial and temporal, and were inspired by exoticism and historicism. Their desire for a return to nature led them to seek inspiration in popular traditions and promote poets who either reflected the aspirations of the people or were part of a popular tradition. Lamartine, Sainte-Beuve, Nodier and George Sand enthused about Jasmin and Mistral, who were fêted in Paris. The high regard with which Occitan literature, medieval and contemporary, was held had a strong impact on young people in the region, whose local patriotism was strengthened further by their romantic historicism.

With the rise of the new Romantic school, history no longer concerned itself exclusively with kings and nobles, but also began to deal with the experiences of ordinary people. For the celebrated historian

---

21   Mme de Staël, *De l'Allemagne, Œuvres complètes*, vol. 2 (Geneva: Slatkine reprints, 1967), p. 61.

Augustin Thierry, Bretons and people from Provence could not accept the history of the French who had oppressed their ancestors as their 'national history'. In 1828, when Guizot returned to the Chair of Modern History at the Sorbonne,[22] his first lecture was on Occitan civilisation and the Crusade against the Albigensians that destroyed the democratic society that had been established in the South of France. During the Restoration, evidence began to emerge of the strength of this southern democracy, and there were denunciations of the fanaticism that had led to the violent suppression of the Albigensians.

This fresh interest in history and literature helped to give new life to minority cultures. In the aftermath of the nationalist revolutions of 1848, the Felibrige was founded by a group of poets who wished to keep the Occitan linguistic heritage alive and create a greater understanding of it outside Languedoc.[23]

The most brilliant writer in this group was Frédéric Mistral, who was awarded the 1904 Nobel Prize for Literature. When he was asked to enter politics, Mistral declined, but at the same time reaffirmed the ideal of a revival of the Provençal nation that had been crushed by the centralised state.[24] He insisted in his memoirs that what spurred him to found the Felibrige was the necessity of creating a local racial identity in Provence by means of a revival of the region's natural, historical language, which had been annihilated by the hostility to it found in the education system.[25]

French nationalism became completely dominant after 1871. The country expanded its colonial empire to compensate for the shame of defeat in the Franco-Prussian war, and there was nobody willing to contest the policy of administrative and cultural centralisation. Members of the Felibrige sought refuge in a purely linguistic resistance far removed

---

22   He had been suspended since 1822 because of the controversial nature of his teaching.
23   H. Jeanjean, 'Romantisme et Nationalisme: Perspectives Occitanes', in J. West-Sooby (ed.), *Les Enjeux de la Modernité: Problèmes d'identité et d'idéologie dans la littérature du XIXème siècle* (Melbourne: Monash Romance Studies 2, 1997), pp. 27.
24   A. Rey, *Frédéric Mistral, poète Républicain* (Cavaillon: Imprimerie Mistral, 1929), p. 37.
25   F. Mistral, *Mémoires et Récits* (Paris: Plon, 1906), p. 132.

from social and economic realities, and based on a glorification of the past. Although part of the Felibrige movement split away to form what came to be called the 'Red Felibrige', the majority, as with most movements in the regional renaissance at the time, attached themselves to the French right. In the 1930s Charles Maurras, a prominent member of the Felibrige, was also the leader of the extreme-right-wing nationalist and royalist organisation *Action Française*. Later he participated actively in the Vichy regime.

The 1944 liberation was marked by a feeling of triumphant French nationalism. The Occitanists who had fought alongside the Resistance, whatever their ideological orientation, fell into what Balzagues called 'the trap of French Nationalism'.[26] The leadership of the cultural organisation they created, the Institute d'Études Occitanes (IEO), was made up solely of intellectuals, mainly academics. Because of the close ties they had with the French left, they were not prepared to accept in their midst anyone subscribing to the separatist/nationalist ideologies they regarded as threats to French unity.

Before the Second World War the Occitan movement was divided between two tendencies. The left movement was led by Camproux, the director of *Occitania* who wanted an autonomous Occitania within a federal France. He was opposed to the nation state and aligned himself with the Catalan and Basque Republicans. The other part of the movement was led by Maurras and pursued an extreme right-wing agenda. During the War this movement joined the Pétain government, who represented the anti-Jacobin tendency in France. Pétain was a Maurrassien, and as early as 1941 his domestic policies were very close to the ideas enunciated by Mistral after 1870. On the other side, preparatory work for the IEO, which replaced the SEO (Société d'Études Occitanes), was done in the Resistance by Max Rouquette, René Nelli, Ismaël Girard and Tristan Tzara.

---

26   G. Balzagues, 'Les organisations occitanes', *Les Temps Modernes*, August–September 1973, pp. 140–62.

The Impact of the Decolonisation Debate

As Indochina, Algeria and Madagascar rebelled against their French
colonial masters after the Second World War, a number of books were
published exploring the nature of colonisation. Octave Mannoni's *Psychologie de la colonisation* (1950), Frantz Fanon's *Peau noire, masques
blancs* (1952), Aimé Césaire's *Discours sur le colonialisme* (1955) and
Albert Memmi's *Portrait du colonisé* (1957) spearheaded the intellectual
soul-searching that gave new vigour to nationalist ideas, not only in the
colonies themselves, but also in some regions of France. In the Occitan
movement François Fontan expounded his thesis of a separatist nationalism in 1954, the year that saw the French defeat in Indochina and the
beginning of the Algerian War of Independence. The following year the
prominent academic Pierre Bec read a manifesto along the same nationalist lines at the General Assembly of the IEO.

The impact of these ideas, and of the debates they provoked, was
increased by the fact that they brought together three separate concerns:
the necessity for the colonised to re-establish their own understanding of
historical truth, the economic basis of colonisation and, most important
of all, the need to establish psychological profiles of the colonised and
the colonisers, as well as an understanding of the interdependence of the
two groups and their interactions. Each of these concerns found an echo
in Occitania, and the result was a new wave of radicals re-appraising
their own historical, social and economic situation, as well as reaching a
better understanding of the reasons for the failure of their predecessors.

Césaire saw the results of colonisation not as the progress proclaimed by the colonisers, but as 'sociétés vidées d'elles-mêmes, de cultures
piétinées, d'institutions minées, de terres confisquées, de religions assas-
sinées, de magnificences artistiques anéanties, d'extraordinaires possi-
bilités supprimées'.[27] Occitans recognised their own experience in these
words. When Césaire denounced the massacres and tortures inflicted
upon the conquered, Occitans could name hundreds of such events from
their own history, beside the most obvious examples of Béziers and

27   A. Césaire, *Discours sur le colonialisme* (*Présence Africaine*, 1955), pp. 19–20.

Bram.[28] A French historian not known for his sympathy with regionalist ideas wrote that the Crusade against the Albigensians was not a civil war, as the Count of Toulouse was not French, and that the French 'ont massacré, tué, violé. En l'occurrence les Français, ce sont les S.S.'[29] For Césaire, in the twentieth century every bourgeois citizen had the potential to be a Hitler. Indeed, he argued that Hitler was regarded as an unique monster not so much on account of his crimes against humanity, but because he used methods that the colonialists had only used previously against the Algerians, Indians and Africans, and applied them in Europe.[30] The French had eradicated similar acts committed in the past by French soldiers from their collective memory, and also from the collective memories of the societies they colonised. In the same way, they refused to acknowledge the similarities between the methods of the Gestapo and those used by the French army in the 1950s when it was fighting against various liberation movements in the colonies.

The initial studies made by the nineteenth-century Romantic historians who denounced the destruction of the democratic system existing in the South of France, the extreme brutality of the Crusade against the Albigensians and the rewriting of history had already given impetus to the deconstruction of the propaganda that had been imposed upon the Bretons, Occitans and Corsicans by the education system. As was the case with all other colonised peoples, 'la mémoire que l'on donne aux individus n'est pas celle de leur peuple et l'histoire qu'on leur enseigne n'est pas la leur.'[31] 'Our ancestors the Gauls were tall and blond,' was the first history lesson that every child had to learn by rote. It became increasingly apparent that this was as ridiculous in Corsica or Occitania as it was in Central Africa. The new movement for the re-appropriation of Occitan history by the Occitans was given further momentum after the

28 Béziers was the first town to fall to the Crusaders in 1209. The whole population was killed: about 20,000 people, including 8,000 women and children who died when the cathedral in which they had taken refuge was burnt down. After taking the weakly defended village of Bram in 1210, Simon de Montfort ordered that 100 men should have their eyes gouged out and their noses cut off. They were sent off under the guidance of the one man who had been allowed to keep one of his eyes in order to spread terror through the region.

29 A. Decaux, *L'Éducation Nationale*, 17 March 1966.

30 Césaire, p. 12.

31 A. Memmi, *Portrait du colonisé* (Paris: Payot, 1973), pp. 133–4.

failed revolution of 1968. In the following years several books were published analysing the events and the processes that had led to the colonisation of the region.[32] However, it was clear that this re-appropriation of history alone was not enough to overcome the alienation of the colonised and create a clear awareness of economic and social realities. The inferiority complex of the colonised is the consequence of a double process in which, firstly, their economic inferiority is established and, secondly, they learn to accept that inferiority unquestioningly.[33]

The Occitan writers compared the struggles of those oppressed by colonialism to the struggles of those oppressed by the class system. The relationship between peoples of different nations as colonisers/colonised was equated to the relationship between the bourgeoisie and proletariat within one nation.[34] This argument stressed the dialectical psychological relationship between the colonised and their colonisers.

In 1959, at a time when the Algerian war was increasing in intensity, Fontan founded the first Occitanist political party, the Occitan Nationalist Party (PNO). This separatist group actively supported the Algerian Liberation Movement and French deserters. One of the reasons for this support was Fontan's belief that the psychological shock that would follow the independence of Algeria would raise the consciousness of the Occitan people and therefore eradicate French nationalism in the South of France. As Manonni pointed out, Europeans have a tendency to compensate for any perceived inferiority by asserting their own superiority.[35] The colonised and dispossessed within France came to accept their oppressed condition as they took up positions in the French colonial service and became oppressors in other parts of the world.[36] Economically ex-

---

32   These publications include: A. Armengaud *et al.*, *Histoire d'Occitanie* (Paris: Hachette, 1979); A. Dupuy, *Petite encyclopédie occitane* (Montpellier: Saber, 1972); J. Larzac, *Descolonisar l'istoria occitana Tolosa* (IEO, A Tots, 1977); M. Roquebert, *L'Épopée cathare* (Toulouse: Privat, 1970).

33   F. Fanon, *Peau noire, masques blancs* (Paris: Le Seuil, 1952), p. 10.

34   Memmi, p. 103.

35   O. Manonni, *Prospéro et Caliban: psychologie de la colonisation* (Paris: Éditions universitaires), p. 67.

36   In Mongo Beti's famous novel *Le roi Miraculé* (Paris: Buchet-Chastel, 1958), all the colonists are the product of colonisation: one of the administrators is half-Vietnamese, the others come from the Caribbean and Corsica, while the missionaries are from Brittany and Alsace.

ploited and used politically to defend interests that they did not, objective-ly, share, they tended to outbid the original coloniser.[37] Fontan hoped that the removal of this option of psychological compensation would prompt a new growth of political awareness in Occitania.

Occitans were among 'ces millions d'hommes à qui on a inculqué le complexe d'infériorité.'[38] As a result of the destruction of the local culture, they were only able to create a sense of identity by locating themselves within the discourse of the 'civilising nation'.[39] Their native tongue, whatever its past glories may have been, only transmitted an impoverished oral culture and did not offer any grasp of the most import-ant aspects of modern society. The language that has been humiliated and crushed by the colonisers comes to be despised by the colonised themselves. Ashamed of it, they hide it from strangers, functioning only in the coloniser's language. As a result, colonial bilingualism is a lin-guistic tragedy that cannot be compared to a state of diglossia in which a popular idiom and a high-status official language coexist peacefully, even though there is a perceived hierarchy in their usage.[40]

The nineteenth-century Occitan writers were aware of the import-ance and the urgency of reviving their language, but they were not able to realise that the principle guiding them was that the first ambition of the colonised is to equal the prestigious model offered by the coloniser, to look like it to the point of disappearing in it.[41] Two examples confirm this proposition.

Although he was a great admirer of Jasmin, Sainte-Beuve, the influ-ential writer and literary critic, expressed considerable reservations about the early political poems written by the Occitan writer. He justified his arguments linguistically: the political ideas enunciated by Jasmin are modern, but as Gascon, a dialect of Occitan, is a language without mod-ern vocabulary, it is unable to express these ideas. In order to do so Jasmin is obliged to use a number of forms borrowed from French, sacrificing the authenticity and purity of his language as he does so. Sainte-Beuve's ideas on language were based on the theories developed by the Jacobins

37 Memmi, p. 45.
38 Césaire, p. 20.
39 Fanon, p. 16.
40 Fanon, pp. 136–7.
41 Fanon, p. 149.

during the French Revolution.[42] What is more surprising is that Jasmin, who had worked hard to achieve authenticity in his language, accepted the validity of this criticism and deeply interiorised these representations of his own language as a dominated and limited language that had been imposed arbitrarily by a French writer with no knowledge whatsoever of Occitan.[43]

Mistral went to Paris for the first time in 1858 in order to publish there his first major work, *Mirèio*. It was printed with a French translation, showing that his first priority was success with a Parisian readership. Both Jasmin and Mistral were celebrated because they appeared to be the guardians of obsolete traditions and customs within which they were prepared to confine themselves. By contrast, Victor Gélu, whose political poems denouncing social injustices and ecclesiastical hypocrisy were sung during the Marseilles Commune and influenced the young Émile Zola, was condemned by the courts for 'outrages against public morals'.

These new and detailed studies of the nature of colonisation gave minority groups an understanding of the nexus between the colonised and the coloniser. The gulf separating the economic development of northern and southern France in the early 1960s was widening rapidly. The analysis of the PNO, which argued that there was an essential equivalence between the economy of Occitania and the economies of the French colonies, appeared to be well founded. The PNO's membership may always have been relatively small, but it was still an extremely important force in the Occitan movement because it was the only group to describe itself as separatist and call for moves to break away from French nationalism. It exerted a lateral force on the Occitan movement as a whole, and on the IEO, in particular. During the winter of 1961–2, which saw the entire population of the Decazeville region mobilised in support of the coal miners following the announcement that their mines would be closing, several members of the IEO led by Robert Lafont created the Occitan Committee of Studies and Action (COEA). It condemned what it called 'interior colonisation', stressing the Occitan character of the political and socio-economic struggles taking place in Occitania.

42   They argued as follows: French was the only language that could transmit the ideas and the core values of the Revolution, while other languages, because they were not modern, could only propagate counter-revolutionary ideologies.
43   C. Torreilles, 'Sainte-Beuve et Jasmin', *Lengas*, 26, 1989, p. 116.

The Loi Toubon

The Loi Toubon, an apparently innocuous piece of legislation, was a major part of the colonialist linguistic policy discussed above. This becomes apparent when the decrees implementing the law are taken into account, as well as the way it has been interpreted by various authorities in the light of the 1992 amendment to Article 2 of the French Constitution. This amendment, which was supported by all the political parties, inserted the statement 'French is the language of the Republic' into the Constitution. During the parliamentary debates on the proposal, some members of the French Parliament tried to insert the phrase 'with all due respect to France's regional languages and cultures'. The Garde des Sceaux[44] formally opposed the motion. This refusal to compromise, which was encouraged by the government, strengthened the discriminatory effect of the law against minority languages, which had previously been tolerated, but now became officially illegal.[45] Speaking for the government, Alain Lamassoure, the then Minister for Budgetary Affairs, claimed that Article 2 could never be used against regional languages.[46] Only a few months later he used this very article to justify the government's decision to exclude all regional publications not written in French from an aid scheme for the regional weekly press set up in 1995.

La Setmana, a weekly magazine written in Occitan, argued that this decision violated the right to freedom of expression. It categorically rejected this discrimination on the basis of the language, adding that, 'la libertat de pensar, d'escríver e d'informar ne's pòt ps apariar dab ua volontat d'empachar l'expression d'ua cultura e d'ua lenga.'[47]

The Loi Toubon did not mention regional languages. However, a circular published on 20 March 1996 to explain the details of the law specified that French was compulsory for all the broadcast media, cinema

---

44 The French equivalent of the British Lord Chancellor.
45 *La Setmana*, 47, 11 April 1996.
46 Article 2 stipulates that French is the language of the France. It appears to have been used in several instances to hinder the use of regional languages.
47 David Grosclaude, 'Libertat d'expression', *La Setmana*, 56, 13 June 1996: 'The freedom to think, to write and to disseminate information cannot coexist with a will to prevent the articulation of a culture and a language.'

and video or sound recordings, publicity materials, and business and public meetings. No attempt was made to differentiate between regional languages and foreign languages, implying that Occitan, Breton and Catalan are as dangerous to the survival of French as English. Whereas funds for the promotion of French abroad were reduced by 15% in the 1996 Budget, new funding was found for this discriminatory linguistic policy. In particular, the Délégation Générale à la Langue Française, for which the Minister for Culture is responsible, created the position of Counsellor for French in each administrative region of France. The ministry urged local government bodies and all organisations dedicated to the 'defence of the French language' to do their best to ensure that the Loi Toubon was implemented in full.[48] This hard-line approach bore fruit when a business was sentenced to a FF 1,000 fine for failing to observe the Loi Toubon following a complaint made by an association for the defence of the French language.[49] In April 1996 the Prefect of Pyrénées Orientales sent a circular to all the mayors in his *Département*, explaining how the Loi Toubon should be applied. This representative of state power declared that organisations that had received state funding and then, for example, organised congresses, seminars or conferences, published reviews, or signed contracts in any language other than French would have to repay part, or all, of grants they had received. There were protests from outraged Catalan groups, while Miquel Reniu, the Director of Linguistic Policy in Catalonia, commented in a letter published in *Aviu*, the Barcelona daily newspaper, that 'it was strange to see that the country that invented Human Rights, does not respect them.'[50] These irrational and excessive reactions can only be explained by an analysis of the serious problems that a combination of legislation on administrative decentralisation in France and the establishment of the European Union has caused recent governments.

48   'Francofonia: Orientacion novèla de la politica lingüistica', *La Setmana*, 46, 4 April 1996.
49   'Francofonia: Orientacion novèla de la politica lingüistica'.
50   'Las reaccions a la letra prefectora', *La Setmana*, 49, 25 April 1996.

The Impact of Europe

The founding of the European Union has had important legislative consequences. The European Court of Justice is building a new supranational judicial order, based on a system of jurisprudence that applies to all countries that have signed relevant treaties: 'bien qu'elle s'en défende, ce travail dans les marges des articles fondateurs fait de cette institution judiciaire un creuset législatif.'[51] As European law takes precedence over national legislation, judges in the member states are able to base their rulings upon the decisions of the European Court of Justice, the European Commission or the Council of Europe. In any jurisdiction, judges can (and sometimes must) refer matters to the European Court, allowing them to revise many aspects of national law.

As the highest French court dealing with conflicts between individuals and the administration, the Conseil d'État has had to take a clear stance with regard to problems arising from the harmonisation of French law with European law. In his end-of-year Report, Marceau Long, Vice-President of the Conseil d'État, mentioned the precedent set by the Nicolo ruling of 20 October 1989.[52] The newspaper *Libération* commented on the historic nature of this event,[53] which marked the transition from the precedence of national legislation to the precedence of European law. This was a development that France had resisted for more than 22 years.

It has always been clear that the legislative and executive powers of the European Union would increase to the detriment of the powers of the individual nation states. The meeting of the Council of Europe on 16–17 June 1997 strengthened the powers of the European Parliament.

> Le tandem franco-allemand n'était pas sur la même longueur d'ondes: Paris préférant privilégier les prérogatives des parlements nationaux [...] Bonn optant pour la stratégie inverse. Amsterdam a tranché en donnant raison aux Allemands.'[54]

51   Jean Palestel, 'Treize super juges pour les douze', *Libération*, 25 May 1990.
52   *Rapport public 1989. Études et Documents du Conseil d'État*, no. 41, La Documentation Française, 1990.
53   Jean Quatremer, 'Le Conseil d'État dans les eaux internationales', *Libération*, 1 June 1990.
54   'La montée en puissance du Parlement européen', *Dernières Nouvelles d'Alsace*, 29 June 1997.

The collapse of the Communist regimes in Central and Eastern Europe and the civil war in the former Yugoslavia have ensured that the question of minority rights has been high on the European agenda. It was one of the main issues at the Copenhagen Conference on the Human Dimension in June 1990, where agreement was reached on a list of rights to be conferred on minorities.[55] The OSCE, the Council of Europe and the European Union now co-ordinate their efforts with a view to developing a coherent system for the protection of minority rights in spite of the disagreements that have arisen over definitions of the nature, and even the very concept, of a 'national minority'.

All the national constitutions of member states of the European Union that refer to questions of language have provisions with regard to territorial linguistic minorities. Article 6 of the Italian Constitution compels the authorities to 'protect the linguistic minorities of the country.' Though Article 3 of the Spanish Constitution states that *Castillano* is the official language of the country, it also notes that other languages may have an official status in autonomous communities, and that it is the duty of the state to protect all these languages. In a bid to strengthen its centralised state, France has therefore become the only country in the European Union with a constitution that names one official language without referring to other languages that have been used historically within its borders.

On the other hand, moves to strengthen the cross-border structures of the European Union inevitably weaken the powers of the individual nation states, a tendency that has been exacerbated in France by the process of decentralisation that has taken place in recent years.

The Impact of Decentralisation

Although the policy of regionalisation was launched under Pompidou in 1972, decentralisation became a reality with legislation passed in 1982 and 1984 that gave the French regions a major role and established

55   F. Benoît-Rohmer, *The Minority Question in Europe* (Strasbourg: Council of Europe, 1996).

regional councils responsible for regional planning. The regional councils were also given extensive powers to make cultural and economic policy. The European Union and the process of regionalisation have combined to create new synergies. Inter-regional co-operation is common within France, but sometimes takes on an international dimension as well, since regional councils have been given the authority to organise regular contacts with decentralised foreign administrative bodies that share common borders with their regions, though only in certain policy areas.

As soon as the results of the first regional elections, held in March 1986, became known, the presidents of Midi-Pyrénées, Languedoc-Roussillon and Aquitaine met with Jordi Pujol, the President of the Spanish *Generalitat* of Catalonia. This was a sign of a revival of the strong cultural and economic ties between Occitans and Catalans in the past. The effect was to overturn the defeat of Muret (1213) and the Treaty of the Pyrenees (1659), which had artificially divided the two communities.

Following his imprisonment in 1960, Jordi Pujol had become the main representative of Catalan identity. President of the *Generalitat* since 1980, he had taken a particular interest in linguistic matters, as is evidenced by developments in Catalonia:

> today bilingualism is in place at all levels of education. Catalan is the preferred language of local administrations and has become an official language within European institutions. The Generalitat launched two television channels (since 23 April 1996 television and radio programmes have been transmitted all over Europe by satellite) and the Catalan press has seen spectacular development.[56]

This re-conquest of its cultural and linguistic identity by an economically vigorous Catalonia at a time when European markets and borders are opening inevitably had direct consequences north of the border. In North Catalonia

> la pressió econòmica i la importància cultural i política de Barcelona provoquen canvis en les mentalitats nord-catalanes: la llengua del pagès s'esta convertint en llengua del comerç e del poder, i recobra i redescobreix el prestigi perdut. Una

56   J.-C. Morera, *Histoire de la Catalogne* (Paris: L'Harmattan, 1992), p. 162.

nova dinàmica pot originar el desenvolupament econòmic en un marc euroregional i europeu molt més favorable als interessos de Catalunya Nord.'[57]

Cross-border exchanges have taken on a new dimension as new agreements, both cultural and economic, come into effect.[58] The responsibility for cultural developments given to the regions has enabled them to take a number of initiatives to support regional languages. While a survey of regional councils in Occitania showed that they dealt very unevenly with minority cultures,[59] the budget allocated to Occitan and Catalan by Languedoc-Roussillon has steadily increased to FF 17.5 million in 1998. For several years this region's policy of promoting minority languages has been broadly endorsed by all political parties,[60] though it may be jeopardised in future if the National Front continues to perform strongly in elections.

Regionalisation and the European Union have combined to give some hope to members of minorities anxious to protect their languages. Although minority languages have become illegal in France, these same languages enjoy official status in countries where they are spoken by even smaller minorities, e.g. Occitan in Spain (Val d'Aran) and Italy (Occitan-speaking valleys in the Alps), and Catalan and Basque in Spain. The Occitanists who, by a large majority, previously opposed both European integration and French regionalisation have come to recognise the benefits that these changes may bring.

57   *Qui sem els Catalans del Nord* (Perpignan: Associaciò Arrels, 1992), p. 106. 'The
      strong economic environment and the cultural importance of Barcelona has pro-
      voked changes in North Catalan thinking: the language of the peasant has become
      the language of business and power, and is recovering its lost prestige. This new
      dynamism may be the starting point for economic developments within the region-
      al European market and the whole European market that will be more auspicious
      for North Catalonia.'
58   The Euroregion encompassing Catalonia, Midi-Pyrénées and Languedoc-Rous-
      sillon was established on 10 October 1991 in Perpignan.
59   *Occitans!*, 82, January–February 1998.
60   E. Hammel, *Aide-Mémoire: Langues et cultures régionales et Région Languedoc-
      Roussillon 1985–1996* (Perpignan: El Trabucaire, 1996).

The Militants' Change of Heart

The crisis in the wine-growing region of Languedoc during the 1970s provided ample evidence to the Occitan movement that the Common Market was dominated by the large wholesalers and that it was official policy to eradicate the wine industry in the region. The European regulations were seen as a premeditated plan put in place to institutionalise the ruin of the South of France by encouraging the unchecked and fraudulent import of wines from Italy and other countries over the Italian border. [61] The 1976 riots encouraged the anti-European sentiments felt by the Occitanists as they forged close links with the leaders of the winemakers. The Occitanists were also bitterly opposed to the legislation on decentralisation passed between 1982 and 1984, when the organisation of the proposed regions was manipulated by the central government in Paris and took no account of the linguistic, cultural and historical identities of the regions. These policies proved to be short-sighted and changes were introduced to make the new authorities more sensitive to local needs.

In the 1980s it became apparent that the radicals' hope of eliminating the very factors that allowed the *status quo* to continue – the tolerance of the oppressed themselves towards the oppression they faced[62] – was receding. As Eugen Weber had shown, between 1870 and 1914 the inhabitants of provincial, rural France became French.[63] While, as all linguistic studies indicate, Occitans were, and still are, attached to their language, since 80% are in favour of it being taught in schools,[64] they are not prepared to challenge the legitimacy of the French state. The majority of the Occitan movement slowly began to abandon uncompromising positions that were looking increasingly utopian and took up more pragmatic attitudes.[65]

61   M. Le Bris, *Occitanie: Volem Viure!* (Paris: Gallimard, 1974).
62   Memmi, p. 117.
63   E. Weber, *La fin des terroirs* (Paris: Fayard, 1983).
64   E. Hammel and P. Gardy, *L'occitan en Languedoc-Roussillon* (Perpignan: Trabucaire, 1991).
65   H. Jeanjean, *De l'Utopie au Pragmatisme? Le mouvement occitan 1976 –1990* (Perpignan: Trabucaire, 1992).

The cultural role of the Euroregion was defined at a meeting of the presidents of the regional governments concerned in February 1989. Some Occitanists were quick to appreciate the new possibilities offered by such realignments. The very same year the Tarn departmental section of the IEO organised the first exhibition of products from Tarn at the international fair in Girona, Albi's twin city. Links were organised between Occitan and Catalan groups whose economic interests were similar or complementary, and more and more people became aware of the close links between the two languages. The ease with which speakers of the two languages were able to communicate led to a rapid expansion of economic exchanges. Following this first successful experience, the IEO-Tarn embarked on a vast project that included a colloquium exploring the synergy between cultural identity and economic development.[66] As a cultural organisation, the IEO demonstrated that the new economic and political situation could be used successfully by the Occitanist movement, provided that it was prepared to collaborate with the various strata of government, local, departmental and regional, as well as other economic partners. The small minority of Occitanists who saw the potential of Europe in the late 1980s were joined by the vast majority of the movement in the mid-1990s. This change of attitude was accelerated by a series of initiatives taken by the European Union, including policies implemented at the legislative level, the establishment of support structures, such as the European Bureau for Lesser Used Languages, and financial aid given to projects promoting minority languages. The intransigence of French governments, whatever their political ideology, when dealing with the minority question in both the international and national arenas, has served only to hasten this shift of emphasis on the part of the Occitanist movement.

In spite of some minor local successes, Occitanists have only had very limited political influence, but what influence they have had has been greatly enhanced by the various programmes supporting minorities instituted by European Union organisations.

The Council of Europe and the European Parliament have always defended a concept of Europe based upon respect, solidarity and the promotion of the linguistic and cultural heritage of all ethnic and cultural

66   IEO-Tarn (coll.), *Identitat Culturala e dinamisme economic* (Albi: IEO, 1992).

groups. Article 128, title IX, culture of the Maastricht Treaty states: 'The Community shall contribute to the flowering of the cultures of the Member States, while respecting their national and regional diversity and at the same time bringing the common cultural heritage to the fore.'[67] European activities in support of minorities have steadily increased and the various European institutions are pushing for greater recognition of minority languages by the member states. Three different events that took place in a single month, March 1996,[68] illustrate the kind of pressure being applied:

1. In March, in Catana, the Committee of the Regions stressed that the importance and value of minority languages traditionally spoken in the member states were not sufficiently recognised in the Maastricht Treaty. It called on the President of the European Commission to ensure that any new treaty incorporate a declaration recognising the importance and the value of these languages for the peoples of Europe and make it incumbent upon the member states to respect and promote those languages.
2. On 13 March the European Parliament in Strasbourg adopted the Dury–Maij–Weggens Report on the reform of the European institutions. Article 4.13, on minorities, calls for the recognition of cultural and linguistic diversity, and the protection of traditional minorities and their languages.
3. On 29 March the Turin Conference sought to redefine the political future of the European Union. According to Allan Wynne Jones, then President of the European Bureau for Lesser Used Languages, the protection of cultural and linguistic minorities will be at the heart of the new challenges faced by the Union.

---

67   The European Bureau for Lesser Used Languages, *Key Words: A Step into the World of Lesser Used Languages* (Brussels: 1995), p. 35.
68   'La conferència de Turin e las minoritats d'Euròpa', *La Setmana*, 50, 2 May 1996.

The Charter for Minority Languages

Confronted with these new realities, France continues to lock itself into a defensive linguistic policy. For instance, in 1989 France refused to sign the article referring to minority languages in the International Convention on the Rights of the Child.[69] The European Charter for Regional or Minority Languages was adopted on 5 November 1992. It set targets for the use of minority languages in various fields of public life, such as education, justice and public administration. It came into effect on 1 March 1998 after Switzerland became the fifth member of the Council of Europe to ratify it,[70] though 17 countries had already signed it. The drafting committee had left a great deal of latitude for the member states in order to facilitate its wide acceptance. For example, Article 2 of the Charter stipulates that, though all the states have to abide by the objectives and the principles of the Charter once they have ratified it, they can still maintain reservations about one or several articles of the Charter. Countries are only obliged to endorse 35 out of the 68 measures intended to support minority languages.

Many politicians in France have publicly urged the French government to sign the Charter, but some only did so under pressure from their constituencies and changed their minds once they were in Paris, or exploited administrative difficulties to renege on their promises.

In an address made in Brittany on 29 May 1996, President Chirac said that he was in favour of the use of regional languages. Alain Juppé, his Prime Minister at the time, declared that his government would look into the legal feasibility of France signing the Charter. In February 1997, the Conseil d'État opposed this move, invoking Article 2 of the Constitution. Lionel Jospin was under the same pressure after his victory in the 1997 elections, and asked for a report to be drawn up. This was finally

---

69   France refused to sign the article stating that children from linguistic minorities
      have a right to be taught in their own language. Its representatives argued that, as
      there were no minorities in France, it did not have to sign that article.
70   The countries that had already ratified the Charter were Norway, Finland, Hungary
      and The Netherlands.

presented to him on 1 July 1998.[71] It recommended that the French government sign the Charter and that a constitutional expert be called upon to assess the compatibility of the Charter's various articles with the French Constitution.

Guy Carcassonne presented his report on 9 October 1998.[72] He found that, as about 50 of the articles in the Charter were compatible with the French Constitution, no problems would be posed if France signed it, provided that careful safeguards were established. Jospin declared: 'The time when national unity and the pluralism of regional cultures seemed antagonistic is over.'[73] Under strong pressure, the French Government finally signed the Charter on 7 May 1999, agreeing to endorse 39 measures. However, parliamentary opposition to its ratification was soon growing across the political spectrum. Four days after the French government signed the Charter, Jean-Luc Mélanchon, a Socialist senator, expressed his feelings by quoting Saint-Just's famous words, 'l'obscurantisme parle breton, la raison parle français,' while one of his colleagues proclaimed that the text meant 'le retour des Chouans'.[74] In any case, the Charter never even came before the Parliament for ratification, as, on 16 June 1999 the Conseil constitutionnel declared the agreement to be incompatible with the French Constitution, confirming the earlier decision made by the Conseil d'État. The Prime Minister, Lionel Jospin, asked President Chirac, who has the sole power to initiate a revision of the Constitution, to amend it by adding an article that would enable Parliament to ratify the Charter. The President refused: in the European elections held in June 1999 a third of the electorate had voted for '*souverainiste*' lists. These 'supporters of national sovereignty' have polarised the political debate on nationality questions, transcending the traditional divisions between right and left. The Republican Left, led by Chevènement, and the anti-European Right, with Pasqua as its main leader, regard the Charter as a threat to the very identity of France.

71   Bernard Poignant, *Langues et Cultures Régionales*, report presented to Lionel Jospin, French Prime Minister, 1 July 1998.

72   Guy Carcassonne, *Étude sur la compatibilité entre La Charte européenne des langues régionales ou minoritaires et la Constitution*, September 1998.

73   J.-L. Andreani and G. Dupont, 'La France devrait ratifier la Charte européenne des langues régionales en 1999', *Le Monde*, 9 October 1998.

74   'Sénateurs sans-culottes', *Le Canard Enchaîné*, 19 May 1999.

During the debate held in the French Assembly on the introduction of the amendment to Article 2 of the Constitution, some of the speeches delivered were extremely revealing of the ideological justifications for its introduction. The speakers made clear that it had been proposed as a consequence of the fears engendered in France by the signing of the Maastricht Treaty and the process of European integration that would follow on from it. Mr Lamassoure, speaking for the government, explained that the measure was particularly necessary on account of the fact that language problems would become more acute as Europe continued to expand. In future, he argued, Europe would only recognise two or three official languages; this article would ensure that French was one of them. This begs the question: Which official languages would be retained? English, German and French? Europe was built on the basis of the equality of all its member states and its cohesion is a result of the general acceptance of this principle. The desire to give French a privileged status therefore undermines the very principles that have helped the European Union to achieve so much.

In 1996, in the name of the Comité Européen pour le Respect des Cultures et des Langues en Europe (CERCLE), the association Le Droit de Comprendre launched an appeal in the French daily press for 'a humanistic, multilingual Europe, rich with cultural diversity'. The text certainly started by defending the status of all European languages since it was intended to mobilise support for 'multilingualism' and against English becoming 'the only language'. Nonetheless, the signatories to this appeal soon showed that their concept of pluralism was very limited: in their view, linguistic diversity only related to national languages, and there was a need for limits to be imposed so that only a 'reasonable number' of languages were used for official business.

Once again, the authors sheltered behind what they presented as a defence of multilingualism in order to seek a privileged status for their own language at the expense of other languages they judged to be inferior. The hypocrisy of the arguments that they claimed were put forward to defend multilingualism is betrayed by the record of recent French governments, which have all opposed multilingualism within France, just like their predecessors over the preceding four centuries.

Will Jospin's promises signal a change of policy? In spite of all the undertakings given before the 1981 elections, nothing of great signifi-

cance was achieved during the ten years of 'Mitterrand's reign'.[75] Giving
the key position of Minister for the Interior to a hard-line Jacobin, Jean-
Pierre Chevènement,[76] was unanimously seen as a catastrophic move by
all commentators favourably inclined towards regionalism. In a speech
made in Perpignan on 23 August 1998, Chevènement, 'the most sinister
and repugnant politician in the whole of democratic Europe',[77] not only
said that there was no possibility of minority languages being recognised
in France, but also attacked the Spanish constitutional model and its
autonomous regions.

France is seeking to use legislation and administrative circulars to
build a linguistic Maginot line that will protect it from the changes
occurring in the rest of the world. Its political leaders refuse to acknowledge current political, historical, technological and economic realities.
In the future its linguistic policy is bound to antagonise the rest of Europe,
just as it has radicalised some members of its minorities.[78] This policy is
therefore bound to be counterproductive in the long term.

Paradoxically, the inevitable failure of the current policy might be
the only chance for the French language to survive. French culture and
the French language owe much of their vitality to the fact that they
originally emerged from a mosaic of languages and cultures. In the last
few decades French literature has been relatively undistinguished. This
lack of creativity has run closely in parallel with the decline of the
country's regional languages. A linguistic policy aiming to support real

75   Jeanjean, *De l'Utopie au Pragmatisme?* pp. 87–92.
76   As Minister for Education under Mitterrand, Chevènement presided over a reform
      of the school curriculum intended to reinforce the ideologies of the nation state
      and centralism. He strongly opposed any acceptance by the Government of the
      notion of the 'Corsican people', a step that would have broken the deadlock in the
      negotiations with the Corsican separatist movement.
77   '[E]l polític més sinistre i repugnant de tota l'Europa democràtica'. A. Quintà,
      'Chevènement i nosaltres', *Avui*, 17 October 1998.
78   Some regionalist radicals are starting to question the use of French. On an Occitan
      Internet group a message entitled 'Cal gardar lo francès?' ('Is it necessary to keep
      French?') argued that 'within a few years English will be compulsory for business
      while, on the other hand, we want to preserve our beloved Occitan. Is it therefore
      necessary to keep French? We have two languages. Is it necessary to teach French
      to our children? Wouldn't it be better to give them a bilingual education in English
      and Occitan?'

multilingualism within France may be the only way to give the French language the new dynamism it sorely needs if it is to maintain its place as a world language.

Richard Wakely

French in Belgium: Belgian French, French Belgium

There were early examples of French/*francien* being used in both the Walloon and Flemish areas of the territory that is now Belgium,[1] i.e. the linguistic boundary has never stopped the use of French from spreading north.[2] The oldest *charte* in French/*francien* was drawn up in Chièvres (Hainaut) in 1194.[3] As a written language and *langue de culture*, French was, of course, widely used early on in various parts of Europe. However, its use (for example by the Burgundian court) does not indicate that it was widely spoken in its *francien* form: indeed, until schooling spread, Belgian languages were largely dialectal. The situation in the south was diglossic French [H(igh)]/Wallon or Picard [L(ow)], the latter being 'parlers romans du nord',[4] while Flanders, having resisted an attempt by the Dutch King to make Dutch the official language in 1823, moved

---

1   I shall use the terms 'Wallonie/Walloon' and 'Flanders/Flemish' in their modern meanings, referring to the two main halves of Belgium and their inhabitants, but excluding Brussels and the small German-speaking areas in the east. 'Wallonie' is a relatively recent coinage; historically both expressions had more restricted application within present-day Belgium (and 'Flanders' still includes an area of northern France).

2   See Sera De Vriendt and Pete Van de Craen, *Bilingualism in Belgium: A History and an Appraisal*, CLCS Occasional Paper 23 (Dublin: Trinity College, 1990); and Maurice Piron, 'Le français en Belgique', in Gérald Antoine and Robert Martin (eds), *Histoire de la langue française 1880–1914* (Paris: CNRS Éditions, 1985), p. 369.

3   See Jean-Marie Klinkenberg, 'Le français en Belgique', in Antoine and Martin, p. 732; and Claude Thiry, 'L'émergence du français. Le Moyen Âge et le XVIe siècle', in Daniel Blampain, André Goosse, Jean-Marie Klinkenberg and Marc Wilmet (eds), *Le français en Belgique* (Louvain-la-Neuve: Duculot and Ministère de la Communauté française de Belgique [Service de la langue française], 1997), p. 105.

4   Jean Lechanteur, 'Les dialectes', in Blampain *et al.*, *Le français en Belgique*, p. 83.

from a diglossic situation French [H]/Flemish [L], through one of French AND Dutch [H]/Flemish [L] to one of Dutch [H]/Flemish [L].[5]

When Belgium was founded as a separate state in 1830, the provisional government made French the official language. The following year the constitution made the choice of language *facultatif*, but in practice French was for some time the sole official language, as it was the language of the educated and the – mainly urban – bourgeoisie, as well as the ruling classes. At the time many hoped that Flanders would eventually switch over to French by means of a process that has been labelled *colonialisme intérieur*, in which a population (whose language was in any case viewed by the dominant group as a 'dialect') would shift from being monolingual in one language to being monolingual in another via a period of bilingualism.[6] This did not happen, and the situation changed rapidly from 1840 onwards, with the spread of Dutch/Flemish literacy accompanied by a growing Flemish consciousness that, in some ways, has not reached its final 'extent' to this day. From the second half of the nineteenth century, i.e. from the beginnings of the *taalstrijd* (*lutte des langues*), language questions have figured regularly on the political agenda.

During roughly the same period, Brussels, though surrounded by the Flemish-speaking parts of Brabant, became a city with a French-speaking majority (bad French, according to Baudelaire, who noted that Flemish was used to swear at servants). In 1846 60% of the population had Flemish as first language, but by 1947 (the year of the last census to

---

5   See Maurice Piron, 'Le français en Belgique' in Albert Valdman (ed.), *Le français hors de France* (Paris: Champion, 1979), pp. 201–21; Marc Wilmet, 'Le français de Belgique: fiction ou réalité', in Emmanuelle Labeau (ed.), *France–Belgique: des frères ennemis de la langue de chez nous?* (Quebec: Université Laval, 2000), p. 8; Bruno Bernard, 'Le français dans la région bruxelloise', in Blampain *et al.*, *Le français en Belgique*, p. 249; and Béatrice Nieberding, 'L'enseignement du français à Anvers après 1850', in Richard Wakely, Gisèle Kahn and Nadia Minerva (eds), *Profils d'enseignants, d'étudiants et d'institutions d'enseignement des langues vivantes de 1850 à 1950* (Paris, SIHFLES, 1995), pp. 103–15.
6   Louis-Jean Calvet, *Linguistique et colonialisme: petit traité de glottophagie* (Paris: Payot, 1974), especially pp. 45ff, 60ff. For an account of developments in Flanders, see Dominique Willems, 'Le français en Flandre', in Blampain *et al.*, *Le français en Belgique*, p. 265.

pose questions on language,[7] since the Flemish parties preferred not to see any official statistics showing that Brussels was majority French-speaking) this had dropped to 24%.[8] In 1920 only six of the 19 communes of Brussels were majority French-speaking, whereas by 1947 all of them were.[9] Herremans, an *échevin* in one of the communes, said that, although he welcomed documents and letters in either language, he only actually received them in French.[10] The 19 communes and the two main (increasingly monolingual) regions were determined in 1932, and the current linguistic boundary fixed in 1962/63.[11]

Today, the official status of Brussels is bilingual. Opinions vary as to what the current French-speaking population is, with some putting it as high as 90%, but it is also a cosmopolitan, multilingual city. Firstly, since it is surrounded by Flemish Brabant, 'Bruxelles est plus flamande à midi qu'à minuit,' given the number of commuters. Secondly, the presence of European institutions (there are as many as 10,000 'Eurocrats') and international businesses gives English a role, one that is exploited by some Belgians who use English as a neutral language when they are unsure which national language to use.[12] Thirdly, Brussels is the centre

7   See Hugo Baetens Beardsmore, 'Le contact des langues à Bruxelles', in Valdman, *Le français hors de France*, pp. 223–47; and Ronald Wardhaugh, *Languages in Competition* (Oxford: Blackwell, 1987), p. 206.

8   Figures quoted in Maurice-Pierre Herremans, 'Besoins et exigences en français à Bruxelles, dans le domaine socio-politique', in Eddy Rosseel (ed.), *La langue française dans le pays du Bénélux: besoins et exigences* (Brussels: AIMAV, 1982), p. 31.

9   Bernard, 'Le français dans la région bruxelloise', p. 248.

10 Herremans, 'Besoins et exigences en français à Bruxelles, dans le domaine socio-politique', pp. 32–3.

11 Bernard, 'Le français dans la région bruxelloise', pp. 249–50. For further discussion, and also for the text of the 1963 law (in English), see Elizabeth Sherman Swing, *Bilingualism and Linguistic Segregation in the Schools of Brussels* (Quebec: CIRB/IRCB, 1980).

12 For the ambivalent attitudes to English, see Jean Dierickx, 'Le français et l'anglais', in Blampain *et al.*, *Le français en Belgique*, pp. 312–5; Hendrickx, 'Le français dans les secteurs financier et industriel en Flandre', in Rosseel, *La langue française dans le pays du Bénélux: besoins et exigences*, pp. 72–4; and Michel Francard, 'Le français en Wallonie', in Blampain *et al.*, *Le français en Belgique*, p. 233, who speaks of 'courtoisie linguistique' leading to the use of English as a neutral language.

for immigrant communities in Belgium,[13] though these groups tend to prefer French to Dutch, especially where they have a Latin (Italian, Spanish, Portuguese) or North African (mainly Moroccan) background. Nonetheless, from the hardline Flemish point of view, Brussels is within Flanders, and people there who choose to speak French or other languages are a minority, whose language rights should be limited to those guaranteed by declarations of human rights and similar documents.[14] Many French-speakers make use of the *principe de personnalité*, which has precedence in Brussels over the *principe de territorialité*, which prevails elsewhere, and send their children to Dutch-speaking schools to ensure they are fluent in the 'other' language. Leman found that

> in recent years the proportion of new enrolments in Dutch-language kindergartens in Brussels were divided as follows: about 35% of new enrolments came from homogeneous Dutch-language families, about 30% from mixed-language families [i.e. only one Dutch-speaking parent, the family environment being French], about 20% from homogeneous French-language families, and about 15% from foreign families.[15]

These statistics show how the decision that Brussels should become officially bilingual has had some unexpected results, with only just over one-third of the school population in Dutch-medium schools using Dutch as their home language! All children are exposed to French outside class as the 'language of the street', and the results at the end of six years show that non-Belgian children are as good at Dutch as Belgian children brought up with other languages.

In addition to the above arrangements, there are the so-called *communes à facilités* around Brussels, where schooling and other facilities can be provided in French, provided there is sufficient demand.[16] Similar

13   Figures quoted in Joseph Pollain, 'Les migrants et le français', in Rosseel, *La langue française dans le pays du Bénélux: besoins et exigences*, p. 104.
14   Claude Javeau, 'Le français dans la région bruxelloise', in Blampain *et al.*, *Le français en Belgique*, pp. 251–3.
15   Johan Leman, 'The Bicultural Programmes in the Dutch-Language School System in Brussels', in Hugo Baetens Beardsmore (ed.), *European Models of Bilingual Education* (Clevedon: Multilingual Matters, 1993), pp. 86–100.
16   See Xavier Mabille, 'La question linguistique dans l'histoire politique de la Belgique', and especially the map provided, in Blampain *et al.*, *Le français en Belgique*, p. 444.

rules apply in *communes* along the linguistic boundary fixed in 1963, where the 'other' language should in all cases be the second one to be taught.

At the unitary state level, French-speakers are less numerous than Dutch/Flemish speakers and therefore, in any situation of conflict, the final decision, unless the Belgian government has devolved power to the regions, will always inevitably go in favour of the Flemish community. Since the latter, despite gains in power over the last decades, still feel resentful of the situation in the past when the language was recognised only with difficulty and there was a widespread attitude that French was linguistically and culturally superior to Dutch/Flemish, demands for complete autonomy persist. We can see those attitudes in, for example, some of Jacques Brel's songs,[17] and in various literary and other works.[18] In the early 1960s Flemish movements organised a *Mars op Brussel* ('March on Brussels'). The demonstrators were greeted by hostile placards bearing slogans like *KEER NAAR UW DORP!* ('go back to your village', i.e. 'you Flemish peasant'). This anti-Flemish feeling was partly fuelled by encouragement given (for their own reasons) by the Germans to Flemish movements during both World Wars.[19]

Despite the official monolingualism of the two main regions of present-day federal Belgium, we should not forget that French is also a (minority) language in Flanders. On account of its use by the bourgeoisie it was seen, especially in the nineteenth century, as the language of social progress and was adopted by numerous families. Many Francophone writers, such as Maeterlinck and Verhaeren, had their roots in Flanders. Internal migration contributed to the building up of a Francophone pop-

---

17 Especially in 'Les F...', in which the *Flamingants* are accused of being 'Nazis durant les guerres et catholiques entre elles'. In 'Les Flamandes' Brel is less virulent, but still treats his targets as dull and priest-ridden. See Jacques Brel, *Oeuvre intégrale* (Paris: Laffont, 1982, 1986), pp. 173, 342.

18 As with the mob that simply had to eat *brioche*, the solution to the problems of the Flemish is for them to learn French! See Barbara Van der Eecken, 'Jean Muno, *L'Histoire exécrable d'un héros brabançon* et les rapports transfrontaliers', in Labeau, *France–Belgique: des frères ennemis de la langue de chez nous?* pp. 120–1.

19 See Xavier Mabille, 'La question linguistique dans l'histoire politique de la Belgique', p. 438.

ulation still in existence: there are estimates of 40,000 Francophones in
Antwerp to this day (most of them bilingual).[20] It is therefore still possible, in spite of a certain amount of disapproval, to be both Flemish and
French-speaking. Alongside this situation, the majority of the Flemish
are said to have greater *maturité bilingue* than the Walloons. They are
now happy in *Algemeen beschaafd Nederlands* (general, *cultivé* Dutch)
and are equally happy to speak French, along with English, German and
other 'foreign' languages, all of which are useful for their jobs.[21] Their
confidence is even greater in that, except in Brussels, few Walloons are
fluent in Dutch and those that attempt to speak it often sound ridiculous.
Despite some gains by English, French continues to be the first 'foreign'
language chosen in Flanders schools, even if nowadays few teachers are
native speakers of the language they teach, so that the general impression
is that the levels of competence are dropping.[22]

   Of course, all this follows a history of conflict, which is by no means
over.[23] Apart from the key dates leading from the recognition of Dutch as
an official language (1898), via increasing regionalisation (1921, 1932)
and federalisation (the country's current political structure dates from
1993), landmarks in this history include the painful events that led to the
University of Ghent moving to Dutch-only instruction (1930) and the
division of the University of Louvain into two institutions based in Leu-
ven and Louvain-la-Neuve in 1968 following a campaign under the
slogan *Walen buiten!* ('Walloons out!'). This was accompanied by a
parallel division of the Free University of Brussels into the Université

20   Jean-Marc Trouille, 'Néerlandais et français: le bras de fer linguistique', in Labeau,
      France–Belgique: des frères ennemis de la langue de chez nous? p. 54.
21   See Jean-Marc Dewaele, 'Néerlandophones–Francophones en Belgique: liberté,
      égalité, fraternité', in Labeau, *France–Belgique: des frères ennemis de la langue
      de chez nous?* pp. 39–44. He speaks from personal experience and takes the term
      maturité bilingue from Hugo Baetens Beardsmore. See also Willems, 'Le français
      en Flandre', pp. 268–72; and Herremans, 'Besoins et exigences en français à
      Bruxelles, dans le domaine socio-politique', p. 35.
22   Eddy Rosseel, 'Le français en Flandre: situations et besoins dans le monde de
      l'éducation', in Rosseel, *La langue française dans le pays du Bénélux: besoins et
      exigences*, pp. 78–9; and Dewaele, 'Néerlandophones–Francophones en Belgique:
      liberté, égalité, fraternité', pp. 45–6.
23   Useful dates in Willems, 'Le français en Flandre', pp. 262ff; and Mabille, 'La
      question linguistique dans l'histoire politique de la Belgique', pp. 434–46.

Libre de Bruxelles and the Vrije Universiteit Brussel.[24] The area known
as les Fourons is probably better known among the wider public. This
area was attached to the (Flemish) province of Limburg when the linguistic boundary was fixed in 1962, but it regularly votes for a Francophone mayor and council, and for the 'Retour à Liège'. It appears that
until boundaries were fixed the area was happily multilingual (French/
Walloon; Dutch/Flemish; German). However, the combination of the
fixing of the boundary and the area's (re-)integration into Limburg polarised opinion in the area, forcing families and individuals to decide where
their loyalties lay, leading to greater monolingualism in each of the two
groups.[25]

Belgian French

Despite the fact that French was the only language widely written in
1830, literacy in the population of Wallonie was no more widespread
than in the Flemish area. Consequently, dialects persisted there,[26] and
although they are now sometimes stated to be moribund (associated as
elsewhere with the aged and people in rural areas or socially 'low' occupations), their existence is still attested and, increasingly, defended.[27]
We need to stress that the dialects are plural: a common view is that the
local variety of French is *wallon*. In fact, there are different types of
wallon, and it should be noted that both *picard* and *wallon* are spoken on
both sides of the state border, as maps show,[28] so they are dialects of both
Belgium and France.

24   See Wardhaugh, *Languages in Competition*, pp. 206–7; Hendrickx, 'Le français
     dans les secteurs financier et industriel en Flandre', p. 71; and Francine Debreucq,
     'La tradition pédagogique', in Blampain *et al.*, *Le français en Belgique*, p. 376.
25   See Jean-Marie Klinkenberg, 'Le cas de Fouron', in Blampain *et al.*, *Le français
     en Belgique*, pp. 273–4; and Mabille, 'La question linguistique dans l'histoire
     politique de la Belgique', pp. 442–3.
26   See Francard, 'Le français en Wallonie', p. 231.
27   See the web pages of Jean-Claude (Djan-Clôde) Somja at: http://www.walon.open.
     net.ma/somja.home.
28   See Blampain *et al.*, *Le français en Belgique*, pp. 85, 87, 89, 95.

There are similar standardising tendencies on the other side of the Belgian linguistic border. The politically correct term for the language of Flanders is *Nederlands* (Dutch) rather than *Vlaams* (Flemish). This leads to problems similar to those found in Switzerland (see Charnley in this volume): a student of mine, British but brought up and schooled in French in Brussels, reported to me how delighted she had been, as a young girl, to learn that she was also going to be taught Dutch at school. After a few lessons, she tried her Dutch out on the children of a Flemish family down the street, only to find that her Dutch did not fit with their language use. Only *beschaafd Nederlands* (*'cultivé* Dutch') may be taught, despite the consequences. This reinforces the idea (see elsewhere in this chapter) that each of the national languages is increasingly treated as 'foreign' in the 'other' region.

Divergence, dialectal or otherwise, from the norm and, above all, consciousness of that divergence lead to lack of confidence. The lack of confidence in their French has led Belgians to seek correctness. This search goes back a long way: as early as 1806 Poyart published a volume listing *Flandricismes, wallonismes et expressions impropres*[29] (and one notes that both halves of the country are deemed responsible for the improprieties). Other works appeared in the course of the nineteenth century and well into the twentieth. Amongst many titles, the one I like best is *Les 600 expressions vicieuses belges*.[30] Theoretical linguistic thought tended to be absent from such works but, from around 1900 on there is evidence of greater academic reflectiveness, and by 1905 Cohen was noting that a local Belgian standard was appearing, independent of the dialects. The existence of a local standard is confirmed by recent work.[31]

---

29   See for example Piron, 'Le français en Belgique', p. 371.
30   By Victor Galand, published in 1891. See Piron, 'Le français en Belgique', p. 372, which also includes a useful list of works. Other lists can be found in Emmanuelle Labeau, 'N'est-il bon bec que de Paris?', in Labeau, *France-Belgique: des frères ennemis de la langue de chez nous?* p. 92; and Michel Trousson and Michel Berré, 'La tradition des grammairiens belges', in Blampain *et al.*, *Le français en Belgique*, pp. 352–8.
31   See Marie-Louise Moreau, 'Le bon français de Belgique', in Blampain *et al.*, *Le français en Belgique*, pp. 395, 399.

In the twentieth century Belgian linguistic *mauvaise conscience*[32] produced Grevisse,[33] Hanse and Doppagne, to name but a few. For a long time, the general attitude was that the items listed were, if not condemned, then at least to be avoided in careful usage. This was the era not only of *Bon Usage* but also of *Chasse aux Belgicismes* (see below). However, despite a continued interest in correctness, there has been a growth in confidence in both local and general Belgian usage. And some of the old guard have openly acknowledged that times have changed. Hanse, author of *Dictionnaire des difficultés grammaticales et lexicologiques*, spoke in 1988 of *une plus saine conception* of the variety of usage, across registers and styles, and, especially, across different areas of the French-speaking world. He praised the fact that studies had been carried out '*sans* [...] *aucun critère normatif*', and he is glad to put an end to *guerre* and *chasse*, while warning school pupils that regional words are not necessarily exportable.[34] More recently, Doppagne[35] has traced the evolution of attitudes to correctness. He refers to the *Quinzaine du bon langage*, held annually from 1962 on, during which a *faute* was denounced every day of the fortnight. He mentions his collaboration with Hanse and Bourgeois-Gielen on *La Chasse aux Belgicismes* (which appeared in 1971) and was followed by other similar volumes. He had acquired the title 'Monsieur Bon Langage' and realised that attitudes to correctness had changed when he attended (incognito) an event at which he saw himself burnt in effigy! His later work has been more of the *constater sans conseiller* type and he has found himself being invited to contribute Belgian terms to general dictionaries of French. He remarks:

32   See Wilmet, 'Le français de Belgique: fiction ou réalité', pp. 20–1.
33   Grevisse's work was originally aimed at a school audience, but has been used by linguists and the public at large. See Trousson and Berré, 'La tradition des grammairiens belges', pp. 358ff.
34   Joseph Hanse, 'Le français dit universel et les belgicismes', in Jacques Lemaire (ed.), *Le français et les Belges* (Brussels: Éditions de l'Université de Bruxelles, 1989), pp. 79–85.
35   Albert Doppagne, 'Notes (personnelles) sur le français en Belgique romane de 1954 à nos jours', unpublished paper presented at the conference *Les Belges: enregistreurs de tous les usages*, University of Edinburgh, Centre de recherches francophones belges, April 2000.

Il n'est plus question de diriger la langue: les mots sont épinglés avec le sens qu'on leur donne en Belgique. La notion de collecte a eu raison de celles de chasse ou d'interdiction.

This is all linked to the question of *insécurité linguistique*. Pierre Swiggers says:

L'insécurité linguistique peut être définie comme un sentiment socialisé d'aliénation: d'une part, par rapport à un modèle qu'on ne maîtrise pas/plus, et d'autre part, par rapport à sa propre production, qu'on veut refouler ou forclore.[36]

In everyday terms, 'La Faute [...] de français guette le Belge francophone à chaque mot écrit, à chaque parole prononcée. Le péché a beau être véniel, il s'obstine à le voir mortel.'[37] In Belgium, these feelings are linked to the common factors of social status and education, and relate (of course) to the Parisian model. This in turn affects the status of Brussels. The city's position as national capital does not make it a 'linguistic capital', the 'true' one being a short ride away on the Thalys international express service. Part of the insecurity comes from the idea that the French, even if referred to pejoratively as *fransquillons*, will find Belgian French comic. They enjoy finding it comic, which is one important factor which explains the success of *Le Mariage de Mlle Beulemans* on the Paris stage, as well as that of Pagnol's *Provençaux*.[38] This insecurity leads, or has historically led, both to exaggerated over-use of language, the so-called *sur-écriture* of which (Flemish Francophone) writers like Verhaeren and de Ghelderode have sometimes been accused,[39] and also to silence, according to the principle that 'qui a perdu sa langue ne trouve plus ses mots.'[40] Insecurity is probably lower among the young and, even though recent studies still show large numbers of people wanting to be better at French, there is no desire to sound like a Parisian. Once again, we see the usual effects of diglossia (after-effects, since the differences

36   Quoted in Labeau, 'N'est-il bon bec que de Paris?' p. 88. Everyone is insecure: the Wallons with regard to French, the Flemish with regard to Dutch and the Cantons de l'est with regard to German. See Debreucq, 'La tradition pédagogique', p. 377.
37   Trousson and Berré, 'La tradition des grammairiens belges', p. 362.
38   See Labeau, 'N'est-il bon bec que de Paris?', p. 94.
39   See Piron, 'Le français en Belgique', p. 379.
40   Francard, 'Le français en Wallonie', p. 237.

between varieties are somewhat residual and there is a High Belgian variety): the High (Parisian) version is more official, and is felt to be cold and distant, whereas the Low version is warm and friendly.[41] This is exploited by a weekly electronic information site called *Radio Belche*,[42] thus assuming a phonological identity long thought to be one imposed by snobbish Frenchmen.

The preceding remark about pronunciation points to the fact that accents persist, though Brel once sang 'J'ai perdu l'accent bruxellois/ D'ailleurs plus personne n'a cet accent-là/sauf Brel à la télévision.'[43] This is of course common, as accents are often kept after dialects have disappeared. In any case, the features of *wallon* speech are also found in northern French accents, such as the use of [w] and the absence of the standard French semi-vowel in *huit* (pronounced as if spelt *ouit*). Wilmet says that Belgians sound Parisian when they are in the South of France, as if they come from Lille when they are in Paris, and as if they come from Mons when they are in Lille, i.e. they are always from somewhere to the north.[44]

As far as vocabulary is concerned, there are of course differences due to the existence of two separate states, France and Belgium. Among such *statalismes* are items that either do not exist in France or that existed historically, often with a different meaning, such as *échevin*, *athénée* and *kot*. There are also internal differences, with the Montois using a different word form of referent from the Liégeois, but, in general, Wilmet[45] reckons that few items are known to ALL Belgians and NOT known at all in France. Piron[46] says that the distinctive vocabulary of French-speaking Belgium is less than 300 items. Such items, given the usual effects of diglossia, tend to be used in Low varieties.[47] However, as discussed above, the *chasse aux belgicismes* has died down, partly because of greater

41   Dominique Lafontaine, 'Les attitudes et représentations linguistiques', in Blampain *et al.*, *Le français en Belgique*, pp. 384–9.
42   More details can be found at http://www.radiobelche.cediti.be.
43   Jacques Brel, 'Les Bonbons 67', in Brel, *Oeuvre intégrale*, p. 311.
44   Wilmet, 'Le français de Belgique: fiction ou réalité', p. 15.
45   Wilmet, 'Le français de Belgique: fiction ou réalité', pp. 15–16.
46   Piron, 'Le français en Belgique', p. 376.
47   Piron, 'Le français en Belgique', p. 378; and Wilmet, 'Le français de Belgique: fiction ou réalité', p. 10.

confidence within Belgium, but partly because of changes within *la francophonie*, where current tendencies are more centrifugal than centripetal.[48] In this context, where defence of French as an international language does not preclude the defence of local particularities,[49] greater acceptance of one or more local varieties has had two principal results. Firstly, although books like *Le Bon Usage* continue to appear, their tone is now rather less general and more linguistic (compare Grevisse with Grevisse as revised by André Goosse, the *norme* is *évoluant, réactualisée*).[50] Secondly, Belgians no longer wish to suppress their linguistic heritage, but are happy to see strip cartoons and advertisements for McDonald's restaurants appear in (a version of) dialect. (McDonald's is of course exploiting the fact that Low varieties are associated with the warmth and intimacy felt within a particular social group when they put up signs saying *Rin qu'po lès Lîdjwès!* ('Rien que pour les Liégeois!').[51]

The French of Brussels is somewhat separate, given the bilingual nature of the city and, even more importantly, its relatively recent move from majority Flemish-speaking to majority French-speaking (see above). Maybe because of its mixed history, Pohl says that the French of Brussels is some of the best and some of the worst.[52]

Among the positive moves to study, adapt and propagate Belgian French, we may list VALIBEL (Variétés linguistiques du français en Belgique), BELTEX (a corpus based on Francophone Belgian publications since 1830) and the Centre de recherche TERMISTI (which does terminological work). A long chapter by Garsou[53] gives an account of the move from purely defensive actions (against *fautes*, against English

48   Wilmet, 'Le français de Belgique: fiction ou réalité', p. 14; and Jean-Marie Klinkenberg, 'Les arts de la langue', in Blampain *et al.*, *Le français en Belgique*, pp. 403–4.

49   Jacques Pohl, 'Le français à Bruxelles: besoins et exigences', in Rosseel, *La langue française dans le pays du Bénélux: besoins et exigences*, pp. 39–40.

50   Terms used in Dan Van Raemdonck, 'J'enregistre, tu corsètes, il façonne', unpublished paper presented at the conference *Les Belges: enregistreurs de tous les usages*, University of Edinburgh, Centre de recherches francophones belges, April 2000.

51   Reproduced in Blampain *et al.*, *Le français en Belgique*, p. 93.

52   Pohl, 'Le français à Bruxelles: besoins et exigences', p. 39.

53   Martine Garsou, 'La promotion du français en Communauté française de Belgique', in Blampain *et al.*, *Le français en Belgique*, pp. 459–81.

and reacting to Flemish moves) to the more active and pro-active scene that we see today. Although the current federal structure only dates back to 1993, there has been a Communauté française for some 30 years now, its web pages[54] advertising events like *La langue française en fête*. Garsou lists a significant number of organisations, some more public than others, such as la Maison de la Francité, la Fondation Charles Plisnier and l'Office du bon langage. While it is true that some of these bodies were originally involved in the *chasse aux fautes*, with regular publications listing incorrect forms, times have changed (though the *championnats d'orthographe* founded in 1972 by Doppagne and Hanse are still popular). Since 1989 there has been a *Charte de la langue française*, le Conseil de la langue française, founded in 1985, has tried to take *actions concrètes* rather than defensive ones, there is a Service de la langue française (part of the Ministère de la Culture et des Affaires Sociales) that publishes the excellent series *Français & Société*, and we must not forget the Académie royale de langue et de littérature françaises.

Furthermore, Belgium has participated in the greater opening-up of *la francophonie*, and has collaborated with others in projects such as *la réforme de l'orthographe, la féminisation des noms de métiers* and the development of terminology in areas particularly threatened by English hegemony, such as economics and science.

French Belgium

Belgium's current federal structure (1993) is complex: there are three 'communities' (Flemish, Walloon and German) and three main 'regions' (Flanders, Wallonie and Bruxelles-Capitale). This system was of course put in place by the central government, which set up the current structure and defined the rights of each region, though Flanders almost immediately merged its community and its region, something viewed as a sensible move by many Walloons, who see their own community as weak. There are also various commissions and courts at central level that rule on

54   http://www.cfwb.be.

regional questions, including language problems, that require central supervision. Maybe none of this would have been needed if the Francophones had realised, say in 1932, that the Flemish could always impose their will, given their numerical dominance, and had accepted state bilingualism at an earlier stage.[55]

The question of identity is posed by the fact that one of the main *instances* of the French-speaking part of Belgium does not call itself the *Communauté francophone de Wallonie-Bruxelles* but rather the *Communauté française de Wallonie-Bruxelles*. Given the importance of language in the debate on the structure of Belgium, the difference is certainly not just a matter of semantics (in so far as any such distinction can ever be purely semantic).

So, will there always be a Belgium? The British are sometimes accused by the French of having invented the country, presumably because a fairer outcome of the Napoleonic wars would have been a (Francophone?) Belgium remaining part of France, especially as Willem I's reign (union with The Netherlands, 1815–30) was unpopular even in Flanders. To come to the present, I heard an elderly Belgian tourist speaking to some of his countrymen in a holiday resort in Spain. After talking about the Second World War and common experiences of hardship, he finished by saying: 'Mais pour la jeune génération, la Belgique, qu'est-ce que c'est?' The implication of his words and tone was that Belgium did not represent very much for young people. Flemish pressure for ever greater autonomy (currently for the devolution of control over social security) has led the Walloons to reflect on their future. And books, articles and web pages with titles like 'Divorce à la Belge', 'La Belgique va-t-elle mourir?' can easily be found.[56] This reflects a common perception that there has been a failure to make this *état sans nation*[57] into such a nation. The *jacobin* French tendency has been to say 'we are a nation so all citizens must master the national language', whereas the main

---

55   See François Tulkens, 'La législation linguistique', in Blampain *et al.*, *Le français en Belgique*, pp. 451ff.
56   See for example http://www.lire.fr for a review by G. Rolin of a book by D. Pavy; or Bernard Remiche, 'L'État fédéral en péril: Divorce à la belge', *Le Monde Diplomatique*, February 1997, p. 11.
57   See Trousson and Berré, 'La tradition des grammairiens belges', p. 337.

(Flemish) Belgian movement has said 'our language reflects our culture and our community must in turn be recognised through autonomy if not independence'. This polarisation has led (though not only for such political reasons) to identity being increasingly associated with the standard version of both languages.

So what should Wallonie do? There are organisations such as the *Mouvement wallon pour le Retour à la France*, based in Liège, whose adherents are commonly known as *rattachistes* (or sometimes *réunionnistes*). These groups organise a yearly celebration of *le quatorze juillet*, including tricolore sashes.[58] It is not exactly by chance that their headquarters is in Liège: the city was the seat of a Prince-Bishop who, with his double function, represented the *ancien régime* so completely that, when the Revolution broke out in France, its ideas rapidly reached Liège, where a mini-revolution took place on 18 August 1789. A few years later, 'à Liège, le peintre Defrance dirigea la destruction méthodique de la cathédrale Saint-Lambert, l'une des plus prestigieuses du pays.'[59] Imagine that Notre-Dame or Reims cathedral had been destroyed and never rebuilt. Despite these revolutionary ideas and the presence of standard French as a *langue de référence*, there is some doubt as to whether incorporation into France was actually welcome.[60] More recently, a separatist political party, the *Rassemblement Wallonie-France* has been founded and has had some electoral success.

Thus, the question is being posed, and not necessarily by extremists (or in a desperate way): will Francophone Belgium one day look for a home within the Republic *une et indivisible*? If the separationists have their way, the Flanders region of Belgium will one day declare independence (despite the appeals of King Albert II, whose throne would obviously be threatened by a split in the kingdom), and then what will Wallonie do? This problem, with its possible answer ('join France'), is clearly presented by a leaflet printed in 1994 that reads, '*La Flandre prépare*

58 A fact noted in the French press, for example: 'A Liège, le 14 juillet de la "Wallonie française". Marianne et Napoléon à l'honneur chez les partisans du rattachement', *Libération*, 16 July 1997, p. 6.
59 Georges-Henri Dumont, *Histoire de la Belgique* (Brussels, Le Cri, 1997), p. 390.
60 See Dumont, *Histoire de la Belgique*, pp. 385–400; and Daniel Droixhe, 'Le français au XVIIe et XVIIIe siècles', in Blampain *et al.*, *Le français en Belgique*, pp. 148ff.

son avenir. Et vous?' A sticker distributed at the same time shows Belgium split into two, with the two halves drifting apart and with the red, white and blue of the *tricolore* extending to cover Wallonie. Some commentators, including linguists, and not just *rattachistes*, are beginning to see the likelihood of a future split as a chance to form some kind of alliance with France, which might lead to incorporation. This is largely based on feelings of *appartenance*, i.e. on the notion that 'ceux qui gomment les différences entre le français de France et celui de Belgique se sentent ou se veulent proches de la France,' whereas 'les chantres de la belgitude ou de l'âme wallonne, occupés à dresser pierre à pierre les remparts de leur petit bastion'[61] are in a parallel situation to the Flemish who seek independence but not union with The Netherlands (while some Flemish politicians encourage an historical view which says 'there has always been a Flanders', i.e. a distinct entity with an independent cultural heritage).[62] Belgium seems to be following what Grillo sees as the normal direction of modern nationalism, namely refusing *Gesellschaft* ('society') and preferring, or returning to, *Gemeinschaft* (small united community). This is linked to divergent (centrifugal) rather than convergent (centripetal) tendencies.[63] These tendencies are not dampened by the fact that the two Belgian groups meet along an extensive border and mingle in a major city, where the threat (if there is one) could be seen as coming from English and globalisation rather than from the 'other' Belgian language and community. The *rattachistes* (*Rassemblement Wallonie-France, Liste FRANCE*, etc.) may be seen as trying to (re-)constitute a *Gesellschaft* by wishing to join France.

From the French viewpoint, one can imagine the horror of some republicans at the idea that France might receive some four million citizens who are used to having a king and for whom the separation of Church and State was only briefly (for about four years from 1879) a remote possibility (though Wallonie has tended to be more *anticléricale*

61   Wilmet, 'Le français de Belgique: fiction ou réalité', pp. 7–8.
62   For a somewhat hostile view of these ideas, see Stef Slembrouck and Jan Blommaert, 'La construction politico-rhétorique d'une nation flamande', in Anne Morelli (ed.), *Les grands mythes de l'histoire de Belgique, de Flandre et de Wallonie* (Brussels: Éditions Vie Ouvrière, 1995), pp. 263–80.
63   R. D. Grillo, *Dominant Languages: Language and Hierarchy in Britain and France* (Cambridge: Cambridge University Press, 1989), pp. 22–3, 63ff.

than Flanders). Could the whole of Francophone Belgium be added to the three departments (Bas-Rhin, Haut-Rhin and Moselle) where the Concordat is still in force and religious education is obligatory? Certainly, there are historical as well as recent indications that some French politicians at least might view an application to join France favourably. De Gaulle, in a letter written to the *recteur* of the Université de Louvain in 1968 (i.e. at the moment when the University was about to divide, see above), wrote:

> Si un jour, une autorité représentative de la Wallonie s'adressait officiellement à la France, ce jour-là de grand coeur, nous répondrions favorablement à une demande qui aurait toutes les apparences de la légitimité.[64]

Such a welcome will presumably become easier as France devolves more powers to its regions.

Maybe this will never happen, and the Flemish will come to think that they are better off as part of a larger unit that, in any case, they dominate numerically. Dewaele says,

> Il me semble que les politiciens flamands, à force de lutter pour l'égalité de leur langue avec le français, à force de se battre contre les classes dominantes francophones pour obtenir une liberté culturelle et politique, risquent d'avoir perdu de vue le principe de fraternité avec la communauté francophone en Belgique. L'ensemble de la population flamande n'est probablement pas aussi radicale que ses politiciens.[65]

This is the heart of the issue. Is Dumont right when he says that, whoever controlled the country (the Spanish, Austrians, French or Dutch), the Belgians 'sont restés eux-mêmes'?[66] Feelings of detestation are clearly still strong amongst many Flemish. On the western outskirts of Brussels, in one of the *communes à facilités*, one can (or could) read a slogan posted in large letters at the top of a large building: *Dilbeek, waar Vlamingen THUIS zijn...* ('Dilbeek, where Flemings are at home/*chez eux*'),[67]

64   Quoted in Labeau, *France–Belgique: des frères ennemis de la langue de chez nous?* introduction.
65   Dewaele, 'Néerlandophones – Francophones en Belgique: liberté, égalité, fraternité', p. 46.
66   Dumont, *Histoire de la Belgique*, p. 6.
67   See photo in Blampain *et al.*, *Le français en Belgique*, p. 451.

i.e. 'you've arrived back on home soil after leaving horrible, French-
(and English-) dominated Brussels'.

Brussels is a problem, as already stated. Some of the web pages I
have consulted on Wallonie quite explicitly accept that Brussels, despite
its largely French-speaking population, may not join with Wallonie if
the region is integrated into France. As the *compte rendu* of a conference
on *La Wallonie au futur* held in Mons in 1998 puts it, 'Une question reste
controversée: *la relation à Bruxelles*. L'alliance (sous diverses formes)
est incontournable pour certains, problématique pour d'autres.'[68] Though
I have never lived in Belgium, I cannot see that the Flemish would agree
to one of the suggestions I have seen on the *Parti FRANCE* or *Liste
FRANCE* web pages,[69] namely that the Brussels area should first define
itself (presumably the surrounding communes would have to opt in or
out of a 'greater Brussels'), and then choose from three options: to be
part of Flanders, to be part of Wallonie or to become a 'free' European
City with EU guarantees. Or is a pact possible, with Wallonie agreeing
that Brussels is part of Flanders while the Flemish agree that French is
its main language – and would the people of Brussels be happy with that
solution? I doubt it. In general, one has the feeling that there are plenty
of people trying to find a way forward that is based on some agreed
commonality of feeling, while trying to avoid purely negative reactions
to community strife. If plays can have characters in search of an author,
Belgium has (would-be) authors in search of one or more characters.
These see three ways forward: in one, the *status quo* is kept, perhaps
with further devolution of powers; in the second, Flanders and Wallonie
separate (with Brussels doing what?) and the resulting small *Gemein
schaft*-type units are seen as viable within a Europe of the regions; in the
third, whatever Flanders and Brussels do, Wallonie seeks its fortune in
association with, and maybe through incorporation into, France.

---

68   http://www.wallonie-en-ligne.net/Wallonie-Futur-4.
69   http://www.ksurf.net/%7Eopcommunication1/rattachistes.homepage.htm.

Conclusion

Whatever the political uncertainties (and linguistic insecurity has dropped as political insecurity has grown), French in Belgium is in excellent
heart. Francard says,

> La position de force du français ne paraît aucunement menacée en Wallonie. Ni
> par les parlers régionaux, le plus souvent déliquescents; ni par le néerlandais, dont
> le poids objectif sur la scène internationale n'est en rien comparable; ni par l'alle-
> mand qui, pour la majorité des aînés, reste associé à des souvenirs douloureux.[70]

Things may be more varied in Brussels, and French is disappearing as a
first (or home) language in Flanders, but this does not seriously affect
the vibrancy of the French language as used in Belgium, and not only in
the French-speaking areas. So whatever happens with regard to the role
of English as a world language, and whatever passport the Belgian Francophones may one day carry, the northern marches of European Franco-
phonia are safe in their mouths.

70   Francard, 'Le français en Wallonie', p. 233.

Joy Charnley

Le point de vue suisse romand: The French Language in Switzerland

It is often said jokingly that 'les Suisses s'entendent parce qu'ils ne se comprennent pas', and it is indeed the case that communication between the country's various language groups is not as good as many outside Switzerland may believe. Thus, commentators have remarked gloomily that 'les communautés linguistiques n'ont guère vécu ensemble. Elles se sont développées parallèlement, mais sans entretenir beaucoup de contacts,'[1] and that the peace that reigns between Switzerland's linguistic groups is 'basée davantage sur l'indifférence que sur l'échange'.[2] One of the factors militating against better communication is quite simply that 'le pur bilinguisme ou le trilinguisme est beaucoup moins fréquent en Suisse que l'étranger n'est enclin à le supposer.'[3] This, combined with the historical tendency for French speakers to look towards Paris, while Italian speakers look to Milan and German speakers to their northern neighbour, has meant that on the whole these cultures do not face one another; rather they 'stand back to back looking towards the outside.'[4] Some have taken this lack of linguistic unity as an indication that it is impossible for Switzerland to ever constitute a country, a view controversially expressed by Charles-Ferdinand Ramuz in 1937 when he claimed that 'c'est une accablante entreprise que d'expliquer un peuple, surtout quand il n'existe pas. Mais comment voulez-vous qu'il existât puisque

---

1 René Knüsel, *Les minorités ethnolinguistiques autochtones à territoire: l'exemple du cas helvétique* (Lausanne: Payot, 1994), p. 247.
2 Didier Froidevaux, 'Helvétie multilingue ou Suisses monolingues?', *Europe*, May 1995, p. 162.
3 Manfred Gsteiger, *La nouvelle littérature romande* (Vevey: Galland, 1978), p. 177.
4 Rolf Kieser, 'Post Festum: The Four Literatures of Contemporary Switzerland', *The Literary Review*, Summer 1993, p. 439.

la Suisse parle trois langues.'[5] Although the advocates of the opposing view, those who agree with Denis de Rougemont that 'nous refusons d'admettre la théorie selon laquelle la race déterminerait l'État et les frontières de celui-ci,'[6] have continued to hold sway, tensions between the various language groups are evident and the feeling that Switzerland exists 'en dépit des divergences linguistiques' rather than because of them, is widely shared.[7]

Linguistic Diversity

The writer Maurice Chappaz wrote figuratively of a link between 'les trois Suisses' (the historic founders of Switzerland in 1291, and all of course German-speakers) and 'les trois langues' spoken in the country.[8] In the context of the 700-year-old Confederation, this multilingualism is, however, very recent, since it only began with the short-lived Napoleonic creation, the *République Helvétique* (1798–1803), was confirmed by the arrival of four French-speaking cantons in the early-nineteenth century (Vaud in 1803, Geneva, Neuchâtel and Valais in 1815), and written into the Constitution that formed the basis of the modern Swiss state in 1848.[9]

5   Quoted in Alfred Berchtold, 'Un débat des années trente. Ramuz et l'existence de la Suisse', *Alliance culturelle romande,* 23 November 1977. See also Jacques Mercanton's views on Switzerland and language in David Bevan, *Écrivains d'aujourd'hui. La littérature romande en vingt entretiens* (Lausanne: Éditions 24 Heures, 1986).
6   Berchtold, 'Un débat des années trente. Ramuz et l'existence de la Suisse'.
7   Pierre Knecht, 'La Suisse et la francophonie de demain', in Jean-Pierre Vouga and Max Ernst Hodel (eds), *La Suisse face à ses langues* (Aarau: Sauerländer, 1990), p. 135.
8   Quoted in Gsteiger, *La nouvelle littérature romande*, p. 199.
9   It should be noted that bilingual Fribourg (where French was spoken in the town and German in the countryside) had been a member of the Confederation since 1481. See the interesting consideration of Fribourg's efforts to prove its Germanic credentials by Walter Haas in Robert Schläpfer (ed.), *La Suisse aux quatre langues* (Carouge-Geneva: Zoé, 1985), pp. 60–2.

Today, of Switzerland's 26 cantons and half-cantons,[10] 17 are German-speaking, 4 Francophone, 1 Italian-speaking, 3 bilingual (French/German: Valais, Bern and Fribourg) and one trilingual (German/Italian/Romansch: Graubünden). Furthermore, the country is more or less evenly divided between Catholicism (43%) and Protestantism (47%).[11] French, German and Italian have the status of 'official' languages, that is to say that they are the languages used in official documents and citizens' dealings with the administration. The country's four 'national' languages are French, German, Italian and Romansch, which gained this symbolic status in 1938. Spoken only in the valleys of Graubünden in Eastern Switzerland, Romansch is very much a language under siege and in need of help. It was officially recognised as a means of communication between Romansch speakers and the state in 1996, and a constitutional amendment further reinforced support for both Romansch and Italian in 1999.[12]

In spite of this strong official support, as well as the efforts of the Lia rumantscha (formed in 1919) and the creation in the 1980s of a unified written form of the language known as rumantsch grischun (since there are five variants of the spoken form),[13] the percentage of the population speaking Romansch has tended to decline steadily, as indicated by the results of the 1990 census (Table 1).[14]

10   For historical reasons the cantons of Appenzell, Basle and Unterwalden are divided into two half-cantons.
11   For details see Philippe Rossillon (ed.), *Atlas de la langue française* (Paris: Bordas, 1995), pp. 60–3; Jonathan Steinberg, *Why Switzerland?* 2nd edn (Cambridge: Cambridge University Press: 1996), p. 206.
12   Didier Froidevaux, 'L'article 116 de la Constitution fédérale et la politique linguistique suisse', in *L'état des langues en Suisse* (Institut romand de recherches et de documentation pédagogique, 1996), p. 41.
13   Victor Ruffy and Frances Trezevant Honegger, 'La question des langues: le profil bas des partis', in Vouga and Hodel, *La Suisse face à ses langues*, p. 199.
14   Taken from Georges Lüdi *et al.*, *Le paysage linguistique de la Suisse* (Bern: Office fédéral de la statistique, 1997), p. 641. In connection with this, however, see Gabriel Mützenberg's positive comments on the current state of Romansch in 'Éloge du plurilinguisme', *Le Passe-muraille*, 19–20, July 1995.

Language	Total population (%)	Swiss population (%)
German	63.6	73.4
French	19.2	20.5
Italian	7.6	4.1
Romansch	0.6	0.7
Others	8.9	1.3

Table1:   Languages in Switzerland.

The languages most spoken by the 19.3% of the population who are not Swiss are currently Italian (23.7%), Serbo-Croat (13.8%) and Portuguese (9.8%).[15]

In spite of the movement of populations and the evident dominance of German, which is spoken by two-thirds of the population, 'les frontières linguistiques se sont à peine déplacées depuis plusieurs siècles,'[16] and this is largely due to the concept of 'la territorialité'. First alluded to in 1932, but not included in an article of the constitution,[17] territoriality gives each canton the right to determine which language or languages can officially be used on its territory and hence means that the *status quo* cannot be changed simply by an influx of speakers of another language. This is especially important in bilingual cantons, such as Valais and Fribourg, along the 'frontière des langues' where a resident Francophone population might feel threatened by the arrival of a large number of German-speakers. The obligation on incomers to speak the language of their adopted canton and educate their children in that language encourages assimilation and keeps the language frontiers stable, thus helping to reduce tensions.[18]

15   For a complete list, see the statistics published in *Le Temps*, 27 June 2000, p. 7.
16   Gsteiger, *La nouvelle littérature romande*, p. 179.
17   Knüsel, *Les minorités ethnolinguistiques autochtones à territoire: l'exemple du cas helvétique*, p. 243.
18   On this issue, see Iso Camartin, in Schläpfer, p. 263; Anne Schnetzer, 'Les petits Romands de Zurich sont condamnés à l'intégration', *Journal de Genève*, 21 July 1993; Uli Windisch, *Les relations quotidiennes entre Romands et Suisses allemands: les cantons bilingues de Fribourg et du Valais*, 2 vols (Lausanne: Payot, 1992).

French in Switzerland

French speakers in Switzerland find themselves in a sense 'doublement minoritaires', firstly with regard to the rest of Switzerland, where the majority speaks German, and secondly in their relations with France, where 'les petits Suisses' have traditionally been viewed with a certain amount of condescension. Earlier this century, for example, Ramuz's efforts to imitate the specific rhythm and intonation of *romand* speech in his novels were met with outcry in France. Supposedly written in a 'langage fort fatigant', his works were described as examples of 'le noir charabia' (Ernest Tisserand), displaying a 'mépris absolu de la syntaxe' (*La Revue Contemporaine*).[19] A natural consequence of such criticism is that *Suisses romands* often do not feel they 'own' their language, since they are aware of a certain pressure to adhere to the norms in order to avoid criticism from the French and the accusation that their language has been 'Germanised'. Indeed, in some quarters, much is made of the prevalence of (and need to combat) 'le français fédéral', the term used to describe official texts badly translated from the original German:

> les habitants de la Suisse romande n'ont qu'un droit de possession limité sur la langue française. [...] leur identité culturelle [...] ne se conçoit guère sans un profond attachement à la norme du français.[20]

Similarly, this fear can make them hesitant to be inventive with the language, as some have very strongly interiorised the idea that 'le bon usage' is dictated by Paris and that 'tout ce qui ne figure pas dans le dictionnaire n'est pas français.'[21] In addition, their minority status within

19   As a recent response to this, see Jacques Chessex's views on those who failed because they tried to write 'en gommant tous les provincialismes', unlike Ramuz, who 'est devenu quelqu'un parce qu'il n'était pas comme eux et parce que jusqu'au bout il a tenu le coup,' *Revue Neuchâteloise*, 54, Spring 1971, p. 28.

20   Pierre Knecht, in Schläpfer, p. 164.

21   Knecht, in Schläpfer, p. 166; and Knecht, 'Le français en Suisse romande: aspects linguistiques et sociolinguistiques', in Albert Valdman (ed.), *Le Français hors de France* (Paris: Champion, 1979), p. 251. See also Gsteiger, *La nouvelle littérature romande*, p. 179. It is also apposite to point out that German in Switzerland is of course in its turn influenced by French, as evidenced by expressions such as 'merci viel mal', which is used in place of the Standard German 'Danke schön'.

the country and the emphasis placed on 'la cohabitation' mean that in the past *Suisses romands* have been tentative about becoming too involved in enterprises that set them apart from other Swiss, as illustrated until recently by their hesitant relationship with *la Francophonie* and French culture in general:

> Tout militantisme linguistique lui [à la Suisse] fait peur, parce qu'il risque de conduire à des conflits qui pourraient mettre en danger la cohésion nationale.[22]

> Switzerland as a nation can proclaim its diversity, as long as its various components don't broadcast their identities, or simply their taste for the culture and the language to which they are attached [...] too loudly.[23]

However, this traditional inferiority complex, felt in literature as well as in the realm of language, is diminishing, and regional differences are being increasingly recognised and valorised.[24] This is well illustrated by the publication (and considerable success) of the *Dictionnaire suisse romand*, which catalogues words and expressions specific to *Suisse romande* and gives lively examples of their usage.[25] These 'helvétismes' include hangovers from dialectical use ('je n'ai personne vu', 'roiller' for 'pleuvoir', 's'encoubler' for 's'empêtrer', 'gouille' for 'flaque'); Germanisms ('poutser' meaning 'nettoyer', 'fatre' from 'Vater', 'yass', a card game, 'foehn' for 'sèche-cheveux'); terms denoting specifically *romand* institutions ('syndic/que' meaning 'maire', 'conseil fédéral' for 'gouvernement'); and throw-backs to old-French usage ('il faut lui aider', 'septante', or 'dîner' in the sense of 'déjeuner').[26] Naturally, differences also exist between 'French' and 'Swiss' pronunciation, and sounds that

22   Knecht, 'La Suisse et la francophonie de demain', p. 135.
23   Étienne Barilier, 'A Culture or a Nation?', *Literary Review*, Summer 1993, p. 510.
24   Gsteiger, *La nouvelle littérature romande*, p. 180.
25   André Thibault (ed.), *Dictionnaire suisse romand* (Carouge-Geneva: Zoé, 1997). An indication of the increasing value placed on local variants comes in the subtitle, 'une contribution au trésor des vocabulaires francophones'.
26   For more examples, see Knecht, in Schläpfer, pp. 161–3; and Henriette Walter, *Le Français d'ici, de là, de là-bas* (Paris: JC Lattès, 1998), pp. 160–2.

are tending to disappear in France (such as the distinction between 'pour-rai' and 'pourrais', 'ot' and 'aut' as in 'abricot' and 'artichaut') are still preserved in Switzerland.[27] It is, however, inaccurate to speak, as many French observers often do, of 'l'accent suisse', since no feature is found throughout the entire region, and each canton has its own particular accent. Some words and expressions are indeed canton-specific: for example, 'huitante' is used in Vaud, whereas other French-speaking cantons employ 'quatre-vingts' like the French, and depending on the canton the word used for 'mayor' may be 'syndic/que' (Vaud and Fribourg), 'maire' (Geneva and Jura) or 'président/e' (Neuchâtel and Valais). In addition, certain traits cannot technically be described as 'Swiss', since they are shared by French provinces close to Switzerland, such as Franche-Comté.[28]

Although Ramuz was criticised (inaccurately) for supposedly employing 'le patois', dialects have in fact been dying out in *Suisse romande* since the eighteenth century. They disappeared in Geneva around 1750, and in Lausanne and Neuchâtel around 1800. In 1987 it was estimated that only about 1–2 % of the population spoke dialect (essentially in the three Catholic cantons of Fribourg, Jura and Valais), a figure that was thought to have fallen below 1% seven years later.[29] Several arguments have been put forward to explain this decline: the impact of the Reformation, with its emphasis on reading the Bible and preaching in French, the influence and prestige of French, France's heavily centralising tendencies and the French Revolution's belief in the promotion of equality through the use of a common language.[30] What has been described by purists as a 'langage impropre et indigent'[31] has in recent years met with support

---

27   Knecht, in Schläpfer, p. 160.
28   Knecht, 'Le français en Suisse romande: aspects linguistiques et sociolinguistiques', p. 252.
29   Knecht, in Schläpfer, p. 143; Steinberg, *Why Switzerland?* pp. 151, 157; Michel Burger, 'La tradition linguistique vernaculaire en Suisse romande: les patois', in Valdman, p. 266.
30   Knüsel, *Les minorités ethnolinguistiques autochtones à territoire: l'exemple du cas helvétique*, pp. 176, 205.
31   Pierre Kohler, *La littérature d'aujourd'hui dans la Suisse romande* (Lausanne: Payot, 1923), p. 8.

from enthusiasts who wish to promote its use through associations such
as the Fédération des patoisants romands, the publication of journals
(*L'Ami du Patois*, for example, which is published in the Canton of
Fribourg four times a year), as well as dictionaries and grammars, such
as *Le parler jurassien* (1990) and *Le patois vaudois* (1979). However,
the various 'patois romands' can now more or less be considered 'langues
mortes' in *Suisse romande*. This is, no doubt, the reason why official
attitudes have softened, and the authorities take a relaxed approach to
their promotion.[32]

The fact that the *Suisses romands* are the only group in Switzerland
not to have a 'second' language in the form of a dialect is significant, for
this makes their relationship to language different from that of the other
three language groups present in the country. The mother tongue of Swiss
Germans is *Schwyzerdütsch*, but at school they also learn *Hochdeutsch*
('Standard German'); Italian speakers speak a local patois as well as the
Lombardy dialect and Standard Italian; several forms of spoken Romansch (recently unified in the written form called rumantsch grischun)
exist, and in addition all Romansch speakers learn German and possibly
Italian. Though the use of dialect in Italian-speaking Switzerland is
clearly limited to the private domain, and Standard Italian (or another
language) will be used with 'outsiders', this is not the case in German-
speaking Switzerland. Historically encouraged by the less centralised
nature of Germany in comparison with France, dialect is creeping into
more and more spheres of life, and what has been dubbed the 'Mundart-
welle' or 'vague dialectale' has in recent years created considerable
tension between the two main language groups.[33]

Controversy around the increasing use of 'Mundart' or 'Dialekt' (a
word that interestingly has none of the negative connotations of 'patois'
and is tellingly contrasted with 'le bon allemand' in *Suisse romande*),
has tended to reopen the debate about the so-called 'Röstigraben', the
'fossé' or 'barrière des langues' between French- and German-speaking
Switzerland, which many believe to be widening, even if it is still no-

32   Knüsel, *Les minorités ethnolinguistiques autochtones à territoire: l'exemple du
      cas helvétique*, p. 176.
33   Steinberg, *Why Switzerland?* pp. 129–62; and José Ribeaud, 'Les langues de la
      division', *Feuxcroisés*, 1, 1999, p. 218.

where near as alarming as during the First World War.[34] The problem
centres around the fact that, whereas the German-speakers see *Schwyzerdütsch*, their mother tongue, as central to their identity and a way even
now of distancing themselves from Germany, for *Suisses romands*, who
learn *Hochdeutsch* at school, it is simply yet another barrier that increases
communication difficulties. It may indeed seem a little absurd that the
German learnt in the French-speaking cantons is not in fact the version
in daily use in Switzerland, and hence when a *Romand* attempts to
communicate in German with a Swiss German both are effectively speaking a foreign language! For it is the case that *Hochdeutsch* is considered
by Swiss Germans to be more or less a foreign language with which
many are not at ease and to which French or even English may be preferred.[35] Indeed, the very term used in Switzerland to designate Standard
German, *Schriftdeutsch* ('written German'), indicates that it is perceived
to be a written language used only in formal circumstances. Even that is
changing, however, since areas traditionally reserved for *Hochdeutsch*,
such as the media and universities, are gradually being invaded by dialect,
increasingly excluding those who do not speak it. Does this then mean
that *Suisses romands* should learn dialect, as has been suggested in some
quarters? If so, which particular variant, since there are many?[36] What

34 Marcel Schwander quotes figures of 27.3% of French-speakers and 9.3% of Ger-
    man speakers who believe the gap is widening, in 'La Suisse – pont entre les
    cultures?', in *Warum brauchen wir unsere Landessprachen? Pourquoi avons-nous
    besoin de nos langues nationales?* (Académie suisse des Sciences Humaines,
    1987), p. 40. On the divisions during the First World War, see Steinberg, *Why
    Switzerland?* pp. 54–5; Du Bois, 'Mythe et réalité du fossé pendant la première
    guerre mondiale', in Pierre Du Bois (ed.), *Union et division des Suisses. Les
    relations entre Alémaniques, Romands et Tessinois aux XIXe et XXe siècles*,
    (Lausanne: Aire, 1983), pp. 65–91; Nicolas Meienberg, *Le délire général. L'armée
    suisse sous influence*, translated by Monique Picard (Carouge-Geneva: Zoé, 1988),
    pp. 36–56; Carl Spitteler, *Notre point de vue suisse*, translated by Catherine Guil-
    land (Carouge-Geneva: Zoé, 1995).
35 Roland Ris, 'L'évolution linguistique en Suisse alémanique et son impact sur la
    Suisse romande', in Du Bois, *Union et division des Suisses. Les relations entre
    Alémaniques, Romands et Tessinois aux XIXe et XXe siècles*, p. 181; Steinberg,
    Why Switzerland? p. 134.
36 See Haas, in Schläpfer, p. 70, on the variety of dialects and the differences between
    them.

about the inevitably negative reaction to the fact that this language would
be of no practical use outside Switzerland?

There are thus problems posed by the increasing use of dialect,
which distances (and potentially isolates) Swiss Germans not only from
Germans (one of the aims of the Bund Schwyzertütsch, founded in 1938),
but also unfortunately from the French-speaking Swiss. Some German-
speakers have attempted to stem the tide by forming associations such as
the Deutschschweizerischer Sprachverein in defence of the German language, but the most vociferous reactions have come from French-speakers, who maintain that national cohesion is threatened by the development
of dialect.[37] As early as 1946 Paul André was speaking of 'l'hégémonie
de l'allemand',[38] and more recently Clovis Lugon and the Mouvement
populaire romand have written in apocalyptic tones about creeping 'Germanisation' in Switzerland.[39] Intricate measures are in place to ensure
adequate representation for all language groups at a federal level, and it
has even been said that 'il serait difficile de trouver un autre État où la
première langue d'un cinquième de la population soit en position aussi
égalitaire,'[40] but this does not prevent some from feeling that they are the
eternal underdogs.

Others point out that it is not just this 'engouement immodéré pour
le dialecte' that poses a problem but also 'l'impérialisme linguistique
américain'[41] that is encouraging many to think that learning English as a
first foreign language would be more useful than learning other national
languages, as is currently the case.[42] However, the adoption of English as
a '*lingua franca*' would clearly be widely perceived as an admission of

---

37   Iso Camartin, in Schläpfer, p. 273.
38   In *La Suisse française, terre alémanique?* (Montreux: Éditions Transjuranes,
      1946), p. 89.
39   Clovis Lugon, *Quand la Suisse française s'éveillera* (Geneva: Perret-Gentil, 1983);
      Mouvement Populaire Romand, 'Le Manifeste Romand', *L'Ethnie française*,
      24(3), September 1984, pp. 162–71; Froidevaux, 'Helvétie multilingue ou Suisses
      monolingues?', p. 159.
40   Knecht, 'Le français en Suisse romande: aspects linguistiques et sociolinguist-
      iques', p. 251.
41   Ribeaud, 'Les langues de la division', p. 214.
42   See Knüsel, *Les minorités ethnolinguistiques autochtones à territoire: l'exemple
      du cas helvétique*, p. 254: Schwander, *Warum brauchen wir unsere Landesssprach-
      en? Pourquoi avons-nous besoin de nos langues nationales?* p. 40 (who quotes

failure in multicultural, multilingual Switzerland and would constitute an earthquake of massive proportions in the area of language policy. In their defence, Swiss Germans sometimes accuse *Romands* of a certain 'paresse linguistique'[43] when faced with learning German, a phenomenon that is perhaps related to the ambivalent feelings experienced towards the dominance of German-speaking Switzerland in economic matters, and the belief that *Hochdeutsch* is not generally well received in *Suisse alémanique* and hence of limited practical use.

These tensions have been reinforced in recent years by the clear splits in voting patterns that have appeared between the two main language groups, particularly on Europe and on issues of individual freedom, which have led French-speakers to feel they will always be outvoted on important questions. The vote against joining the European Economic Area on 6 December 1992 has gone down in Swiss history as one of the lowest points in relations between the two groups, with 72% of *Romands* voting in favour and 56% of *Alémaniques* against.[44] Although not on the same scale as the gulf that opened up during the First World War, such divisions are worrying for the Swiss and the results are carefully analysed and broken down by linguistic region following each 'votation', especially those on politically sensitive issues.

Clearly, there will be no easy solutions: it is likely that in the future French-speakers will need to become more aware of the centrality of dialect for Swiss Germans, whereas the Swiss Germans will perhaps need to become more sensitive to the issue of the *Hochdeutsch/Mundart* divide and the particular problems it poses for *Romands*.

---

figures of 65% of *Romands* and 58% of *Alémaniques* in favour of learning English as a first foreign language); and Ribeaud, 'Les langues de la division', p. 214. See also the results of the survey published in *L'Hebdo*, 21 April 1994, p. 81, concerning the relative importance accorded to various subjects. This shows that in both French- and German-speaking Switzerland English rates more highly than any of the national languages.

43   Froidevaux, 'Helvétie multilingue ou Suisses monolingues?', p. 157.
44   For further discussion of this issue and its importance, see Camartin, in Schläpfer, pp. 278–80; Knüsel, *Les minorités ethnolinguistiques autochtones à territoire: l'exemple du cas helvétique*, pp. 261–331; and Steinberg, *Why Switzerland?* p. 108.

The Jura Crisis

The crisis in the Jura serves as a good illustration of the extreme linguistic divisions that exist in some areas, the reactions to them and the solutions found.[45] The Jura is a French-speaking region in the north-west corner of Switzerland, composed of three mainly Catholic and three mainly Protestant districts. Its problems began in 1815, when the territory, which had previously belonged to the Prince-Bishop of Basle, was transferred to Bern (a Protestant, German-speaking canton), as 'compensation' for Bern's loss of Vaud, which had just become an autonomous canton within the Confederation, having been under Bernese rule since 1536. During the nineteenth and early-twentieth centuries German speakers moved into the area, changing the linguistic balance, and the rumbling resentment about being ruled by the Bernese finally came to a head in 1947, when a French-speaker was denied election to the cantonal executive simply because he was Francophone. This event sparked the creation of the autonomy movement, the Rassemblement jurassien, led by Roland Béguelin, which quickly gathered momentum and was supported in due course by writers like Alexandre Voisard (author of the famous 'Ode au pays qui ne veut pas mourir') and Jean Cuttat. In response, groups were formed to defend the *status quo* (the Union des patriotes jurassiens) or propose a 'middle way' (the Mouvement pour l'Unité du Jura). A series of referendums on autonomy were held (and lost by those in favour of independence) during the 1950s and 1960s, following which there was a move to direct action on the part of the separatists' youth wing, formed in 1962 and known as 'les Béliers', whose aim was summed up by their slogan: 'Jura libre'.

A first breakthrough came in 1970, when a change in the Constitution of the Canton of Bern made it possible to organise a referendum on

---

45   For further background information on the Jura Crisis, see Kenneth D. McRae, *Conflict and Compromise in Multilingual Societies: Switzerland* (Waterloo: Wilfred Laurier U.P., 1983), pp. 185–213; Alain Pichard, *La Romandie n'existe pas* (Lausanne: Éditions 24 Heures, 1978); Steinberg, *Why Switzerland?* pp. 89–98; Uli Windisch, 'D'un fédéralisme entropique à un fédéralisme de la complexité active', in Du Bois, *Union et division des Suisses. Les relations entre Alémaniques, Romands et Tessinois aux XIXe et XXe siècles*, pp. 216–25.

autonomy in which only *Jurassiens* would vote, and the autonomists were eventually successful on 23 June 1974, when the region voted for separation in a referendum with a 90% turnout. This was, however, not the end of the matter, since a counter-group, opposed to separation and known as 'les Sangliers', was formed, and violence ensued. The three southern districts, which are closer to Bern geographically and mainly Protestant, voted once again in March 1975, registering their desire to remain within the Canton of Bern, a decision that was initially unacceptable to the hardline separatists who wanted all of the territory traditionally considered *jurassien*. There were more votes, for example, in September 1975 in communes that had voted differently from the majority of their district, and more violence occurred, but in September 1978 the process was finally concluded with the vote by the rest of Switzerland approving the creation of a new canton on 1 January 1979.

As this brief account indicates, the Jura Crisis illustrated the Swiss political process at work: the slow, methodical consultation of all the parties concerned, in order to find a solution that is acceptable to all and sensitive to local differences. Less positively, it also emphasises once again the deep divisions that exist in the country between speakers of different languages (and to some extent between different religions) and seems almost a microcosm of the national stage, on which French-speakers (represented here by the *Jurassiens*) feel ignored and unimportant, and view the German speakers (here, the Bernese) as arrogant and insensitive.

'Bâtisseurs de passerelles'

Amongst all this talk of division and tension, it is, however, important to remember that much positive work is being done to foster links between Switzerland's four national languages, even if it is still often the case that exchange remains far too limited:

> Les auteurs de ces quatre régions linguistiques ne se connaissent pas bien, lisent à peine les livres de collègues qui écrivent dans une des autres langues; de ce fait,

ils ne se font ni mal ni bien, ne sont au fond pas du tout influencés les uns par les autres.[46]

Pro Helvetia, founded in 1939 and in a sense the Swiss equivalent of a Ministry for Culture, is central to efforts to provide support for authors, finance translations and bring writers of different languages together. Emphasis has been placed on translations between the national languages published in the 'Collection CH' (established in 1974 and subsidised by Pro Helvetia and the cantons as well as receiving private funding) or by publishing houses like Zoé (Geneva), Limmat (Zurich) and L'Âge d'Homme (Lausanne). Writers themselves often work as translators for other writers (in *Suisse romande* Yvette Z'Graggen and Étienne Barilier have translated from both German and Italian, Adrien Pasquali from Italian), and work in this area has found academic support from the Centre de traduction littéraire, which was established in Lausanne in 1989.[47] Furthermore, daily newspapers, such as *Le Temps* and the *Neue Zürcher Zeitung*, and weeklies such as *L'Hebdo* and *Die Weltwoche*, attempt to make writers from the other language groups better known to their readers; similar aims are pursued by journals such as the Lausanne-based *Écriture*, while *Passages* publishes regular thematic issues in Switzerland's official languages as well as in English. Writers from the different language groups have the opportunity to meet in forums such as the Journées littéraires de Soleure or Solothurner Literaturtage (established in 1979) and also have links via the 'Groupe d'Olten', which was founded in 1971 by a group of writers who disagreed with the right-wing stance being taken at that time by the Société Suisse des Écrivains and its President, Maurice Zermatten.

In spite of these efforts, both links and understanding between writers in the various language groups remain inadequate in the eyes of many. Some candidly admit to a limited interest in, and knowledge of, Swiss writers who write in other languages, and 'la situation pluriculturelle de la Suisse, en principe appréciée, ne débouche pas sur un échange

---

46   Kurt Marti, 'Ma mauvaise conscience', *Écriture*, 37, Spring 1991, p. 113. Similar
      views are expressed in Gsteiger, *La nouvelle littérature romande*, p. 197.
47   Isabelle Rüf, 'Les traducteurs, bâtisseurs de passerelles', *Feuxcroisés*, 1, 1999,
      pp. 39–53; Edgar Tripet, 'Littérature et politique culturelle', *Europe*, May 1995,
      pp. 167–73.

ou sur une confrontation créatrice.'[48] In universities the literatures of Switzerland are studied in parallel rather than comparatively, and, paradoxically, many Swiss German writers only become known and read in *Suisse romande* once they have been translated, published and accepted in France, a phenomenon described by one critic as 'l'absurdité de la réception indirecte et de la communication détournée'.[49] Theoretically, the situation in Switzerland should make *Romands* more aware of other cultures, but in fact, as discussed above, indifference and a tendency to look outwards rather than towards one another continue to characterise the relations between the language groups in Switzerland, and 'la crise d'identité que la Suisse traverse depuis la fin des années 1980 n'a pas – ou pas encore – rassemblé les écrivains des quatre langues sur la place publique helvétique.'[50]

Conclusion

The ongoing tensions between language groups in Switzerland, particularly between French- and German-speakers (although Italian- and Romansch-speakers also to some extent feel threatened by the 'Germanisation' of their respective cantons)[51] lead some to conclude that the country appears incapable of seeing its cultural plurality in a positive light. Thus, Knüsel lambasts Switzerland's 'incapacité [...] à tirer profit de sa pluralité, aujourd'hui encore perçue plus comme un handicap que comme une

---

48 Gérard Froidevaux, 'Réception et relations: la littérature romande et les autres littératures suisses', in Roger Francillon (ed.), *Histoire de la littérature en Suisse romande*, 4 (Lausanne: Payot, 1999), pp. 375–6. See also the comments of various writers on this issue in Bevan, *Écrivains d'aujourd'hui. La littérature romande en vingt entretiens*.

49 Froidevaux, 'Réception et relations: la littérature romande et les autres littératures suisses', p. 374.

50 Froidevaux, 'Réception et relations: la littérature romande et les autres littératures suisses', p. 385.

51 Froidevaux, 'Helvétie multilingue ou Suisses monolingues?', p. 163.

richesse'[52] and predicts gloomily that 'à l'avenir [...] la Suisse ne constituera pas un modèle de gestion dynamique de la pluralité culturelle.'[53] Yet all are agreed that better communication and understanding are vital if the country is to emerge unscathed from the period of crisis and self-doubt that it is currently experiencing following revelations about 'Nazi Gold' and Swiss attitudes to refugees during the Second World War.

Not only does plurality need to be perceived positively rather than negatively, the component parts of Switzerland also have to realise that, one way or another, they all need each other, and each element plays a part in the entity that is Switzerland. Interdependency has to replace what has been called 'cette indifférence non conflictuelle'[54] and all have to accept that 'sans les minorités linguistiques – ou sans la majorité alémanique – la Suisse n'existerait plus.'[55] Thus, the German-speaking majority need the other languages as a further means of distinguishing themselves from Germany; without Italian and Romansch speakers the *Romands* would all too easily be engulfed by *Suisse alémanique*; Italian speakers in the Ticino and Graubünden have greater influence and representation than they could possibly hope for as part of Italy;[56] and the very existence of Romansch as a language and culture is ensured by the Swiss federal state (note the granting of 'national language' status in 1938 and recent changes to the Constitution), since Romansch has no 'big brother' to look to, unlike the other three cultures.[57]

To some extent integrated into the wider Francophone community and yet in so many ways unavoidably peripheral to it, *Suisse romande* finds itself in a somewhat confusing position. *Romands* speak French and yet are not French, they share a nationality but not a language with

52   Knüsel, *Les minorités ethnolinguistiques autochtones à territoire: l'exemple du cas helvétique*, p. 258.

53   Knüsel, *Les minorités ethnolinguistiques autochtones à territoire: l'exemple du cas helvétique*, p. 248.

54   Froidevaux, 'Réception et relations: la littérature romande et les autres littératures suisses', p. 373.

55   Schwander, *Warum brauchen wir unsere Landessprachen? Pourquoi avons-nous besoin de nos langues nationales?* p. 45.

56   See Steinberg, *Why Switzerland?* p. 146, for figures regarding the percentage of Italian-speaking federal employees (around 7.6%) compared to their relative weight within the Swiss population (about 4%).

57   See Mützenberg, 'Éloge du plurilinguisme'.

their fellow Swiss, they 'live in a country that cannot be a culture, and in a culture that cannot be their nation.'[58] The strong desire for cohesion and the avoidance of internal splits have always been guiding forces in Switzerland, but the country's inclination to remain on the sidelines as an observer, thought by Spitteler in 1914 to be the way to preserve the country's coherence, is increasingly perceived as negative and unsustainable.[59] It remains to be seen, however, whether the twenty-first century will see Switzerland overcome its current fears and divides, notably over its place in Europe, and really become a land where 'les cultures s'ouvrent les unes aux autres' in practice as well as in theory and where plurilingualism is indeed 'une inspiration positive, un modèle'.[60]

58   Barilier, 'A Culture or a Nation?', p. 511.
59   See Spitteler, *Notre point de vue suisse*, p. 29, where he describes Switzerland's neutral observer status as 'une faveur spéciale du sort'.
60   Mützenberg, 'Éloge du plurilinguisme'.

Maeve Conrick*

Language Policy and Gender Issues in Contemporary French

Issues related to language and gender, and especially the representation of women by language, have been the subject of significant debate in recent decades, especially in the final decades of the twentieth century, due principally to the increased demands for change emanating from feminist groups. Responding to the demands of various groups of interested parties has kept policymakers busy, forcing them to confront the wider representation of women not only socially but also linguistically. Nowhere has the debate been more controversial than in the area of the representation of women's professional activities. The linguistic problems posed by the need to address and refer to women in their professional capacities has become more acute with the greater access that women have achieved to a much wider range of occupations than was previously the case. How these problems are manifested linguistically depends to some extent on the typology of individual languages. The existence of grammatical gender in some languages (e.g. French, Spanish, Italian and German) and its absence in others (e.g. English) has led to different approaches being brought to bear on linguistic policy regarding the question of professional titles. It would be erroneous to think that the absence of grammatical gender (and the consequential necessity for grammatical gender agreements) in English means that English is somehow exempt from difficulties with regard to the inclusion of women in descriptions of occupational categories. It means simply that problems in English are of a different nature. If anything, the debate on language and gender issues generally has been more focused on English than on

* The financial support of the Canadian Government Faculty Research Award is gratefully acknowledged.

any other language, though this is for socio-historical rather than wholly linguistic reasons.[1]

In a language with grammatical gender, like French, categories based on grammatical gender are such a fundamental feature of the morphological structure of the language that choice of 'feminine' or 'masculine' is inescapable, even in relatively short, syntactically simple, messages. Consequently, at all levels of usage, gender (in its broadest sense) issues are impossible to ignore. The linguist Claude Tatilon refers to grammatical gender as 'ce damné genre grammatical' and to the whole question of eliminating sexism as 'redoutable pour le français' because of its existence in French.[2]

This chapter examines the progress of feminisation, notably in Canada and France, looking at the case for feminisation as well as reaction to the ensuing debate, especially from the Académie française and the print media. Guidelines issued by the Office de la langue française du Québec (OLF) are compared with practice by reference to a corpus of data collected from three Canadian Francophone newspapers, *La Presse* and *Le Devoir* (Montreal), and *Le Droit* (Ottawa-Hull).

Feminisation and 'la francophonie'

Though there are other issues surrounding the representation of women linguistically in French, the area of professional or occupational titles (and related forms of address) is generally the one that has been pursued

1 For discussion of issues relevant to English, see Maeve Conrick, 'Linguistic Intervention, Prescriptivism and Purism: Some Issues in the Non-Sexist Language Debate', *Teangeolas: Journal of the Linguistics Institute of Ireland*, 36, 1997, pp. 22–8, and *Womanspeak* (Dublin: Marino Books/Mercier Press, 1999).

2 Claude Tatilon, 'Une optique sur la féminisation', *On Good Terms/En bons termes*, Fall/Autumn 1999, pp. 1–2, p. 1: 'Même si cette question est redoutable pour le français – où le genre grammatical est inévitable [...] autant l'admettre d'entrée en jeu, les résultats obtenus ne seront jamais aussi nets qu'en anglais. (Toujours ce damné genre grammatical!)' See also Claude Tatilon, 'La langue, le discours et l'égalité', *La Linguistique*, 32(2), 1996, pp. 133–43, and 'Un genre bien à elles', *La Linguistique*, 34(1), 1998, pp. 107–12.

most energetically in Francophone countries, where debate has focused primarily on the feminisation of titles.[3] It could be argued that this concentration on feminisation as the most important – and sometimes the only – goal pursued by those seeking linguistic reform of French on feminist principles, obscures two important facts:

(1) lack of feminisation is not the only possible example of sexist language practices; and
(2) implementation of feminisation would not eliminate all linguistic discrimination.

Notwithstanding these caveats, most of the pressure for reform of French has focused on feminisation as the central tenet of proposals for change. Two of the central issues in the feminisation debate in French are:

(1) should professional titles and forms of address be changed?; and
(2) if so, how should change be implemented?

Both of these areas are indeed controversial, since there is no general agreement that occupational titles should be feminised. Even among those who agree in principle with feminisation, there is disagreement on what exact form it should take.

There may also be some confusion with regard to terminology, especially when 'la féminisation' is used on its own, as opposed to in the phrases 'la féminisation des titres' or 'la féminisation des textes'. The word 'féminisation' is sometimes used with the narrow meaning of the creation (or addition) of feminine forms and associated morphological changes ('féminisation des titres'), which contribute to the linguistic visibility of women. 'Féminisation' may also be used as a sort of umbrella term, with the much wider meaning of 'inclusive language', thus incorporating various processes of 'neutralisation' ('féminisation des textes').[4]

---

3   For discussion of a wide range of other issues concerning non-sexist language in French see Marina Yaguello, *Les mots et les femmes* (Paris: Payot, 1978); Céline Labrosse, *"Soit dites en passant" chronique sur le sexisme dans la langue* (Quebec, Université Laval: Le GREMF édite, 1990), and *Pour une grammaire non sexiste* (Montreal: Les Éditions du remue-ménage, 1996).

4   The term 'neutralisation' overlaps partly with some of the ways in which the term 'non-sexist' language is used in English.

For the purposes of this chapter, I will generally use the term 'féminisation' with its wider meaning.

The Francophone community in Canada has taken a lead in this
domain and discussion on 'la féminisation' has been ongoing since the
late 1970s. This leading role began on 28 July 1979 with the publication
in the *Gazette Officielle du Québec* of the first 'Avis de recommandation'
concerning feminisation from the Office de la langue française (OLF).
Other recommendations followed on 28 March 1981 and 24 March 1984,
and guidelines were published in 1986 and 1991.[5] These developments
have been widely reported, for example, by Cardinal (1996), Parent
(1994) and Vachon-L'Heureux (1992).[6] Other countries and regions with
a Francophone population followed suit, and guidelines were published
in Switzerland in 1991[7] and in Belgium in 1994.[8] Many organisations in
Quebec and in Canada generally, including government departments and
universities, have formulated their own policies on the issue and published their own guidelines.[9] The Federal Government published a set of

5   Office de la langue française (OLF), *Titres et fonctions au féminin: essais d'orien-
     tation de l'usage* (Quebec: Publications du Québec, 1986), and Office de la langue
     française, Monique Biron et al. (eds), *Au féminin: guide de féminisation des titres
     de fonction et de textes* (Quebec: Publications du Québec, 1991).
6   Linda Cardinal, 'Des voies/voix en écho, le français dans les études féministes en
     milieu francophone québécois et non québécois', in Jürgen Erfurt (ed.), *De la
     polyphonie à la symphonie: méthodes, théories et faits de la recherche pluridisci-
     plinaire sur le français au Canada* (Leipzig: Leipziger Universitätsverlag, 1996),
     pp. 165–82; Monique Parent, 'Féminisation et masculinisation des titres de profes-
     sion au Québec', *La Linguistique*, 30(2), 1994, pp. 123–35; and Pierrette Vachon
     L'Heureux, 'Quinze ans de féminisation au Québec: de 1976 à 1991', *Recherches
     féministes*, 5(1), 1992, pp. 139–42.
7   Thérèse Moreau, *Dictionnaire féminin-masculin des professions, des titres et des
     fonctions* (Geneva: Métropolis, 1991). A revised and updated edition has been
     published more recently: *Le Nouveau dictionnaire féminin-masculin des profes-
     sions, des titres et des fonctions* (Geneva: Métropolis, 1999).
8   Communauté française de Belgique, Service de la langue française, Direction
     générale de la culture et de la communication and Conseil supérieur de la langue
     française, *Mettre au féminin: guide de féminisation des noms de métier, fonction,
     grade ou titre* (Belgium: 1994).
9   For example, Air Canada, Services linguistiques, Section Terminologie, *La rédac-
     tion française non sexiste* (Montréal: 1990); Emploi et Immigration Canada/
     Employment and Immigration Canada, *La féminisation des titres de profession*

guidelines in 1986, entitled: *Féminisation: Lignes directrices pour la rédaction des textes.*[10] At an international level, in 1990 UNESCO published guidelines that are now in their third edition.[11]

In Canada, though there are numerous texts defining policies and outlining suggestions for the application of feminisation, relatively little has been written about the background events leading to the adoption and implementation of decisions. The article by Lamothe and Labrosse entitled 'Un fragment du féminisme québécois des années 80: la féminisation linguistique', published in a special issue of *Recherches féministes* (Lamothe and Labrosse, 1992), is an exception, as it gives a short history of the feminisation process at l'Université du Québec à Montréal (UQAM). If one simply reads policies and guidelines on feminisation, one could get the impression that the process was accomplished very smoothly, with widespread agreement from all quarters. This is somewhat at variance with anecdotal evidence, which suggests that feminisation was not embraced with equal delight by everyone. Nonetheless, the

de la *Classification canadienne descriptive des professions* (Ottawa: Direction des systèmes nationaux d'analyse et de classification des professions, 1985); Fédération canadienne des enseignantes et des enseignants, *Pour le traitement égalitaire des femmes et des hommes dans les communications écrites. Guide de rédaction* (Ottawa: Fédération canadienne des enseignantes et des enseignants, 1990); Hydro-Québec, Vice-présidence Information, Direction Édition et Production, *Féminins des titres et fonctions* (Quebec: 1986); Justice Canada, *Directives visant à l'élimination des stéréotypes sexuels dans les communications du ministère* (Ottawa: Justice Canada, 1984).

10   Secrétariat d'État, *Féminisation: Lignes directrices pour la rédaction des textes* (Ottawa: Secrétariat d'État, 1986). Contrary to normal practice, there is no equivalent English version: 'This guide deals with the particular difficulties related to the elimination of sexual stereotyping in French. Because these specific problems do not arise in English, there is no English-language equivalent to this guide.' (Introductory Note).

11   UNESCO, *Pour l'égalité des sexes dans le langage/Guidelines on Gender-Neutral Language*, 3rd edn (Paris: UNESCO, 1999). See also Pierre Bouchard, Noëlle Guilloton, Pierrette Vachon-L'Heureux, Jean-François De Pietro, Marie-José Béguelin, Marie-Josèphe Mathieu and Marie-Louise Moreau, *La féminisation des noms de métier, fonctions, grades ou titres, au Québec, en Suisse romande, en France et en Communauté française de Belgique*, Collection Français et Société 10 (Belgique: Service de la langue française/Ministère de la communauté française/Éditions Duculot, 1999), for an international overview.

general success of feminisation in Canada and in other Francophone countries contrasts sharply with its relative lack of success in France. According to Marie-Éva de Villers: 'ici [au Québec], la féminisation est entrée dans les moeurs.'[12]

The Feminisation Debate in France

In France the debate on feminisation still rages, fuelled especially by opposition from the Académie française. An analysis of the history of attempts to feminise shows that they were often greeted with strong criticism, not to say derision. The fate of feminisation in France is described in two articles in *La Linguistique*[13] by Anne-Marie Houdebine (-Gravaud), one of seven French linguists who were members of the 'Commission de terminologie' set up in 1984 by the then Ministre des droits de la femme, Yvette Roudy, with the writer Benoîte Groult presiding. The setting up and workings of the Commission gave rise to a high degree of public controversy and heated debate in the media. During the period in which the Commission was working (1984–6), articles appeared regularly in *Le Monde*, representing both sides of the argument. Articles supporting the Commission's activities included 'Des mots pour la dire',[14] while those condemning its activities had titles like 'L'Académie contre Mme Roudy'.[15] The Commission's recommendation that titles should be feminised was accepted by the then Prime Minister, Laurent Fabius, who, in a circular in the *Journal Officiel* dated 11 March 1986, prescribed their use in all documents emanating from public ad-

---

12   Directrice de la qualité de la communication at the École des hautes études commerciales in Montreal, quoted in André Pratte, 'La féminisation des titres d'emploi progresse', *La Presse*, 8 March 2000.
13   Anne-Marie Houdebine, 'Le français au féminin', *La Linguistique*, 23(1), 1987, pp. 13–34; Anne-Marie Houdebine(-Gravaud), 'Sur la féminisation des noms de métier en français contemporain', *Recherches féministes*, 5(1), 1992, pp. 153–9.
14   Christiane Chombeau, 'Des mots pour la dire', *Le Monde*, 29 April 1984.
15   *Le Monde*, 'L'Académie contre Mme Roudy', 20 June 1984.

ministration.[16] The fact that the Commission's findings were not welcomed by the Académie française was a major drawback. A declaration condemning feminisation was published, drafted by two members of the Académie, George Dumézil and Claude Lévi-Strauss, and it resulted in the Commission's recommendations not being implemented. The Académie saw its preventative role as a triumph.

The situation changed significantly over a decade later when seven women Ministers in Lionel Jospin's Government – Martine Aubry, Marie-George Buffet, Michelle Demessine, Élisabeth Guigou, Ségolène Royal, Catherine Trautmann and Dominique Voynet – insisted on being referred to as 'Madame *la* Ministre'. They were supported by the Prime Minister and the President with the result that the controversy surfaced again in late 1997 and continued into 1998. Newspaper articles appeared in the press with inflammatory titles like 'Lionel Jospin et Jacques Chirac militants du féminisme grammatical'.[17] The reaction from the Académie française was predictable. On this occasion, three senior members, Maurice Druon, Hélène d'Encausse and Hector Biancotti, respectively 'secrétaire perpétuel', 'directeur en exercice' and 'chancelier', published an open letter to President Jacques Chirac in *Le Figaro*, appealing to him to help put a stop to 'une affaire qui [...] porte atteinte à la langue française'. In so doing they reiterated what had been the guiding principle of the Académie's previous objections to the Commission Roudy's findings:

> [C'est] le genre dit *masculin*, ou genre *non marqué*, et qu'on peut appeler également *extensif*, qui [a] presque toujours la capacité de représenter à lui seul les éléments relevant de l'un et l'autre genre.[18]

Reaction to this letter and its contents came from a wide spectrum of interested parties, for example from the linguist and co-director of *Le Robert* Dictionaries, Josette Rey-Debove,[19] and from the writer and aca-

16 Laurent Fabius, 'Circulaire du 11 mars 1986 relative à la féminisation des noms de métier, fonction, grade ou titre', *Journal officiel de la république française*, 16 March 1986, p. 4267.
17 Rafaële Rivais, 'Lionel Jospin et Jacques Chirac militants du féminisme grammatical', *Le Monde*, 19 December 1997.
18 Maurice Druon, Hélène d'Encausse and Hector Biancotti, *Le Figaro*, 9 January 1998.
19 Josette Rey-Debove, 'Madame "la" ministre', *Le Monde*, 14 January 1998.

demic Michelle Coquillat,[20] writing in *Le Monde*, and in Canada from Marie-Éva de Villers in *Le Devoir*.[21] The French linguist Marina Yaguello describes the situation in France as follows: 'La France est l'un des derniers pays où la féminisation des titres fait encore débat.'[22]

Finally, despite the Académie's opposition, Lionel Jospin published a circular on feminisation, dated 6 March 1998, in the *Journal Officiel*, in which he reactivated the policy on feminisation of titles originally instituted by Laurent Fabius:

> Voilà plus de dix ans, le 11 mars 1986, mon prédécesseur, Laurent Fabius, adressait aux membres du Gouvernement une circulaire prescrivant la féminisation des noms de métier, fonction, grade ou titre dans les textes réglementaires et dans tous les documents officiels émanant des administrations et établissements publics de l'État.
>
> Cette circulaire n'a jamais été abrogée mais elle n'a guère été appliquée jusqu'à ce que les femmes appartenant à l'actuel Gouvernement décident de revendiquer pour leur compte la féminisation du titre de ministre. Elles ont ainsi engagé un mouvement qu'il faut poursuivre afin que la féminisation des appellations professionnelles entre irrévocablement dans nos moeurs.[23]

The OLF, which bases much of its language policy decisions and recommendations on speaker usage, plays a somewhat different role in Quebec from that of the Académie française in France, which adopts a strongly prescriptive role. The Académie sees itself as one of the last bastions protecting the French language from outside 'interference', whether that 'attack' is believed to come from the influence of English or from feminists promoting gender equality. Houdebine sums up these differences in approach as follows:

> L'Académie française en France et L'Office de la langue française au Québec n'entretiennent pas le même rapport avec les usagers et les usagères; non plus que

---

20   Michèle Coquillat, 'Académie et misogynie', *Le Monde*, 20 January 1998.

21   Marie-Éva de Villers, 'Un mal qui répand la terreur', *Le Devoir*, 27 January 1998. See also Céline Labrosse, 'Au sujet de madame l'académicien', *Le Devoir*, 11 March 1998.

22   Marina Yaguello, *Le Monde*, 7 July 1998. See also Marina Yaguello, 'Madame la Ministre', *Petits faits de langue* (Paris: Éditions du Seuil, 1998), pp. 118–39.

23   'Circulaire du 6 mars 1998 relative à la féminisation des noms de métier, fonction, grade ou titre', *Journal Officiel*, 57, 8 March 1998, NOR: PRMX9802741C.

le Commissariat de la Langue Française en France. L'Office québécois est beaucoup plus sensible aux usages réels de la langue que ne le sont nos institutions, en
particulier L'Académie dont la tradition conservatrice puriste et prescriptive n'est
plus à démontrer.[24]

Consequently, feminisation is far more visible in Francophone countries
other than France. In their letter to Jacques Chirac of 9 January 1998
(quoted above), Maurice Druon, Hélène d'Encausse and Hector Biancotti
adopt a familiar, rather disparaging tone when they refer to the tendency
in Quebec and Francophone Belgium to feminise titles:

On peut regretter que, cédant à des influences démagogiques, certains de nos amis
québécois incitent à écrire: 'une auteure', 'une professeure', 'une écrivaine', ou
encore que les autorités francophones belges, pour faire pièce à une initiative
flamande équivalente, aient pris une décision linguistiquement fort contestée, qui
conduirait à appeler 'entraîneuse' une femme chargée de l'entraînement d'une
équipe sportive, ou à gratifier les femmes appartenant aux brigades de lutte contre
l'incendie de l'appellation de 'sapeuses-pompières'.

The predominant response of other Francophone countries (and of some
circles in France) has tended to regard such attitudes as mistaken, old-
fashioned and detrimental to the position, and promotion, of French as a
modern language adapted (or adapting) to the requirements of the modern
world.

The Case for Feminisation

Usage in Quebec has been particularly innovative in several areas despite
a long-standing 'sentiment d'insécurité linguistique vis-à-vis de la métro-
pole française'.[25] Quebec has given a strong lead and other Francophone
communities and countries have taken up the linguistic challenge of

24   Houdebine, 'Le français au féminin', p. 16.
25   André Lapierre 'À propos du discours lexicographique québécois', Dieter Kremer
      and Alf Monjour (eds), *Studia ex Hilaritate, Mélanges de linguistique et d'ono-
      mastique sardes et romanes offerts à Heinz Jürgen Wolf* (Paris: Klincksieck, 1995–
      6), pp. 233–46 (p. 233).

modernising the French language, with confidence in the ability of the language to cope with the changes necessary. Most guidelines take as their starting point the basic principle that the French language already has ample resources to carry through feminisation without the need to resort to non-traditional forms or processes. In his preface to the 1991 guide on feminisation the president of the OLF, Jean-Claude Rondeau, stresses that the guide 'met en valeur toutes les ressources dont dispose la langue française pour répondre aux exigences de la langue moderne.'[26] In fact, far from being radical proposals, most suggestions on feminisation rely heavily on generalising the morphological processes that already characterise grammatical gender in French.[27] In that sense, it is not so much a case of attempting to impose bizarre neologisms, it is rather a case of filling existing gaps in the French lexis by coining feminine forms along already established lines.

There appears to be no satisfactory reason why masculine/feminine pairs should exist for some occupations, but not for others. The obvious historical explanation is that feminine titles did not exist, and did not need to be created, when women tended to be poorly represented (if they were represented at all) in certain careers and professions. Titles for teachers at primary and secondary level provide an interesting example of differential (linguistic) treatment. Why should the feminine of 'instituteur' (the well-attested and uncontroversial 'institutrice') be acceptable, if a feminine form of 'professeur' is not? Why should this remain the case when, in fact, feminising 'un professeur' is a very simple morphological operation, since it can be accomplished (without change in pronunciation) as either 'une professeur' or 'une professeure'.[28] The most convincing sociolinguistic explanation advanced thus far in the discussion is the suggestion that the existence of a feminine term correlates with low status; in other words, the higher up the social scale an occupation, the less likely it is to have a feminine title. This hypothesis would

---

26   OLF, *Au féminin: guide de féminisation des titres de fonction et de textes*, p. 6.
27   A notable exception is Céline Labrosse, who makes more radical suggestions, such as 'la réactivation de formes et de règles antérieures; l'exploitation de tournures en émergence dans les dictionnaires ainsi que la création de mots nouveaux'. Labrosse, *Pour une grammaire non sexiste*, p. 9.
28   At a pragmatic level, in the absence of a feminine form, students will tend to use the colloquial term 'la prof' when their teacher is a woman.

seem to be reasonably justified, for example in the case of the titles for teachers cited above, and it merits further investigation. In practice, guidelines have sought to 'equalise' at least the linguistic representation of professions, by filling in gaps in the lexis where only a masculine form existed previously.

The achievement of feminisation in its fullest sense involves not only changes at the level of language, i.e. morphological and syntactical changes, it also necessitates changes at the broader level of discourse. The level of language occupied most attention in the early days of feminisation, when the filling of gaps in the lexis was the major focus of interest. Subsequently, attention was paid to the wider repercussions of feminisation in terms of the construction of texts. There are two main theoretical possibilities for filling lexical gaps: it can be done either by derivation or by composition. The more common of the two processes is derivation, which is usually achieved along traditional morphological lines, as exemplified in pairs like 'directeur/directrice', 'doyen/doyenne', 'enseignant/enseignante'. Most cases that arise may be dealt with satisfactorily by reference to the morphological rules for creating feminines as detailed in any traditional French grammar text.

However, dealing exclusively with the issues that arise at the purely morphological level is not of itself sufficient to account for all phenomena that are found in French. This is in large part due to the repercussions of grammatical gender agreement in French, since the gender of individual terms affects other grammatical features of sentences or larger blocks of language. Difficulties created by such grammatical gender agreements at intra-sentential or inter-sentential level are not created by the feminisation process *per se*; they already exist in many sentences attested in French where the grammatical gender of a term may be at odds with a female referent. Consequently, using existing masculines as generics may result in grammatical problems. As Marie-Éva de Villers points out:

> Non seulement les femmes ne se reconnaissent pas dans les désignations masculines, mais sur le plan grammatical, l'emploi des titres masculins pour des titulaires féminines donne lieu à des incongruités multiples.[29]

---

29   Marie-Éva de Villers, 'Un mal qui répand la terreur', *Le Devoir*, 27 January 1998.

Marino Yaguello adverted to this difficulty 20 years earlier, focusing on the problems inherent in the lack of feminine forms for occupations where women were – even then – well represented, using the following example: 'Nous aimons bien *ce professeur*, mais *elle* va nous quitter.'[30]

The lack of a feminine equivalent for 'professeur' leads to a grammatical 'disagreement' between the masculine noun ('professeur'), and the anaphoric feminine pronoun ('elle'). Many similar examples may be found in print as well as in the spoken context. The following sentences headed an article in *Le Monde* in 1998:

> *Pionnière* de la lutte des femmes algériennes, *ce professeur* de français devenu journaliste a vu son courage récompensé par le prix Olof-Palme et par le prix Sakharov des droits de l'homme, décerné par le Parlement européen. 'La Nation', l'hebdomadaire qu'*elle* dirige, est interdit de parution depuis décembre 1996.[31]

The italicised forms illustrate in more detail exactly the same problems as those identified in the previous example by Yaguello: the difficulty of trying to 'fit' a female referent into a grammatically masculine category. The use of a feminine form of 'professeur' would certainly have eliminated the grammatical ambiguity in both cases.

There are even more striking examples of the problems created by the lack of feminine titles in French when there is occasion to refer to female referents fulfilling biological functions that are only possible for females, such as becoming pregnant or giving birth. Céline Labrosse provides the example 'Un pompier a accouché la semaine dernière', which leaves the reader with the impression that a man has given birth![32] An even more celebrated example is provided by 'l'affaire Prieur'. The event in question involved the repatriation to France of 'le capitaine Prieur', one of the French navy officers implicated in the sinking of the Greenpeace ship the *Rainbow Warrior*, who had been exiled to an atoll in Polynesia. She was allowed to return to France in 1988 on account of her pregnancy. The difficulties in reporting her repatriation were aggravated by the problem of trying to explain, without sabotaging grammatic-

30   Yaguello, *Les mots et les femmes*, p. 130 (emphasis added).
31   These sentences are quoted from *Le Monde*, 'Salima Ghezali, le défi du dialogue', 20 February 1998 (emphasis added).
32   Labrosse, *"Soit dites en passant" chronique sur le sexisme dans la langue*, p. 3.

al accuracy, that 'le capitaine' was pregnant. The only possible adjectival form available to describe the situation is the feminine 'enceinte', a form that – for obvious biological reasons – exists only in the feminine. The Prime Minister Jacques Chirac's office announced the news in the following terms, privileging semantic coherence over grammatical accuracy, since the masculine noun blatantly disagrees with the feminine adjective: '*Le* capitaine Prieur est actuellement *enceinte* et l'accord prévoyait que, dans ces circonstances, *elle* pouvait être rapatriée à Paris.'

The print media dealt with this grammatical problem in various ways, mostly by trying to avoid the unhappy coincidence of masculine and feminine forms.[33] The simplest solution would have been to feminise 'le capitaine' to 'la capitaine', thereby ensuring agreement with subsequent feminine forms and respecting the rules of grammatical gender agreement in French. Examples of the kind described above amply illustrate that feminisation is not necessarily the source of problems; on the contrary, it may be a way of solving existing difficulties.

Proposals made with regard to the feminisation of titles generally involve derivation, using the current resources of French morphology. This is usually stated expressly in the various published guides. For example, Hélène Dumais asserts that, 'À chaque titre peut et doit correspondre un titre féminin, formé selon les règles traditionnelles de la langue française.'[34] Those who resist feminisation in principle often wilfully misrepresent what is involved by suggesting completely false feminines like 'dimanchesse' and 'les températures maximelles'. Houdebine quotes from a text published in *Le Monde* on 28 April 1984 that contains a series of completely ridiculous false feminines, which are used to ridicule genuine attempts at feminisation:

> La première femme qui sera élue *cheftaine* de l'État aura ainsi devant elle une *septennate* pour tenir avec la *gouvernemente*, les *engageaisons* de sa *program-*

33 For full treatment of how these issues were dealt with by the print media see Marina Yaguello, *En écoutant parler la langue* (Paris: Éditions du Seuil, 1991), pp. 18–24; and Suzanne Fleischman, 'The Battle of Feminism and *Bon Usage*: Instituting Nonsexist Usage in French', *The French Review*, 70(6), May 1997, pp. 834–44.

34 Hélène Dumais, 'Pour un genre à part entière', *Recherches féministes*, 5(1), 1992, pp. 169–74.

mature électorale, et conduire la France sur les *chemines* de la *progressesse* dont elle a tant *besoigne*.[35]

In practice, feminised forms fill existing lacunae in the French lexis, thereby alleviating the grammatical – and consequently communicative – difficulties of denoting female referents.

Guidelines on Feminisation

Guidelines typically recommend the formation of new feminines by derivation, based on traditional grammatical rules for written French, such as 'add *e* to the masculine'. Another method is simply to use the masculine form accompanied by a feminine determiner, i.e. with the title being used as an epicene. This is particularly straightforward when the ending is 'e' as in 'le dentiste'/'la dentiste'. This solution has the enormous advantage of minimising morphological intervention, and there is no alteration in pronunciation. Taking both of these processes into account, arguments along the lines that suggestions for feminisation are somehow an 'attack' on the intrinsic structure of the French language are difficult to sustain.

Feminisation of Titles

The following points sketch briefly examples of the six major morphological categories involved.[36]

---

35   This extract from *Le Monde* and the previous examples are quoted from Houdebine, 'Le français au féminin', p. 22. Opponents of non-sexist language in English demonstrated a similar reaction by suggesting (ludicrously) that proponents of change would wish to replace the words 'history' and 'mandate' with 'herstory' and 'persondate'.

36   This description follows the guidelines detailed in OLF, *Au féminin: guide de féminisation des titres de fonction et de textes*.

1. Nouns ending with 'e'. This category is for the most part composed of epicenes, where gender is marked by a change of determiner, as in 'la capitaine', 'la juge' and 'la pilote'. Obviously, pronunciation and spelling of the lexical item remain the same.

2. Nouns ending with 'l'. The regular feminine of these nouns is formed by adding 'e', and in some cases, by doubling the 'l'. Examples are: 'une caporale', 'une industrielle'. This category does not require any change in pronunciation, only in orthography.

3. Nouns ending with 'n'. This group is feminised by adding 'e' and, in some cases, by doubling the 'n', e.g. 'une écrivaine', 'une chirurgienne'. In these instances, a change in pronunciation accompanies the change in orthography, though it is fully in line with already existing masculine/feminine pairs.

    There are two obvious exceptions, where following the traditional rule for forming the feminine would mean that the new form would coincide with an existing term in the lexis, designating the fields of activity, i.e. 'la marine' and 'la médecine'. To avoid confusion, it is usually recommended that these forms follow the rule for epicenes, i.e. that they should be, respectively, 'la marin' and 'la médecin'.

4. Nouns ending with 'r'. Many of these nouns require a change in pronunciation as well as in orthography. They may be divided into three subcategories:
    (i) Nouns ending with 'er' and 'ier'. Such nouns follow the usual morphological rules of changing 'er' to 'ère' and 'ier' to 'ière', on the model of 'berger'/'bergère', 'ouvrier'/'ouvrière'. The result is forms like the following: 'une bouchère', 'une officière'.
    (ii) Nouns ending with 'eur'. The most usual form for 'eur' is 'euse', as in, for example, 'une fournisseuse', 'une chercheuse'. There are exceptions to this general rule, largely for the very commendable reason that alternatives have already been adopted in usage. In Quebec, for example, the forms 'professeure', 'gouverneure' and 'ingénieure' are in use, so the OLF, very sensibly, advises that, 'Il ne faut pas créer inutilement de

nouveaux féminins'.[37] The treatment of 'professeur' is an example of how the approach towards individual items varies across 'la francophonie'. While Quebec decided on 'la professeure', the francophone community in Belgium opted for 'la professeur', hence categorising 'professeur' as an epicene.[38]

(iii) Nouns ending in 'teur'. There are two possibilities in this category, either 'teuse' (e.g. 'chanteuse') or 'trice' (e.g. 'actrice'). The general rule in cases of uncertainty is: if a present participle can be formed by replacing 'eur' with 'ant', the feminine should be 'teuse', otherwise it should be 'trice'. There are cases where two or more forms exist in common use, for example the feminines of 'auteur', 'sculpteur' and 'docteur'; in these cases, the OLF recommends 'une auteure', 'une sculpteure' and 'une docteur'.[39]

5.   Nouns ending in 't' or 'd'. Here the feminine is generally obtained by adding 'e', as in 'une agente', 'une commandante', with some exceptions such as 'une matelot' and 'une substitut' treated as epicenes.

6.   Nouns ending in 'é', 'f' and 'is'. Nouns ending in 'é' take 'e', as in 'une députée', 'une chargée de cours'. Nouns in 'is' take 'e' except for 'commis', which is treated as an epicene. Those in 'f' become 've' except for 'chef', which remains an epicene. Other possibilities such as 'cheffe' or 'cheffesse' are rejected by the OLF as 'insolites ou ironiques'.[40] Indeed, many critics of feminisation

37   OLF, *Au féminin: guide de féminisation des titres de fonction et de textes,* p. 12.
38   The history of a feminine form of *professeur* in Quebec indicates how much change in usage there has been in roughly 20 years. In a survey carried out in Quebec in 1983 by Hélène Dumais analysing knowledge and use of feminine professional titles, not one of the 40 respondents supplied 'une professeure' as the feminine of 'un professeur'. In fact, 65% of respondents opted for 'pas de forme féminine', while, among those who did provide a feminine, the most popular one was 'une professeur' (15%). Hélène Dumais, 'La féminisation des noms de profession', *Québec français,* December 1983, pp. 30–3.
39   The feminine 'doctoresse' has largely fallen out of use. *Le Petit Robert* lists it as 'vieilli'.
40   OLF, *Au féminin: guide de féminisation des titres de fonction et de textes,* p. 13.

have used as examples the various possible feminine forms of 'chef',
including 'cheffe', 'cheffesse' and 'cheftaine'.

Feminisation of Texts

Guidelines are not normally confined to suggestions on a purely morphological basis, due largely to the fact that if feminisation is implemented
only at this level the results will have rather limited acceptability. Much
criticism of feminisation stems from the incidence of continual repetition,
which does indeed make texts long and unwieldy. Arguments about the
requirements of good style have to be taken on board and consequently,
at the level of discourse, greater ingenuity is needed if texts are to be
elegantly constructed as well as inclusive. Attention to the macro level
of text composition, while desirable syntactically and stylistically, does
of course mean that drafters of written texts, if they are to accomplish
the task successfully, have to give further thought to the process beyond
simply adding in a few feminines here and there.

The overall principles in the OLF guide are: 'la qualité avant toute
chose [...] la clarté du message et la cohérence de l'écriture'.[41] Consequently, the document focuses on how to compose texts as efficiently
and elegantly as possible, while at the same time making them inclusive
of women and men. Two principles are advocated:

- l'écriture des formes des deux genres, en toutes lettres;
- le recours aux termes génériques et aux tournures neutres.[42]

The first of these two principles means that all forms of truncation are to
be avoided: 'L'emploi de finales féminines entre parenthèses et le recours
aux traits obliques, tirets, virgules ou autres signes graphiques sont à
rejeter'. The result is that the following forms are not approved:

- les ingénieur(e)s retraité(e)s
- les étudiant/e/s inscrit/e/s;
- les chirurgien.ne.s;
- les directeur-trice-s.[43]

41 OLF, *Au féminin: guide de féminisation des titres de fonction et de textes*, p. 15.
42 OLF, *Au féminin: guide de féminisation des titres de fonction et de textes*, p. 15.
43 OLF, *Au féminin: guide de féminisation des titres de fonction et de textes*, p. 16.

These are rejected not only because they are contrary to grammatical usage, but also because they reduce the readability of texts. The fact that these are the reasons cited should reassure those who see all forms of feminisation as an assault on French grammar, detrimental to the construction of coherent, stylish texts. Various procedures are outlined, having regard to the criterion of readability, including: 'suppression de l'article et de l'adjectif', 'utilisation de l'ellipse', 'coordination sans répétition' and 'reprise par les pronoms'.

The second principle quoted above deals with the use of generic terms and neutral turns of phrase: 'le recours aux termes génériques et aux tournures neutres'. The generics referred to are those that can designate either a woman or a man, such as 'une personne', 'la direction' and 'la présidence', and collectives like 'le personnel', 'le corps professoral' and 'la clientèle'. Neutral turns of phrase include the use of infinitival or nominal forms, to eliminate the need to repeat 'il ou elle' frequently. For example, in listing duties required of a candidate for a post being advertised, instead of the description:

> – il ou elle planifie le cheminement et la qualité des réponses […]
> – il ou elle supervise le traitement des plaintes […]
> – il ou elle effectue des recherches sur les nouvelles lois

it is possible to avoid repetition of gender specific markers and neutralise the text by listing the tasks as:

> – planifier […] superviser […] effectuer,
> (or)
> – planification […] supervision […] recherche.[44]

These models for the feminisation of texts are more in line with approaches taken in English, where neutralisation has been the overwhelmingly preferred method of attempting to make language more inclusive. In fact, what has happened in French as a consequence of feminisation of titles, i.e. the greater visibility of gender and gender markers, has been very much at odds with the move in English to reduce the overall

44   These examples have been adapted from OLF, *Au féminin: guide de féminisation des titres de fonction et de textes*, pp. 22–3.
45   OLF, *Au féminin: guide de féminisation des titres de fonction et de textes*.

visibility of gender and gender markers. For example, English oppositions like 'actor/actress', 'poet/poetess' and 'author/authoress' have been rejected in favour of the single unmarked forms 'actor', 'poet' and 'author'. So, while the general objectives of feminist reformers in both languages coincide, the methods by which they aim to achieve their objectives are, in some instances, diametrically opposed.

Implementation of Feminisation

While the existence of guidelines demonstrates a positive climate of opinion, it is essential to test the factual situation by reference to samples of data. With a view to determining the actual rate of occurrence of feminisation in a particular type of text, i.e. employment advertisements in newspapers, data was collected from the 'Professions et carrières' sections of three Francophone newspapers: *La Presse*, *Le Devoir* and *Le Droit*. Collection of data took place over two periods of approximately one month, March 1997 and May 1998. This data was examined in the light of the recommendations of the OLF guide,[45] with the objective of ascertaining the extent to which feminisation is implemented and which methods are used.

The OLF guide contains a total of 475 professional titles for women.[46] The guide is not intended to be exhaustive and, in fact, the data included 44 unlisted titles:

> Aides-cuisiniers, aviseurs légaux, chimiste organicien(ne), clinicien(ne), comptable, concepteurs de logiciel, designers, développeurs de logiciels, distributeur, échantillonneur, éditeur-éditrice, environnementaliste, ergonome, ergothérapeutes, fiscalistes, formateur-formatrice, généraliste, graphiste, historien, hydrogéologue, intégrateurs de systèmes, investigateur, leaders, météorologistes, météorologue, orthophoniste, personnes-ressources, pharmacologue, physiothérapeute, planificateur, professionnel, psychologue, QA et QC ingénieurs, quantity surveyors, spé-

---

46   This is a relatively small number of titles since the *National Occupation Classification (NOC)/Classification nationale des professions*, published by Employment and Immigration Canada, lists over 25,000 titles.

cialiste, statisticien(ne), technologue, télémarketer, télévendeurs, thérapeutes, trade marketing manager, trésorier municipal, webmaster principal, webmestre.

The reasons for the absence of most of the examples above are self-evident. Some of them are English terms (e.g. 'quantity surveyors', 'trade marketing manager', 'webmaster') and others are calques of English terms (e.g. 'personnes-ressources'). These forms are integrated somewhat incongruously into the grammatical structures of French, either in the heading or in the text that follows (e.g. 'QA et QC ingénieurs', 'webmaster principal'). Others refer not so much to the title of a post but rather to the functions of a post (e.g. 'développeur' 'spécialiste'). New titles are being created very rapidly, especially in the field of information technology, giving rise to a whole range of neologisms (e.g. 'concepteurs de logiciel', 'télémarketer', 'télévendeurs', 'webmestre'[47]). In this context, the prefixes 'télé-' and 'ergo-' seem to be particularly productive.

From the point of view of feminisation, all theoretical possibilities are represented in the data, from advertisements where there is no effort at feminisation, to those that follow the OLF guidelines to the letter, along with many shades of grey in between.

No Feminisation

Some of the advertisements collected use only masculine titles, though they are, presumably, being used generically. These include:

acheteurs, adjoint, administrateur, agent, aides-cuisiniers, aides-pâtissiers, analyste financier, analystes-développeurs, animateur, assistant, associé, auditeur, aviseurs, avocat, cadres supérieurs, chargé de -, chauffeurs, chef, chercheurs, commis, concepteurs, conseiller, consultant, contrôleur, coordonnateur, correcteurs, courtiers, designers, dessinateur, directeur, distributeur, échantillonneur, éducateur, enseignants, estimateur, ferblantier, formateurs, gérant, historien, ingénieur, inté-

47   The term 'webmestre' appears in the OLF website document *Vocabulaire d'Internet Plus*, which is based on the second edition of *Vocabulaire d'Internet*, launched on 18 March 1997, revised and expanded by Marcel Bergeron, Corinne Kempa and Yolande Perron, 'terminologues à la Direction des services linguistiques'. A note explains the reasons for its choice: 'Le néologisme *webmestre* possède plusieurs qualités: il est épicène, court et concilie l'ancien et le moderne puisqu'il tire ses racines du terme *Web* et du terme *vaguemestre* [...]'.

grateurs, investigateur, leaders, maîtres de langues, mécaniciens, moniteur, outilleur, planificateur, plombier, préposé, président, procureur, professeur, profes-
sionnels, programmeur, recruteur, rédacteur, relecteurs, représentant, superviseur,
surintendant, surveillant, technicien, télémarketer, télévendeurs, traducteurs, trésorier, vendeurs, vérificateur, vice-président, vice-principal, vice-recteur.

While some advertisements make no effort at all in the direction of
feminisation, others point out (frequently at the bottom of the advertisement) that the post is open to women and men. Many of those advertisements that do not feminise display a certain amount of linguistic
insecurity, in that they tend to add disclaimers explaining why they have
not done so. Some drafters are keen to point out that while their language
may appear exclusive, their intentions are not. The following are typical
examples:

> N.B. Le genre masculin est utilisé sans aucune discrimination et dans le seul but
> d'alléger le texte. (*La Presse*, 1 March 1997)

> 'Le genre masculin est utilisé par souci d'allégement du texte. On doit l'interpréter
> dans son sens générique, à moins d'indication contraire.' (*Le Droit*, 2 May 1998)

One of the surprising things about the last advertisement (for 'chargés
de cours' at l'Université du Québec à Hull) is that a university placed it
and, in general, universities tend to feminise. This specific formulation
reappears in other advertisements placed by the same university, for
example, at the end of an advertisement for a 'professeur suppléant',[48]
and it is preceded by the assurance 'Poste accessible aux femmes et aux
hommes'. Even if the reason feminisation is not implemented is to save
space, an alternative like that quoted above does not exhibit any advantages with regard to length.

Other forms of feminisation appear to be still current, despite the
fact that they are not recommended by any set of guidelines and appear
to be rather sloppy attempts at inclusiveness. They include the addition
of the words 'homme ou femme' as in:

> Directeur – homme ou femme (*Le Droit*, 29 March 1997)

> Analyste des risques politiques (homme ou femme)[49] (*La Presse*, 2 May 1998)

48 *La Presse*, 9 May 1998.

When analysing the forms (listed at the beginning of this section) that
are used as masculines only, it is obvious that there is no intrinsic linguistic reason why they could not have been feminised. Almost all of the
terms could easily have been feminised in line with the recommendations
of the OLF. Indeed, feminines of some of these forms existed in French
long before the advent of the feminisation process, e.g. 'enseignante'
and 'directrice'. Among the examples of words borrowed from English,
used only in the masculine, are 'leaders' and 'designers',[50] in which the
ending '-er' has the same phonetic structure as 'eur', i.e. is pronounced
[œʀ]. Consequently, they could be feminised as 'leadeuses' and 'design-
euses'. Some of the masculine forms refer to traditionally male occupations (e.g. 'ferblantier', mécaniciens', 'outilleur', 'plombier').

There are also examples in the data of the opposite case: forms that
appear only in the feminine, predictably for posts which are traditionally female, as in 'infirmières bachelières' and 'auxiliaires familiales'.[51]
Advertising in these gender-exclusive ways indicates that not all employers seek to adhere to the much-quoted 'principe d'équité en matière
d'emploi'.

An interesting linguistic turning of the tables is the use of a feminine
as generic, where the feminine is deemed to include the masculine:

> Conseillère syndicale […]

> La forme féminine dans le texte désigne aussi bien les hommes que les femmes.
> (*La Presse*, 23 May 1998)

This example is an unusual, not to say radical, one, since feminine forms
are not usually used generically. This is true of both French and English.
For example, while the terms 'actor'/'acteur' may be used to refer to
both male actors and also to all actors both male and female, the terms
'actress'/'actrice' may only be used to denote female actors and not all
actors.

---

49   The addition of 'homme ou femme' is unnecessary here, since 'analyste' is an
     epicene. In this instance, it may have been added to the heading because the rest of
     the advertisement is composed using exclusively masculines.
50   'Designer' is classified by *Le Petit Robert* as an Americanism that first appeared
     in 1969. 'Leader' is listed, though not with a business meaning.
51   *La Presse*, 29 March 1997.

Epicenes

The data contains many examples of epicenes ending in 'e' and also exceptions from other categories, like 'chef', 'commis' and 'médecin':

> analyste, analyste-conseil, architectes, archiviste, auxiliaires, bibliothécaire, biolo- giste, cadres supérieurs, capitaine, chef, chimiste, commis, commissaire, comp- table, économiste, environnementaliste, ergonome, ergothérapeutes, fiscalistes, généraliste en ressources humaines, gestionnaire, graphiste, hydrogéologue, ma- chinistes, maîtres de langues, médecin, météorologistes, météorologue, optomé- triste, orthophoniste, pharmacologue, physiothérapeute, psychologue, responsable de classe, secrétaire, secrétaire réceptionniste, spécialiste, stagiaires, technologue/ métallurgiste, thérapeutes.

In the case of epicenes, there is no orthographic difference between feminine and masculine. Consequently, whether they are indeed being used with reference to both genders is sometimes not clear until the body of the advertisement, or by reference to accompanying determiners if there are any. All theoretical possibilities are attested in the corpus. Some examples are clearly epicenes:

> analyste principal(e) (*La Presse*, 8 March 1997)
> chimiste organicien(ne) (*La Presse*, 23 May 1998)
> secrétaire médical(e) (*Le Droit*, 30 May 1998)
> un(e) orthophoniste (*La Presse*, 9 May 1998)
> une ou un capitaine d'avion-citerne (*La Presse*, 9 May 1998)[52]
> un(e) comptable (*La Presse*, 9 May 1998)
> assistant(e)-contrôleur(e) [...] chef de la logistique [...] technicien(ne) à la formula- tion [...] directeur(trice) de programme de recherches [...] (*La Presse*, 9 May 1998)[53]

Others, clearly are not being used as epicenes, either on the evidence of accompanying determiners or from the fact that they appear in a list of terms where all the other terms are masculine:

52 This advertisement was placed by the Gouvernement du Québec, so it is not surprising to find that they adhere to their own guidelines. Their practice on feminisation is highlighted by the appearance at the top of the advertisement of the legend 'pour l'équité en emploi', in letters of equal size to those used for 'Gouvernement du Québec'.

53 This list is quoted from a lengthy advertisement, placed by Axcan Pharma, in which all titles are feminised.

cadres supérieurs (*La Presse*, 9 May 1998)
machinistes recherchés (*La Presse*, 23 May 1998)
un psychologue (*Le Droit*, 23 May 1998)
analyste-programmeur principal (*La Presse*, 1 March 1997)
chef de service [...] analystes [...] analystes/programmeurs [...] spécialiste de réseau (*La Presse*, 9 May 1998)
responsable du service des travaux actuariels [...] un postulant [...] le candidat élu [...] (*Le Devoir*, 14 March 1997)
spécialistes en méthodologie client-serveur [...] chercheurs [...] rédacteur [...] formateurs [...] (*La Presse*, 1 March 1997).

Epicene terms offer an ideal method for composing an inclusive text. This is achieved in many cases by the use of the epicene along with some of the devices advocated by the OLF guide for feminising texts, including 'tournures neutres' (e.g. the use of infinitives and nouns). The following example illustrates how these principles are put into practice:

responsable de classe:
– sommaire de la fonction: être responsable des activités reliées à [...]
– qualifications et aptitudes requises: diplôme universitaire, souci d'excellence, disponibilité et flexibilité, maîtrise du français etc.
– conditions de travail: rémunération et avantages sociaux [...] (*La Presse*, 1 March 1997).

Another way of avoiding the need to use formulations such as ' le candidat ou la candidate [...]', with the attendant problem of having to use (and maybe repeat) the third person singular pronouns 'il ou elle', is the use of the first and second person pronouns 'nous' and 'vous' and the possessive adjectives 'nos' and 'vos'. This happens typically when employers detail their requirements under the heading 'nos exigences' and 'vos responsabilités'.

The title 'chef' is included in the epicene category by the OLF guide. In practice it is used as an epicene or as a masculine only. The 'cheffe' referred to in the title of Moreau's article 'Attention la cheffe arrive!' (Moreau, 1992) has not arrived as there is only one example in the corpus of 'chef' being feminised as 'cheffe', in the following advertisement by a large engineering and construction company:

chef(fe) de projet adjoint(e), chef(fe) d'équipe (*La Presse*, 9 May 1998).[54]

54   The company, SNC-Lavalin Inc., describes itself in the advertisement as 'une des plus importantes sociétes d'ingénierie et de construction au Canada'.

Feminised Advertisements

The epicene category discussed in the previous section provides some of the best examples of gender-inclusive advertisements. Among the feminised advertisements, excluding the category of epicenes, are:

> acheteur(euse), adjoint(e) d'actuariat, administrateur(trice), agente ou agent, associé(e)s en recherche clinique, avocat(e), chargé(e) d'affaires, chercheur(e), clinicien(ne), conseiller(ère), coordonnateur-trice, dessinateur(trice), directeur ou directrice, doyenne-doyen, échantillonneur(e), éditeur-éditrice, éducateur(trice), enquêteuse ou enquêteur, enseignant(e), estimateur(trice), formateurs(trices), gérant(e), infirmière ou infirmier, ingénieur(e), inspecteur/ inspectrice, instructeur(trice), pharmacien(ne), préposé(e), professeur-e, professionnel(le), programmeur(e)/(euse), recruteur(euse), rédacteur(trice), représentant(e), réviseur[e], répartiteur(trice), superviseur(e), technicien, traducteurs/traductrices, travailleur(euse) social(e), vendeur(se)s, vérificateur(trice), vice- président(e).

There is much variety in the type and level of post listed. Consequently, it does not appear on this evidence that the status of the post is the major factor determining whether or not the title is feminised. Though 'vice-principal' and 'vice-recteur' (which appear in *Le Devoir*[55]) are not feminised, there are several examples of feminised 'vice-président(e)' in all three newspapers.

There is considerable variation in the amount of feminisation and in the form that it takes. Sometimes only the heading is feminised and the rest of the advertisement reverts to masculine only, e.g.:

> directrice générale ou directeur général [...] préoccupé par la réussite des élèves [...] vous êtes reconnu [...] les candidats joindront à leur curriculum vitae [...] (*Le Devoir*, 24 March 1997).

In other cases, both genders are used consistently throughout the text, though they are rarely written out in full:

> inspecteur/inspectrice [...] le/la titulaire [...] (*Le Droit*, 1 March 1997)
> directeur(trice) des finances de l'administration [...] le(la) candidat(e) choisi(e)

55 The advertisement for a 'Vice-principal (enseignement)' at McGill University appears in *Le Devoir* (11 May 1998) and that for a 'Vice-recteur à l'enseignement et à la recherche' at the Université du Québec à Chicoutimi in the same newspaper (29 May 1998).

[…] il est souhaitable qu'il(elle) connaisse les lois régissant les pensions de retraite
[…] (*Le Droit*, 30 May 1998)
informaticien(ne)s […] vous êtes diplômé(e) […] (*La Presse*, 2 May 1998).

The principle of 'l'écriture des formes des deux genres, en toutes lettres' is not respected in the overwhelming majority of cases (with some notable exceptions, such as the Gouvernement du Québec and the Université de Montréal). Many examples are truncated in various ways, whether by the use of parentheses (e.g. 'représentant(e) médical(e)'), slashes (e.g. 'directeur/trice'), full stops (e.g. 'agent.e de projet') or dashes (e.g. 'professeur-e substitut'). By far the most common is the use of parentheses. It is easy to understand why truncation should be so prevalent in newspaper employment advertisements, because space is at a premium. However, it is obviously inadvisable in cases where not writing out the feminine in full leads to a morphological anomaly. In one of the examples from the corpus, 'un poste de professeur(e) régulier(e)',[56] the feminine ending should be 'ère', not 'ere', a fact that is obscured by the use of truncation. Such careless feminisation plays into the hands of those who are convinced that feminisation is destructive of the grammatical structures of French.

There is evidence of variation in the form of some feminines, most particularly in those ending in 'eur' and 'teur'. For example, 'enquêteur' is realised as either 'enquêteuse' or 'enquêteure' and, similarly, 'programmeur' is feminised as either 'programmeuse' or 'programmeure'. The only example of the feminine of 'chercheur' in the corpus is 'chercheure' (rather than the recommended 'chercheuse'). It appears that there is indeed a tendency to féminise forms ending in 'eur' by adding an 'e', on the model of 'professeur'/'professeure', rather than by changing 'eur' to 'euse'. Gaston Bernier of the Bibliothèque de l'Assemblée nationale, in an article on the subject, makes reference to a request sent by another librarian to the OLF for the feminine of 'catalogueur' to be 'catalogueure' rather than 'catalogueuse', which might be perceived as 'trop vert, trop rugueux'.[57] The OLF guide suggests that there is reluctance to use 'euse' because

---

56   *Le Devoir*, 14 March 1997.
57   Gaston Bernier, ' "Catalogueuse", avez-vous dit?', *Documentations et bibliothèques*, 45(2), April–June 1999, p. 83.

il y a une valeur péjorative attachée parfois aux féminins en –*euse* et que la résistance à employer ces formes est plus forte lorsqu'il s'agit de professions de type intellectuel. Il en résulte un flottement, une concurrence de formes. [58]

There is also an unusual case of 'directeur' being feminised as 'directeur(e)',[59] despite the long established existence of 'directrice'. One can conclude that the feminine of nouns ending in 'eur' is not fixed, and that there seems to be a tendency to feminise by adding 'e', which has the obvious advantage of maintaining the same pronunciation for both genders.

Many of the feminised advertisements observe the guidelines on feminisation of titles closely, but not slavishly, and make creative use of the suggestions made for feminising texts. Advertisements for 'personnel enseignant' and 'un poste de direction générale' (using 'tournures neutres') are common along with other techniques for avoiding repetition of 'il ou elle' such as the use of the second person 'vous' in place of the third person. The result is that many advertisements are both inclusive and well formulated, avoiding the major pitfall of feminising by only adding in a feminine form to accompany every masculine. The Gouvernement du Québec gives a lead on this by providing the masculine and feminine titles in the heading and following it up with 'tournures neutres':

> agente ou agent de secrétariat […] attributions […] conditions d'admission […] période d'inscription (*Le Droit*, 23 May 1998)
> enquêteuse ou enquêteur en matières frauduleuses, grade stagiaire […] principales fonctions […] conditions d'admission, inscription, information […] (*Le Droit*, 30 May 1998)
> technicienne ou technicien en foresterie et en gestion du territoire […] principales fonctions […] (*Le Droit*, 9 May 1998).

Other employers have followed the principles of feminisation (titles and texts) to the letter, including writing everything out in full. A notable example is the Université de Montréal, whose advertisements are drafted along similar lines to those of the Gouvernement du Québec. The following is one of many examples from the corpus:

58　OLF, *Au féminin: guide de féminisation des titres de fonction et de textes*, p. 11.
59　*Le Droit*, 23 May 1998. The advertisement is for a 'directeur(e) à l'enseignement', Institut de la haute technologie, La Cité collegiale, Ottawa.

Professeure ou professeur d'études françaises [...] fonctions [...] exigences [...]
traitement [...] date d'entrée en fonction [...] (*Le Droit*, 30 May 1998).

The clarity and suitability to purpose of such advertisements gives
the lie to any notion that feminisation leads to unwieldy, woolly texts.
Even the layout is frequently easier to follow, since functions, conditions
of employment and other necessary information appear in the form of
lists, rather than in a more closely packed continuous text.

Frequent use is also made of generic terms such as 'les personnes
intéressées' and collectives like 'le personnel':

la personne recherchée possède [...] les personnes désireuses de se porter candidates [...] (*Le Devoir*, 3 March 1997)
personnel enseignant (*La Presse*, 16 May 1998).

There is also a tendency to phrase the title in a neutral way, as in
'un poste de direction générale' or simply 'direction générale'. The
neutral formulation is not, however, necessarily continued into the body
of the advertisement. In one case where the heading is 'direction générale', the subsequent text uses the formulation 'directeur général'.[60]
Clearly, the use of 'tournures neutres' may not always be attributed to a
desire to feminise.

Some employers completely avoid referring to a job title and prefer
instead to invite or challenge applicants to join them:

Joignez-vous à notre équipe! [...] nous voulons vous rencontrer! (*Le Droit*, 9 May
1998)
Si vous recherchez des défis, nous en avons à vous proposer. (*La Presse*, 8 March
1997)
J'ai besoin de toi! [...] homme/femme [...] carrière dans la vente automobile [...]
Du Portage n'embauche que des gagnant(e)s (*Le Droit*, 1 March 1997)
Une proposition d'affaires [...]
Partir en affaires c'est bien, avec nous c'est mieux. (*Le Droit*, 2 May 1998).

Employers who adopt this approach tend to be those involved in
fields like marketing and information technology, utilising a very direct,

60 This advertisement was placed by the Société Saint-Jean-Baptiste de Montréal,
which describes itself as: 'vouée à l'indépendance économique, politique, culturelle et sociale du Québec [...]. Aussi connue pour la défense du français, de l'histoire, de la culture québécoise et de l'éducation [...]' *Le Devoir*, 29 May 1998.

first or second person approach, presumably to attract dynamic applicants, lured by the company's display of its own dynamism. In a competitive market, they may also emphasise the attractions of the position, rather than the requirements of successful candidates. Défense nationale/National Defence adopts the technique of neutralisation, using second person verbs to appeal directly to the public, under the heading 'Du savoir en réserve':

> Certains soirs et week-ends, vous releverez des défis et apprendrez sur le terrain. Vous rencontrerez des gens intéressants. Et en plus, vous serez payé. Faites un choix intelligent. Joignez-vous à la Réserve des communications [...] (*Le Droit*, 1 March 1997).

Large multinational companies like Bayer only need to feature their company name and logo to be instantly recognisable, and to have immediate impact, so it is often unnecessary to specify exactly what they require in large letters in a heading that includes the job title. One of their advertisements features in large letters, in the style of a mission statement, the sentences: 'On peut. Et on agit.'[61] It is not until the second paragraph that the small print specifies what the company is actually looking for: 'chefs de file des ventes'. The rest of the advertisement is formulated using masculine generics, so that one may not conclude that either avoidance of specification of title or use of neutral formulations indicates a desire to feminise; their use may simply coincide with a particular marketing strategy.

Conclusion

In France, the debate on feminisation is ongoing, with only very sporadic use of feminised professional titles. There are, however, some signs of change, one of which is the lead given by government ministers in their adoption of the title 'la ministre'. The appearance of an article in the journal *Défense de la langue française* supporting the use of 'la ministre'

61   *La Presse*, 2 May 1998.

is evidence that even in traditionally conservative contexts the issues are at least being voiced and debated.[62]

Implementation of feminisation is well advanced in Francophone Canada. The data from Canadian newspapers shows that feminised employment advertisements are commonplace, though there is widespread variation in how feminisation is actually realised. Some examples display more than one form in use, indicating a change in progress, with the final form not yet fixed. Usage will eventually determine which of the forms becomes established. The most significant departure from the OLF guidelines is the pervasiveness of truncation, in various forms. This is likely to be the result of space – and consequently cost – saving, given the text type. The data does not support the argument that feminisation makes texts less readable. There are many examples of advertisements that utilise the full range of possibilities, and that are clear and to the point. Much use is made of the neutralising devices recommended by the OLF. Jean-Claude Rondeau (then President of the OLF) is keen to point out in his preface to the OLF guide, in a non-directive way, that 'la féminisation des textes demeure toujours facultative.'[63] Notwithstanding the OLF's broadly facilitative rather than authoritarian role, the Office certainly gives a strong lead on feminisation of both titles and texts in all examples of its own advertisements in the corpus.

It is abundantly clear that the French language does possess all the necessary morphological and syntactic resources to implement feminisation. There is no reason why the addition of forms that were previously lacking should not be considered an enrichment of the lexis of French, the result of a natural linguistic process following on the need to express new realities. Many feminised forms have passed almost unobtrusively into usage in Canada and elsewhere, with the result that, according to Patricia Niedzwiecki, '[elles] dérangent si peu que l'on s'en aperçoit à peine, tant elles apparaissent, en réalité, naturelles.'[64] The time seems to

62 Paul Teyssier, 'Madame *la* Ministre?', *Défense de la Langue Française*, 187, January–February–March 1998, pp. 22–5. The editors of the journal are careful to point out nonetheless that 'en règle générale, les articles de cette revue n'engagent que leur auteur' (p. 22).

63 OLF, *Au féminin: guide de féminisation des titres de fonction et de textes*, p. 5.

64 Patricia Niedzwiecki, *Au féminin! Code de féminisation à l'usage de la francophonie* (Paris: Éditions A.-G. Nizet, 1994), note de l'auteure.

have come when it is possible, in the words of the Secrétariat d'Éat du Canada, to:

> offrir aux femmes la possibilité de dire, d'exprimer et d'être nommées suivant leur sexe. Jusqu'à maintenant, la langue française s'est montrée peu empressée à donner à la femme une plus grande visibilité. Le français possède cependant les ressources nécessaires pour effectuer les changements qui s'imposent. Sans rien sacrifier à l'accessibilité et à la lisibilité des textes, il est possible, en respectant certaines règles, de donner aux femmes la place qui leur revient. Tout est affaire de bons sens et de bon vouloir.[65]

In his introduction to *Au feminin!* by Patricia Niedzwiecki, the then Président de l'Assemblée de la Commission communautaire française de Belgique, Serge Moureaux, refers to the dynamic nature of language and the inevitability of language change in the following terms: 'Souvenons-nous qu'une langue qui n'évolue plus, se fige d'abord, pour mourir ensuite.'[66]. It would indeed be very ironic if those who charge themselves with the task of preserving the French language in a 'pure' state (thereby opposing any attempt at feminisation) were to contribute ultimately to its fossilisation.

On balance, the forces of 'la francophonie', at least in Europe and Canada, seem to be lined up in this debate on the opposite side from mainland France. For example, forms like 'la ministre', 'la doyenne' or 'la députée' used in both written or oral contexts have become so well established that they scarcely provoke comment in Canada. The existence of institutional policies in universities, companies and elsewhere is also significant. Despite pockets of resistance, the case seems to have been proven. In linguistic terms, it would be impossible to turn back the clock to the situation pre-1970. One could legitimately argue that these linguistic changes are a mark of vibrancy and regeneration in Canadian French, in particular Quebec French. The fact that this challenge has been embraced and the process largely brought to fruition shows that the French language is more than capable of representing the changing social realities of the beginning of the twenty-first century. Such a sign of life should indeed counteract exaggerated rumours of its demise.

---

65   Secrétariat d'État du Canada, p. 1.
66   Serge Moureaux, 'Avant-propos', in Niedzwiecki.

MAEVE CONRICK

French in the Americas

The history of French in the Americas may be traced back to the arrival of Jacques Cartier on the shores of the Saint Lawrence in 1534. It was not until a century later that the French language became established in Quebec and Acadia (the present day Nova Scotia, New Brunswick and Prince Edward Island). By far the greatest concentration of Francophones in the Americas is still to be found in Canada, where the Francophone population has reached 6.7 million (or 23.5% of the total population), according to the most recent census in 1996.[1] The number of people in Canada as a whole with French as mother tongue continues to increase: in 1996 it was up 2% from 1991 and 16% from 1971. However, Francophones are a minority in terms of the overall population of Canada, which numbers 17.1 million (or 59.8%) English-speakers. In addition to this, the fact that Canada's nearest neighbour is the United States, with its overwhelmingly Anglophone population, means that the Francophone population is geographically (and some would say ideologically) surrounded by an Anglophone culture. This situation has led to a marked defensiveness on the part of Francophones in Canada and especially in Quebec, where 86% of the country's Francophones are concentrated. Many Quebecers see themselves as the standard bearers of French tradition, culture and identity in America, and language has become one of the linchpins of this identity, and often the defining feature. Consequently, it is almost impossible to separate the linguistic from the political.

Canada, more particularly Quebec, is the most significant Francophone presence in the Americas, not only because of its superiority in terms of numbers of speakers, but also in view of the significant role that Quebec has played on the international Francophone stage. French is

---

1 Unless otherwise stated, these and other statistics quoted subsequently are based on information from the Census 1996, available on the Statistics Canada website at www.statcan.ca.

also present in many other parts of the Americas, in the overseas French Departments of Guadeloupe, Martinique and French Guyana, and the 'collectivité territoriale' of St-Pierre-et-Miquelon, as well as in Haiti, St Lucia, Dominica and the USA. This chapter analyses the current situation of French in the Americas, taking as its starting point the position of French in Canada, especially Quebec.

The Situation of French in Canada

French settlement in Canada took place particularly during the seventeenth century. Most emigrants to Acadia originated in the Haut-Poitou region of Western France. The linguistic homogeneity of these emigrants explains the present-day existence of many traits that are characteristic of Poitou in the speech patterns of their descendants.[2] Emigrants to Quebec came from a wider number of regions, including Normandy, Maine and the Île de France and, consequently, Quebec French does not display the same level of linguistic homogeneity. It would be beyond the scope of this chapter to provide a detailed description of the historical origins and development of French in the Americas;[3] suffice to say that the history of French in Canada is intimately linked to the changing political situation. Probably the most significant political event was the Treaty of Paris of 1763, whereby France ceded 'La Nouvelle France', as

2   Henriette Walter, *Le français d'ici, de là, de là-bas* (Paris: JC Lattès, 1998), points out that the present-day Francophone population of Acadia is descended from only about 89 families who emigrated there during the first half of the seventeenth century (p. 214). René Guindon and Pierre Poulin, *Francophones in Canada: A Community of Interests*, New Canadian Perspectives Series (Canada: Canadian Heritage, 1996), also discuss the ancestral origins of French Canadians and give examples of two large families, the LeBlancs in Acadia, who derive from one ancestor, and the Gagnons in Quebec, who derive from three brothers and a cousin (pp. 4–10).

3   There are many sources of historical descriptions of French in Canada. See for example Albert Valdman, *Le français hors de France* (Paris: Éditions Honoré, 1979), and Henriette Walter.

the colony was then called, to England. This treaty meant that English became the official language. Another important event from the point of view of the spread of French in North America was the deportation of rebellious Acadians in 1755, which is referred to as 'Le Grand Dérangement' and was a result of the Treaty of Utrecht, which had ceded Acadia to England in 1713.[4] Some of the Acadians found refuge and settled in Louisiana, where they were called 'Cajuns', a form of the French word 'Acadiens'. Even brief historical references provide ample evidence to prove that conflict with regard to language issues is not a recent phenomenon, but one that dates back many centuries. In Canada, these issues have been addressed at the level of the Federal Government of Canada, and also at the provincial level, especially in Quebec. Present-day Canada is a federal democracy of provinces and territories with a population of over 28.5 million. It has two official languages, English and French, which together constitute the mother tongues of 83.3% of the total population (see Table 1).[5] Of the non-official languages (spoken as first languages by 16.6% of the population), the most important is Chinese (2.6%), followed by Italian, German and Spanish.[6]

Date	English	French	Non-official language
1971	60.1%	26.9%	13.0%
1996	59.8%	23.5%	16.6%

Source: Census of Canada, Statistics Canada

Table 1:   Canada by Mother Tongue.

4   See, for example, Vincent Lucci, *Phonologie de l'Acadien* (Montreal: Didier, 1972), pp. 1–10, for further historical and linguistic background information. The trials and tribulations of the Acadians were immortalised in Longfellow's *Evangeline*.

5   Mother tongue is defined as the first language learned at home in childhood and still understood by the individual at the time of the census.

6   For a list of most predominant non-official languages as mother tongue and home language figures see *Canada Year Book 1999* (Canada: Statistics Canada, 1998), pp. 99–100). The list varies in the home language category, giving in order, Chinese, Italian and Punjabi.

French in Canada: The Legislative Framework

Language legislation in Canada emanates from both federal and provincial sources. One of the most significant Canadian federal initiatives of the 1960s was The Royal Commission on Bilingualism and Biculturalism, which was set up in 1963.[7] Its remit was to:

> inquire into and report upon the existing state of bilingualism and biculturalism in Canada and to recommend what steps should be taken to develop the Canadian Confederation on the basis of an equal partnership between the two founding races, taking into account the contribution made by other ethnic groups to the enrichment of Canada [...].[8]

The Federal Government's reaction was to pass the first Official Languages Act (1969), which, *inter alia*, established English and French as the official languages of Canada and imposed duties on federal institutions to provide services in both languages. The Act also created the post of Commissioner of Official Languages, with a remit akin to that of an ombudsperson for official languages, with powers to investigate complaints regarding the implementation of the Act.

At the Provincial level, in 1969 the Quebec Government adopted Bill 63, Loi pour promouvoir la langue française au Québec. This Bill included provisions, such as making the teaching of French obligatory in English-speaking schools and redefining the remit of the Office de la langue française, which had been established in 1961. Other legislative initiatives followed. Quebec adopted its own Loi sur la langue officielle (Bill 22) in 1974, making French the official language of Quebec and

7 See Barbara Burnaby, 'Language Policies in Canada', in Michael Herriman and Barbara Burnaby (eds), *Language Policy in English-dominant Countries: Six Case Studies* (Cleveden: Multilingual Matters, 1996); Stacy Churchill, *Official Languages in Canada: Changing the Linguistic Landscape* (Canada: Canadian Heritage, 1998); Michael O'Keefe, *Francophone Minorities: Assimilation and Community Vitality* (Canada: Canadian Heritage, 1998).

8 *Royal Commission on Bilingualism and Biculturalism*, 1967, p. 173. Cited in Burnaby, p. 163.

introducing measures imposing the use of French in public advertisements. This was followed by the very significant and controversial Bill 101, Charte de la langue française,[9] which was proposed by the Parti Québécois government of René Lévesque and adopted by the Assemblée nationale of Quebec in 1977. Its stated objectives were:

> faire du français la langue de l'État et de la Loi aussi bien que la langue normale et habituelle du travail, de l'enseignement, des communications, du commerce et des affaires.[10]

Bill 101 marked a turning point in the official promotion of monolingualism in Quebec, stressing the priority of French in key institutions.[11] It was thus a significant declaration of intent with regard to assuring the position and development of French in the province. It also created mechanisms for overseeing the application of the law, namely the Conseil de la langue française (CLF) and the Commission de surveillance de la langue française (from 1983 the Commission de protection de la langue française [CPLF]), and further defined the role of the Office de la langue française (OLF). The remit of these organisations is defined as follows:

> Un Office de la langue française est institué pour définir et conduire la politique québécoise en matière de recherche linguistique et de terminologie et pour veiller à ce que le français devienne, le plus tôt possible, la langue des communications, du travail, du commerce et des affaires dans l'Administration et les entreprises.[12]

> Un Conseil de la langue française est institué pour conseiller le ministre sur la politique québécoise de la langue française et sur toute question relative à l'interprétation et à l'application de la […] loi.[13]

---

9 See *Canada. Patrimoine canadien* (Department of Justice Canada: 1998), pp. 367–420, for the full text of the Charter.
10 *Canada. Patrimoine canadien*, p. 367. An English translation is available in *Canada. Canadian Heritage* (Department of Justice Canada, 1998), p. 385.
11 Bill 101 was substantially modified by Bill 57 (1983), Bill 178 (1988), Bill 86 (1993) and Bill 40 (1997).
12 *Canada. Patrimoine canadien*, p. 395.
13 *Canada. Patrimoine canadien*, p. 412.

[Une] Commission de protection de la langue française [est] chargée d'assurer le respect de la [...] loi.[14]

The enforcement role of the CPLF includes the levying of fines and the granting of temporary exemptions from some of the provisions of the Bill. For example, in 1999 a total of 44 fines were imposed ranging from $50 to $1000. In 2000 44 fines had been imposed by the middle of July, and temporary exemptions until various dates in 2000 and 2001 were in force under Articles 151 and 153 in respect of 16 companies.[15]

The Constitution Act of 1982, incorporating the Canadian Charter of Rights and Freedoms, had major implications for Quebec, rendering some of the provisions of its linguistic legislation unconstitutional. The Act gave constitutional status to the position of English and French as official languages, as well as guaranteeing minority language education rights to speakers of French or English, as the case may be, in provinces in which they constituted a minority.[16] Section 23 of the Canadian Charter, Minority Language Educational Rights, states that:

(1) Citizens of Canada a) whose first language learned and still understood is that of the English or French linguistic minority population of the province in which they reside or, b) who have received their primary school instruction in Canada in English or French and reside in a province where the language in which they received that instruction is the language of the English or French linguistic minority population of the province, have the right to have their children receive primary and secondary instruction in that language in that province. (2) Citizens of Canada of whom any child has received or is receiving primary or secondary instruction

14 *Canada. Patrimoine canadien*, p. 408. The roles and mandates of these organisations have not remained static. For example, the Commission de protection de la langue française was abolished by Bill 86 in 1993 and reinstated by Bill 40 in 1997. See Gaston Cholette, *L'action internationale du Québec en matière linguistique: coopération avec la France et la francophonie de 1961 à 1995* (Quebec: Les Presses de l'Université Laval, 1997), and the OLF website for further details. There is also a fourth Commission, La Commission de toponymie, whose role is to advise on place names.
15 Details of all fines and exemptions are listed on the CPLF website. Companies holding temporary exemptions include Adidas, Les Brasseries Molson, Nike Canada and Russell Stover Candies Inc.
16 In Canada, the term 'minority language' refers *only* to English or French where they are spoken by a minority in a particular province. Consequently, it does not refer to languages spoken by other minority communities.

in English or French in Canada, have the right to have all their children receive primary and secondary school instruction in the same language.[17]

Another significant federal measure was the passing of The Official Languages Act 1988, which replaced the 1969 Act, taking into account the various developments since its enactment, especially those resulting from the Canadian Charter of Rights and Freedoms of 1982. In Section 41, the Government of Canada committed itself to:

a)   enhancing the vitality of the English and French linguistic minority communities in Canada and supporting and assisting their development; and
b)   fostering the full recognition and use of both English and French in Canadian society.[18]

Despite the provisions of the various legislative measures, the reality falls somewhat short of the ideal picture that one might gain from the sentiments and aspirations contained in federal legislation. In practice, in Canada, though bilingualism has increased, it is still true that the vast majority of French speakers are located in Quebec (86% according to the 1996 Census) and that Quebec is the most bilingual province. Also, more than three-quarters of Francophones outside Quebec live in the neighbouring provinces of New Brunswick and Ontario (76%). As a result, the vast majority of the Francophone population is solidly concentrated in the eastern provinces. This situation is confirmed by the statistical data collected by the census of population and published by Statistics Canada.

17   See The Canadian Charter of Rights and Freedoms, Sections 16–22, Official Languages of Canada, and Section 23, Minority Language Educational Rights. These rights are tempered by Section 3, which states: 'The right of citizens of Canada under subsections (1) and (2) to have their children receive primary and secondary school instruction in the language of the English or French linguistic minority population of a province a) applies wherever in the province the number of children of citizens who have such a right is sufficient to warrant the provision to them out of public funds of minority language instruction; and b) includes, where the number of those children so warrants, the right to have them receive that instruction in minority language educational facilities provided out of public funds.'
18   See O'Keefe, pp. 57–9, for the texts of the Official Languages of Canada sections (16–22) of the Canadian Charter of Rights and Freedoms and Part VII, Sections 41–44 of the Official Languages Act (1998).

The Current Linguistic Situation in Canada

Language Data in the Census

It is relatively unusual for countries to ask for data on language in their census forms. Even those that do usually ask for only very rudimentary information. The Canadian census makes available a wealth of information on the linguistic situation in Canada, providing data in three major categories: Mother Tongue, Home Language and Knowledge of Official Languages. Home language is defined as the language spoken most often at home by the individual at the time of the census. Knowledge of official languages refers to the ability to conduct a conversation in one or both languages.

On the basis of the most recent Census in 1996, one of the major changes highlighted by Statistics Canada is that, though the numbers of people speaking both English and French as their mother tongues increased, the proportion of the total population they represent had declined (see Table 1). Accordingly, the proportion of people with a mother tongue other than English or French increased from 13% in 1971 to nearly 17% in 1996 (4.7 million). This change is attributed to two factors: the number of immigrants, as well as the proportion of immigrants with a mother tongue other than English or French, trends steadily sustained up to and during the 1990s. Overall, the numbers paint a picture of an increasingly multilingual country. The situation in Quebec is of particular interest, given the political upheavals and language planning measures of the last few decades.

Census Data for Quebec

Mother Tongue

The Census data for Quebec over the last 25-year cycle reveals overall increases in both the numbers and percentages of Francophones (see Table 2). Another very striking feature is the fact that the percentage of allophones (speakers of non-official languages) has overtaken that of

Date	French	English	Non-official language
1971	80.7%	13.1%	6.2%
1996	81.5%	8.8%	9.7%

Source: Census of Canada, Statistics Canada

Table 2:   Quebec, Mother Tongue.

Anglophones, in stark contrast to the position in 1971, when there were more than twice as many Anglophones as allophones.

Home Language

The percentage of those with French as home language increased in Quebec between 1971 and 1996 from 80.8% to 82.8%, while the numbers with English as home language declined from 14.7% to 10.8% (see Table 3). The 'Home Language' statistics give a more accurate[19] account of the linguistic picture than the 'mother tongue' category, since it illustrates

Date	French	English	Non-official language
1971	80.8%	14.7%	4.5%
1996	82.8%	10.8%	6.4%

Source: Census of Canada, Statistics Canada.

Table 3:   Quebec, Home Language.

shifts from the mother tongue, which are significant, especially in the case of immigrants. The percentages point to a language shift towards French, with net gains of 39% among French-speakers. Consequently, according to Statistics Canada:

> French is becoming more attractive to allophones. Among those who did shift to either English or French, an increasing proportion were shifting to French: 39% in 1996, compared with 37% in 1991 and 29% in 1971.

19   See Churchill, p. 8, for a discussion of the limitations of classification by mother tongue.

These figures point to a measure of success of the linguistic policies adopted by Quebec in order to reverse the process of anglicisation, especially among speakers of non-official languages.

Knowledge of Official Languages

The 1996 Census indicates that English–French bilingualism in Canada is generally on the increase. Seventeen per cent of the population (4.8 million people) could speak both official languages in 1996, as opposed to 13% (2.9 million) in 1971. Quebec is notable as the province with the highest rate of bilingualism, with percentages rising from 27.6% in 1971 to 37.8% in 1996. The next most bilingual provinces are, not surprisingly, New Brunswick, with 33% in 1996 (as compared to 22% in 1971), and Ontario, with 12% in 1996 (as compared to 9% in 1971; see Table 6).

Between 1971 and 1996 there was a remarkable change in the ability of Quebec allophones to speak French. In 1996 69% could speak French, whereas 66% were able to speak English, in contrast to the situation in 1971, when only 47% of allophones could speak French and 69% were able to speak English (Table 4).[20] This reflects the tendency mentioned above of allophones to shift more towards French than previously.

Among the 25 census metropolitan areas in Canada, Montreal has the highest percentage of bilinguals (almost half, 49.7%) followed by Ottawa-Hull (44%). This is not a cause for celebration among *Québécois* intent on promoting French, since a gain in English–French bilingualism means, in effect, an increase in the numbers who can speak English. The

Date	French	English
1971	47%	69%
1996	69%	66%

Source: Census of Canada, Statistics Canada

Table 4:   Quebec, Knowledge of Official Languages, Allophones.

20   For a discussion of the correlation between knowledge of official languages and period of immigration, see Louise Marmen and Jean-Pierre Corbeil, *Languages in Canada: 1996* (Canada: Canadian Heritage and Statistics Canada, 1999), pp. 59–64.

situation of the French language in Montreal has long been the object of concern because of the position of the Communauté urbaine de Montréal (CUM) as the biggest centre of population in Quebec.[21] It is not unusual to see headlines proclaiming that 'Le français recule à Montréal'.[22] What this particular headline fails to mention is that the Anglophone population is also declining and in even greater percentage terms, though not in quite the same numbers as for Francophones (Table 5).

	1981	1996	Variation	%
Francophones	1,055,588	963,870	−91,718	−3.44
Anglophones	474,420	443,195	−31,225	−6.58
Allophones	230,114	342,440	+112,326	+48.90

Sources: *Québec Info*, Spring–Summer 1999; Census of Canada.

Table 5:   Total Population of the Communauté urbaine de Montréal (CUM).

The losses to both official languages are the result of the very significant increase in numbers of the allophone population. The figures also show that 282,420 of the immigrants use their mother tongue – more significantly – as their home language, so that a language shift has not taken place to either of the official languages. Consequently, Montreal is, *de facto*, a highly multilingual community, with all that that implies in terms of language contact. There are many services offered by non-profit organisations like SANQI (Service d'aide aux Néo-québécois et immigrants) in a variety of languages, including Creole, Spanish, Tamil and some African languages, as well as in French and English. SANQI's mission is to 'fournir aux Néo-québécois et immigrants tous services

21   Many sociolinguistic studies have been carried out on Montreal French. See Maeve Conrick, Review of Michelle Daveluy (ed.), *Culture: Canadian Anthropology Society*, XIV: 2, 1994, special issue on the French language in Quebec, in *Journal of French Language Studies*, 8: 2, September, 1998, pp. 259–60, for a review of a collection of important articles emanating from research on Montreal corpora.

22   *Québec Info*, Spring-Summer 1999. The article is based on a demographic analysis by Marc Termote on Statistics Canada data for 1981–1996, reported in *Le Devoir*, 29–30 March 1999.

afin de faciliter leur adaptation et leur intégration à la société québécoise.'[23] Much is made of the policy of integration, which presupposes
the acquisition of French and the ability to use it at least in the public
domain, even if it is not used as frequently in the private domain as a
home language. Since many *Néo-québécois* and immigrants retain their
mother tongue as their home language (as discussed above), this makes
for a situation where different languages are used depending on whether
the context is public or private. It also means, inevitably, that the characteristics of a multilingual society are apparent in the ways in which
languages are spoken, with evidence of phenomena such as code-mix-
ing[24] and code-switching.[25]

French in Canada outside Quebec

The Francophone (French-as-mother-tongue) population in Canada outside Quebec is just under one million. It declined by 0.6% from 976,000
to 970,000 between 1991 and 1996. As noted above, the majority of
Francophones outside Quebec (76%) are found in the eastern provinces
of New Brunswick and Ontario. In 1996 there were about 242,000 Francophones (33.2% of the population) in New Brunswick and about 500,000
in Ontario (4.7% of the population). In both cases there was a drop in the
percentage of Francophones between 1991 and 1996. An interesting fact
is that outside New Brunswick (and Quebec) French is very much in the
minority in all other provinces, with less than 5% of the population.
Even in Ontario, where the numbers of Francophones are relatively large,

23   See the SANQI website: www.info-internet.net/~sanqi/bienvenu.html.
24   'In bilingualism, the transfer of linguistic elements from one language into an-
      other.' William Bright (ed.), *International Encyclopedia of Linguistics*, vol. 3
      (New York and Oxford: Oxford University Press, 1992), p. 284.
25   'The use by a speaker of more than one language, dialect, or variety during a
      conversation, depending on such factors as audience and topic (conversational
      switching); also, the differential use of languages or varieties depending on the
      situation (situational switching).' Bright, p. 284.

the overall proportion of Francophones is still less than 5%. Francophone minorities tend also to be concentrated in particular areas within each province.[26]

The numbers of the population speaking French as home language outside Quebec also declined in the five years from 1991 to 1996, from 637,000 to 619,000. In percentage terms, the proportion of French-as-home-language speakers declined from 4% to 3% in the 25 years from 1971 to 1996. Table 6 shows the situation of French in the provinces and territories of Canada outside Quebec according to the 1996 Census.

Province/ Territory	Mother Tongue	Home Language	English–French Bilingualism
Newfoundland	0.5%	0.2%	3.9%
PEI	4.3%	2.3%	11%
Nova Scotia	4.0%	2.3%	9.3%
New Brunswick	33.2%	30.5%	32.6%
Ontario	4.7%	2.9%	11.6%
Manitoba	4.5%	2.1%	9.4%
Saskatchewan	2.0%	0.6%	5.2%
Alberta	2.1%	0.7%	6.7%
British Columbia	1.5%	0.5%	6.7%
Yukon	3.8%	1.8%	10.5%
NWT	2.2%	1.0%	6.3%

Source: Census of Canada. Statistics Canada.
(Note: PEI = Prince Edward Island; NWT = North West Territories).

Table 6:   French in Canada Outside Quebec, 1996.

These figures confirm the overall position of French as a minority language in all provinces of Canada outside Quebec. Notwithstanding this situation, a number of initiatives are in place pursuant to the status of French as one of the two official languages. These include the Office of the Commissioner of Official Languages and Official Languages Support Programs, one of which is a publishing programme.[27]

26   See O'Keefe, pp. 36-37.
27   See the following websites: http://www.ocol-clo.gc.ca and http://www.pch.gc.ca/offlang/off/French.

Outside the political and legislative contexts there are also many points of contact between the various Francophone groups across Canada. Guindon and Poulin refer to their common ancestral origins:

> Use of the expression 'our little cousins from Quebec' or 'our cousins in the other provinces of Canada' to refer to our fellow French-speaking citizens is thus more than an affectionate turn of phrase. The great majority of Francophones in Canada are in fact united by kinship ties of varying degrees of closeness, which create the feeling of belonging to a 'big family'.[28]

Despite this somewhat idealised view of the situation, relationships between Quebec and Francophones in the rest of Canada have not always been smooth. There has been resentment in some quarters because elements of the political leadership in Quebec have often been seen to plough their own furrow in pursuit of the goal of independence from Canada, thereby appearing to abandon the interests of other Francophones in the rest of Canada and elsewhere in America. Claude Poirier expresses this point of view as follows:

> Occupés à se définir eux-mêmes, les Québécois ont graduellement perdu de vue les autres communautés francophones du continent et ils éprouvent aujourd'hui de la difficulté à percevoir l'identité différente de chacune de ces communautés et à comprendre leurs aspirations.[29]

The status of Acadia is particularly problematic, since the area does not constitute an established political entity, in contrast to Quebec. Louder, Trépanier and Waddell refer to it as 'un territoire imaginaire, donc sans frontières'.[30] Some Francophones in Acadia pursue the objective of giving it some legal status, while others consider the possibility of annexation to Quebec. Since, despite the referenda, the question of the

28 Guindon and Poulin, p. 4.
29 Claude Poirier (co-ordinating editor), with the collaboration of Aurélien Boivin, Cécile Trépanier and Claude Verrault, *Langue, espace, société. Les variétés du français en Amérique du Nord* (Quebec: Les Presses de l'Université Laval, 1994), p. vii.
30 Dean Louder, Cécile Trépanier and Eric Waddell, 'La francophonie nord-américaine. Mise en place et processus de diffusion géographique', in Poirier, pp. 185–200 (p. 194).

sovereignty of Quebec has not yet been resolved to the satisfaction of all parties, any change in the current status of Acadia is unlikely.

Hundreds of organised Francophone groups exist in Canada, and not only in Quebec and Acadia. They include groups of business people, young people, women's groups and seniors. There are municipal associations, such as the Association française des municipalités de l'Ontario (AFMO) and the Manitoba Association of Bilingual Municipalities (MABM). There have also been strong contacts in the sporting arena, for example between the Société des jeux de l'Acadie (SJA), which includes Acadians from New Brunswick, Prince Edward Island and Nova Scotia, and the Société des jeux du Québec and Sport-Québec. Francophones from outside Quebec and Acadia have been included in these games: Guindon and Poulin (1998: 43) report representation from outside these provinces at the 1991 SJA finals and at the Académie internationale de la jeunesse in 1994.[31] There are also numerous cultural and educational links and centres. Among many examples is the Université de Moncton (New Brunswick), which has a Centre d'études acadiennes, a Musée acadien and a Chaire d'études acadiennes, and publishes and distributes the journal *Contact-Acadie*.[32] On the international stage, the choice of New Brunswick as the co-host with Canada, and Moncton, New Brunswick as the venue, for the most recent Sommet de la francophonie (3–5 September 1999) considerably enhanced the profile of Acadia and of Francophone Canada generally.

Status of Canadian French

It is obvious from the review of legislation and the census data presented above that the linguistic situation in Quebec altered significantly in the last four decades of the twentieth century. During that time, Quebec showed a marked desire to assert its Francophone identity, thereby redefining itself in relation to the rest of Canada and indeed the rest of the

31   Guindon and Poulin, p. 43.
32   See its website at http://www.francoidentitaire.ca

world, including France. The fact that language is such a central element
of Quebec's self-definition has meant that matters linguistic have been
the object of great, not to say obsessive, attention in both the public and
private domains.[33] The specific characteristics of its language have come
under the microscope, in particular the issue of what should be the norm
of reference. As a general linguistic rule, the variety of a language that
ultimately becomes the prestige norm is the variety used by the socially
most prestigious group.[34] In the case of Francophone populations outside
France, this is a particularly difficult issue, since Standard (Parisian)
French remains the prestige norm for many Francophones around the
world. The debate about the 'quality' of its French has been ongoing in
Quebec, with widespread disagreement about its relative standing, especially with regard to Standard French. For a long time all local varieties
of French, especially 'joual', were downgraded, not just by people outside Quebec, but, more significantly, by Quebecers themselves. Many
sociolinguistic studies of attitudes to language carried out in the 1960s
provide strong evidence of how negatively Quebecers saw themselves at
that point in their history. Richard Bourhis reports one example that

> [...] using a dialogue refinement of the matched-guise technique, showed that
> French-Canadian listeners rated a French-Canadian speaker to be more intelligent
> and educated when she switched to Standard French than when she maintained
> her Québécois-style French.[35]

As well as sociolinguistic evidence, there is also plenty of anecdotal
evidence of negativity towards the quality of French spoken in Quebec.
In 1968 Pierre Trudeau, then Minister for Justice, described it as 'lousy

---

33   See Chantal Bouchard, *La langue et le nombril. Histoire d'une obsession québéc-
     oise* (Quebec: Fides, 1998), for discussion on the role of language in the construc-
     tion of Quebec identity.
34   See Conrick, 'Norm and standard as models in second language acquisition', in
     Angela Chambers and Dónall P. Ó Baoill (eds), *Intercultural Communication and
     Language Learning* (Dublin: Royal Irish Academy/Irish Association for Applied
     Linguistics, 1999), pp. 175–86, for a discussion of norm and standard in the
     acquisition of French as a second language.
35   Richard Y. Bourhis, 'Language Policies and Language Attitudes: Le Monde de la
     Francophonie', in Nikolas Coupland and Adam Jaworski (eds), *Sociolinguistics:
     A Reader and Coursebook* (London: Macmillan, 1997), pp. 306–22 (p. 318).

French'. He added that the Federal Government in Ottawa should not give more powers to Quebec until it could teach better French in schools, thus explicitly linking language quality and political rights.

In the years since the 1960s there has been fundamental change in how Quebecers see themselves. They have reconstructed their identity, reversing almost entirely the lack of prestige that had been associated previously with speaking French. This evolution was marked linguistically by a change in the title they used to identify themselves from 'Canadiens français' to 'Québécois'. This change carried enormous symbolic weight, indicating that they were no longer defining themselves as a minority within Canada, but as a majority within their own context in Quebec. The result is a new self-confidence and vitality not only culturally and politically, but linguistically as well. In the 1990s sociolinguistic studies[36] showed the greater acceptability of *Québécois* French and a tendency no longer to measure it against Standard French as the norm of reference.[37]

The question of the precise linguistic characteristics of Standard *Québécois* French is still under discussion. The various language bodies provide leadership and guidance on linguistic issues and forms, especially in the lexical area, where the language needs to respond to the challenges that new technologies and new social realities present. In terms of linguistic features, the problem is to strike a balance between mutual comprehensibility by Francophones internationally and the retention of local characteristics. According to Bourhis, the process of standardisation is already well under way:

> [I]t would seem that of all the francophone communities beyond France, Quebec has the demographic and institutional means needed to imbue its own middle-class Québécois-style French with as much prestige as Standard French. In this sense, the emerging strong position of Québécois French relative to Standard French is becoming more similar to the strong position of American English relative to the British Standard [...].[38]

36   See Bourhis for further discussion of changes in attitudes between the 1960s and 1990s.
37   Salien, Jean-Marie, 'Quebec French: Attitudes and Pedagogical Perspectives', *The Modern Language Journal*, 82, 1998, pp. 95–102, disagrees and argues that attitudes to Quebec French are still largely negative.
38   Bourhis, p. 318.

The international standing of Quebec French has also been enhanced by a number of factors, including its role in the international
organisation of 'la francophonie'. In France, the approach that Quebec
has taken to language planning, especially in its legislative framework,
is considered by many to set a worthy example for others, including
France itself. France followed Quebec's lead by passing an amendment
to Article 2 of the French Constitution in 1992, declaring that 'la langue
de la République est le français'.[39] A very significant point was that the
intended wording of the amendment, 'le français est la langue de la
République,' had to be changed due to opposition from language organisations, especially in Quebec, which objected to the proprietorial attitude
to the language that it displayed on the part of France. This is another
indicator of the self-confidence of Quebec in its international status,
ironically in relation to France, which had been its point of reference for
so long and the focus of many of its linguistic insecurities. Quebec is
also admired in France for its resistance to the influx of anglicisms. The
Loi Toubon adopted in France in 1994 covered some of the same ground
as Bill 101 (1977) in Quebec. Another area where Quebec has given an
international lead is its response to the linguistic challenges posed by the
need to expand the representation of women by feminising titles and
forms of address.[40] There has been a certain amount of turning of the
tables with regard to language planning, with France following the lead
of Quebec rather than the other way round, as might have been expected.
It would seem that the status of Quebec as an international player in the
Francophone world is assured.

39   See Lynne Wilcox, 'The Amendment to Article 2 of the Constitution: An Equivocal
      Interpretation of Linguistic Pluralism', in *Modern and Contemporary France*,
      NS2: 3, 1994, pp. 269–78.
40   See Conrick in this volume for a detailed discussion of the feminisation process in
      Canada.

French in the DOM-TOMs

In the overseas French Departments (Départements et territoires d'outre-mer)[41] of Guadeloupe, Martinique and French Guyana[42] and the 'collectivité territoriale' of St-Pierre-et-Miquelon the status of the French language is, of course, that of the official language. These regions are certainly not monolingual: in St-Pierre-et-Miquelon French coexists with English and in the three other cases with a French-based Creole,[43] Lesser Antillean Creole French. Inevitably, situations of diglossia and bilingualism arise from such language contact.

The islands of St-Pierre-et-Miquelon lie off the south coast of Newfoundland, Canada. In 1985 they became a 'collectivité territoriale'.[44] Historically, the origins of its inhabitants are not homogenous, and include Breton and Basque fishermen who settled there during the seventeenth century and Acadian refugees who arrived after 'le Grand Dérangement' of 1755. There were also settlers from Newfoundland, who were originally English-speaking and acquired French.[45] The most recent census conducted in France in 1999 and published by INSEE (Institut National de la Statistique et des Études Économiques) puts the number of inhabitants at 6,316.[46] Contemporary French in St Pierre-et-Miquelon shows evidence of lexical particularities, having an extensive marine

41   General information on the DOM-TOMs is available on the French Government website http://www.outre-mer.gouv.fr.
42   They became French Departments as a result of the Loi du 19 mars 1946.
43   'A creole is a pidgin language which has become the mother tongue of a community.' David Crystal, *The Cambridge Encyclopedia of Language* (Cambridge: Cambridge University Press, 1991), p. 336.
44   The islands changed hands between colonial powers on several occasions, reverting finally to France in 1814 as a result of the Treaty of Paris. They became a TOM in 1946 and a DOM in 1976, before becoming a 'collectivité territoriale' in 1985.
45   See Walter, p. 217.
46   See Jean-Pierre Le Gleau and Donald Castaing, *Le recensement de la population à Saint-Pierre-et-Miquelon* (Paris: INSEE, 2000). Census information for French territories in this and the next two sections is quoted from data published by INSEE.

vocabulary, and it also shows signs of the influence of the Anglophone population in nearby Newfoundland.

The populations of Guadeloupe and Martinique (The French Antilles) are larger, with the 1999 figures standing at 422,496 and 381,427 respectively. These islands were colonised during the seventeenth century by settlers from the west and north of France, and these regions of origin are responsible for an important substratum of the French spoken there today. The linguistic situation on the islands was substantially influenced by the development of Creoles, a consequence of the presence of people who had been forcibly removed from Africa and brought to work on the plantations. In 1979 speakers of Lesser Antillean Creole French were reported to number around 335,000 in Guadeloupe and 325,000 in Martinique. Most people speak Creole as their first language, and the co-existence of French and Creole gives rise to a situation of diglossia, with French as the language of the dominant, prestigious culture as opposed to the dominated Creole. In a sociolinguistic study of French and Creole in Martinique conducted in 1979, Jardel suggested three major types of attitude to these languages in contact:

> Le premier type montre une assimilation à la culture dominante, qui fait que le prestige se mesure encore en termes de francisation ou d'européanisation. Il y a adoption de la langue française et rejet du patois créole appartenant au monde noir dévalorisant. Le deuxième type, au contraire, refuse l'assimilation, refuse le système de valeurs du monde blanc dominant. Cela se traduit par un retour vers le folklore, vers l'Afrique avec affirmation d'une négritude et réhabilitation du créole, élément essentiel de differenciation vis-à-vis de la métropole. Enfin, le troisième type d'attitude cherche à dépasser les oppositions précédentes, en intégrant les apports de l'Afrique, de l'Amérique des Plantations et de la France.[47]

French Guyana, in the north-east of South America between Brazil and Surinam, has a more diverse linguistic and ethnic composition than Guadeloupe and Martinique. It is probably best known internationally for two reasons, firstly the presence of the infamous Devil's Island prison between 1852 and 1945, and secondly the establishment of a rocket-launch site at the Centre national des études spatiales (Cnes) in 1983.

---

47   Jean-Pierre Jardel, 'Français et créole dans le conflit interculturel à la Martinique', in Valdman, pp. 145–63 (p. 159).

The 1999 census shows an increase in population from 114,678 in 1990 to the current level of 157,213, a figure that represents the highest growth in population of any French department. The population has widely diverse origins, including Guyanese Creoles (about 40%), Amerindians[48] (about 3%)and metropolitan French (about 12%). Almost 40% of the population is of Chinese, Lebanese, Brazilian, Haitian or Surinamian origin. Altogether, about ten languages are represented.[49] French Guyanese Creole was reported to have about 50,000 speakers in 1977.[50] Over one third of the population in the capital, Cayenne, speak Creole as their first language, with a much higher percentage in rural areas, and the majority of speakers are bilingual in French to some degree. Accurate and up to date figures are difficult to establish. Creole is not taught in schools, so it remains a vernacular language, with relatively low status.

French in Haiti, St Lucia and Dominica

The political status of Haiti is of a completely different order from that of its neighbours Guadeloupe and Martinique, in that it has been an independent republic since 1804. It had become a French colony in 1697 and retained French as the only official language, used in administration, the courts, education and international relations. For most speakers, French is a second language learned at school, and spoken and read by only about 10% of the population. The vernacular language is Haitian Creole French, which has three main varieties, spoken by all Haitians (around 5,740,000 in 1982).[51] It was given legal and educational status in 1961. The figure for Creole as the only language spoken is as high as 95%.[52]

48 The Amerindian languages are Arawak, Palikúr, Galibi, Wayana, Wayampi and Emerillon.
49 See http://www.sil.org/ethnologue/countries/FreG.html for a full list.
50 Bright, p. 229; Crystal, p. 336.
51 Bright (p. 230) also reports about 112,000 speakers of Haitian Creole French in the Dominican Republic in 1982.
52 See Pradel Pompilus, 'La langue française en Haïti', in Valdman, pp. 119–43, for a description of the linguistic traits of Haitian French.

St Lucia has been an independent state since 1979, having changed hands between France and England on numerous occasions during its history. It has retained an associate membership of the British Commonwealth. It has an estimated population of over 150,000, with about 121,000 speaking Lesser Antillean Creole French and less than 10% understanding Standard French.[53]

Dominica, a member of the British Commonwealth, has a population of about 87,000, of whom about 83,000 speak Lesser Antillean Creole French, and, as in St Lucia, English is the official language. The situation of Standard French is similar to that of St Lucia, since it is understood by no more than 10% of the population. Along with Haiti, St Lucia and Dominica are members of 'La Francophonie', Dominica having been a member since 1979 and St Lucia an associate member since 1981.

French in the USA

The greatest density of French speakers in the USA is to be found in the state of Louisiana, where French is the second official language. French is also present in other parts of the country, mainly in the states of New England,[54] though the geographical distribution of speakers is very scattered. The most recent US Census in 1990 asked the following questions about language:

> Does this person speak a language other than English at home?
> What is this language?
> (For those who speak another language) How well does this person speak English?
> – very well, well, not well, not at all.[55]

53   Bright, p. 230.
54   See Gérard-J. Brault, 'Le français en Nouvelle-Angleterre', in Valdman, pp. 75–91; and Louise Péloquin, 'Une langue doublement dominée: le français en Nouvelle-Angleterre', *Francophonies d'Amérique*, 1, 1991, pp. 133–44.
55   This and other statistical information for the USA is based on data available from the US Census Bureau, whose website may be accessed at: http://www.census.gov/population/www/socdemo/lang_use.html.

United States (total)	230,445,777
English only	198,600,798
Total non-English	31,844,979
Spanish (ranked 1)	17,339,172
French (ranked 2)	1,702,176
Cajun (ranked 49)	33,670

Source: US Bureau of the Census, 1990 Census of Population, CPHL-133.

Table 7:   Language Spoken at Home by Persons 5 Years and Over, United States, 1990.

The amount of information requested (the same questions as were asked in 1980)[56] does not quite match the level of detail of the Canadian census. However, the data does provide some useful information on language use. The top 50 languages other than English are ranked in order of total number of speakers (see Table 7).

As is obvious from the figures in Table 7, French is very much a minority language in the US, very far behind Spanish, which ranks as the number one language other than English with the highest number of speakers.

It is interesting too to look at the statistics for the ability to speak English. These figures show that the vast majority of French speakers also speak English either very well (1,226,043) or well (318,409). The same is true for Cajun speakers, of whom 23,834 speak English very well and 7,577 speak it well. Consequently, the level of bilingualism is very high, as is the level of integration into Anglophone US culture.

The data provided by state gives composite figures for French and Creole, so they are not quite as useful in determining numbers of speakers of the different varieties. However, as a total is given for French including Creoles in the USA (1,930,404), it is possible to determine the total number of Creole speakers by subtracting the numbers for French and Cajun listed in Table 7, thus arriving at a figure of 194,558. The 15 states with the highest numbers of speakers of French, including Creoles, are listed in Table 8.

---

56   In earlier censuses questions were about 'mother tongue' or were aimed at particular groups (e.g. those born outside the US).

Louisiana	261,678
New York	236,099
Florida	194,783
California	132,657
Massachusetts	124,973
Maine	81,012
Texas	64,585
Connecticut	53,586
New Jersey	52,351
New Hampshire	51,284
Ohio	46,075
Pennsylvania	45,515
Illinois	43,070
Virginia	40,353
Maryland	39,484

Source: US Bureau of the Census, 1990 Census of Population, CPHL-96.

Table 8:   French and Creoles Spoken at Home by Persons 5 Years and Over, United States, 1990.

Louisiana

As evidenced in Table 8, Louisiana is the state with the most significant numbers of French speakers. They are to be found in about 26 parishes (counties) of south-western Louisiana.[57] Historically, the French language is part of a long tradition in the state, going back to settlers in the seventeenth and eighteenth centuries. Probably the most significant historical event influencing the linguistic direction of French in Louisiana was 'Le Grand Dérangement', which resulted in an influx of Acadians in the middle of the eighteenth century. In order to distinguish these from the original settlers, they were called 'Cajuns' (from 'Acadiens'). The fortunes of French in the state have been somewhat varied, given the political upheavals that have characterised its history. The Louisiana Purchase of 1803, when Napoleon sold Louisiana to the Americans, meant that the French settlers became American citizens. Following a period of official bilingualism, English became the official language in 1864. Subsequently, various measures were aimed at the assimilation of

57   See Marilyn J. Conwell and Alphonse Juilland, *Louisiana French Grammar* (The Hague: Mouton, 1963), p. 19.

the Cajuns. For example, in 1921 the use of French was banned in schools by the Louisiana State Constitution.

The status of French changed in 1968 with the recognition of French as the second official language and the foundation of CODOFIL (Conseil pour le développement du français en Louisiane), which has been responsible for a cultural revival in recent decades. Its aims are to promote the use of French in Louisiana and to raise awareness of French identity among Cajuns. It is assisted in these objectives by French Government programmes, including the provision of teachers and teacher training. There has also been a significant increase in the amount of French programming on television and radio, partly from France and partly with locally produced programmes in Cajun French or Creole. In New England, CODOFINE (The Council for the Development of French in New England) plays a similar role to that of CODOFIL, though the historical and geographical circumstances are dissimilar.

As well as Standard French, two main varieties are spoken in Louisiana: Acadian/Cajun French (the most dominant) and Louisiana French Creole. The term 'Louisiana French', though it is used frequently, is rather ambiguous, in that it is sometimes used to refer to Acadian/Cajun French[58] and at other times to refer to Standard French as spoken in Louisiana.[59] It is also difficult to establish numbers of speakers of different varieties, with estimates varying widely from one source to another. The census data, as discussed above, is not sufficiently detailed. In 1990 CODOFIL carried out a survey, which found that 58% of Francophones spoke Cajun French, 33% Standard French and 9% Creole French.

It is difficult not to be rather pessimistic about the chances of survival for French in Louisiana and the USA in general, despite the gallant efforts of the various organisations that exist to promote it. The effects of the omnipresence of the Anglophone world are even more evident in the USA than they are in Canada, where the existence of a majority French province, Quebec, is a distinct advantage in the survival stakes. The diversity of forms and varieties in Louisiana also presents problems, as does the fact that French is primarily a spoken language, with low literacy levels. The 1990 CODOFIL survey referred to above suggests that 34.3%

58   Conwell and Juilland.
59   Hosea Phillips, 'Le français de la Louisiane', in Valdman, pp. 95–110.

of Francophones could read French, but only 8.4% could read it fluently. Other reports suggest that the numbers are very much lower.[60]

Conclusion

The French presence in the Americas goes back to the sixteenth century, though its fortunes have waxed and waned during the ensuing centuries. The future of French in the Americas is very much linked to the future of Quebec as the largest Francophone centre on the continent. If French is to survive in the Americas, it must survive in Quebec. Outside Canada, the future of French is very uncertain. Obviously, the status of French as the official language in the DOM-TOMs assures its continuing presence, as long as their status as an integral part of the French Republic is maintained. In these and other areas in the Americas the linguistic situation is complicated by the presence of French-based Creoles spoken as first languages, and low levels of literacy. Attempts to consider the future of French inevitably raise the question of which variety of French is under discussion. The picture is very different, depending on whether the object of discussion is Standard French, the metropolitan norm, or the Creole languages historically linked with French.

The future of French in Quebec seems assured, despite the concerns that continue to be expressed by *Québécois*. The evidence shows that its position is strong, and that the various language planning measures undertaken by the Quebec Government have largely succeeded in ensuring the viability of a Francophone community in a majority Anglophone state on the American continent. The census data shows growth in the numbers of Francophones and, more significantly, an increasing shift towards French among immigrants to Quebec. The situation is not so positive in other Francophone areas in Canada, where Francophones are

60   Eleven years earlier Phillips's estimate was much less encouraging: 'La plupart des francophones de la Louisiane ne savent que parler le français; bien entendu, ils comprennent le français parlé. Il y a sans doute quelques centaines de personnes qui savent le lire. Le petit nombre qui savent l'écrire ne le font, malheureusement, qu'à l'occasion.' Phillips, p. 105.

very much in the minority. There is an increasing concentration of Francophones in Quebec. While this strengthens the situation of French in Quebec, the unfortunate corollary is that it diminishes its position elsewhere. Quebec continues to demonstrate its strength as a cultural, political and economic force, a point of reference for all Francophones in the Americas, with the French language – its own emerging Quebec Standard – as its central defining feature. Of the three original French colonies (Quebec, Acadia and Louisiana) it is the one that has managed to retain its Francophone identity most successfully, since French is represented not only in the private domain, but also, more importantly, in public life. Louder, Trépanier and Waddell emphasise the central role of Quebec and sum up the presence of French in the Americas as follows:

> Trois anciennes colonies d'une France démissionnaire, précocement transformées en solides foyers américains, qui ont vu à travers les soubresauts de leur histoire une partie de leur population partir vers un ailleurs. Comme des araignées qui ont tissé leur toile, ces foyers et leurs diasporas constituent aujourd'hui la toile de fond sur laquelle se trame le destin d'une Amérique française contemporaine – un vaste archipel au centre duquel se situe la grosse île du Québec entourée d'une poussière d' îlots essaimés aux quatre vents, chacun ayant son identité propre.[61]

61 Louder, Trépanier and Waddell, p. 200.

PETER BROWN, CHANTAL CROZET, TONY LIDDICOAT AND LOUISE
MAURER

French in Australia: Policies and Practices

Australia has been very active in its development of language policy
documents, with numerous reports and policy statements appearing almost on an annual basis since the first official languages policy was
adopted in 1987. While none of the policies deals explicitly with French,
the place of French in Australian education can be ascertained by examining these documents. In order to understand the place of French
(and of languages in general) in Australian education, it is necessary to
examine some of the history that led to the development of the nation's
first languages' policy.

An examination of early government documents relating to education shows a rather suspicious view of languages, and from about 1870,
when the colonial governments began to involve themselves in education,
the main emphasis appears to have been placed on restricting their study.[1]
Within this context, French fared quite well. Having transported its
prestige in Britain to the Australian colonies, French was one of the most
widely taught of the small number of languages available in nineteenth-
century Australia, with Latin and German also having a strong presence.

The restrictions on languages in the public domain were continued
and strengthened during the period following the First World War. Limitations placed on the use of foreign languages in the press during wartime
persisted long after 1918 and, in some cases, survived until the 1970s,
with even 'community' languages being required to submit an English
translation of their local newspapers. At the same time, study of languages was usually compulsory for at least part of secondary education

---

1   Michael Clyne, 'Australia's Language Policies: Are We Going Backwards?', in
    A. J. Liddicoat (ed.), *Language Planning and Language Policy in Australia* (Mel-
    bourne: Applied Linguistics Association of Australia, 1991); A. J. Liddicoat, 'The
    Narrowing Focus – Australia's Changing Language Policy', *Babel*, 31(1), 1996.

(High School). In the largest State, New South Wales, for instance, High Schools were categorised as two-language, one-language and no-language schools.[2] Thus, while languages may have had a severely limited place in the life of the Australian community, language study retained its position in academic education during the interwar period, with French as the most widely taught language.

While languages continued as school subjects during this period, the general restrictions placed on language use in society seem to have had an impact on the perception of languages in Australia. Language teaching was not typically conceived in terms of a need to use the language. Australia was distant, both geographically and culturally, from Europe, and the use of languages other than English was limited within Australia. Language learning in this context becomes primarily an academic exercise, with an emphasis on the written language and little general perception of a need to use languages for communication.

This scepticism about languages moved to more direct antagonism in the 1960s following the release of the Wyndham Report,[3] which examined the changing nature of secondary education in New South Wales. It argued that previous models of education had been designed for the cultivation of an élite and were no longer appropriate for the educational needs of the 1950s and beyond. Languages in particular were strongly associated with this élitism in the report and suffered in the restructuring of the education system. Languages are not included in Wyndham's formulations of what constituted a 'general education' and they were no longer considered part of the compulsory core curriculum. Languages were not even included as areas that would need specialist teachers in some parts of Wyndham's proposal.[4]

An immediate impact of the restructuring undertaken in response to the Wyndham Report was a gradual increase in the range of languages offered, as more languages spoken by immigrant groups were introduced

2   K. Croft and R. MacPherson, 'The Evolution of Languages Administrative Policies in New South Wales: 1962–1979', *Australian Review of Applied Linguistics*, 14(1).
3   H. Wyndham, *Report of the Committee Appointed to Survey Education in New South Wales* (Sydney: Government Printer, 1957).
4   Croft and MacPherson, 'The Evolution of Languages Administrative Policies in New South Wales: 1962–1979'.

into schools. These languages were perceived as less élitist and more practical than the languages that had been taught previously, such as French. Accordingly, this increase in the range of languages was accompanied by a decline in the study of the 'traditional' languages: French and German. According to Croft and MacPherson,[5] the number of students sitting the Higher School Certificate[6] examinations in French dropped immediately from 31% of all candidates in 1967 (the last cohort under the 'traditional' model) to 26% in 1968 (the first cohort under the new system). By the 1970s, however, French was not the only language to have suffered, with overall numbers of students studying languages beginning to decline.

While the Wyndham Report dealt only with education in New South Wales, the perceptions of education it represented influenced educational planning in all the other States, with similar results around the country. By the early 1980s commentators were beginning to signal serious problems for language teaching in Australia due to the extent of the decline in enrolment for language courses.[7] In 1967 47% of candidates for final secondary examinations in Australia sat a language examination,[8] while by 1988 this number had dropped to only about 8%.[9] It should be noted that French remained the most widely studied language in Australia throughout this period of decline, although it was to be overtaken by Japanese in the 1990s.

The marked reduction in language students, accompanied by pressure from ethnic communities and language professionals, as well as the official adoption of multiculturalism as the basis of the country's social policy, led to a perception that a national languages policy was needed in Australia. In response, the Senate Standing Committee for Education

5   Croft and MacPherson, 'The Evolution of Languages Administrative Policies in New South Wales: 1962–1979'.
6   The Higher School Certificate is an external examination taken in the final year of secondary school (High School).The terminology for this examination varies around Australia.
7   T. Quinn, 'A National Language Policy', *Babel*, 14(1), 1982.
8   O. Wykes and M. King, *Teaching Foreign Languages in Australia* (Melbourne: ACER, 1968).
9   Australian Federal Ministry of Education, 1989.

and the Arts prepared a report on language policy needs. This report[10] presented a very ambitious programme for policymaking, but failed to make an impact on actual government policy, probably because of its wide scope and 106 separate recommendations.

In 1987 a more focused report[11] was adopted as Australia's official language policy as the National Policy on Languages (NPL). The NPL covered four broad language objectives: English; Languages Other Than English (LOTEs); indigenous languages; and language services. It is the second of these objectives that most closely concerns French. The policy made general recommendations about language programmes and the delivery of language teaching with the aim of promoting the learning of a wide range of languages in Australia. However, it singled out nine 'languages of wider teaching' that merited special attention, one of which was French. These were languages that were expected to develop significantly within the Australian educational context. As such, French continues to hold a significant place among languages in education.

The NPL presented four basic justifications for learning languages in Australia:

(1) equity: competence in a range of languages is needed to ensure service provision and access in a multicultural and multilingual society;
(2) economics: Australia needs language skills to compete in global markets;
(3) enrichment: language study is an important part of cognitive, social and cultural development; and
(4) external uses: Australia needs languages to communicate with the rest of the world.

In this context, the significance of French in Australia lies in the last two of these justifications: the traditional justification of language study as an end in itself by providing access to other cultures and the acknowledgement of French as an important language in the international arena, especially in diplomacy. French is not perceived in Australia as

10   *A National Policy on Languages* (Canberra: Australian Government Publishing Service, 1984).
11   Jo Lo Bianco, *National Policy on Languages* (Canberra: Australian Government Publishing Service, 1987).

being necessary to ensure equity, nor is it considered to be an important trade language (though Stanley *et al.*[12] and Lo Bianco and Monteil[13] argue that France is in fact an important trade partner for Australia). While the NPL presented all four justifications as being of equal merit, the first two emerged as the most important.

The National Policy on Languages was reviewed in 1990 and re-placed in 1991 with the Australian Language and Literacy Policy (ALLP).[14] This change of policy after only a few years is indicative of the volatility of language policy in contemporary Australia. The new policy placed an increased emphasis on English and English-language literacy, with a corresponding reduction in emphasis on the other areas of language covered by the NPL. The ALLP reduced the goals for second-language learning from the NPL's rather slogan-like 'A second language for all' to the more bureaucratic: 'The learning of languages other than English must be substantially expanded and improved to enhance educational outcomes and communication both within and outside Australia.'

The ALLP set a target of 25% of all students in the final year of secondary school taking languages and provided funding for this. The funding arrangements were quite interesting. The ALLP established 14 'priority languages', and the Commonwealth government then required each State and Territory government to choose eight languages from the list of 14. Students taking the eight languages designated would attract funding for the relevant State/Territory education system. The end result was a three-tiered system in which some languages gained the symbolic support of the government and were funded, others received only sym-bolic recognition and others were denied both recognition and funding.[15]

12   J. Stanley, D. Ingram and G. Chittick, *The Relationship Between International Trade and Linguistic Competence* (Canberra: Australian Government Publishing Service, 1990).

13   Jo Lo Bianco and Alain Monteil, *French in Australia: New Prospects* (Canberra: CNP Publications, 1990).

14   Department of Employment, Education and Training (DEET), *Australia's Language: A National Language and Literacy Policy for the 1990s* (Canberra: Australian Government Publishing Service, 1991).

15   A. J. Liddicoat, 'Bilingualism: An Introduction', in A. J. Liddicoat (ed.) *Bilingualism and Bilingual Education* (Melbourne: The National Languages and Literacy Institute of Australia [NLLIA], 1991).

French, because of its large candidature, was selected by all states and territories as a priority language and so is firmly located in the first tier.

Another feature of the ALLP is the pre-eminence it gives to economic justifications for language learning.[16] While the cultural prestige of French helped maintain its position in the pantheon of languages, the perceived marginality of France as a trading partner seriously weakened the status of the language in comparison to its closest rival, Japanese. Japanese had come to be perceived as the economic language *par excellence* in Australian rhetoric about language learning. The inability of French, or indeed any European language, to establish a presence in the discourse about language as a significant language of trade was to have important consequences for later developments in language policy. At the level of student numbers, the weakening status of French can be seen from the fact that, since the publication of the ALLP, Japanese has occasionally replaced French as the most widely taught language in Australia.[17]

In 1994 the Council of Australian Governments (COAG) published a new policy document[18] that was designed to stand alongside the language learning provisions of the ALLP. This new document had only two foci: economic justifications for language learning and Asian languages. This new policy sought to change the balance in language programmes that hitherto had been weighted more towards European than Asian languages. The new policy designated four languages, Japanese, Chinese, Indonesian and Korean, as priority languages for education in Australia and set a target of 15% of year 12 students and 60% of year 10 students learning one of the designated languages by 2006. Under this new policy, French has become increasingly marginalised in policy terms.

16   Liddicoat, 'The Narrowing Focus – Australia's Changing Language Policy'.
17   N. Bramley and N. Hanamura, 'The Teaching and Learning of Japanese in Australian Universities: An Overview', in N. Bramley and N. Hanamura (eds), *Issues in the Teaching and Learning of Japanese* (Canberra: Australian Association of Applied Linguistics [ALAA], 1998); H. Marriott, J. V. Neustupny and R. Spence-Brown, *Unlocking Australia's Language Potential: Profiles of 9 Key Languages in Australia: Japanese* (Melbourne: National Languages and Literacy Institute of Australia, 1992).
18   Council of Australian Governments (COAG), *Asian Languages and Australia's Economic Development* (Canberra: Australian Government Publishing Press,1994).

It is now the most important language in the 'Miscellaneous' category and has to compete strenuously to preserve its place as the most widely taught language in Australia. The fall of French from the pre-eminent position it held until the 1980s appears to be essentially tied to the shift in focus of Australia's language policy towards economic objectives[19] and the inability of France to establish itself as an important economic partner in a discourse that has concentrated increasingly on Asia.[20]

Yet despite this, at the primary and secondary school level, French has been associated with some of the most innovative language, indeed educational, programmes in the country, through its place in bilingual schools. These have not only attracted attention for the LOTE skills they develop, but also for the success that their students have enjoyed in the mainstream Australian curriculum. Their patronage, principally by non-French-speaking Australian families, just as French is perceived to be in decline, is a sign both of the residual prestige of French as a language and of a deep ambivalence in Australia towards things French.

French in Action: French–English Bilingual Schools and Immersion Programmes

In order to appreciate the importance of French–Australian bilingual and immersion programmes fully, it is necessary to situate them within the overall language education culture of Australia. As indicated above, the Australian taxonomy of language education roughly encompasses the teaching of English as a native and second language; the teaching of foreign languages, mainly in tertiary institutions, secondary schools and most primary schools; the teaching of community languages in com-munity-based programmes in public schools at primary level and in after-

---

19   See Liddicoat, 'The Narrowing Focus – Australia's Changing Language Policy'.
20   Whilst the government has recently decided that this is programme will in fact be terminated at the end of 2002, without having met its objectives, the study of Asian languages has been greatly expanded as a consequence of it.

hours programmes or in non-government schools; and the teaching of Aboriginal languages. A language may of course belong to more than one category, depending on its prestige and its community base. Italian, for example, is a language that enjoys a mixed-status in Australia as a high-culture language as well as a community language, and to this extent can be considered a 'hybrid',[21] since it is taught in universities and secondary schools, primary insertion programmes and as an after-hours community language. By contrast, French enjoys the status of a language of 'high culture' in Australia, with no significant community representation. As such, it is taught as a foreign language in universities, secondary schools and some primary schools. Bilingual and immersion programmes that provide instruction in both French and English have a relatively high profile, and recruit their clientele mainly from the professional classes.[22]

According to Rado's categorisation of bilingual education in terms of its intended learners,[23] students in French bilingual/immersion programmes in Australia fall under the label of 'cultural bilinguals' as opposed to 'social bilinguals'. Cultural bilinguals are typically monolingual when they start a bilingual programme, whereas social bilinguals already know two languages that they practise in everyday life (one language being typically a minority language). Social bilinguals are all too often in the gradual process of replacing one of their languages (usually their mother tongue or community language) with the dominant language, while the cultural bilinguals tend to be adding a 'prestige' language to their knowledge of the dominant societal language. In Canada this distinction is described as additive vs subtractive bilingualism. Liddicoat[24] argues that 'élite bilingualism' (i.e. a form of additive bilingualism), in which learners acquire their second language formally with

21   J. Lo Bianco, 'Italian, the Most Widely Taught Language. How Much is it Learned?', in A. Bivona (ed.), *Italy Towards 2000* (Melbourne: Victoria University of Technology, 1994), p. 151.
22   P. Cryle, A. Freadman and B. Hanna, *Unlocking Australia's Language Potential: Profiles of 9 Key Languages in Australia: French* (Canberra: National Languages and Literacy Institute of Australia, 1993), p. 86.
23   M. Rado, 'Bilingual Education', in Liddicoat, *Bilingualism and Bilingual Education*, p. 151.
24   Liddicoat, 'Bilingualism: An Introduction', p. 7.

some natural exposure, has always been highly regarded for the cultural enrichment it offers and as a marker of high-quality learning. French–Australian bilingual/immersion programmes represent a form of additive and élite bilingualism that offers a unique education to their clientele of mainly cultural bilinguals.

It should be remembered that Australia has only one official language and no dominant non-English speaking minority. Learning another language is not required for social success, as English is regarded as sufficient in the public and private realms. The challenges bilingual programmes face in Australia are therefore very different to those in Canada and can be best understood within their own national and local linguistic contexts. Such programmes started in Australia in the mid-1980s. Their mode of establishment and curriculum largely depend on the amount and type of support that the schools implementing them derive from different authorities, such as Australian State Departments of Education or the French Ministère de l'Éducation. French bilingual/immersion programmes in schools, such as Telopea Park School (Canberra, Australian Capital Territory) or the Lycée Condorcet (Sydney, New South Wales), which are supported by the French government, are more politically inclined to follow the French curriculum. Schools that are fully within the Australian national school system, such as Camberwell (Melbourne, Victoria) and Benowa (Brisbane, Queensland), have more freedom to develop French immersion programmes suited to their local environment. In what follows, we present the main features of these two approaches to bilingual education involving French.

Telopea Park School (Canberra, Australian Capital Territory)

The bilingual programme started when Telopea Park, in the Australian capital Canberra, became a bi-national French–Australian school in 1984 as a result of an international agreement between the Governments of France and Australia. The school is officially recognised as one of the 385 French schools abroad by the Agence de l'éducation en Français à l'étranger, though only about 8% of the students come from France or other French-speaking countries. Telopea has a truly international character, with one-third of the students born overseas and one-fifth speaking a language other than English at home. Nevertheless, it is also a fully accredited Australian state school, which means that there are no fees for Australian students, and continuing strong community support for the bilingual programme is attested by the increase of the intake in the primary section of the school from 264 students in 1984 to 420 students in 1996.

The bilingual programme starts in the primary section (Kindergarten to year 6: K–6) and continues all the way through high school to year 10. Narrabundah College in the vicinity provides the last two years of the bilingual programme (years 11 and 12). Apart from the K–10 bilingual programme, the school also provides an Australian secondary education in years 7 to 10 for local area students, using English only as the language of instruction.

In the primary section, Kindergarten and year 1 children follow an almost full immersion programme, with instruction in French four days a week and one day in English. In year 2 children are taught in French around 70% of the time. From year 3 to year 6 approximately 50% of the instruction is in French and 50% in English. In the Australian system year 6 is the equivalent of the first year of secondary school (*collège*) in the French system. In consequence, in year 6 children have specialist teachers for subjects taught in French, such as Mathematics, History, Geography and French language. From year 7 to year 10, a 50% French–50% English programme is followed, with all students in both the bilingual and mainstream programmes studying one language other than English or French (if taking part in the bilingual programme). History, History–Geography, Mathematics and Science are taught in French by native-French teachers. The other subjects are taught in English by Australian teachers in classes attended by both bilingual students and students from the mainstream programme. No subject is taught in both languages. So, for example, students learn Mathematics from a French perspective only and Home Economics from an English-Australian perspective only.

Students in the bilingual programme can sit the *Brevet des Collèges* in year 9. At Narrabundah College, Telopea's sister school for the final two years (11–12) of secondary education, students can present the French *Baccalauréat*, the International Baccalaureate and the local Year 12 Certificate. In fact, only a small proportion of students who start schooling in Kindergarten at Telopea Park ultimately sit the French

Baccalaureate. However, this should not be seen as an indication of the failure of the bilingual programme, but rather as a reflection of the interests of the majority of the student population on the programme. These are Australian, not French, nationals, who value the programme for the bilingual skills it provides, rather than the French qualifications they might obtain from it. Indeed, it could be said that the bilingual programme at Telopea Park School is successful overall, but that it is not equally so for all children. According to Duverger's evaluation,[25] it has 'a bright future in terms of the political evolution of the schooling of French children outside France within the framework of the development of globalisation and multiculturalism'. However, a more genuinely harmonised French-Australian curriculum could prevent a certain amount of the 'intellectual wastage' experienced by some children, as noted in Duverger's study.

The Lycée Condorcet (The French School of Sydney, New South Wales)

The structure of the bilingual programme at the Lycée Condorcet in Sydney resembles very closely that of Telopea Park School. The Lycée Condorcet is the responsibility of the French Ministère de l'éducation nationale and the Agence de l'éducation en Français à l'étranger. In 2002, 300 students are enrolled in the pre-school, primary and secondary sections of the school, which provides education up to year 12. Teaching throughout the school is based on bilingual French–English educational principles. However, it is not a bi-national school in the sense of Telopea Park School. Although recognised by the NSW Department of Education since 1994, it is, legally speaking, a French private school run as a private company, and so charges school fees as would a normal Australian private school.

In the pre-school section, children receive a quasi-full immersion programme in French, with supporting instruction in English for non-native speakers of the language. In the primary and secondary section 70% of the teaching is in French and 30% in English. Fluency in French

25   J. Duverger, *Mission Report: Telopea Park School, French–Australian Bi-lingual School* (Canberra: The French Embassy, 1998), p. 10.

is one of the prerequisites for entry into year 1 of the primary section. All curricula in all sections closely follow the official French curriculum. The low number of students who sit the French Baccalaureate in year 12, however, does not match the numbers enrolling in the pre-school section. As in the case of Telopea Park School, the majority of students are not primarily interested in the programme for the opportunity it gives them to acquire French qualifications, despite this being the school's official *raison d' être*.

Camberwell Primary School (Melbourne, Victoria)

The English/French Bilingual Immersion Programme at Camberwell Public Primary School (CPS) was established in 1991. It now has an enrolment of 400 students, who are mostly local children with English-speaking backgrounds. Only around 10% of the children have a Franco-phone parent. The school is entirely bilingual, and provides what can be classified as an 'early partial immersion' education.[26] It differs from the bi-cultural programmes of both Telopea Park and the Lycée Condorcet in that the primary mission of the Camberwell programme is not to maintain the mother tongue of children who have native-French-speaking parents. Rather, the school's ethos is marked by the belief that by learning the French language children will strengthen their ability to communicate more widely on a global scale. The school also recognises the importance for children of receiving a thorough grounding in English, as it endorses the principle that children's proficiency in their first language will influence their success in their second language.

Children receive instruction 45% of the time in French and 55% of the time in English from the start of schooling up until year 6. Mathematics, Physical Education and some Social Science are taught in French. All other subjects are in English. There is a primary focus on learning French through Mathematics. But while CPS is well-known in Melbourne for its bilingual programme, it values its reputation for striving for excellence in teaching the State's curriculum in the designated Eight

26   M. Burston, M. De Courcy, J. Warren and P. Young, 'Learning Through French in Australia', unpublished document (Melbourne: The University of Melbourne, 1996).

Key Learning Areas. As a result, no concessions are made in the school's expectations and standards for subjects taught in French, e.g. Mathematics, though taught in French, is assessed as if it were taught in English. Despite experiencing some difficulty with written tasks in mathematics due to the fact that instruction in French is mainly oral, children at CPS are, according to Burston's report,[27] doing well above the national average in mathematics. However, the school has not yet been established long enough for a full evaluation of its bilingual programme to have been carried out. We can therefore not make any further comment on its success.

Immersion Programmes in Queensland

The first immersion programme in French in Queensland started in 1985 in the Benowa State High School. According to Berthold, the programme developed 'almost by accident'.[28] Some staff members in the school were highly dissatisfied with the generally low levels of language competence displayed by senior students after five years of language study. In order to do something about this situation, they started a first immersion class for a group of volunteer students in year 8 (the first year of secondary education in Queensland). Students were taught Mathematics, Science and Music in French. The programme was quickly extended to both years 8 and 9, and now offers 60% French immersion instruction. Subjects taught in French include Mathematics, Science, Social Science and Physical Education. This programme, widely known in Australia as the 'Benowa model', is remarkable in that it started and flourishes thanks to the continuous efforts of a small group of highly motivated teachers. Berthold, who took an active part in the establishment of the programme, describes the Benowa model in the following words:

> It is an example of a bottom-up initiative which has finally been recognised for what it is – an innovative, effective, challenging programme for children who are

27 Burston, De Courcy, Warren and Young, 'Learning Through French in Australia'.
28 M. Berthold, 'The Concept of Immersion', in M. Berthold (ed.), *Rising to the Bilingual Challenge* (Canberra: The National Languages and Literacy Institute of Australia, 1995), p. 19.

looking for an alternative to traditional secondary schooling which will give them the opportunity to become functionally bilingual – if they make the effort.[29]

In 1991, following the success of the Benowa model, the Department of Education in Queensland decided to pilot similar immersion programmes in two other high schools, one in German, the other in French at Mansfield State High School, and over the past few years the University of Queensland has provided academic support to both the Benowa and Mansfield State schools. More recently, in 1998 an independent school, the Glennie School, started a French immersion programme also based on the Benowa model. A third of the volunteer students on the French programme come from remote rural areas where they have only received instruction via distance education prior to attending the Glennie School. Their first experience of a face-to-face learning environment is therefore all the more challenging in that 60% of their teaching is delivered in a foreign language.

Overall, it is possible to say that, regardless of the conditions under which they develop and the type of curriculum or the degree of immersion they offer, all bilingual immersion programmes in French in Australia tend to attract a similar clientele: students (or parents?) who are primarily looking for a challenge in education, the majority of whom have no prior knowledge of French when they start the programmes. Their main goal is to achieve a functional level of bilingualism that will help them broaden their understanding of the world. As such, French continues to be associated with programmes that are clearly at the forefront of education in Australia. It should, on this basis at least, have a bright qualitative (if less quantitatively impressive) future.

French Studies in Academia

'The history of modern language teaching [in Australia] is virtually the history of the teaching of French.' This statement was made by one

29   Berthold, 'The Concept of Immersion', p. 34.

commentator a generation ago[30] – and with some reason. French had enjoyed a strong, even dominant, position in the Australian educational curriculum for the greater part of a century. It was the first modern language to be introduced into Australian universities, at the same time as modern (English) literature in 1882, and the country's first Chair in modern languages was created in French with G. G. Nicholson's appointment to Sydney University in 1921.[31] However, in the light of the above-mentioned series of changes over the past generation, both in educational policy and in Australia's perception of its global interests, it is clear that what might still have been summarily true from the historical perspective of the early 1960s can hardly be sustained at the beginning of the new millenium. It is the case that French is still more or less on a par with Japanese in terms of overall numbers of language learners, and the recent widespread introduction of language learning in primary schools has been beneficial to French, which is taught to about a quarter of the LOTE learning student population. However, the language is generally in decline in secondary education. French teaching is often confined to NIT (non-institutional time) or simply not available. Furthermore, the number of students enrolled in French at tertiary institutions dropped by 30% during the 1980s,[32] though this downward trend now seems to have been arrested.

This situation highlights a paradox with regard to the current status of languages in the education curriculum, and French in particular. Indeed, while the removal of a LOTE (language other than English) as a compulsory subject in schools and as a requirement for matriculation to University in the 1960s brought about the decline in numbers referred to above, there is evidence[33] to suggest that the language students at Aus-

---

30   D. Hick, *A History of Modern Language Teaching in the Public Schools of N.S.W.*, unpublished thesis, University of New South Wales, 1964, quoted in Cryle, Freadman and Hanna, *Unlocking Australia's Language Potential: Profiles of 9 Key Languages in Australia: French*, p. 6.

31   I. Barko, *Seventy Years of the McCaughey Chair of French* (Sydney: University of Sydney, 1991).

32   B. Leal, *Widening our Horizons: Report of the Review of the Teaching of Modern Languages in Higher Education* (Canberra: Australian Government Publishing Service, 1991).

33   P. Brown, 'Why Are Our Students Learning French? And Other Questions', *Australian Review of Applied Linguistics*, 15, 1996, pp. 29–42.

tralia's universities are again strongly motivated to learn languages, both out of interest and a perception of enhanced employment prospects more than from the mere desire to travel for pleasure. This student group is therefore increasingly heterogeneous in its academic aims, which extend far beyond the traditional career path of teaching. According to Leal,[34] at the start of the 1990s, 40% of third year undergraduate students of French were studying on degree courses other than a straight B.A. A subsequent study[35] showed that only one French student in two was now enrolled on a straight B.A. course (indeed a growing number are not even doing an Arts degree at all), with around 75% of students of French at University studying in the *ab initio* + streams (introduced into Australian university language departments from the 1980s on). This study further showed that students feel that their language courses involve a heavier workload than those of other disciplines, and that they have been poorly prepared for their university course, whether or not they have learnt a language at secondary school. This is noteworthy, particularly in an academic context where administrators (and to some extent academic colleagues) continue to have a limited understanding of what is involved in language learning at University level.

The stabilisation of student enrolment and interest needs to be seen, however, against the background of a budgetary crisis that has taken its toll on the education sector. Australian universities have suffered cuts of between 10 and 20% over the past few years, bringing about significant reductions in course provision, particularly in languages, which are often perceived by university managers as (human) resource-intensive. At the same time, a fratricidal war in the name of commercial competition is going on between Australia's 37 universities, which serve a country with a population of under 20 million. For want of a unified national policy in higher education, and in the context of short-term economic rationalisation, the smaller academic units are particularly vulnerable.

French Departments, historically more important or at least larger than those dedicated to other European languages, are increasingly subject to this logic, with a number of them now living a very precarious

34   Leal, 'Widening our Horizons: Report of the Review of the Teaching of Modern Languages in Higher Education'.
35   Brown, 'Why Are Our Students Learning French? And Other Questions'.

existence, reduced in some cases to three, two or even one full-time
member of academic staff – either within an amalgamated European
Studies area or even as an adjunct to English, where they have not quite
simply been closed altogether (as at Latrobe University in Melbourne or,
as is periodically threatened, at James Cook University in Townsville
and Flinders University in Adelaide). A little over a decade ago there
were a dozen Chairs of French across the 17 universities teaching the
language. Today, there remain only three Chairs of French for Australia's
37 universities. Moreover, it is not only French that is threatened in this
way. Other European languages are suffering even more. Russian has
virtually disappeared, German is in free-fall, Spanish never really got
off the ground and even Italian is in difficulty, and that in a country
where it is a 'community language' due to the presence of hundreds of
thousands of Italian immigrants who have settled in Australia since the
Second World War.

As an academic discipline, French and French studies have historically been a vital and vibrant part of the humanities in Australia. As stated
above, French's prestige enabled it to do well despite the general suspicion of foreign languages.[36] In debates about educational policy and
curricula in the late-nineteenth-century, French and France were seen as
representative of the modern in a land that was moving towards nationhood with an eye to its own mercantile interests and a double-edged
attitude to Britain, which, it should be remembered, had colonised Australia the year before the outbreak of the French Revolution. Academically, too, French was considered progressive. The first professor of
French, Nicholson, defined his profession by rejecting the models derived
from the teaching of classical languages, looking instead to the innovations of philology as the guiding basis of the discipline,[37] the ultimate,
practical aim of which was to achieve fluency in French as a language of
social intercourse. This was the approach of the early Nicholson, at least.
In the latter part of his quarter-century reign over academic French in
Australia he came to focus more on grammar as assimilation of rules,
which found its place in the trend of 'language' learning as a preparation
for the study of literature conceived as *belles-lettres*. With numbers on

36   Liddicoat, 'Bilingualism: An Introduction'.
37   Barko, *Seventy Years of the McCaughey Chair of French*.

its side and a well-developed infrastructure, French remained pre-eminent whatever its methodological basis. However, language-teaching methodology has been changing with increasing rapidity over the last 50 years in Australia, as elsewhere. The post-war model of 'basic French' gave way in the late 1960s to the structural method and the golden age of the language laboratory. Developments in linguistic theory paralleled the subsequent advent of a cognitive approach through to functional–notional syllabus design and the catch-all communicative method, which is still largely dominant, though now subject to a certain amount of revisionism as attempts are made to retrieve the baby if not the bathwater.

Ironically, the period that saw the greatest decline in enrolment at University, the mid-1970s to the mid-1980s, also saw an impressive attempt to renew the shape and variety of the courses on offer. This resulted in a more inter-disciplinary approach driven by developments in structuralist and post-structuralist theory in France. Similarly, there was a widespread extension of French to French studies and the concomitant geographical and political recognition of the importance of French-language culture outside metropolitan France. *La francophonie* (Africa, Quebec, the Caribbean and the Pacific) is now included in the curricula of virtually all French (Studies) programmes in Australia. The French Section at the University of New England has a Documentation Centre in Canadian Studies, with a particular focus on Quebec, and the University of Queensland has been working over the last few years on a vast multidisciplinary 'Resource Kit' on France/French in the Pacific. In this context, it should be remembered that Brisbane is closer to Noumea than it is to Melbourne.

An active visitors programme (thanks, in part, to the support of the French government) underpins this diversity. For instance, in mid-1998 Andreé Makine, the winner of the *Prix Goncourt*, appeared at the Sydney Writers' Festival, as well as lecturing at a number of universities, and a few months later Michel Serres became the first French Academician to visit Australia, when he made a campus tour culminating in his paper (delivered in French) on Ethics and Science to the National Academy of Sciences. Other French philosophers followed in 1999: Alain Badiou, Jacques Derrida (who spoke to a packed, paying, house at Sydney Town Hall), Michèle Le Doeuff. But the traffic is not just one way, and there are moves afoot for exchanges of academic staff between France and

Australia. For students, too, an increasing range of international exchange agreements with French universities and the French University of the Pacific are enabling young Australians to engage in programmes of study abroad, particularly in French at Honours level. To this end, in 1999 the French Government introduced the *Bourses Baudin* scheme (in honour of the navigator who charted Australian waters 200 years ago), offering a dozen undergraduate scholarships (increased to 16 in 2002) for study in France. At graduate level, students have a similar opportunity, either through their Australian award or the two French Government scholarships awarded annually. They may also apply for the 50 positions (increased from 35 in 2000) as *assistants* in French *lycées* and primary schools, and the three in New Caledonia, made available to Australians each year.

Historically, the tyranny of local distance and the traditional territorialism of the Australian States, each with its own prerogatives in education, may have contributed to a certain kind of isolation in the national context. The Australian Society for French Studies (ASFS) was set up in 1993 in a belated attempt to overcome this problem, and its annual conference provides a forum for discussion of academic developments in the discipline as well as scholarship. The papers presented are still predominantly literary in orientation, but literature is conceived as text more than canon. Moreover, there is usually some representation of *la francophonie* (for example, in 1997 the conference was attended by writers and academics from New Caledonia), and there is always a strong emphasis on language studies. A sign of the interest of these deliberations to the wider applied linguistics community is that selected papers from the 1994 conference were published in a special volume of the *Australian Review of Applied Linguistics* (*Issues and Innovations in the Teaching of French*). A recent feature of the Society's conferences has been the considerable number of quality postgraduate research students presenting papers. However, the fact that a good number, if not most of these papers are being delivered in English is a sign of changing times, at least with respect to traditional Australian practice. The Society also intends to create a database of all publications relating to French studies in Australia. Internationally, it has recently expressed its desire to further its links with the Fédération Internationale des Professeurs de Français (FIPF) and to establish closer links with French teachers in the Asia-

Pacific region. Its wider professional profile is therefore poised to expand as its national base contracts.

The ASFS Conference is just one of many held in Australia of concern to scholars of French. Other regular events are those of the Applied Linguistics Association of Australia; the African Studies Association of Australasia and the Pacific (whose 22nd annual conference was organised in November 1999 by French colleagues in Perth); the biennial Australasian Universities' Languages and Literatures (AULLA) conference, where French and Francophone Studies are one of the 14 Sections; the Georges Rudé Seminar devoted to the history and culture of France, including France's Overseas Territories, the proceedings of which are usually published; the biennial Canadian Studies Conference. Numerous other relevant symposia to have taken place in recent years include the tripartite African Year at the Humanities Research Centre (Australian National University, 1995); a conference on the centenary of the cinema and French–Australian connections (1995); a conference on the nuclear question in Franco-Australian relations (Melbourne, 1996), one year after the 'fall out' following President Chirac's decision to resume French nuclear testing; a commemoration of François Mauriac and his era (Macquarie University, Sydney, 1998), and an important celebration of 'The Mallarmé Century' (Melbourne, 1998) to mark the centenary of the poet's death (Australia has made an impressive contribution to Mallarmé studies, 'second only to France', in the words of one of the keynote speakers, the poet and critic Michel Deguy).

Australian French studies also have a rich tradition of publishing. *The Australian Journal of French Studies*[38] has produced three issues a year since 1964, and *Essays in French Literature*[39] has been appearing each November since 1964. The Australasian Association of Languages and Literatures issues a twice-yearly bulletin that has a particular focus on book reviews, while the Australian Society for French Studies launched its semestrial *Carnet austral* in 1994. Another recent initiative of note is the Brisbane-based Boombana Publications, which was founded by a former academic, Jean-Claude Lacherez, and has specialised in French-

38   Wallace Kirsop (ed.) *The Australian Journal of French Studies* (Melbourne: University of Monash).

39   Denis Boak (ed.), *Essays in French Literature* (Perth: University of Western Australia).

language publications since 1991. So far it has published more than 20 books: scholarly works, teaching material and French texts, both in the original and in English translation, ranging from works on the cinema of Marguerite Duras, to literary translations (e.g. Victor Segalen's *Les Immémoriaux*), volumes of literary criticism (e.g. on Gilbert Durand) and works on the evolution of the discipline itself in the Australian context.[40]

In the field of technology, French studies in Australia has been very active in spite of the budgetary constraints discussed above. The 'Oz-French' network (set up by Tim Unwin, formerly of the University of Western Australia, now Professor of French at the University of Bristol) has been in operation since 1993, offering daily e-mail contact with other students and teachers with an interest in the Francophone world in Australia and beyond. Home pages and other websites are commonplace, and surfers are able to use several local collections of Francophone links: a *Guide de l'Internet* (Queensland University of Technology); *Ressources pour l'enseignement du français* (Edith Cowan University, Western Australia); *La francophonie en Australie* (Alliance Française); and *Web-French* (University of Western Australia). Tools of this kind can be very valuable in a country the size of Australia where universities increasingly have several campuses – not to mention the fact that here, as elsewhere, there is currently much talk of the use of the information superhighway for 'flexible on-line learning'.[41]

Furthermore, courtesy of developments in technology, and aided by the international time difference, it is possible to read *Le Monde* and other French newspapers in Australia before they are available in the kiosks of Paris. Similarly, France 2's evening news comes in virtually 'live' via the local multicultural public TV station SBS (Special Broadcasting Service), and TV 5 is now available 24 hours a day. Academics in Australia are also making the most of new forms of publication. For example, Jean-Marie Volet (University of Western Australia, Perth) has created an internationally refereed (bilingual) electronic periodical, *Mots*

40 P. Lane and J. West-Sooby, *Traditions and Mutations in French Studies: The Australian Scene* (Mount Nebo: Boombana Publications, 1997).
41 P. Brown, C. Crozet and C. Trevitt, 'L'Enseignement à distance en Australie : au-delà de l'enjeu géographique', *Revue Internationale d'Education*, 23 (Sèvres: CIEP, Centre National de Documentation Pédagogique, February 2000), pp. 141–7.

pluriels et grands thèmes de notre temps,[42] which engages in debates on major contemporary issues such as AIDS, development and cultural relativism with particular focus on Francophone Africa.

Thus, despite the difficulties that 'French' is currently undergoing in the educational system, reports of its death may prove to be exaggerated. In the meantime, it is certainly leading a busy and productive life.

A History of Ambivalence

The paradoxes and ambiguities surrounding the situation of French in Australia are nothing new, of course, even if they have been given greater exposure in the media and academic literature over the past two decades due to issues such as French nuclear testing, the *Rainbow Warrior* affair, regional tensions in the Pacific, etc. Indeed, some studies have pointed to the existence of a historically well-established set of stereotypes about France, with the positive values attached to France and Frenchness accompanied by a strong and persistent strain of anti-French opinion in Australia. For example, while French is still regarded as a language of prestige, it is not uncommon for it to be seen as a language 'for girls in finishing schools'.[43] Similarly, the number of Australian soldiers who fought and died in Northern France during the First World War holds a particular place in Australian history and collective memory. Yet, the relevance of France to contemporary Australia is not obvious to many and the case for studying French has to be argued against the background of Australia's push towards Asia.[44] A recent cultural example of contradictory feelings towards France concerns the relevance of French

---

42   Jean-Marie Volet (ed.), *Mots pluriels et grands thèmes de notre temps* (Perth: University of Western Australia).

43   Cryle, Freadman and Hanna, *Unlocking Australia's Language Potential: Profiles of 9 Key Languages in Australia: French*, p. 117.

44   B. Leal, 'French–Australian Cultural Links: Suggestions for a Reappraisal', in Lane and West-Sooby, *Traditions and Mutations in French Studies: The Australian Scene*, p. 137.

theory for non-French specialists in an Australian context. On the one hand, the importance assigned to French theory can be construed either as a mere fashionable pursuit[45] or as a symptom of dependence on European ideas – an extension of the cultural cringe felt historically towards Britain and the United States, with the resulting perception of a one-sided relationship between the two countries.[46] However, on the other hand, it might also be said that Australian intellectuals refer to France in order to 'inflect the nation's cultural history.'[47]

Against this backdrop of ambiguity, the acute difficulties of 1995 between France and Australia in the wake of French nuclear tests in the Pacific have provided the focus of attention for a collaborative Franco-Australian study currently being conducted, 'Xénophobie/xénophilie dans l'espace d'influence franco-australien', which is led by Geneviève Zarate of the Ecole Normale Supérieure de Saint-Cloud in Paris and Professor Peter Cryle of the University of Queensland. This project is examining the images of France disseminated in Australia and images of Australia in France ('the French are arrogant'; 'Australians are easygoing and relaxed', etc.), and is intended as a contribution to an understanding of stereotyped discourse in general. There is no lack of raw material: apart from discussions of the nuclear issue, stereotypes of the French in programmes such as the BBC's *Allo! Allo!* and local television programmes like *The Big Gig* have enjoyed great popularity in Australia.

In the context of this project, an overview of questionnaires recently distributed in colleges and high schools in Brisbane, Sydney, Canberra and Melbourne shows that France is still generally identified in Australia with food, wine, fashion and Paris, while the French language is often associated with the word 'difficulty'. Significantly, the word 'technology' appears very rarely in answers to the question 'What words do you associate with France and the French?', thus showing little awareness of French as a language of economic and industrial importance in the wider contemporary world. It is worth noting, however, that, when given a list of adjectives to grade in relation to the French, a significant proportion

45   K. Murray (ed.), *The Judgement of Paris* (Sydney: Allen & Unwin, 1992).
46   Leal, 'French–Australian Cultural Links: Suggestions for a Reappraisal', pp. 136–7.
47   Cryle, Freadman and Hanna, *Unlocking Australia's Language Potential: Profiles of 9 Key Languages in Australia: French*, p. 20.

of respondents refused to answer, stating that they dealt with French people as individuals and did not want to attach labels to them. This attitude is echoed even in the answers to questions about reactions to the nuclear tests, which found that while the majority of people surveyed felt that this issue had had a negative impact on the way they viewed France, and that they remained mistrustful of the French government, they made a clear distinction between it and French people in general.

In practice, this distinction is not always preserved, however, and again the debate about nuclear testing was marked by the conflation of a number of different concepts that revealed Australian ambivalence towards France. For instance, a detailed linguistic analysis of articles published in the press in Australia during the three months after the decision to restart nuclear testing[48] reveals that, in their accounts of agency and motivation, the journalists (including editorialists, foreign correspondents and commentators) of major Australian newspapers, such as the *Sydney Morning Herald* and *The Australian*, often failed to make clear distinctions between the French President, the French government and the French people. Some journalists based their description and interpretation of events on negative generalisations, attributing character defects and neuroses to the French as a whole. However, it is clear that while the nuclear issue may have brought such attitudes to a head, this kind of francophobia was already present in Australia, and not only in the press, before the resumption of nuclear testing in 1995. That is, it could be said that, in circulating certain representations of France and the French, the press has done no more than exploit and modify what are deep-seated social representations that happened to come to the fore at a time of crisis.

It may also be that, regardless of any particular attitude towards things French, the Australian psyche is currently going through a period of more general crisis, as the country confronts the challenge of its own identity and destiny on several fronts simultaneously: its own prehistory and relations with its indigenous population; its European past as a colony of Britain at a time when it is contemplating moving towards a republic; and its 'multicultural' (largely European) identity in the context of an increasing realisation of its 'place' in Asia and Asian migration to

---

48   E. Rechniewski (forthcoming).

Australia. At present, Australia is therefore dealing with its own unresolved issues and uncertainties. Against this background, it is understandable that France, which is both the historical arch-rival of Anglo-Saxon power (in the Pacific as well as elsewhere), and a familiar, yet romanticised, symbol of all that is very definitely not British in Australian eyes, may attract the bifocal but not always clear vision of a nation in transition that is worried about the way ahead. Indeed, despite Australia's official policy of 'multiculturalism', the ideological climate is not very favourable to the promotion of cultural or linguistic difference at the present time. For example, Pauline Hanson, the leader of the populist One Nation party, which won nearly 25% of the vote in State elections in Queensland in 1998, has expressed concern about what she sees as the possible 'invasion' of Australia by foreigners, who sometimes do not even know English when they first arrive in the country (admittedly, she has Asians particularly in mind). Australia is thus prey to its own doubts, and currently shows a tendency towards introspection, exacerbated by the country's boat-people and asylum seeker 'crisis' and the events of 11 September 2000. In the regional context, too, the nation's voice became fainter after 1997, with the closing of Radio Australia's French language programmes to the Pacific, which had built up a faithful audience over the years in Vanuatu, New Caledonia and French Polynesia.

In the language area itself, this inward-looking mood has recently produced a challenge to LOTEs at the policy level in the form of English literacy policy. In the last few years, English language literacy has come to be seen as an area in crisis in Australian political discourse, and literacy has emerged as a key area for educational funding, with the consequence that it is now being argued that a larger share of the timetable should be allocated to developing English literacy skills. In response to the increased push for literacy, some schools, especially primary schools, are discontinuing language programmes in order to devote more time to literacy work. A new rhetoric is beginning to emerge that represents learning a foreign language as detrimental to the development of adequate levels of literacy in the learner's first language. The historic suspicion of languages discussed above therefore seems to have returned in a new guise. At the moment, however, it is impossible to determine what the overall impact of this emerging discourse will be on language learning in Australia. Whatever the outcome, it is likely to be an important reflection of the future social and cultural directions that the oldest land mass maps out for itself in its attempts to begin a second consecutive century as a new nation.

So where does all this leave French? In short, it is clear that its past pre-eminence is gone for good. Yet, despite the current concentration of language policy in Australia on English literacy and, for assumed economic reasons, the promotion of Asian languages over continental European languages, it seems safe to predict that French has a sound future – at least as far as can be foreseen. To a certain extent, the solid infrastructure for French teaching still present in schools and universities, while less extensive than previously, may stand it in good stead in a climate in which inertia in public policy and the education system is also a factor that is anything but negligible. And again, despite, or perhaps because of, Australian historical ambivalence towards the French phenomenon, French, as a language and culture, retains a very broad, and indeed one could say special, appeal for Australians. Perceived as at once familiar and exotic, romantic and antagonistic, French represents a range of interests and activities, as a language for travel, a language for culture, a language for fine cuisine in an evolving multicultural society relativising its Anglo-Saxon heritage, a language of sophistication with added value in a 'nouveau riche' society; in other words, a language for being non-British, yet also a language for avant-garde developments in bilingual education and for philosophy in the New Humanities. Thus, amidst all the uncertainties and apprehensions besetting the languages field in Australia, it would appear that a kind of complex southern 'auld alliance' (a no doubt unconscious nostalgia for what might have been had La Pérouse reached Sydney before Governor Phillip with his penal colony in 1788, alongside relief that he did not) will assure French a place in this part of the Pacific beyond the existence of the *Territoires d'Outre-Mer* in Australia's 'backyard'.

GABRIELLE PARKER

France and Southern Africa: Culture, Co-operation and Language Policy

The French system of co-operation was comprehensively overhauled in 1998. The new titles adopted in the reorganisation is significant: the country now has a single Ministère des Affaires Étrangères, which includes within its remit Coopération and Francophonie. It is in the context of this new institutional framework, itself reflecting policy changes in response to a 'New World Order', that the evolution of French policy towards Southern Africa in matters of culture, co-operation and language is examined in this chapter. According to the French Ministère des Affaires Étrangères, the three key words that characterise France's African policy are '*Fidélité, adaptation, ouverture*'.[1]

The reformed system presents *la Francophonie* as an essential part of international *coopération* as a result of the values it conveys through its shared culture: co-operation takes place at one and the same time on the linguistic and cultural levels as well as on the economic, social and political levels.[2] Image – and the influence attached to it – is of special importance. That the two missions – co-operation, *Francophonie* – should be yoked together is more important than an acknowledgement of a hitherto implicit reality: co-operation assists the spread of the language, and language acts as a medium for co-operation. It is also a recognition that making this link explicit will help to embed it in the consciousness of all parties participating in the process.

However, the word *Coopération* can have different meanings, depending on the standpoint adopted. For French government officials, it is an investment of goodwill that creates a climate culturally and politically favourable to France and all things French. For a publication like *Le MOCI* (*Moniteur du Commerce International*), the weekly organ of the

1   Cf. 'La politique africaine de la France', *Dossiers d'actualité*, 11 January 2001, p. 1; http://www.diplomatie.fr/actual/dossiers/polafricaine/index.html.
2   See the official document published by the Ministère de la Coopération et de la Francophonie, *Réforme du dispositif français de coopération*, 1998.

Centre Français du Commerce Extérieur, and its readership of entre-
preneurs, co-operation presents itself as a commercial investment, a fair
exchange from which both parties are bound to gain.[3] Both types of co-
operation are expected to bring dividends: it is the nature of the dividend
that is different.

According to officials at the Ministère des Affaires Étrangères,[4] the
old approach to co-operation was preoccupied with 'holding ground' –
occuper le terrain – maintaining France's influence in other countries
and perpetuating the need for France's help. This approach has been
turned upside down. In the cultural domain, for instance, artistic co-
productions help to train local personnel, encourage cultural co-operation
and promote *francophonie*. Various international organisations vie to
reform local educational systems, offering financial support and ensuring
that languages have a place in curricula, with the World Bank, the EDF
(European Development Fund), UNESCO and the EU all in competition
with each other.

Another aspect of the reforms concerns the 'regional' dimension.
The East–West model that collapsed with the break-up of the Soviet
Union has been replaced by a 'regional' model. Furthermore, globalisation, or *la mondialisation*, as the French prefer to call it, has the effect,
inter alia, of altering spatial frames of reference and enlarging their
scope. The world is being structured in 'natural' regions: Southern Africa
is one of them. It is commonly understood as comprising the twelve
member countries that constitute the SADC[5] – Angola, Mozambique,
Zambia, Namibia, Zimbabwe, Tanzania, Botswana, Lesotho, Swaziland,

3   Cf: 'La francophonie économique n'est pas une idée désuète, c'est une réalité', *Le
     MOCI* (*Moniteur du Commerce International*, 310, 6 November 1997, pp. 34–5.
4   Interviews conducted 28–30 October 1998.
5   SADC stands for Southern African Development Community. It was formed in
     1992 following the Windhoek Treaty, which transformed the former SADCC
     (Southern African Development Co-ordination Conference) from a regional fron-
     tier state lobby into a community. In addition to the 12 countries on the mainland,
     Mauritius and the Seychelles Islands in the Indian Ocean were invited to join, and
     the Republic of South Africa was invited to join in 1994 (following the collapse of
     the apartheid regime). La Réunion was invited to participate in the September
     1998 summit held in Mauritius, and Madagascar was accepted as an observer.
     The Democratic Republic of Congo and the Seychelles applied for membership in
     August 1997.

Malawi, Namibia and South Africa. Nevertheless, language policy still tends to be managed by country rather than by region. The budget – which to a degree governs the policies to be put in place – is allocated by the Foreign Affairs ministry on an annual basis.

The whole of Southern Africa is generally considered to be comparatively stable and to pose few political risks:[6] its relative homogeneity, in spite of its diversity, supports this assessment, as do the activities of the various regional organisations that promote dialogue on development, defence, and financial and economic policy.[7] Although the disintegration of the Soviet Union has deprived South Africa of its former strategic role as a self-styled bulwark against Communism (a role that to a certain extent provided an apology for those of her allies who otherwise condemned her), the Southern African region is emerging as a geo-politically important one. In the domain of military co-operation, France has been competing with well-established British and US interests, as well as with Israel, Germany and China. There is a need to reopen markets for private firms and compete for influence at government level. This field of activity gives new meaning to the phrase *champ de coopération* and brings to mind the fact that, prior to the recent restructuring, *coopération* fell within the remit of the Ministère des Armées. In this field, economic and market intelligence overlaps with military intelligence.

A substantial market for military equipment is emerging in Southern Africa, and France has recently negotiated an industrial partnership with military objectives in South Africa.[8] In addition to military equipment, there is a demand for training personnel, both within the UN framework,

6   Bournaud, in M. Aicardi de Saint-Paul (ed.), *Afrique du Sud, Afrique Australe. Interdépendences et antagonismes*, special issue of *Afrique contemporaine*, 184, October–December 1997 (Paris: La Documentation Française), pp. 65ff.

7   For instance, besides the SADC, COMESA (Common Market for Eastern and Southern Africa, created in 1994; from the SACU (Southern African Customs Union), created in 1910, to the CMA (Common Monetary Area), now the MMA (Multilateral Monetary Area), which trades in the South African Rand. The MMA's monetary policy is very much led by the Reserve Bank of South Africa, nominally in consultation with the other Federal Banks.

8   Klen, p. 92. The Republic of South Africa is itself an arms exporter, and earned $216 million in 1997 from trading with 91 clients, according to Heim Marais, 'Conversion musclée à la Real politik', *Le Monde Diplomatique*, March 1999, p. 11, http://monde-diplomatique.fr/1999/03/Maraid/11/11783.html.

and independently. For instance, advanced negotiations were taking place between Paris and Luanda concerning the training of the new Angolan army at the same time as French military specialist engineering forces were helping to train anti-mine personnel and French observers were monitoring the reconciliation process under UN auspices. A French technical detachment is also present in Mozambique. These developments confirm the shift in foreign policy set out by the Ministre des Affaires Étrangères, Hubert Vedrine:

> As far as French military presence in Africa is concerned, France will of course honour its commitments [...]. At the same time, France is also seeking to adapt its military presence. [...]
> I might add that, in future, we shall be concentrating more and more on training actions that will enable African states to take part in peace-keeping forces [...]. Such action will be undertaken in cooperation with the Americans and the British.[9]

The Service militaire adapté (SMA) is another example of French know-how that attracts interest in Southern Africa.[10] The SMA scheme's new approach to military service combines military training with apprenticeships in specific trades that can be put into use in civilian life. France takes pride in the work done by the SMA in the DOM-TOMs.

The new approach to English-speaking Africa constitutes an important policy shift, albeit a gradual one that started in the 1970s, and is by no means one-sided. The United States and the United Kingdom, no longer bound by self-imposed limits on their influence in Africa,[11] and

9   Cf. 'Realism and Initiatives in a Global Environment', *Label France*, 30 January 1998, http://www.france.diplomatie.gouv.fr. Concerning France's commitment to multinational military co operation in Africa in collaboration with the United States and the United Kingdom, see *Le Monde Diplomatique*, March 1998, pp. 20–1, http://www.monde.diplomatique.fr/1998/03/WAUTHIER/10186.html. *The Independent* reported on Robin Cook and Hubert Vedrine's mission to Ghana and Ivory Coast to mark the co-operation in the region between Britain and France as follows: 'The initiative meshes with efforts to boost links between the Commonwealth and *la Francophonie*.' Trade benefits were also mentioned. 'Old colonial rivals work together in Africa', *The Independent*, 3, 814, 8 March 1999, p. 11.
10 See the interest generated in South Africa, Angola and Mozambique following a visit by South African military staff to an SMA unit in La Réunion. Klen, pp. 112–3.
11 The BBC has had no qualms about 'invading' Francophone territory: since 1999, it has been broadcasting in FM to Benin, Burkina-Faso, Congo-Brazzaville, Ivory Coast, Senegal and Madagascar.

President Mitterrand's decision to abandon the old Gaullist doctrine of French non-intervention outside its own *pré carré* during the Rwandan Civil War in 1991 and again in 1994, brought that policy into sharp focus. The collapse of the 'old world order' post-1989 and the end of Apartheid in 1991 seemed to justify this open approach. Conversely, the United States' proposal for an inter-African force that would act in parallel with the UN on the continent, had the effect of setting the Francophone/ Anglophone divide into sharp contrast, even though Christopher Warren's proposal of an African force to respond to crises met with an unenthusiastic reaction from Southern African as well as the IOR (Indian Ocean Rim) countries.

The new Republic of South Africa has stated from the start (1994) that its main priority in foreign affairs is the rest of Southern Africa: its neighbouring states and fellow members of SADC, CPA and COMESA. The emergence of the new South Africa and the anticipated growing influence of the SADC zone were seen as unmissable opportunities that prompted a new *fin-de-siècle* version of the scramble for Africa.

Nelson Mandela visited France in May 1990, June 1991, February 1992 and October 1993 – and many times subsequently, following his election and inauguration as President, in particular to receive an honorary doctorate at the University of Paris I Panthéon-Sorbonne, on 15 July 1996. Thabo Mbeki, then Vice-President, had also visited the country as part of a European Union tour. Following Mandela's election on 9 May 1994, President Mitterrand was the first Western leader to visit the new South Africa in July of the same year. 1996 saw numerous visits on the part of foreign leaders and numerous journeys by Mandela, including one to France in July. President Chirac followed in 1998 with his first tour of Southern Africa, which included Namibia, Mozambique, Angola and the Republic of South Africa.[12] He brought with him 'the most high-powered trade entourage to have visited the country since the end of apartheid'.[13] As well as three ministers, the 40-strong business delega-

12   Namibia, Mozambique and Angola belong to the newly-designated 'pays de la zone prioritaire', which include the former 'pays du champ'. See: *Le Monde diplomatique*, March 1998, p. 21, http://www.monde.diplomatique.fr/1998/03/ WAUTHIER/10186.html.
13   Mary Braid, 'France on a mission to impress', *The Independent*, 22 June 1998, p. 16.

tion also included ELF Oil chief executive, Philippe Jaffre, his counter-part at Total, Thierry Demarest, the head of Alcatel, representatives from Bouygues, Cartier, Dassault, Eurocopter, Thompson CFS, etc., as well as Christian Graeff, chair of the sub-Saharan business group at the CNPF, all lured by the prospect of new trade deals, including defence contracts. Archbishop Desmond Tutu, who was made a *grand officier* of the Legion of Honour on this occasion, stated in his speech of thanks that, in his view, the anti-Apartheid struggle had been based on the achievements of the French Revolution.[14]

Hugo Vedrine, the Ministre des Affaires Étrangères, referred to a shift from paternalism to fraternalism and a judicious mix of aid and trade, thus adroitly situating France within the spirit of the vision of an African Renaissance expressed by the then Vice-President, Thabo Mbeki, and addressing an indirect rebuke to less sensitive American approaches. In the course of his own visit a few months earlier (March 1998), Bill Clinton had angered many in his audience by speaking of 'trade, not aid'. The American official visit had not proved a total success: South African foreign policy towards Libya had been an obstacle, there had been irritations and misunderstandings with regard to protocol, and doubts had been raised about South Africa's ability to guarantee the security arrangements surrounding the visit. In response to continued pressure from the United States for South Africa to cut links with Libya and Cuba, President Mandela made a firm statement on 15 January 1997: 'We will not allow any country, however powerful, to dictate our foreign policy.'[15] However, US interests in South Africa currently represent a quarter of private investment in the country, and the US is the third largest foreign investor after the United Kingdom and Germany;[16] such figures can only exacerbate mutual irritation.

Other players on the scene include Japan and other South East Asian countries: Malaysia and Singapore are poised to conquer Southern African markets (Namibia, for instance). Malaysia owns 30% of Engen, the main oil company in the RSA. Both Nelson Mandela and Frederick de

14   Braid, 'France on a mission to impress'.
15   Gonidec, P.-F., 'Afrique du Sud: une nouvelle politique extérieure?', in *Afrique Contemporaine*, p. 188.
16   Gonidec, P.-F., 'Afrique du Sud: une nouvelle politique extérieure?', in *Afrique Contemporaine*, p. 190.

Klerk (the last State President of the Apartheid regime) visited Malaysia twice, while Malaysian Prime Ministers have made three official visits to South Africa. The long-established Malay community in the Cape is not enough to explain this keen interest. Not only is the Republic of South Africa considered a springboard from which to penetrate the whole of the Southern African market, France is not alone in wishing to promote its culture abroad, and the gains of Islam in a previously mostly Christian country must be seen as an encouraging sign for Malaysia, which has invested substantially in schools and education in South Africa.

The British Prime Minister, Tony Blair, figured among the many foreign leaders who followed these visits by the French. Also, as Secretary of State for Trade and Industry, Peter Mandelson undertook his first overseas trade mission to South Africa in September 1998, 'intent on grabbing a share of the country's £20 billion privatisation programme for British firms'. He was reported as saying that 'there was a huge amount the City had to offer Nelson Mandela's government, based on its wealth of experience over the last 20 years of privatisation in the UK'[17] – know-how that Old Labour would not have boasted about in the past. Among the sectors identified as being of interest were telecommunications, housing, water, energy and transport. President Chirac's retinue a few months earlier gave clues as to France's own assessment of the potential opportunities.

The notion of the Commonwealth – allowed to languish in the Thatcher years – is now enjoying a renaissance, and its 50th anniversary in 1999 was celebrated enthusiastically in London. South Africa rejoined the Commonwealth in 1994.[18] Blair's government placed a strong emphasis on Britain's relations with Africa. The appointment, in August 1999, of the former anti-Apartheid activist, Peter Hain, as a Minister of State at

---

17 *The Independent*, 12 September 1988, Business Section, p. 18.
18 The Apartheid regime had, in advance of the threat of expulsion, left the organisation in 1961. Following the first general elections in which all ethnic groups were able to participate, and the election of Mandela as the first President of the 'new South Africa' (a phrase attributed to Archbishop Tutu), South Africa not only rejoined the Commonwealth, but also the United Nations, UNESCO, the IMF and the World Bank. It became the 53rd member of the Organisation of African Unity and the 10th member of SADC in the same year.

the Foreign & Commonwealth Office was seen as a signal of the British government's commitment to African and Southern African relations.

The current state of the various rivalries was summed up on a map published by *L'Événement du jeudi* in 1997 under the heading: 'Un continent sous influence franco-américaine'. As its title suggests, the map showed countries coloured according to whether they were 'under French influence' – most of the traditionally Francophone countries – 'under American influence' – Botswana, Zimbabwe, South Africa – or 'countries where France and the United States are at loggerheads' such as Angola and Zaire. A number of countries – Zambia, Malawi, Mozambique – were left uncoloured. Hence it was not clear under what influence, if any, they were deemed to labour.[19]

It may be useful at this point to look at current French policy and attitudes towards the region in a historical context. Although the history of France's relations with Southern Africa goes back a long way, relations have been weak and frequently disrupted. In the nineteenth century, the Société des missions évangéliques de Paris decided, independently of any formal, or government, policy, to establish French Protestant missions in Southern Africa. The aim of their first mission, 25 miles east of Cape Town, was 'pour y instruire les esclaves hottentots', who would eventually go and found stations away from the colony once they had been fully trained.[20] Théophile Jousse, himself a former missionary, wrote in his retirement:

> L'Afrique est redevable au protestantisme français de deux bienfaits que l'histoire ne saurait passer sous silence: l'établissement d'une colonie de réfugiés au Cap, et celui d'une mission au Lessouto.[21]

The missionaries established themselves among the Basotho nation in 1833 and extended their work north beyond South Africa's current borders into what is now Lesotho, and parts of Zimbabwe and Zambia.

---

19   *L'Événement du Jeudi*, 3–9 April 1997, p. 13.
20   Théophile Jousse, *La Mission française évangélique au sud de l'Afrique, son origine et son développement jusqu'à nos jours* (Paris: Librairie Fischbacher, 1889), p. 19.
21   Jousse, *La Mission française évangélique au sud de l'Afrique, son origine et son développement jusqu'à nos jours*, p. 28.

Their sole aim was to bring the (reformed) Christian faith to those parts of Africa and – through literacy – to help the peoples they were seeking to convert to record their own histories and cultures. They learnt the local languages in order to be able to communicate; translated the Bible and the Psalms into those languages, and did not seek to teach French or French culture to the natives.[22] Consequently, their influence has been limited to a measure of respect for the memory of these missionaries among individuals aware of their work.[23]

In spite of sentimental attempts to trade on a French inheritance in the Southern Cape – Franschoek, in particular – there is little evidence of Huguenot influence. Indeed, any attempt by the Huguenots to leave their mark was deliberately thwarted almost from the start and soon forgotten. This was partly due to an edict of 1701 forbidding the use of the French language among recent settlers in the Cape Colony.[24] During the Second Boer War (1899–1902) French support for the Boers was suspect and short-lived, and the French settlers who espoused the Boer cause were often nationalistic, opposed to Dreyfus and anglophobe.[25] Since the proclamation of the Republic, in 1948, France's role has been more or less limited to that of a trading partner.

To Afrikaner writers and artists opposed to the racist policies of the Apartheid regime, the representation of France as a haven of liberty and

22 See, in particular, the accounts by Edouard Favre, *François Coillard au Lessouto*, vol. II : *François Coillard, missionnaire au Lessouto (1861–1882)*, and vol. III : *François Coillard, missionnaire au Zambèze (1882–1904)* (Paris: Société des Missions Évangéliques, 1908); and Alfred Casalis, 'Premiers essais de création de littérature indigène au Lessouto', in *Foie et Vie* (1903).
23 Interview with High Commissioner for Lesotho to the United Kingdom, 1998.
24 See, in particular, R. Vigne, in Bach, 1990, pp. 17–36; also Jousse, *La Mission française évangélique au sud de l'Afrique, son origine et son développement jusqu'à nos jours*, pp. 31–2. Still, on 28 June 1998, during President Chirac's official visit, the South African Minister of Foreign Affairs, Alfred Nzo, invited his French counterpart, Hubert Vedrine to be the guest of honour at a ceremony at the Huguenot Memorial in Franschoek, where he unveiled a plaque commemorating the visit as well as the 400th anniversary of the Edict of Nantes, 'symbole de tolérance et de liberté'. The plaque is inscribed in French.
25 J. Marlin, *Les Relations entre la France et la République d'Afrique du Sud* (Paris: Conseil Économique et social, 1995), p. 97.

creativity became symbolic capital in the Bourdieuan sense.[26] Jan Rabie
is credited with this *prise de conscience*, and for starting the trend. Rabie
had lived in France between 1948 and 1955, and his *Een-en-Twintig*
(*Twenty-One*), first published 1956, had a seminal effect, as did, perhaps
more so, his *Ons, die Afgud* (*We, the Idol*) two years later. Others involved
included the writers Elsa Joubert, and, a decade later, André Brink,
Breyten Breytenbach and the painter Erik Laubscher.

The same decades (1950–60s) saw Afrikaner writers translate French
literature into Afrikaans,[27] thus disseminating French poetry and contemporary literature (Camus, Sartre). Conversely, the translation of writers
such as Brink, and later, Gordimer and J. M. Coetzee into French, and
their success, helped create a receptive climate sympathetic to the South
African struggle in France. Discreet support for anti-Apartheid activists,
writers and intellectuals went alongside official political and economic
support for the Apartheid regime itself.[28]

It was not until 1985–6 that the French government decided to
apply economic sanctions and suspend new contracts with South Africa.
France's response to the declaration by the Apartheid regime of a 'state
of emergency' in July 1985 was to recall its ambassador.[29] This period
saw the institution of a new policy of cultural co-operation that was
targeted solely at the 'coloured' and black populations, and culminated
in the official opening of the Soweto branch of the Alliance Française
on 14 July 1989.[30] The mission of this branch was to offer opportunities
for vocational training to township residents. The promotion of the
French language and French culture was not a primary aim. However,

26   See Philippe-Joseph Salazar, 'De Parys à Paris, la littérature afrikaans et ses
      modèles français', in D. Bach, *La France et l'Afrique du Sud. Histoire, mythes et
      enjeux contemporains* (Paris: CREDE-Karthala, 1990), pp. 397–407.
27   Salazar, 'De Parys à Paris, la littérature afrikaans et ses modèles français', pp.
      400–1.
28   For instance, the poet and critic, Breyten Breytenbach lived in France (1960–75),
      and settled there in 1982. Jack Lang, then Minister of Culture, proposed that the
      novelist Alex la Guma (at that time ANC representative in Cuba), be invested
      with the honour of Chevalier des Arts et des Lettres. Unfortunately, the news
      reached La Guma's widow only after the writer's sudden and untimely death on
      that island.
29   Marlin, p. 97.
30   Marlin, p. 98.

this commitment conveyed a message of support and goodwill that fostered a positive attitude towards France. The Alliance Française network had been active throughout the Apartheid years, and had acted as a dynamic instrument for the French embassy's activities in South Africa. The embassy did occasionally become involved in the promotion of the French language and French culture – for instance, through vocational schools that provided training for the disadvantaged – as a way of promoting a positive image of France.

The work of the Alliance in South Africa is of interest since, although it is independent of the French state, the organisation's network of contacts was used to promote and sustain the kind of activities that would normally have been those of parallel networks of government organisations. In a way, this use of an independent network was a result of the reorganisation that had begun a few years earlier when the French ministries involved realised how much of the work done by the Alliances and the French Institutes in matters of language (promotion and teaching) was duplicated, and agreed a division of tasks and responsibilities. The new, restructured ministry has gone further by suggesting that private concerns, with their technical expertise and other resources, must be involved more systematically in all matters pertaining to (a very widely defined sense of) co-operation: 'nous devons apprendre à faire faire' – we must learn to help others to work for themselves – from 'l'humanitaire' to education, training, etc. The CCIP (Chambre de Commerce et d'Industrie de Paris) has been engaged in this work for a long time. It emphasises its commitment to the 'promotion du français des affaires', *inter alia*, since its *raison d'être* in matters of training and education is to promote a French approach to, as well as an understanding of, business and management. Its training programmes, examinations and qualifications form a thriving commercial concern. In business matters, it helps French companies abroad, providing background information and briefings, brokering contacts, and offering facilities for meetings and communications. The CCIP has a presence in South Africa.

In present-day South Africa, the French language and French culture suffer from contradictory perceptions that, to a degree, match the fault-lines of the former Apartheid system: on the one hand, the intelligentsia, English- as well as Afrikaans-speaking, maintain a favourable attitude inspired by what is perceived as a radical tradition; on the other, the rising political élite tends to dismiss what is seen as 'Eurocentric' and irrelevant to African concerns. Such suspicion may be reinforced by traditional schools, such as the Lycée Français Jules Verne in Johannesburg, which has a total of 500 students, just 50 of whom are South African. Its principal describes it as 'a sort of French island in South Africa'.[31] It is an awareness of attitudes like this that has prompted the promotion of French as the language of Francophone Africa, on the one hand, and of French for specific, vocational and professional purposes, on the other – together with opportunities to study and work not in metropolitan France, but in countries of the Indian Ocean (not only in La Réunion, but also in Mauritius and Madagascar), thus emphasising relevance in terms of geographical focus, as well as meeting immediate needs.

South African distrust of French intentions is tempered, however, by an awareness of the advantages – perceived, or real – granted by France to CFA countries, which is perhaps keener in neighbouring SADC countries, since it is metropolitan France and French as the language of Francophone élites that attracts them.[32] According to French officials, there is increasing demand for learning French – especially French for specific purposes – throughout Southern Africa.[33] This follows an intensification of relations with Francophone Africa. President Mandela had expressed the wish that both French and Portuguese would become working languages within SADC. French officials especially welcomed this unexpected request and interpret it as reflecting desire to maintain the status of the country's own languages and reaffirm their importance while showing openness towards other languages as international media.

The growing political and diplomatic exchanges between Francophone, Lusophone and Anglophone African countries afford an opportunity to demonstrate this openness to other languages. The predominant role played by SADC in this expansion of contacts has been a major factor. The extension of membership to non-English-speaking countries

31   *The Sunday Independent* (Johannesburg), Focus on Education supplement, 5 February 1999, p. 5.
32   Interviews in London with the High Commissions of Botswana, Lesotho and Namibia, 1998.
33   Conversations with officials at the Ministère des Affaires Étrangères on 28 October 1998.

raises the issue of language. For instance, the Republic of Congo and the Seychelles are participants; Madagascar is an observer; La Réunion enjoys a special status, while Nigeria has decided to include French in its special curriculum, and Zambia has done the same.

As far as France is concerned, the management of this new demand is decided on an *ad hoc* basis, country by country. The whole of Africa ranks only sixth in order of priority, with countries in the European Union at the top of the list, followed by Central and Eastern Europe, the Maghreb and Mediterranean countries, and Latin America. The resources – financial, human and organisational – allocated to this work are limited. While an overall sum of FF 25 million is allocated for cultural co-operation in South Africa, with another FF 12 million for educational and linguistic co-operation, Benin (for example) gets FF 200 million, while the expenditure on Zambia amounts to a mere FF 2 million.[34] Budgetary constraints mean that projects are limited in those areas that are not deemed to be a priority. In July 1997 the FAC (Fonds d'aide et de coopération) committee allocated FF 6 million to Mozambique for training purposes,[35] the same amount that was allocated to Ivory Coast in the same year. When, after a gap of some 15 years, the teaching of French was reintroduced in educational programmes in 1993, an FF 8 million project was set up. Five thousand learners were enrolled as a result of this investment, and the current FF 6 million project aims to strengthen, extend and establish the teaching of French in Mozambique. FF 9 million were allocated to Angola in the same round in order to renovate a building for the Alliance Française in Luanda, the current premises being small and unsuitable. The proposed new home, the 'Palais de fer' (inspired by Eiffel) is, in fact, a fine example of Angola's architectural heritage. This money was also meant to help set up a multimedia research centre.

The official line is that French simply cannot be ignored – SADC countries cannot do without French. In the autumn of 1998 French was declared one of the SADC's working languages. There is an *engouement* for the language at local level, and officials share this enthusiasm. The French preoccupation is 'la formation des élites', which must be understood in the same sense as it is used in Francophone Africa: *les élites* are

34   Figures provided in interview cited above.
35   Reported in *Information Bulletin*, 5 November 1997.

the minority of local nationals who benefit from the full educational system – in which, in Francophone Africa, of course, all teaching is delivered through the medium of French. If the educated minority of Southern Africa were also fluent in French, that would be a major step forward – so the reasoning goes.

Given, however, that French is not the medium of instruction in these countries, the main priority is language skills for specific purposes. The campaign has two elements: the promotion of the language based on its instrumental uses and its capacity to enhance employability; and the promotion of French culture through a different network in a French–Southern African dialogue of equals. The first element is implemented through a network of Alliances Françaises, which work in partnership with primary and secondary schools, technikons, and universities. Their work supports the linguistic policies devised by the Embassy and the Bureau d'Action Linguistique et Éducative. The Mitchell's Plain Alliance on the outskirts of Cape Town, for instance, works closely with local primary schools, providing courses that aim to encourage young pupils to take French at secondary level. It also helps to train school teachers in the subject, reviews the current syllabus and matric examination,[36] and works on joint programmes in journalism with the Peninsula Technikon in Cape Town, and with the University of the Western Cape School of Government in preparing students for Diplomas with French, offering scholarships to France and to La Réunion. The second element, the promotion of culture on equal terms, receives similar support: 'The role of the Alliance Française is not only to promote French and francophone culture, but also to promote South African culture.'[37]

The image conveyed by the new co-operative approach to *franco-phonie* is that of *partage*. The Mitchell's Plain Alliance Française is a concrete 'place of sharing' situated close to the town's railway station, market and civic amenities. Its moment of glory came with the France–South Africa football match in the 1998 World Cup when 150 taxi drivers crowded round the brand new satellite television set that was broadcasting

---

36   The 'matric' is the final general school-leaving examination – similar to the *baccalauréat* – that concludes schooling; it is taken, more or less, at the level of the *classe de première* (in France) or lower sixth form (in England and Wales).

37   *Alliance Info*, 1, January–March 1999 (newsletter of the Mitchells Plain Alliance Française, written almost entirely in English).

the match live.[38] Anecdotes aside, *francophonie* is now conceived of as an essential element of international co-operation, since it conveys values – business and economic as well as cultural – across frontiers.

Beyond the network of Alliances, the Institut Français pour la recherche en Afrique (IFRA) is present in Harare and Nairobi. The University of Cape Town (UCT) has piloted French for specific purposes in collaboration with the Alliance Française in the city centre.[39] Another sign of interest in French culture comes in the job description for a lecturer in French to be appointed at the University of Botswana: this lecturer would not only be 'responsible for teaching the year three French for practical purposes', but also 'currents of thoughts in the French speaking world, African theatre, and Poetry in French'. Expertise was required in Francophone literature and civilisation, and the ability/experience to teach French for specific purposes was considered to be an advantage.[40]

The cultural dimension, for its part, is kept separate. It is estimated that one out of every four cultural events currently taking place in South Africa is financed or supported by the Institut Français d'Afrique du Sud (IFAS).[41] Unlike most of its counterparts around the world, the IFAS does not offer courses in French, relying on the Alliance Française network for that purpose. IFAS itself concentrates exclusively on cultural work and the Franco-South African cultural dialogue: again a different perspective from that of most Instituts Français, which tend to emphasise the promotion of French culture. IFAS acts as focus for the whole of the Southern African region, and the proximity of its base in Johannesburg to other SADC capital cities – Maputo, Gaborone, Windhoek, Harare, not to mention centres in the Indian Ocean – is an advantage not offered by Cape Town.

The need to study French may not be the primary concern of learners whose main preoccupation is likely to be whether they can afford

---

38   Interview with M. Fabrice Mongiat, Directeur de l'Alliance Française, Mitchell's Plain, February 1999.

39   Since it is the policy to develop French for specific purposes, a *Coopérant* was seconded to this task.

40   *Times Higher Education Supplement*, May 1999, p. 60.

41   Interview with Madame Marie-Claude Messager, Directrice de l'Alliance Française du Cap, February 1999.

bare necessities – starting with basic schooling. The need to integrate French into the syllabus of schools that are already burdened by the demands of multilingual learning is clearly evident to school principals who have to balance the needs of the broader curriculum with the desirability of employing a specialist French teacher. French is an official language of a number of international organisations based in South Africa, and President Mandela's announcement that French would be one of the SADC languages has helped the case for studying the language. The Truth and Reconciliation Commission required a high level of interpreting skills in order to satisfy the needs of the world media – especially in French – as did the World Conference on AIDS that took place in Zambia. Although there is an urgent need for skilled linguists at high-level events of this kind, these transient opportunities do not cut much ice with potential learners in the townships.

An economic dimension is added by agreements with the EU. The SADC countries (and South Africa, in particular) have negotiated extensions of the Lomé Convention, of which the Francophone African countries are already the beneficiaries. The introduction of the Euro has also revived the idea of a single currency for the SADC, a venture that would take place within the dual contexts of the introduction of the Euro and its relationship with the *zone franc* countries on the SADC's borders. There is an awareness that Southern African currencies need to position themselves in relation to a major global player, and to its neighbours already within that framework. The Euro and the convertibility of the franc CFA (the currency of Francophone Africa), which is guaranteed by the French Treasury at the rate of 100 francs CFA = FF 1 (and its equivalent in Euro), are seen as a possible threat to the economy of the SADC region. The counterpart to the CFA already exists: the CMA, formed in 1986, and previously known as the RMA (Rand Monetary Area). It was limited, however, to four countries: South Africa, Lesotho, Swaziland and Namibia.

Although France figures among South Africa's main trading partners, it is ranked 10th in a league in which the United Kingdom comes first, the USA second and Germany third. While its top trading partner on the continent, Zimbabwe, is ranked ninth,[42] South Africa's nearby

42   Source: Gauteng Tourist Agency document.

Francophone neighbours do not even figure in the statistics. Nevertheless, exports to the rest of the continent are on the increase, although this activity is mainly within the SADC. However, the SADC is very keen to expand commerce with the CFA countries, and South Africa has been negotiating with the European Union on a trade agreement. Furthermore, following the end of Apartheid, in April 1997 the European Union extended an invitation to South Africa to subscribe (with a special status) to the Lomé Convention.[43] The original convention (1975) had been signed by 71 ACP (African, Caribbean and Pacific) countries, all of whom (including South Africa) fall under the *champ de compétence* of the French Ministère de la Coopération.

French business intervention in the South African market has not always been a diplomatic success. The water deal brokered by the international consortium SAUR International (a subsidiary of Bouygues), a private–public partnership with the Dolphin Coast municipality, provoked indignation and very strong opposition on the part of the South African Municipal Workers Union (SAMWU), who threatened legal action against the Department of Constitutional Development and Provincial Affairs for approving the deal.[44]

Another factor prompting French interest in South Africa was the fear – or the expectation – that it was poised to 'colonise' its neighbours. In a major feature devoted to South Africa, the *MOCI* assessed the situation as follows:

> Déja dominatrice, l'Afrique du Sud a fait de l'ensemble du continent sa priorité géographique, en attendant d'acquérir une compétitivité industrielle suffisante pour se tourner largement vers la grande exportation. De quoi faire réfléchir les Français qui ont une carte à jouer en coopérant, quand cela est possible, avec les Sud-Africains en zones australe et francophone. Sinon, ils doivent se préparer à affronter des concurrents acharnés à reconquérir 'leur terrain de chasse'. D'autant que l'Afrique du Sud, en adhérant à la Communauté de développement de l'Afrique australe (SADC), est devenue le moteur de l'intégration régionale. Un pays incontournable, à la fois appelé au secours et rejeté. Un pays qui, quoi qu'il en soit, inquiète.[45]

43 Cling, J.-P., 'De la coopération régionale à l'intégration économique', in *Afrique Contemporaine*, p. 131.
44 *The Sunday Independent*, Business Report, 10 February 1999.
45 'L'Afrique du Sud va-t-elle coloniser ses voisins?', *MOCI*, 1234, 23 May 1996, pp. 32–65.

Tension between, for instance, the South African government and the neighbouring states, Zimbabwe and Zambia, confirms this analysis. Then, too, there is also a tendency in South Africa to blame immigration from other SADC (and Francophone) countries for the country's high levels of crime and unemployment. Emigration is not one way – a number of Namibians hold dual Namibian and South African passports, and own farmland, industries, mines, fishing rights, etc.[46] South African citizens have also emigrated to Angola, where co-operation agreements between the two countries are in place with regard to agriculture and animal husbandry, and where South African aid is available for the development of certain crop varieties. South African investors have put a great deal of money into the agro-industries (flour mills, breweries), diamond extraction and mining.[47]

Conversely, the interdependence created by globalisation is illustrated by the British decision in July 1999 to sell the United Kingdom's gold reserves. While this represented an immediate threat to the South African economy, it also confirmed the nagging concern that the various raw materials formerly of prime importance to Western economies no longer have the same strategic weight.

In terms of surface area, population, health statistics, GNP and trade, South Africa dwarfs its neighbours. South Africa alone accounts for 80% of the whole region's economic activity.[48] South Africa's contribution to the world economy may amount to only 0.45%, but compare that figure with the 0.58% for the whole of Southern Africa's share.[49] Its citizens constitute 44% of the population of the SADC countries, and there are some 700,000 migrant workers from other SADC countries in South Africa: their earnings, most of which are repatriated to their home countries, form an important share of the incomes of the states in question.[50] Currency, capital goods and trade movements are intense and increase the dependency of South Africa's neighbours – as does the landlocked situation of many of these countries. These considerations make it imperative for them to be integrated within the South African

46   Châtel, in Aicardi de Saint-Paul, pp. 265–6.
47   Simonet, in Aicardi de Saint-Paul, p. 281.
48   Aicardi de Saint Paul, p. 8.
49   Aicardi de Saint-Paul, p. 9.
50   Hugon, in Aicardi de Saint-Paul, p. 116.

system of logistics. The SADC brings together countries that may not carry the same weight in terms of economic power, but are still equal partners. The Windhoek Treaty (1992) underlined the close relationship between economic and political objectives: the member states pledged to subscribe to similar values and similar economic policies.[51] One of its missions is to promote macro-economic stability throughout the region. In particular, it co-ordinates investment programmes (transport, communications, agriculture, natural resources, the environment, trade, industry and human resources) throughout the region, helping to avoid duplication and waste, and also requires competitive bidding for major projects. Each member state has a specific responsibility for one sector of the economy: e.g. fishing for Namibia, transport for Mozambique, energy for Angola, agricultural research and training for Botswana, finance for South Africa.[52] Interdependence is increased by the members' reliance on customs and excise revenue from the SACU (South African Customs Union).

French interests in the region are all the more at stake since the SADC club includes Mauritius, a member of the rival Francophone organisation. The *MOCI* survey, for its part, pointed to a solution to the perceived South African threat to the *pré carré*: co-operation that would strengthen France's position on traditional markets and extend this partnership to the rest of Southern Africa.[53] The survey also pointed out that, though France needs South Africa in order to make forays into a region where her ignorance of the local languages, culture and business ethos puts French businessmen at a disadvantage, similarly, South African businesses are looking for partnerships with their French counterparts following their own failures to make progress on their own in the CFA zone. Bouygues, EDF and Lafarge are listed as 'present' in South Africa – Lafarge, a world leader in building materials, bought Blue Circle South Africa (ranked third in its sector in the RSA) in July 1998, and Accor, the hospitality chain, has been in South Africa since 1992 and bought Premier Lodge at the end of 1999, thus reinforcing its presence.

51   Gonidec, P.-F., 'Afrique du Sud: une nouvelle politique extérieure?', in *Afrique Contemporaine*, p.182.
52   Châtel, p. 267.
53   'L'Afrique du Sud va-t-elle coloniser ses voisins?', p. 60.

President Chirac's visit in 1998 was not confined to the limits of the Republic of South Africa; and neither are French commercial interests. Bouygues can be found in Lesotho (the Liatse dam project),[54] while Sanofi, Bull, Alcatel and Total have expanded across the whole of the Southern African region. Elf, which exploits a share of Angola's offshore oil reserves (the Dahlia and Girassol wells), has been present in that country since 1980 and (after Chevron) is the second largest operator there.[55] French banks have been expanding from their positions in Francophone Africa. BNP has been trading in South Africa, Namibia and Zimbabwe for some 20 years now, and is currently expanding into Tanzania and Angola. Conversely, the European Union accounts for 40% of the Republic of South Africa's exports and 52% of its foreign investments.[56] The Republic has been a member of the Lomé Convention since the end of Apartheid, albeit with a restricted status, re-negotiation of which started in 1996 and has not yet been completed. The country has also negotiated alternative partnership arrangements within the Indian Ocean Rim (IOR) with Australia, India and Mauritius.

Nelson Mandela left Cardiff empty-handed in 1997 when Britain held the presidency of the European Union. The following year's negotiations in Brussels in September 1998 (the 21st Round) offered three days of hard bargaining. The EU insisted that South Africa drop its remaining protective tariffs against EU industrial exports in return for the opening up of EU markets to South African agricultural goods, including wine. In addition, the EU sought to win access to South African waters for Spanish and Portuguese fishermen.

A candid new approach to the articulation of vested interests is now making itself felt. This can be interpreted as either cynical or refreshingly honest, depending, no doubt, upon the observer's own view of human nature. Archbishop Desmond Tutu set an example when he conceded that the aims and objectives of the Truth and Reconciliation Commission may have been impossibly noble and virtuous for ordinary human beings to achieve. However, the TRC was also the only realistic opportunity of reconciling the country with itself. Therefore, to assert a belief in its

---

54   'L'Afrique du Sud va-t-elle coloniser ses voisins?', p. 61.
55   Simonet, in Aicardi de Saint-Paul, p. 280.
56   Hugon, in Aicardi de Saint-Paul, p. 120.

ability to achieve its objectives was to be naïvely, but also rightly, correct.[57] This claim represented an assertion of faith in the phatic power of language. The Deputy Foreign Minister, Aziz Pahad, explained candidly that it was in South Africa's own, well understood, interests to invest in the rest of Africa, and that the benefits were mutual.[58] This statement bears comparison with Peter Mandelson's comment that he was going to South Africa on behalf of UK Inc. The fact that he is not the only person to have learned this new language is shown by some of the stalwarts of the Francophone movement within the *hexagone*.[59] Having restructured its whole approach to international aid, foreign policy and Francophone affairs in the interests of economy and efficiency, the French government can now state plainly that co-operation is good for the image of France abroad, as well as for the domestic economy; that it generates employment in France; reduces problems related with immigration; and makes people feel good while doing some good.[60]

In a global SWOT (strength; weakness; opportunities; threats) analysis, the 'threats' faced by Southern Africa have been neatly turned into a set of 'opportunities' for the rest of the world to engage in co-operation and investment: from the clearing of mine fields in Angola to converting 'rebel' forces into official military units, from urban crime and immigration to unemployment and income inequalities – expertise based on

57 Mark Gevisser, 'La Commission Vérité et Réconciliation en Débat', in Gervais-Lambony (ed.), *La nouvelle Afrique du Sud*, La Documentation Française, N0810, 1998, pp. 40–2.

58 Interview in *L'Express*, 15 May 1997.

59 The French Attaché Culturel, in an interview conducted in February 1999, in Cape Town, made the following disconcerting observation: 'La francophonie, c'est curieux, c'est quelque chose que je ne sens pas.' He explained that, since the South African Parliament was then in session in Cape Town, he was expending all his energies (and expanding his waistline) lobbying Ministers and MPs as well as local business leaders, trying to win their hearts through the old, tried route of appealing to their stomachs. While there was no doubting his commitment to the promotion of French interests in South Africa, or his knowledge of key players and understanding of the local situation, it was, however, precisely that understanding that prompted his cautious approach to *francophonie*.

60 See the 'Foreword' to the official Ministry document introducing the main features of the *réforme*, signed by both the Minister, Hubert Vedrine, and his délégué à la francophonie. Southern Africa and France speak the same language: co-operation is a virtuous circle.

experience is called for. The dearth of schools and training opportunities in a part of the world with high unemployment and great untapped natural resources (from fisheries, forestry, agriculture and mining to tourism, banking, finance and gambling), affords bright prospects. The geopolitical importance of the region compounds the interest. Not only is it of prime importance within the North–South axis that has been part of French political discourse based on its concept of *francophonie*, and one that has gained further currency through the EU and other international organisations, it is also important in terms of the region's very own ambitions. As Aziz Pahad has stated,[61] the Republic of South Africa's interest in the rest of Africa is 'because our future lies there'. Thabo Mbeki's vision of an African Renaissance is predicated on a scenario in which 'the North' has little part to play beyond its scripted words in the *dialogue nord-sud*. According to Mbeki, the main protagonists will come from the Southern Hemisphere and act through a range of alliances and institutions (IOR, MERCOSUR, etc) in which (starting with similar handicaps and similar assets) the SADC countries can be equal – or even leading – partners.

It is still the case that Africa south of the Sahara is France's third most important area of commercial activity outside the EU, and that South Africa itself ranks just ahead of the Ivory Coast as a trading partner.[62] Furthermore, French initiatives in peacekeeping have led to a number of collaborative undertakings, including military exercises that have brought together France, Britain, the United States and various African states. The third such operation, planned to take place in Tanzania in February 2002, will involve military personnel from Southern Africa and the Indian Ocean Rim, thus touching on another dimension of regional integration and co-operation.[63] In consequence, France's affirmation of its own definition of a 'vocation à l'universalité' through its reformed cultural, scientific and technical system of co-operation[64] is illustrated in Southern Africa.

61   *L'Express*, 15 May 1997.
62   'La politique africaine de la France', p. 2.
63   'La politique africaine de la France', p. 4.
64   'La politique africaine de la France', p. 5.

Patrick Corcoran

Language and Cultural Affiliation in West Africa: The Case of Ahmadou Kourouma

Situating Ahmadou Kourouma in a linguistic or cultural context is not an easy task. He is generally described as an Ivory Coast novelist, but for a variety of reasons Kourouma is a much travelled man. His particular brand of cosmopolitanism may be essentially African, but it nevertheless makes any attempt to categorise him exceptionally difficult. This is true for two chief reasons. Firstly, there is the fact that Kourouma originates from a princely Islamic family, and the family connections and networks that provided a practical infrastructure shaping his early experiences and upbringing bear no correspondence to the national boundaries that students of modern Africa would easily recognise. Secondly, Kourouma has never been reticent about giving voice to his political beliefs and has never shrunk from translating the convictions that flow from these beliefs into actions and decisions that have frequently incurred the wrath of professional politicians in the region. On several occasions, both in the period prior to the wave of African countries gaining independence in the 1960s and subsequently, Kourouma has been obliged to make decisions about how and where to earn his living on the basis of expediency rather than on the basis of free choice. He has frequently seen doors closed on him, both metaphorically, as posts to which he was appointed were suddenly no longer available, and physically, as he endured imprisonment during the period of Houphouët-Boigny's 'faux complots' in the early 1960s. Kourouma himself would be reluctant to employ words like 'exile' to describe his rather nomadic lifestyle,[1] but a good number of self-proclaimed African exiles have often had a less obvious and

---

1   Indeed Kourouma prefaces a comment on the matter of exile with the statement 'When I think about it […]': 'Quand j'y réfléchis, j'ai en effet toujours vécu d'exil en exil […] et en écrivant, je cherchais un peu à reconstituer le monde que j'avais quitté.' Dominique Mataillet, 'Qui êtes-vous Ahmadou Kourouma?', *Sépia*, 17, 1994, p. 5.

pressing need to distance themselves from the régimes they have chosen to 'flee'.

These biographical points are not offered as a way of explaining any aspect of Kourouma's work as a novelist. Instead they are intended to highlight the difficulty of using current vocabulary and current national boundaries in order to situate the man and his work. It could be argued that Kourouma is not so much an 'Ivoirien' as a man who originates from the Malinké people inhabiting the savannah regions of the former French Sudan. Their location on the present-day map of Africa would need to include not only much of Mali but also areas of north-east Senegal, northern Guinea, northern Ivory Coast and parts of Sierra Leone and Burkina Faso. Centred on the Niger river (the Djoliba), the Malinké culture is often claimed to be coterminous with the area in which the shea tree grows: 'les griots disent que font partie de la savane, du Mandingue, toutes les terres sur lesquelles pousse l'arbre de karité.'[2] This rather vague cultural boundary could hardly be more directly linked to natural, geophysical features and less dependent on abstract political distinctions. The Malinké peoples speak a number of closely related languages belonging to the Niger–Congo family: notably Malinké, Bambara, Dioula and Mossi (or Moore). The distinctions between these languages are not enormous, and speakers of each are relatively easily understood by speakers of the others. 'Dioula' is also the name given to a Malinké trader. Often, by the very nature of their occupations, *dioulas* are itinerants, and their language may be seen as a vehicular language distinct from, but having much in common with, both Malinké and Bambara. The distinction between these latter two languages is not related to the geographical origins of the speakers (as is the case with Mossi, for example). It rather reflects a deeper cultural difference within Malinké culture itself. Generally speaking, Malinké speakers have accepted the Muslim religion and are followers of Islamic traditions, while the Bambara are non-Islamised followers of animist beliefs and practices. As Kourouma's work constantly demonstrates, however, Malinké culture displays a high degree of syncretism in matters of religious belief, and the distinctions outlined here should be seen as mere generalisations.

2   Ahmadou Kourouma, *En attendant le vote des bêtes sauvages* (Paris: Seuil, 1998), pp. 135–6.

What they nevertheless clearly serve to underline is the fact that Malinké culture is simultaneously marked by variety – variety in the range of linguistic and cultural practices, including religious practices – and a high degree of homogeneity stemming from a common set of traditions and a deep-seated respect for shared origins.

What should be equally clear is the difficulty in providing any clear analysis as to the current status of Francophone influence within a cultural domain that does not correspond to clear national boundaries but extends across several countries. Given that all these countries have distinct educational and cultural policies, and variable levels of resources to bring to bear on these aspects of political life at the national level, the language situation with regard to French is understandably very different in each state. In the post-colonial context, however, both governmental policies and individual choices relating to language use, inevitably have a political dimension.

The very fact of writing in the language of the former colonial masters has often been problematised, notably by the Kenyan novelist Ngugi Wa Thiong'o, but also by writers from the Francophone diaspora as different as Sembène Ousmane, Sony Labou Tansi and Assia Djebar.[3] How individual writers perceive this question (or whether it continues to be perceived at all) depends on a range of social, political and cultural factors linked to geographical and historical circumstances. Interesting as this general question may be, it is sufficient for our present purposes to say that Kourouma is not generally given to soul-searching in this particular respect. That is to say, the 'language question' is not experienced by Kourouma in its political dimension; it is not problematised as a space within which political struggle is to be located. In various interviews that Kourouma has given over the years he has repeatedly been questioned about his use of language, but the emphasis of the questions as well as his responses has tended to focus primarily on stylistic matters rather than on the politics of post-colonial linguistic choice.

If his first novel, *Les Soleils des Indépendances* (1967),[4] gave the impression that a new voice had emerged in Francophone African writ-

---

3   Cf. Ngugi Wa Thiong'o, 'The Language of African Literature', in *Decolonising the Mind* (London and Nairobi: James Currey/Heinemann Kenya, 1981), pp. 4–33.

4   Ahmadou Kourouma, *Les Soleils des Indépendances* (Paris: Seuil, 1970).

ing, it was in no small measure because of the idiosyncratic style of
French he writes. Kourouma has frequently explained the reason for the
peculiarly hybrid quality of the language he employs, which he describes
in one interview as 'breaking the French language' by translating from
thought processes occurring originally in Malinké: '[J'ai] traduit le malinké en français, en cassant le français pour trouver et restituer le rythme
africain.'[5] This was the process that Makhily Gassama has analysed in
some detail in his book on Kourouma, *La Langue d'Ahmadou Kourouma*.[6] Interestingly enough, his subsequent novels have not attracted
quite the same sort of interest or provoked similar analyses, and Madeleine Borgomano rightly argues that there has been a gradual move away
from the stylistic peculiarities of his first novel towards more standard
forms of French:

> Dans *Monnè*, la langue de Kourouma reste encore un français mûri 'sous le soleil
> d'Afrique', comme l'écrivait si joliment M. Gassama, mais la malinkisation s'est
> nettement atténuée. *En attendant le vote des bêtes sauvages* a poursuivi cette
> évolution vers un assagissement.[7]

This seems to be borne out by Kourouma himself, who explains in a
recent interview that, with the passage of time, he now thinks in French
and that, in order to achieve the same stylistic effects, he would need to
translate in the opposite direction, no longer *from* but *into* Malinké:

> Quand j'écrivais *Les Soleils des Indépendances* je pensais en malinké. […] mais
> quand j'ai fait *Monnè, outrages et défis*, après près de 20 ans en dehors de mon
> pays, j'avais perdu ma langue, j'avais perdu la méthode. Il m'est impossible
> actuellement d'écrire *Les Soleils des Indépendances*. C'est fini […] Je pense en
> français. Il faudrait que je traduise du français en malinké.[8]

5   M. Badday, 'Ahmadou Kourouma: Écrivain africain', *L'Afrique littéraire et artis-
     tique*, 10, 1970.
6   Makhily Gassama, *La Langue d'Ahmadou Kourouma* (Paris: ACCT/Karthala,
     1995). Cf. Christopher Miller, *Theories of Africans* (Chicago: University of Chi-
     cago Press, 1990), especially pp. 201–6.
7   Madeleine Borgomano, *Des Hommes ou des bêtes* (Paris: L'Harmattan, 2000), p.
     167.
8   Patrick Corcoran, 'Entretien avec Ahmadou Kourouma', *ASCALF Bulletin*, no
     24, 2002.
9   Jean-Marc Moura, *Littératures francophones et théorie postcoloniale* (Paris: PUF,
     1999), p. 86.

Kourouma's latest novel, *Allah n'est pas obligé* (2000), confirms what is already apparent in different ways in all the previous novels, namely, that for Kourouma style cannot be dissociated from the search for a voice or for voices that adequately serve to take charge of the narrative they are called upon to embody. The key to an appreciation of Kourouma's language should involve not only focusing on specific linguistic, lexical and syntactic characteristics, but also recognising that such questions of style are inseparably linked to, and motivated by, the narrative strategies and techniques that increasingly structure the novels from *Les Soleils des Indépendances* onwards. Style is not some artificial veneer that can be applied or dispensed with at will. Nor, in the final analysis, is the Malinkisation of the French language and the production of a hybrid 'interlangue'[9] any more authentically 'African' than the more standard forms of language to be found in *Monnè, outrages et défis* (1990). Style in this sense is part and parcel of the search for the voice through which the narrative can be given authentic form. Kourouma hints as much in a recent interview in *Le Monde*:

> J'ai commencé par écrire dans un français académique, mais les personnages ne sortaient pas. Ayant fait des études de mathématiques, je n'éprouvais pas le respect pour la langue française de ceux qui ont une formation classique. Si j'avais étudié les lettres, je n'aurais jamais pu écrire ces romans.[10]

One has only to consider each of the novels in turn with the notion of 'voice' in mind in order to recognise how unswerving Kourouma has been, throughout his career as a novelist, in foregrounding the act of speech and the act of 'prise de parole' as a structuring narrative device. The narrative voice in *Les Soleils des Indépendances* may appear to be that of a conventional third-person narrator, but the register of the narrative voice is usually that of spoken language. The 'Malinkisation' of the language operates partly through the essentially oral style of the third-person narration as well as through the use of dialogue and 'discours indirect libre'. It also includes numerous devices typically associated with oral communication, such as references to proverbs, the use of highly coloured popular images, direct appeals to the reader, the use of

10   Catherine Bédarida, 'Ahmadou Kourouma, le guerrier-griot', *Le Monde*, 1 November 2000, p. 15.

rhetorical questions, repetition and the internal revision of the narrative as it progresses: all of these contribute to what J.-M. Moura has referred to as a 'mise en scène de l'oralité'.[11] Moura might be forgiven for not having made even passing reference to *En attendant le vote des bêtes sauvages* (1998) here, since the latter novel appeared only months before his own book was published. What leaps out from the pages of Kourouma's third novel, however, is the fact that it is structured entirely upon a type of ritualised oral performance, the *donsomona*, involving characters such as the *griot*, Bingo, the *répondeur*, Tiécoura and the implied audience made up of the brotherhood of hunters. This audience also includes characters who figure in the diegesis, such as Koyaga or Maclédio. This is not merely a 'staging of the act of oral communication or of the oral tradition itself' (depending on how Moura's formulation is to be translated), it is a staging of the act of narration as a ritualised and highly self-conscious performance, which narration itself involves a staging of the act of communication, much along the lines described above. The structuring framework of the novel is a meta-narrative that self-referentially explains the principles of its own organisation, as when Bingo directly addresses the listeners/readers to tell them that each of the 'veillées' is dedicated to a key theme: 'Une veillée ne se dit pas sans qu'en sourdine au récit ronronne un thème. La vénération de la tradition est une bonne chose. Ce sera le thème [...] de cette première veillée.'[12] Thus, not only is the audience instructed in how the narrative is produced, organised and structured, it is also given instructions on how best to consume it and how to understand the purposes to which it should be put: the *donsomona* is after all a purification rite, with a very special function.

In his second novel, *Monnè, outrages et défis*, the complex way in which the narrative is organised is also readable in terms of 'voices'. Madeleine Borgomano has analysed the phenomenon in some detail and is prepared to take issue with Kourouma himself when he suggests there are three different 'paroles' in the novel, as she herself identifies five

11   Moura, *Littératures francophones et théorie postcoloniale*, p. 85.
12   Kourouma, *En attendant le vote des bêtes sauvages*, p. 10.

different narrators.[13] Elsewhere, Kourouma is even less disposed to adopt an analytical approach to his narrative technique, commenting simply: 'C'est un livre très complexe parce que […] c'est les gens de Soba qui racontent leur histoire.'[14] The diversity of voices assuming responsibility for the narrative is a clear feature of the technique Kourouma employs in this novel and is reflected in the switch of pronouns that occurs when the third-person narration is interrupted by the use of the first person, 'je', designating the protagonist, Djigui, and, on occasion, Fadoua, or by the use of 'nous', behind which the reader may assume the presence of the 'petit peuple' of the town. The overall effect is rather similar to witnessing a *palabre* or some other form of oral linguistic performance in many voices, but without the 'stage directions' that might have helped the reader to reconstruct the choreography of the narrative. What is certain is that this novel, too, repeats Kourouma's tendency to focus on acts of speech and linguistic performance as a way of structuring narrative form.

In the most recent of Kourouma's novels, *Allah n'est pas obligé*, the polyphonic narration of the earlier works gives way to a narrative that is comparatively unified. The novel has a first-person narrator: the street boy, Birahima, who assumes control of the narrative and directly addresses his readers from the outset. To help him in his task as narrator, Birahima has recourse to four dictionaries to which he constantly refers throughout the course of the novel. The explanation for this, which he gives in the opening pages, associates their use with the need to make the novel accessible to a varied readership:

> Ces dictionnaires me servent à chercher les gros mots, à vérifier les gros mots, et surtout à les expliquer. Il faut expliquer parce que mon blablabla est à lire par toute sorte de gens: des toubabs (toubab signifie blanc) colons, des noirs indigènes sauvages d'Afrique et des francophones de tout gabarit (gabarit signifie genre). Le Larousse et le Petit Robert me permettent […] d'expliquer les gros mots du français de France aux noirs nègres indigènes d'Afrique. L'Inventaire des particularités lexicales du français d'Afrique explique les gros mots africains aux toubabs

13   Referring to a comment made by Kourouma in 'Entretien avec Bernard Magnier', *Notre Librairie*, 103, October–December 1990, she writes: 'Il semble qu'on puisse distinguer dans l'ensemble du roman, non pas trois, mais au moins cinq formes du narrateur.' Madeleine Borgomano, *Ahmadou Kourouma: Le 'guerrier' griot* (Paris: L'Harmattan, 1998), p. 162.

14   Corcoran, 'Entretien avec Ahmadou Kourouma'.

> français de France. Le dictionnaire Harrap's explique les gros mots pidgin à tout
> francophone qui ne comprend rien de rien au pidgin.[15]

Hence, as in the earlier novels, the structuring framework of the narrative is itself integrated within the narrative act, not this time as a staging of the act of oral communication but as a staging of the act of writing. (Birahima specifically states that his 'blablabla' is intended to be read.) Moreover, there are frequent comments through which Birahima self-consciously draws attention to the act of narration, particularly at the end of many of the novel's numbered sections. At the end of the second section, for example, we have:

> Moi non plus, je ne suis pas obligé de parler, de raconter ma chienne de vie,
> de fouiller dictionnaire sur dictionnaire. J'en ai marre; je m'arrête ici pour au-
> jourd'hui. Qu'on aille se faire foutre![16]

The references to the various dictionaries that punctuate Birahima's narrative can be seen as having a number of distinct functions. They constantly remind the reader of the fact that the narrator's voice is a hybrid one, and that both his language and the culture expressed through it may require an act of translation in order to become comprehensible. In this sense, the dictionary glosses obliquely and implicitly call to mind the varied elements of the audience to whom the narrative purports to address itself, and they indirectly include that audience in the narrative as Birahima's omnipresent interlocutors. The glosses also foreground the very process of selection, through which the narrative is constituted as a series of choices that ultimately enhance or hinder the possibilities of success in establishing communication. In order to make the 'other' understandable, difference has to become in some way assimilable. The dictionary glosses represent a naïve effort to ensure the 'other' becomes readable; Birahima is at least attempting to make his story comprehensible. But as the horrific subject matter of the narrative unfolds with its account of tribal war and the atrocities that go with it, it becomes clear that 'otherness' in this context is not merely 'cultural difference', but more precisely a whole world of brutalising experiences and opaque

15   Ahmadou Kourouma, *Allah n'est pas obligé* (Paris: Seuil, 2000), p. 11.
16   Kourouma, *Allah n'est pas obligé*, p. 101.

motivations that risk becoming illegible once divorced from their own special context. How to communicate cultural 'otherness', how to make an alien culture 'readable' to outsiders are questions that seem to be transformed, in this novel, into an attempt to communicate and make readable the radical 'otherness' that is the experience of the arbitrary and gratuitous violence of war as seen through the consciousness of a child. The dictionary glosses are perhaps a way of allowing the child to focus on language issues rather than the realities they 'cover'. They act as a screen or filter that allows raw experience to be constantly mediated by language, and invested with explicative and interpretative discourse before being delivered to the plurality of audiences that await it. Thinking oneself into the culture of another is as difficult a task as trying to imagine the horrors of war from the comfort of one's own fireside. They are worlds apart. And like the dictionary glosses, the novel's foregrounding of the act of narration provides a way of ensuring that the events narrated move that little bit further into the background; like 'cultural difference' the horrors of war have to be subjected to mediation. They have to be processed and pass through the filter of the act of narration before they can be consumed.

And this is perhaps what makes the dictionary glosses ultimately irrelevant and, in the long run, something of an irritant to the reader. Perhaps they even end up telling us more about how dictionaries work, about how essentially pleonastic they are as they multiply discourses on experience without necessarily increasing the possibility of improving understanding and empathy. Birahima himself seems to understand this on occasion, as the following example suggests:

> C'était un centre de rééducation. (Dans le Petit Robert, rééducation signifie action de rééduquer, c'est-à-dire la rééducation. Walahé! Parfois le Petit Robert aussi se fout du monde.)[17]

The dictionary glosses are merely one type of repetitive intervention that characterises Birahima's narrative style. They cannot be considered independently from a second, equally frequent type of interjection: the obscenities that also punctuate the narrative with great regularity. Indeed, both types of interjection are in different ways concerned with 'gros

17   Kourouma, *Allah n'est pas obligé*, p. 74.

mots'. The 'gros mots' Birahima checks in the dictionaries are the 'big words' and concepts he feels he needs to gloss as he reaches out to his interlocutors. The 'gros mots' that provide Birahima's own commentary on his experiences are simply obscene expressions that seem to be pointing back at himself, reminding readers that the narrator is an insolent and impudent street urchin whose experience as a boy soldier has led him into a life where murder and the use of hard drugs are commonplace. When he explains this characteristic of his narrative style, in the opening pages of the novel, he is at pains to stress the difference between himself, an authentic Malinké, and those Africans who have been assimilated to French language and culture:

> [Je] suis insolent, incorrect comme barbe d'un bouc et parle comme un salopard. Je dis pas comme les nègres noirs africains indigènes bien cravatés: merde! putain! salaud! J'emploie les mots malinkés comme faforo! (Faforo! signifie sexe de mon père ou de ton père.) Comme gnamokodé! (Gnamokodé! signifie bâtard ou bâtardise.) Comme Walahé! (Walahé! signifie Au nom d'Allah.) Les Malinkés, c'est ma race à moi.[18]

As was the case in the earlier novels, the particular style that Kourouma assigns to the voice of Birahima is heavily, almost self-consciously marked. We have already seen that Kourouma refers in interviews to the process of translating from, or into, Malinké or French, as the case may be, as a way of describing the process involved in the search for a voice through which the narrative may be given shape. It is probably not surprising therefore, that the notion of translation and the use of dictionaries should play such a dominant role in Birahima's narrative strategies. These strategies actually turn out, in the final pages of the novel, to be symbolically significant. We learn that the young narrator has inherited the dictionaries from an interpreter whose name was Varrassouba Diabaté and who originated from his native village of Togobala. As Birahima explains: 'C'était un Malinké et, chez les Malinkés, lorsque quelqu'un porte le nom de Diabaté, il est de la caste des griots'.[19] The self-confessed insolent, uncouth, verbally-challenged narrator would appear to be the inheritor of a noble Malinké tradition. His position as last in the line of

18   Kourouma, *Allah n'est pas obligé*, p. 10.
19   Kourouma, *Allah n'est pas obligé*, pp. 229–30.

the renowned 'maîtres de la parole'[20] provides a mocking confirmation of the decadence of Malinké culture.[21]

Part of the irony here, of course, is the fact that Birahima himself would not make the connections that Kourouma is inviting his readers to make. Proud as he is of belonging to the Malinké race, Birahima lacks the maturity and experience to see that the Malinké world view he represents in the novel is being swamped in the morass of moral and ethical turpitude that cannot be dissociated from the upheaval of tribal war. The references to Malinké beliefs and practices that pepper the novel fail to provide a meaningful structure within which a child such as Birahima can grow. On the contrary, war has reduced his existence to a degree zero of precariousness, exemplified perhaps by the fate of Kik, for whom Birahima takes the trouble to offer the following *oraison funèbre*:

> Kik regagna la concession familiale et trouva son père égorgé, son frère égorgé, sa mère et sa soeur violées et les têtes fracassées. Tous ses parents proches et éloignés morts. Et quand on n'a plus personne sur terre, ni père ni mère ni frère ni soeur, et qu'on est petit, un petit mignon dans un pays foutu et barbare où tout le monde s'égorge, que fait-on?
>
> Bien sûr on devient un enfant-soldat, un small-soldier, un child-soldier pour manger et pour égorger aussi à son tour; il n'y a que ça qui reste.[22]

Even the search for understanding (and the constant recourse to the authority and security of the dictionaries is perhaps another futile gesture in this direction) repeatedly peters out with the circular argument that things are as they are because that is the way Allah wants them to be. As the title constantly reminds us, Allah is not obliged to be fair in all the things he does.

Kourouma may be prepared to be frank about the decadence of Malinké culture, as appears to be the case in *Les Soleils des Indépendances* and *Monnè, outrages et défis*, but the bankruptcy of traditional

---

20   Cf. Camara Laye, *Le Maître de la parole* (Paris: Plon, 1978).

21   Kourouma's personal identification with Malinké culture and traditions never prevents his analysis of them from being extremely critical and often ironic. In the interview with Dominique Mataillet he comments, 'C'est en effet une société quelque peu décadente. Une société dépassée, qui vit avec des mythes.' Dominique Mataillet, 'Qui êtes-vous Ahmadou Kourouma?', p. 4.

22   Kourouma, *Allah n'est pas obligé*, p. 100.

Malinké belief systems is by no means the central message of *Allah n'est pas obligé*. In all of his novels, Kourouma writes about the everyday predicament of his fellow Africans as they attempt to feed and clothe themselves, and seek to make their way in a world where historical, political and economic circumstances have stacked the cards against their succeeding. They may appear to cling to belief systems that provide little help in solving their problems, but Kourouma is not interested in passing judgement on such systems any more than he seeks to judge Fama, Djigui, Koyaga or Birahima.[23] The cultural context within which his characters operate is a 'given' to be explained, illustrated and dramatised, not some accidental feature of their lives of exotic interest to Western readers or historical interest to Africans themselves. Ultimately, this cultural context is merely one element of the story, and the meanings and values it carries within it are constantly and ironically challenged by the suggestion that there are other positions to be understood and other cultures vying for dominance. In fact, Kourouma makes it impossible to experience Malinké culture in an unadulterated form. It has to be read through the prism of alien cultural realities and juxtaposed to other ways of viewing the world. For all his hankering after a lost past, Fama has little choice but to live in the 'modern' world and constantly faces the pressure to adapt. Similarly, in *Monnè, outrages et défis* it is Djigui's world view that remains the central focus of the novel, and this tends to marginalise the forces that are combining to drive political change in Africa. So it is not the focus on Malinké culture that is the prime interest in Kourouma's novels, it is the richer question of the relationships that exist between the Malinké world view and other ways of understanding experience.

The points at which cultures are depicted as coming into contact are therefore worthy of particular attention. Leaving aside language and specifically linguistic issues for the moment, it nevertheless remains true that instances of cultural contact (or more accurately the difficulties experienced in seeking to bridge cultures) are a regular feature of the diegesis in Kourouma's novels. In both of his first two novels, for instance, there are examples of 'frontier crossings' that have particular, even poignant significance as moments of cultural contact.

23   The protagonists of Kourouma's four novels to date listed in chronological order.

The first of these occurs towards the end of *Les Soleils des Indépendances* when Fama, who has been released from prison (itself a 'frontier crossing' of sorts), finally turns his back on the capital and heads for his native village, Togobala. His journey is interrupted at the bridge crossing the river that separates the two fictional modern-day republics of the Côte des Ébènes and Nikinai. Tensions between the two countries are so great that the frontier has been closed. Fama, as prince of the region straddling the two countries, known in pre-Independence days as Horodougou, refuses to accept this as a reason for delay. His refusal is simultaneously a refusal of modern geopolitical realities, notably the very existence of this frontier and the existence of the two republics that embody this redrawing of the map, and a refusal of the historical process itself, which has seen his own traditional power base, already undermined by colonialism, subsequently replaced by a new dispensation in post-Independence Africa (namely the one-party states). Fama's response is to ignore the closed frontier and set off across the bridge, before lowering himself over the parapet on the other side. Shots ring out at the same time as the sacred crocodiles, disturbed by Fama, move into action. Fama is mortally wounded by a crocodile, retrieved from the bank by Nikinai soldiers and dispatched to the nearest town. He dies *en route*, close to the town of Togobala, thus confirming the prediction made earlier in the novel that the last of the Doumbouya dynasty would end his days in his native village in Horodougou.

It would be wrong to suggest that this scene is open to two different readings. However, Kourouma manages to control the narrative's development in a very subtle way so that two different views of a single set of narrative events are respected and made possible. On the one hand, this is an account of a prosaic border incident – an insignificant skirmish in which soldiers on both sides open fire because they think they are being attacked. The incident is triggered by an old man without the requisite papers, who was due to be evacuated back to the capital, and who ends up being attacked by crocodiles. But the prosaic details provided in this account of the incident are interwoven with a narrative voice that has an almost epic quality, and recognises and acknowledges both Fama's princely status and his claims to stand above the petty politics of the modern world. This is achieved partly through switches in the narrative perspective. From one sentence to the next, Kourouma switches from an objective third-person narration of practical details to a 'discours indirect libre', which allows the reader access to Fama's own views on what is unfolding. This can be easily tracked by printing the objective narration in italics and the indirect voice of Fama in normal type:

> Fama était dans le Horodougou, jamais il ne devait accepter d'en sortir. *La grille de fils de fer barbelés était à quelques pas. Une porte y était faite du côté du parapet gauche.* Un Doumbouya, un vrai, père Doumbouya, mère Doumbouya, avait-il besoin de l'autorisation de tous les bâtards de fils de chiens et d'esclaves pour aller à Togobala? Évidemment non. *Fama, le plus tranquillement du monde, comme s'il entrait dans son jardin, tira la porte et se trouva sur le pont.*[24]

Accompanying these switches in the way the narrative is focused is a narrative voice that eschews any concerns for the prosaic practical realities of the incident. It involves a third-person narration, but one that foregrounds the natural world and has something of a timeless quality about it. This narrative voice recounts events not as a chronological sequence, but rather as a coming to fruition of events that have been long awaited, have been foreseen and are inevitable.

> Et comme toujours dans le Horodougou en pareille circonstance, ce furent les animaux sauvages qui les premiers comprirent la portée historique du cri de l'homme, du grognement de la bête et du coup de fusil qui venaient troubler le matin. [...] Les forêts multiplièrent les échos, déclenchèrent des vents pour transporter aux villages les plus reculés et aux tombes les plus profondes le cri que venait de pousser le dernier Doumbouya. Et dans tout le Horodougou les échos du cri, du grognement et du fusil déclenchèrent la même panique et les mêmes stupeurs.[25]

Within this narrative perspective the reader is made aware that the events recounted have a wider, almost metaphysical, significance and portray matters of great import. As the gunfire ceases and silence falls, the return to calm can be read on two levels. The skirmish has finished,

---

24   Kourouma, *Les Soleils des Indépendances*, pp. 198–9. A second example: 'Les gros caïmans sacrés flottaient dans l'eau ou se réchauffaient sur les bancs de sable. Les caïmans sacrés du Horodougou n'oseront s'attaquer au dernier descendant des Doumbouya.' *Les Soleils des Indépendances*, p. 200.
25   Kourouma, *Les Soleils des Indépendances*, pp. 200–1.

or the predictions about the end of the Doumbouya dynasty are being fulfilled: 'Les coups de feu s'arrêtèrent. Mais le matin était troublé. Tout le Horodougou était inconsolable, parce que la dynastie Doumbouya finissait.'[26]

A second example of a particularly significant moment of cultural contact is to be found in the opening pages of *Monnè, outrages et défis*, when the invading French troops enter the town of Soba, catching the defending townsfolk and their prince, Djigui, completely unawares.[27] There is a deep irony about the way this scene is presented, not least because this simulacrum of a conquest is the only first-hand portrayal in the novel of an incident supposedly from the renowned Samorian wars of resistance to the French. The Malinké people continue to look back to Samory with great pride, but the circumstances of Djigui's defeat could hardly be less heroic. All Djigui's efforts have been directed to the construction of a defensive mound around the town. The French troops simply by-pass these defences and enter the town by the sacred hill of Kouroufi, which Djigui has not bothered to include in his defensive plans because he believes it to be protected by the spirits of the ancestors and its strong magical properties. A boundary that exists in a powerful way for Djigui and his people has no reality whatsoever within the mental universe of the invading troops. The boundary belongs to a world view rooted in cultural practices that have no meaning for the newcomers. The shock of the collision of cultures is thus portrayed through the mutual incomprehensibility of the two sides. There is no conflict in military terms, and, indeed, had Djigui succeeded in joining battle with the French, the shocking effect of their arrival in Soba would have been far less successfully portrayed than is the case in this depiction of their peaceful entry into the town.

The meeting between Djigui and the French troops is narrated in such a way as to emphasise the collision of cultures that is the key to understanding this scene:

---

26 Kourouma, *Les Soleils des Indépendances*, p. 202.
27 Cf. Patrick Corcoran, 'Cultural ambivalence in the novels of Ahmadou Kourouma', in *The Changing Frontiers of 'Francophonie'* (Oxford/Bern: Peter Lang, forthcoming 2002).

De l'immense chantier montait une clameur de chants, de cris et de prières qui avait appelé des charognards plus noirs et gros que ceux qui évoluent habituellement dans les cieux du Mandingue. Djigui le remarqua sans y attacher de signification. Les sorciers lançaient contre les Nazaréens les plus terribles sorts; les marabouts les maudissaient avec les versets les plus secrets; les griots louangeaient le roi. Les sbires administraient des coups aux bâtisseurs. La légende prétend que, ce jour-là, le soleil était immense et écrasant.

C'est quand Djigui arriva en tête de l'escorte du côté de Kouroufi, au bout du chantier, qu'il trouva, arrêtée, une colonne française. La vraie colonne française, en tête à cheval, le capitaine et le lieutenant blancs, casque colonial et costume blancs, le pistolet à la ceinture, les jumelles et le sifflet en sautoir, l'interprète à droite des Blancs.[28]

The description of the moments leading up to the meeting are narrated almost as a celebration of time-honoured Malinké cultural practices. The narrative voice has an epic quality about it as it details the role and functions of the various actors directly or indirectly involved in the work of constructing the defensive mound. Djigui's blind faith in the rightness of his tactics is an affirmation of the cultural beliefs that inform his whole life. His interpretation of the manifest destiny of the dynasty to which he belongs and the people under his rule has led him to choose this strategy. The shock registered at the sight of the French troops is conveyed through a sudden change in the narrative focus. Details of the almost ritualised behaviour of the people of Soba give way to the prosaic description of physical objects and people, with the emphasis on their real rather than magical properties: 'la vraie colonne française'.

The difference between Djigui's world and the world of the invading forces is symbolically inscribed in the novel as the ability or the failure to recognise the boundary represented by the sacred hill of Kouroufi. The crossing of the boundary by the French troops marks not only a military conquest and the end of Djigui's effective political control of Soba, it also constitutes a challenge to the Malinké system of cultural hermeneutics through which the world was interpreted and meanings ascribed to events. It is for this reason that the arrival of the French is seen by the griot, Diabaté, as ushering in a new world order with its own language and symbols which he must learn to decipher: 'Chaque fois que les mots changent de sens et les choses de symboles, je retourne à la

---

28   Ahmadou Kourouma, *Monnè, outrages et défis* (Paris: Seuil, 1970), pp. 33–4.

terre qui m'a vu naître pour tout recommencer: réapprendre l'histoire et les nouveaux noms des hommes, des animaux et des choses.'[29] In a sense, this acknowledgement of the new dispensation is something which Djigui can never bring himself to make. French hegemony may be a political reality but Djigui manages to live a life of politico-cultural denial, co-cooned in a parallel universe that preserves its own codes and its own rituals.

In Kourouma's treatment of both Fama and Djigui the contact between cultures is depicted in a subtle and ultimately ambivalent way. The historical reality of the French colonial presence is not disputed, however much the foregrounding of outmoded Malinké views tends to push historical reality into the background. Similarly, the contention that traditional Malinké culture is essentially decadent and an outmoded tool for interacting with the world would appear to be omnipresent, particularly in the theme of sterility that pervades *Les Soleils des Indépendances*.[30] The rear-guard actions led by Fama and Djigui in defence of the Malinké world view are doomed to failure, but in each case the way in which they are portrayed as failing reads more like an affirmation than a rejection of Malinké traditional beliefs. Fama's refusal to acknowledge the existence of the frontier between Côte des Ébènes and Nikinai makes it possible for the novel to conclude with the fulfilment of the predictions about the end of the Doumbouya dynasty. Against all the odds, Malinké hermeneutics turns out to be an effective tool for reading the world. Likewise, the narrative voice through which Djigui's death is recounted at the end of *Monnè, outrages et défis* is the voice associated with the magical hermeneutics of the Malinké world view:

> La vie venait de quitter Djigui; il ne passa pas les limites de Soba: les nombreux sortilèges qu'ils avaient enfouis dans le sol de la ville et le sang des sacrifices avec lesquels les Keita avaient arrosé ce sol ne l'avaient pas permis.[31]

---

29 Kourouma, *Monnè, outrages et défis*, p. 41.

30 Cf. 'La stérilité de fait dans laquelle disparaît Fama est le symbole de la fin définitive de l'espèce des chefs traditionnels et, au-delà, le symbole de la *disparition d'une époque*.' (Emphasis in original.) Jean-Claude Nicolas, *'Les Soleils des Indépendances' d'Ahmadou Kourouma* (Issy-les Moulineaux: Éditions Saint-Paul, 1985), p. 103.

31 Kourouma, *Monnè, outrages et défis*, p. 278.

It is not only through the *topos* of 'border crossings' or by the deployment of subtle narrative techniques and strategies that Kourouma cultivates ambivalence with regard to cultural values and cultural affiliation. As we have already seen in the case of the griot, Diabaté, the communicative possibilities of language itself are ultimately the issue when cultures collide. This fact is amply illustrated by the role of the interpreter, Soumaré, in *Monnè, outrages et défis*. Far from acting as a self-effacing channel of communication through which the colonial masters convey their will to the colonised people of Soba, Soumaré is a hybrid creature who gives voice to hybrid linguistic creations and even more frequently to hybridised cultural concepts. He neither translates nor seeks to find equivalences in order to explain the message of the Whites, but rather creates his own imagery and his own version of the message as, for example, when he explains what colonisation means and how the system will operate:

> le grand dessein de la colonisation [...] s'appelait la civilisation que, faute de mot correspondant, il traduisit par 'devenir toubab'. Les mots firent sursauter Djigui. L'interprète rassura tout le monde en expliquant que civiliser ne signifie pas christianiser. La civilisation c'est gagner de l'argent des Blancs. Le grand dessein de la colonisation est de faire gagner de l'argent à tous les indigènes.[32]

Soumaré's way of acting as a bridge between the two cultures involves a process of creating a third version of the realities he is called upon to express. His way of conceptualising and explaining the colonisation process has a sort of independent authority about it, and both his economic status and the power he wields within the social hierarchy seem to flow from the very distinctiveness of the hybrid linguistic creations that appear throughout the novel. In short, Soumaré appears to be a

---

Kourouma, *Monnè, outrages et défis*, p. 57. The narrative voice once again reflects the essentially hybrid nature of the communication process. This passage begins as a form of reported speech, switches to a third-person narrative in mid-sentence and goes on to employ verbs in the present tense: a strategy one would assume to be indicative of direct speech.

living embodiment of the characteristics that Bhabha ascribes to the concept of the Third Space.[33]

Frequently, therefore, Soumaré's attempts at interpretation are a source of misunderstandings[34] and indeed, often involve intentional deception, as when he refuses to translate Djigui's words to the French captain at their first meeting. He explains to Djigui: 'Comme tous les Keita tu es un fanfaron irréaliste. Je n'ai pas traduit un traître mot de tes rodomontades.'[35] The reason why Soumaré feels free to take such liberties, not only with Djigui but with his office as interpreter, is firmly rooted in a Malinké tradition, which the colonisers would have struggled to comprehend. Soumaré and Djigui are in fact bound together in the special clan relationship of *sanankounya*,[36] which makes each a *frère de plaisanterie* to the other. The relationship has a number of features: each may speak openly and mockingly to the other without either being able to take offence at, or seek redress for, what has been said; they may not harm each other, and they are duty-bound to honour their peculiar alliance and offer each other help and assistance.

What is involved here is, in fact, a ritualised speech relationship, which effectively ensures that the dissident, ironic voice cannot be stifled. Soumaré is able to say what he likes to Djigui without ever having the slightest fear of the consequences. Much the same sort of ritualised

33 'It is only when we understand that all cultural statements and systems are constructed in this contradictory and ambivalent space of enunciation, that we begin to understand why hierarchical claims to the inherent originality or "purity" of cultures are untenable. [...] It is that Third Space, though unrepresentable in itself, which constitutes the discursive conditions of enunciation that ensure that the meaning and symbols of culture have no primordial unity or fixity; that even the same signs can be appropriated, translated, rehistoricized and read anew.' Homi Bhabha, 'The Commitment to Theory', in *The Location of Culture* (London and New York: Routledge, 1994), p. 37.

34 Cf. Borgomano, *Ahmadou Kourouma: Le 'guerrier' griot*, pp. 168–75.

35 Kourouma, *Monnè, outrages et défis*, p. 36.

36 'La "Sanankounya" est une alliance particulière qui permet d'échanger des plaisanteries ou de se dire des vérités sans que cela puisse tirer à conséquence ni entraîner de suites fâcheuses. [...] La sanankounya (appelée par certains ethnologues "parenté à plaisanterie" ou "libération catharsique") peut exister entre deux individus, deux ethnies ou deux pays.' Ahmadou Hampaté Bâ, *L'Étrange Destin de Wangrin* (Paris: UGE: 10/18, 1992), p. 448, note 204.

relationship exists between Bingo, the griot (and chief narrator of *En attendant le vote des bêtes sauvages*), and Tiécoura, the apprentice-griot or *cordoua*, whose role is to act as respondent to the narrator.[37] More often than not his interventions are marked by their brutal honesty, as he summarises Bingo's narrative without any attempt at euphemism or circumlocution, or by the comic and usually ironic tone of his mocking commentaries on the narrative that is unfolding. Here the dissident voice is in a privileged position: Tiécoura is untouchable and therefore free to say what he pleases in the manner and tone of his own choosing. This careful ritualisation of the act of enunciation serves to create a screen between the act of narration and the bloody events that constitute the narrative: it is as though the brutality of the dictator, Koyaga, and the bloodshed and violence that are the leitmotifs of the account of his life exist in a world that is divorced from the world in which the purificatory rite of the *donsomana* is taking place.

Writing in 1990 about *Les Soleils des Indépendances*, Christopher Miller was quick to pick up on the Bakhtinian qualities of the narrative, describing it as a 'carnavalesque arena in which competing voices perform; no single voice is able to dominate or silence the others,'[38] and going on to mention 'the "unofficial", antiauthoritarian, and antiunitary power of Kourouma's novel'.[39] These qualities of the first novel recur in the later works, but with an increasing tendency towards a ritualisation of the act of enunciation. As we have seen, such ritual may provide a framework for the act of narration itself, or it may appear as a mere event within the narrative, but the intention remains that of creating a safe space from within which the voice of 'dissidence' may constitute its own hybrid version of reality and give utterance to it. The appeal that Kourouma thus makes to Malinké culture as a way of providing a vehicle for the process of ritualisation seems to go beyond Bakhtin. It is not so much a case of opposing 'official' and 'unofficial' forms of language and

---

37   'Un cordoua est un initié en phase purificatoire, en phase cathartique. Tiécoura
       est un cordoua et comme tout cordoua il fait le bouffon, le pître, le fou. Il se
       permet tout et il n'y a rien qu'on ne lui pardonne pas.' Kourouma, *En attendant le
       vote des bêtes sauvages*, p. 10.
38   Miller, *Theories of Africans*, p. 237.
39   Miller, *Theories of Africans*, p. 238.

thought,[40] as of using language and thought that can be ascribed to competing versions of 'officialdom'. Malinké culture, traditions and beliefs sit alongside non-Malinké elements (including the novel form itself and the French language) in order to force the reader to accept the need for 'code-switching', a step that is necessary before a reading can take place at all. This raises the question of whose language and whose cultural frame of reference is to be taken as the accepted, official version of language and culture.

There is, of course, no answer to such a question. Nevertheless, in the novels of Kourouma, Malinké language and culture on the one hand, and French language and culture on the other, would appear to exist in an ironic relationship of mutual dependency. Like 'frères de plaisanterie', each is the source of discourses that call into question orthodoxies, challenge received wisdom and ultimately subvert the discourse of the other. Such is the dialectic of this process that it is not possible to associate Kourouma's work with any given ideological stance. His politics are a matter of finding an appropriate rhetoric with which to say the scandalous nature of the unsayable, whether this be the scandal of colonial rule, the scandal of post-Independence African dictatorships or the scandal of child-soldiers in more recent tribal and inter-ethnic conflicts in Africa. 'Rien en soi n'est bon, rien en soi n'est mauvais. C'est la parole qui transfigure un fait en bien ou le tourne en mal,' Fama cynically thinks at one point.[41] However, Kourouma's task is not to endorse or contradict such a statement. Rather, he offers his readers illustrations of how language both generates the cultural and ideological realities that structure our sense of identity, and is itself shaped by them.

40   Miller, *Theories of Africans*, p. 238, note 85.
41   Kourouma, *Les Soleils des Indépendances*, p. 109.

Dawn Marley

Diversity and Uniformity: Linguistic Fact and Fiction in Morocco

Morocco is a multilingual country, whose complex sociolinguistic landscape is characterised by bilingualism and diglossia. Officially, however, it has one national and official language, 'Arabic'. Arabisation has consistently been the basis of Moroccan language policy since Independence in 1956, and yet the language of Arabisation has never been the mother tongue of any Moroccan. The vast majority of Moroccans actually speak a dialect of Moroccan Arabic or a variety of Berber, while French is widely used in education, business and commerce, the media and elsewhere.

This chapter will briefly describe the sociolinguistic reality of the country and then examine the political and ideological motivation behind a language policy that ignores it. It will also consider the cultural tensions created by such a policy and in particular will look at the role of the two languages that represent major obstacles to Arabisation: French and Berber. These two languages are associated with cultures that are perceived as antagonistic towards 'national' culture, for very different reasons. French is an exogenous language, initially imposed on the country by a colonial power and now representing modern, Western culture, whereas Berber is the indigenous language, predating Arabic in Morocco and representing an arguably more 'authentic' traditional culture. In their different ways, both languages create problems, linguistic and cultural, for language policymakers in Morocco, as their continuing presence undermines the fiction of Arabic as the sole national language, uniting the country in a uniform culture, and draws attention to the sociolinguistic and cultural diversity that is regarded by many as an important part of Morocco's national character.

Sociolinguistic Reality

This section will briefly describe the sociolinguistic landscape of Morocco, taking each of the languages in turn and explaining their cultural and social significance. The languages will be examined in chronological order, starting with Berber, generally acknowledged as the indigenous language of the area, then Arabic, which was introduced in the seventh century, and finally French, which was introduced at the end of the nineteenth century and imposed on the country during the French Protectorate between 1912 and 1956.

Berber is the term used by Europeans to refer to the indigenous languages of the Maghreb, spoken not only in Morocco but also in Algeria, a small part of Tunisia and parts of adjoining sub-Saharan countries. The term covers a large number of related, but not all mutually intelligible languages of the Hamito-Semitic family, which are distantly related to Arabic. Most Berber speakers in Morocco belong to one of three main groups: Tashelhit, Tamazight and Tarifit, which are spoken in three distinct regions of the country. There are no official statistics for Berber speakers, since Moroccan censuses have not, until 1993, included a question about language, and so figures have been advanced based on information from the *Carte des Tribus* and the *Carte Administrative*. On this basis, Boukous[1] estimates Berber speakers as 50% of the rural population in Morocco and 40% of the overall population. The Summer Institute of Linguistics[2] gives the following conservative estimates for numbers of speakers of the main three dialect groups in Morocco in 1991, adding that a survey is needed: Tashelhit: 2,300,000; Tamazight: 1,900,000; and Tarifit: 1,500,000. It is not only numbers of speakers that are imprecise; any information about Berber languages is difficult to obtain due to their lowly status and lack of written form in Morocco. Although a Berber script (Tifinagh) does exist and is increasingly used in the modern cultural movement, this script has never been used in

---

1   A. Boukous, 'La langue berbère: maintien et changement', *International Journal of the Sociology of Language*, 112, 1995, pp. 9–28.
2   B. F. Grimes (ed.), *Ethnologue* (Summer Institute of Linguistics, 1996).

Morocco, and Berber speakers have only ever become literate through Arabic.

For centuries Berber has co-existed with Arabic in a situation of diglossia (in the extended sense of the term used by Fishman),[3] with Berber acting as the L language that is used in everyday domestic and agricultural life, and oral culture (songs and storytelling), but has no place in education, administration or, obviously, religion, where Arabic is used. Despite its lack of prestige compared to Arabic, it has nonetheless remained 'une langue à valeur symbolique qui façonne l'imaginaire des berbérophones et définit leur identité culturelle collective face à l'altérité.'[4] Its importance is evident from the very fact that it has survived fourteen centuries of competition from Arabic. Although the Berbers embraced Islam when Arab invaders brought it to North Africa in the seventh century, and revered Arabic as the language of divine revelation, they did not automatically become Arabic-speakers. Arabic-speakers did eventually become the majority population in Morocco, but, though Berbers have become bilingual they have not abandoned their own language and associated culture.

The survival of Berber languages over fourteen centuries may, however, have much to do with the fact that Berber communities have mainly lived in remote mountain areas and have had limited contact with anyone outside their own community. In modern times this is changing, particularly with the growth in compulsory education and the phenomenon of rural exodus. Like so many minority languages in modern states, Berber suffers from its image as the language of the uneducated and backward peasant, whereas Arabic is seen as the language of social promotion. The Berber heritage has also suffered the same fate as did regional languages in France in the Republican education system, that of being systematically ignored or presented in a pejorative way, thus further undermining any sense of pride in Berber identity. According to Ziri,[5]

---

3   J. A. Fishman, *Sociolinguistics: A Brief Introduction* (Rowley: Newbury House, 1971).
4   Boukous, 'La langue berbère: maintien et changement', p. 11.
5   R. R. Ziri, 'Le mouvement amazigh ou la réalité d'un Maroc oublié', *Parimazigh*, 5, February 2000.

'[l]'école et les médias ont été utilisées systématiquement pour faire croire aux Berbères qu'ils n'existent plus, aussi majoritaires soient-ils!' These factors have led to an apparently irreversible decline in Berber languages, which have been increasingly marginalised in recent years. This decline, however, is to a certain extent countered by the growing awareness of the value of Berber language and culture, and conscious attempts to maintain their vitality. The very process of marginalisation has caused what Boukous[6] refers to as 'un éveil identitaire qui donne naissance à un mouvement de revendications s'inscrivant dans le cadre des Droits de l'homme.' There is a growing Berber cultural movement, at the local, national and international levels, which will be discussed in some detail below (pp. 378–84).

By contrast, Arabic has for centuries been the language of prestige in Morocco, but the term 'Arabic' has so far been used in quotation marks due to its ambiguity. The term covers a wide range of varieties of language, described by a bewildering number of terms that will not be discussed here,[7] but can be summarised as 'Classical' and 'Dialectal'. In general, 'Classical' is used to refer to the written, standardised language, while 'dialectal' refers to the spoken, non-standardised variety. In Morocco the dialectal form of Arabic is significantly different to the standard in terms of vocabulary, grammar and pronunciation, and therefore the standard form is effectively a foreign language. Although the constitution does not specify which variety is meant when it refers to Arabic as the national language, it is the standard written form that is taught in schools, used in all government institutions and the media, and promoted as the official language, despite the fact that it is not a national language inasmuch as it is never spoken as a mother tongue.

This fact is rarely mentioned publicly, but in recent years the taboo seems to have lifted slightly: it was acknowledged by the Ministre de

---

6   A. Boukous, 'La langue et culture amazighes: entre la plénitude du fait et la vacuité du droit', p. 24, *Prologues, revue maghrébine du livre*, no.17, été 1999.

7   See A. Youssi, 'The Moroccan Triglossia: Facts and Implications', *International Journal of the Sociology of Language*, 112, 1995, pp. 29–43; F. Laroussi and F. Madray-Lesigne, 'Plurilinguisme et identités au Maghreb', in D. Marley, M.-A. Hintze and G. Parker (eds), *Linguistic Identities and Policies in France and the French-Speaking World* (London: AFLS/CiLT, 1998), pp. 193–204.

l'Éducation Nationale, Rachid Ben Mokhtar, in his official speech to the Conference of Moroccan French Teachers in 1998: 'Il faut reconnaître que nous avons un problème de langue. Nous avons une langue nationale qui n'est pas la langue maternelle bien qu'elles se rapprochent.'[8] The following year an article appeared in the national press, asking why the debate on Arabisation could not be more open and demanding an admission that 'Classical' Arabic is a foreign language for Moroccans, who speak 'Moroccan Arabic', a language that officially does not exist.[9] Despite the official silence on the subject, linguists have for many years been examining the relationship between Moroccan Arabic and the national language. Mouhssine, for example, claimed that the 'duality' that exists between Dialectal and Classical Arabic is the 'fondement même de la personnalité arabe',[10] and that the Classical language has been able to remain 'pure' and unchanged because the dialects have taken on the role of dealing with everyday life and changes in society. Moroccans, like other Arabic speakers, see their own language as a 'deviant' or 'impure' form of the 'true' Arabic language, yet if they were to use this Classical language for everyday life it would soon lose its 'purity'. At present, the situation of diglossia, which has existed for centuries, continues, with Moroccan Arabic as the L language, and Classical Arabic as H, used for religion and all written purposes. However, this situation is changing, according to Boukous.[11] He claims that yet another variety of Arabic is coming into existence, which he calls *arabe médian*. It is used by educated speakers in formal or semi-formal circumstances, for example on radio and television, in order to avoid both Classical Arabic and Moroccan dialect; the former, either because they do not speak it well enough, or because it sounds pedantic, and the latter because it can sound vulgar. Thus it appears that the Classical–Dialectal diglossia is becoming triglossia, with *arabe médian* serving a particular purpose for situations where neither of the other two alternatives is appropriate.

A complex sociolinguistic situation, with widespread diglossia and bilingualism, thus obtained for several centuries, and was further compli-

8   *Recherches Pédagogiques*, 1998, p. 16.
9   Ben Abbes Taarji, 'Et si on apprenait le dialecte', *L'Opinion*, 1999.
10   O. Mouhssine, 'Ambivalence du discours sur l'arabisation', *International Journal of the Sociology of Language*, 112, 1995, p. 52.

cated by European colonisation from the mid-nineteenth century. Spanish
had been spoken in northern regions of Morocco from about the fifteenth
century, following the end of the *Reconquista*, when Muslims and Jews
fled Spain and took refuge there. From the mid-nineteenth century, the
Spanish colonised parts of Morocco, thus increasing the importance of
the Spanish language in certain areas, mainly the north. It was French,
however, the language of the European Protectors from 1912 to 1956,
that quickly made a significant impact on the national sociolinguistic
landscape. During the Protectorate French became a new H language,
and even after independence it has continued to be a language of prestige.
Clearly, French could not usurp the place of Arabic in religious contexts,
but it did become the language of administration and education, and was
learnt by a very small minority of Moroccans. Since Independence,
however, a far greater percentage of the Moroccan population has been
educated, at first bilingually, later in Arabic, but with French featuring in
the curriculum as first foreign language from the third year, and so the
number of French speakers, or potential French speakers, is greater than
ever. Although French is not mentioned at all in the Moroccan constitution, and is never even referred to officially as 'second language', it is
often referred to as a 'langue étrangère privilégiée' or even '*la* langue
étrangère',[12] and in reality it dominates in certain domains, particularly
in commerce and finance, science and technology, and increasingly in
the growing sector of the media. It also continues to be vital for any
position of importance in the private or public sector, and is seen as the
language of social and professional success.

From this brief outline of the sociolinguistic landscape of Morocco,
it is clear that imposing standard Arabic as the only official language
was always bound to meet with opposition, as people had – and still
have – very valid reasons for not wanting to adopt Standard Arabic as
their language. In terms of everyday communication, they see no reason
to give up their mother tongues, and in terms of work and communication

11   A. Boukous, *Société, langues et cultures au Maroc. Enjeux symboliques* (Rabat:
      Publications de la Faculté des Lettres et des Sciences Humaines-Rabat, 1995), p.
      35.
12   H. Esmili, 'Statut, usage et rôle du français au Maroc', in S. Abou and K. Haddad
      (eds), *Une Francophonie différentielle* (Paris: L'Harmattan, 1994), p. 395.

with the outside world generally, French appears to be better adapted and more useful in the modern world. Few Moroccans would dispute the importance of Arabic as a vital symbol of Moroccan national identity, yet in practice many Moroccans have a serious problem with their official language, and hesitations and opposition from various sources have, from the outset, marked official language policy. The next section will examine the factors that help to explain a language policy that seems destined to achieve only partial success.

The Grounds for the Policy of Arabisation

After 44 years of French rule, during which time French had been the official language, the development of a language policy was one of the primary issues facing the newly independent Moroccan government in 1956. Whereas many African countries formerly under French rule adopted French as the official language, Morocco, in common with Tunisia and Algeria, opted to replace French with Arabic, and thus embarked upon a policy of Arabisation, a policy seen as central to the building of an independent nation. However, despite the official discourse in favour of Arabisation, its implementation has not always been so consistent, a fact observed by linguists, among others. Grandguillaume, assessing the situation in 1983, noted that

> à cette forte affirmation de la légitimité d'une langue nationale correspond une lenteur dans la mise en œuvre, l'expérience d'une extrême difficulté à se détacher du français, voire parfois la conscience d'une sourde résistance au processus engagé, d'un complexe d'attirance et de répulsion pour l'arabe, qui fait que [...] la pratique passée, présente et prévisible est une insertion toujours plus grande dans une position de bilinguisme.[13]

More recently, Boukous summed up Moroccan language policy as a

13   G. Grandguillaume, *Arabisation et politique linguistique au Maghreb* (Paris: Maisonneuve et Larose, 1983), p. 29.

compromis pragmatique [...] entre la francophonie et l'arabisation [...] Cette situation reflète les ambivalences d'une PL [politique linguistique] qui tergiverse entre les pesanteurs de *l'authenticité* et les aspirations à la *modernité*, ce en quoi elle est plus symbolique et idéologique que rationnelle et efficiente.[14]

There are a number of reasons for both the insistence on the import-ance of Arabisation in theory and for the tendency to maintain bilin-gualism in practice. This section will aim to explain why Arabisation is seen as such a vital basis for Moroccan language policy by those in power, and why their actions do not always match their words.

Arabisation is first and foremost promoted as the cultural counter-part of political and economic independence, a means of liberation from dependency on colonial cultural models. Morocco has been a Muslim country for centuries, and the reinstitution of Arabic was an assertion of its Arabo-Islamic identity. Arabisation was thus promoted as being the only way to restore the 'authentic' identity of the country. This would appear to be an indisputable basis for a language policy and one that would be popular and beneficial for all concerned, were it not for the fact that the form of Arabic used is not the form spoken by Moroccans. As discussed in the previous section, Standard Arabic is effectively a foreign language for most Moroccans, even though it is linguistically closely related to Moroccan Dialectal Arabic. Reinstating Arabic as the language of administration, education and the media certainly was a means of asserting independence from France, but although 'cultural independence' was a genuine ideological motivation, it was by no means the only motivating factor. The following paragraphs examine other factors less frequently mentioned by the policymakers.

Perhaps the most important of these is the pursuit and maintenance of power. As Grandguillaume observed, if Arabisation is 'un élément indispensable d'une construction nationale' it is also 'l'un des moyens par lesquels un pouvoir national établit et renforce son contrôle sur l'ensemble de la population.'[15] Boukous states bluntly that those already in power 'définissent une PL [politique linguistique] dont les choix visent

14   A. Boukous, *Dominance et différence: essai sur les enjeux symboliques au Maroc* (Casablanca: Éditions Le Fennec, 1999), p. 61.

15   Grandguillaume, *Arabisation et politique linguistique au Maghreb*, p. 34.

la sélection sociale en déterminant les règles d'accès au groupe des élites.'[16]

The idea that Arabisation restores an authentic identity makes it popular with the masses, who believe that they are thus liberated from foreign oppression, and will enjoy greater equality of opportunity than before. Those in power, however, promote Arabisation apparently from purely ideological motives, but also in the knowledge that French continues to be a necessary requisite for social and professional success, and that they can assure their own hold on power by educating their children bilingually. The policy of Arabisation, with *de facto* bilingualism in key sectors, thus fits Cooper's framework of language planning as the pursuit and maintenance of power:

> To the extent that cooperation of the mass is a prerequisite for the maintenance of elites and to the extent that benefits to the mass encourage cooperation with elites, the latter are well-advised to channel benefits to the former or *at least give the appearance of doing so.*[17]

To the illiterate masses, Arabisation was a purely symbolic policy, since they had never learnt French in the first place. Nevertheless, they were led to believe that they would benefit from Arabisation, as it would liberate them from French cultural oppression. Most Moroccans are therefore in favour of Arabisation because they see it as an important expression of cultural independence, but in actual fact they do not necessarily benefit from it, as it is the bilingually educated élites who continue to obtain the best posts in almost all walks of life.

A further indication that the traditional élite uses Arabisation in the pursuit and maintenance of power is suggested by Boukous.[18] He points out that official discourse claims that Arabisation means returning Arabic to the status it held before the Protectorate, yet the vast majority of Moroccans never knew Standard Arabic, being illiterate, and the small élite who did learn the language continued to do so in the Franco-Muslim

16 Boukous, *Dominance et différence: essai sur les enjeux symboliques au Maroc*, p. 53.

17 R. Cooper, *Language Planning and Social Change* (Cambridge: Cambridge University Press, 1989), p. 83. Emphasis added.

18 Boukous, *Dominance et différence: essai sur les enjeux symboliques au Maroc*, p. 77.

schools set up by the French. Thus the argument that Arabic was taken away from Moroccans is an invalid one, which was used by the traditional élite in order to regain the power they had lost during the Protectorate.

Another openly stated objective of Arabisation is to unite the country. Such an objective is common to language policies in many newly independent states, as the idea of linguistic unity provides a strong symbol of an independent nation and unites the people behind their leaders. The government of independent Morocco legitimised its power by claiming to represent and further the national cause, using the national language as a potent symbol of that cause. As Cooper points out, language can be the supreme symbol of a national cause (what he calls the 'common destiny'), or may even be 'manipulated to help create the *perception* of a common destiny'.[19] In other words, one language can be so presented that people will believe it symbolises their national culture, even though they do not actually speak or even understand it. In fact, Arabic represents a unifying force at two levels, symbolising both Islam and the nation. As the language of divine revelation, it represents and unites all Muslim believers in the mythical Islamic *Umma*; at national level it overtly symbolises self-affirmation against foreigners, notably the French, and covertly symbolises unity against the diversity of dialects. One logical consequence of this would appear to be the eventual disappearance of other languages – Dialectal Arabic and Berber languages – and the ethnic assimilation of Berbers.

The eradication of Arabic and Berber vernaculars has not been explicitly stated as an objective of Arabisation, but it would be the logical long-term result of the policy, since it is hard to see the value of a national language that nobody speaks or understands. Boukous goes so far as to say that 'dans le discours nationaliste, l'arabisation a aussi un objectif assimilationiste.'[20] The non-recognition of Berber languages and culture, their exclusion from the education system and their marginalisation in the media are not the results of a *de jure* decision, but are nevertheless seen as necessary to the construction of the nation state, where linguistic and cultural diversity are perceived as dangers. In pursuing a policy of

19   Cooper, *Language Planning and Social Change*, p. 86.
20   Boukous, *Dominance et différence: essai sur les enjeux symboliques au Maroc*, p. 77.

linguistic unity, Morocco thus appears to be following the example of France, where linguistic unity has symbolised national unity for centuries. It has also had the effect of undermining to the point of almost total extinction all languages other than French. It has often been argued that not only was this necessary for national unity, but also that French language and culture were inherently superior to the regional languages and cultures. Arabic has an immediate advantage in this type of argument, as it is already revered as a superior language for religious reasons, which makes it all the easier to persuade people that it is the only appropriate language for use in a Muslim state. Ziri points out that appealing to people's religious feeling has been successful in boosting a sense of Arab identity in Morocco:

> L'arabité et l'Islam se sont confondues pour ne plus être qu'un seul et unique repère identitaire. Les Marocains sont musulmans donc arabes! Le berbère n'est qu'un particularisme régional sans aucun statut, si ce n'est celui de l'infériorité et de l'ignorance.[21]

To conclude this discussion of the ideology behind Arabisation, the idea of national identity needs to be explored a little further. Arabisation has been promoted as the way to restore an 'authentic' national identity, but 'authenticity' is not easy to define. Essentially, the restoration of Arabic as the official language represented the return to a more traditional Islamic identity, but there are two major problems with this. Firstly it assumes that pre-colonial society was exclusively Arabic-speaking and Islamic, ignoring the substantial Berber population; secondly it ignores the fact that all living cultures are subject to change, and that the changes that Moroccan society had undergone during the colonial period could not simply be forgotten. Moroccans did wish to reaffirm their own cultural identity as an Arabo-Islamic people, yet they did not want to lose the undoubted benefits that contact with French had brought them, namely an introduction to the world of modern science and technology and Western consumer civilisation. Arabisation therefore needed both to restore Arabic to its former status as the official language, representing

---

21   Ziri, 'Le mouvement amazigh ou la réalité d'un Maroc oublié'.

Morocco's Islamic past, but also to make it the vehicle of modernity, expressing the values of an outside culture, and incorporating them into Moroccan identity. The idea that 40 years of exposure to an outside culture could simply be forgotten, particularly when it represented so many attractive benefits, and when contacts with it – through immigration, commerce and other means – were to remain so great, was unrealistic.

Inevitably, the issue of national identity was not resolved following Independence. Tahar Ben Jelloun[22] acknowledges that there was a need for a redefinition of national identity after the colonial era, but claims that simply imposing an Arabo-Islamic identity is to deny the richness and diversity of Moroccan culture, which has always been influenced from inside by Berber, Jewish and Bedouin cultures, and has been open to French and other European influences. The various different elements that had always co-existed were made to feel out of place, and the attempt to impose uniformity actually led to cultural antagonisms. The fact that Berber militants are ever more vociferous within Morocco and elsewhere, and that French continues to be the language of choice in a number of important domains underlines the fact that Arabic does not appear to be an adequate means of expressing modern Moroccan identity. Mouhssine suggests that the ambiguity of the role of Arabic is symbolic of the very nature of Moroccan society. She refers to a number of observers who have drawn attention to the cultural crisis being suffered by Moroccan society and concludes that 'la langue constitue elle-même un enjeu: enjeu culturel où l'arabisation devient porteuse de toutes les contradictions qui travaillent la société.'[23] She also points out, like so many other researchers, that the issue of identity is problematic in Morocco because there are several elements to be taken into account, not least the different languages spoken by Moroccans.

---

22   T. Ben Jelloun, 'Défendre la diversité culturelle', in Y. Lacoste and C. Lacoste (eds), *Maghreb: peuples et civilisations* (Paris: La Découverte, 1995), pp. 94–6.
23   Mouhssine, 'Ambivalence du discours sur l'arabisation', p. 46.

Major Developments in Moroccan Language Policy since Independence

Although Arabisation is seen as desirable and the ultimate goal of Moroccan language policy, even within the ranks of power there are differences of opinion as to how this should be achieved. On the one hand, the Istiqlal party represents those in favour of rapid and total Arabisation, while on the other, the late King Hassan II took a more pragmatic approach. On a number of occasions he spoke publicly in favour of bilingualism; in 1978, for example, before a parliamentary commission, he said 'Nous sommes pour l'arabisation. Mais si elle est un devoir, le bilinguisme est une nécessité.'[24] A decade later he was quoted in a national newspaper[25] as saying:

> Je considère que ceux qui ne cessent d'appeler à l'arabisation ne sont pas encore libérés car leur esprit est encore bourré d'infériorité [...] Le fait que je parle la langue française – et j'aurais aimé parler d'autres langues – ne signifie pas que je suis encore sous le Protectorat des Français.

More recently he gave a press conference on international French television advocating a balanced bilingualism.[26] The Mouvement Populaire, led by Mahjoubi Aherdane, is also in favour of maintaining Arabic–French bilingualism, while including calls for the teaching of Berber languages.

In contrast to this approach, Istiqlal and allied groups have, at different times, sought to put pressure on the government to drive forward the Arabisation process, for example in 1970, when they circulated the *Manifeste des Ouléma, intellectuels et des hommes de pensée*, a protest against bilingualism that gathered more than 500 signatures and was published in the national press.[27] In 1973 a communiqué demanded the Arabisation of the whole education system, the administration and public life.

24   Quoted in Mouhssine, 'Ambivalence du discours sur l'arabisation', p. 49.
25   *L'Opinion*, 1988.
26   TV5, 17 September 1995, quoted in Boukous, *Dominance et différence: essai sur les enjeux symboliques au Maroc*, p. 79.
27   *L'Opinion*, 8 August 1970.

Despite such differences, which have often led to hesitations over how to proceed, the government has implemented the policy of Arabisation, firstly by giving Arabic official status, and then by creating a legislative framework to support that status. There exists a large corpus of laws relating to language policy, of which the most important are listed by Boukous[28] and reproduced here.

1957:   Education Minister Mohammed El Fassi decides on the progressive Arabisation of primary education.
1958:   Following the failure of the previous reform, arithmetic and science return to being taught in French at primary level.
1959:   The report of the Commission Nationale de l'Éducation et de la Culture reaffirms the *absolute necessity* of studying Arabic, but also advises maintaining Arabic–French bilingualism, even at primary level, and therefore also at higher levels.
1959:   The doctrine of national education is drawn up by Education Minister Abdelkarim Benjelloun. The principles are unification, Arabisation, generalisation and Moroccanisation.
1960:   Arabisation of the administration by M. Boucetta.
1960–4:   Five-year plan opts for a progressive Arabisation of primary education between 1958 and 1964, with French being taught for ten hours a week.
1965–7:   Three-year plan delays the Arabisation of secondary education; only history and geography are to be Arabised, but Arabic sections are created in higher education.
1965:   The use of Arabic is made obligatory in courts of law.
1967:   Primary education is completely Arabised.
1970:   *Colloque d'Ifrane.* The King recommends that the four principles outlined in 1959 should be applied in the following order: Moroccanisation, then Arabisation, then generalisation and lastly unification.

28   Boukous, *Dominance et différence: essai sur les enjeux symboliques au Maroc*, pp. 65–7.

1968–72: Five-year plan confirms the Arabisation of primary education and boosts the Arabisation of secondary schooling, especially of philosophy.

1973–7: Five-year plan sees the beginning of the Arabisation of human and social sciences in higher education. A. Laraki defines educational policy as education through 'the Arabic language, the Muslim religion and Moroccan humanism'.

1978–80: Three-year plan opts for the total Arabisation of sciences in secondary education over the next few years. The King makes a speech before the Parliamentary Commission for National Education, where he underlines the need to maintain French–Arabic bilingualism in education.

1983: Arabisation of secondary education is completed.

1986–94: Measures are put in place to cope with the problems faced by Arabised school-leavers going into scientific disciplines at university.

1990: The first cohort of fully Arabised school-leavers.

1994: The king recommends the teaching of Berber dialects in his speech to mark the 'Fête du Trône' on 3 March.

1995: The Commission Nationale de la Réforme de l'Enseignement recommends the complete Arabisation of the whole education system. The King declares himself opposed to 'systematic and blind Arabisation of the education system'.

In addition to the legislative framework, a number of organisations have been set up to assist in the implementation of language policy. Again, Boukous[29] lists the most important, which are given here.

1959: Creation of the Conseil Supérieur de l'Éducation Nationale.

1960: Creation of the Institut d'Études et de Recherches pour l'Arabisation.

1961: Creation of a ministerial commission to study the problems in the education system.

29   Boukous, *Dominance et différence: essai sur les enjeux symboliques au Maroc*, p. 68.

1961:   Meeting of the Congress of Arab States devoted to Arab-
            isation.
1963:   'La semaine de l'arabisation'.
1964:   National conference on education, whose recommendations
            represent the nationalist vision of language policy.
1969:   Conference of Maghrebian education ministers on the nor-
            malisation of vocabulary, the Arabisation of primary educa-
            tion and the adaptation of Arabic for science teaching.
1989:   Study days devoted to preparing Arabised school-leavers to
            study science at university.

Numerous *ad hoc* commissions have also been created within the Ministère de l'Éducation Nationale to deal with the educational implications
of Arabisation and the creation of appropriate teaching materials. The
result of all this activity is that primary and secondary education are
now fully Arabised, as are the social and human sciences at university
level, while science and technology are still taught in French at University level. In the administration, technical departments still function in
French, while Arabic is the working language of legal, social and cultural
departments.

    In addition to these organisations, a language planning institution
was set up in 1960, the Institut d'Études et de Recherches pour l'Arabisation (I.E.R.A.), which had a number of aims, all of which could be
classified, in Haugen's terms,[30] as 'elaboration of function of the Arabic
language', i.e. making Standard Arabic an adequate tool for teaching
and administration in Morocco. The creation of the I.E.R.A. was a recognition of the twin objectives of Arabisation: to return Arabic to its pre-
colonial status and to give it a new role as the vehicle of modern science
and technology. It is the second objective that has proved a stumbling
block to total Arabisation, for two main reasons. Firstly, French is readily
available and is already adapted to this task; secondly, Arabic suffers
from two major drawbacks: the lack of vocabulary and the need to reform
the script (traditionally vowels are not included, and letters have three or
even four different forms, depending on their place in the word, making

---

30   E. Haugen, 'Dialect, Language, Nation', *American Anthropologist*, 68, 1966, pp.
      922–35.

comprehension and printing difficult). Although these problems have often seemed insurmountable, and the use of French so much easier, in recent years significant progress has been made, largely as a result of the work of Ahmed Lakhdar-Ghazal, who created a method for the development of scientific terminology in Arabic in 1976 and also devised a reformed script. This script, however, has never been used, much to the disappointment of some commentators, such as Ben Abbes Taarji,[31] who believes that if it could be brought into general use it would vastly improve the levels of literacy in Morocco. At present the illiteracy rates leave much room for improvement, being 43.7% for the whole population aged 15 and above, with male illiteracy at 56% and female illiteracy at 31%, according to estimates made in 1995.[32]

This account of the legal and operational framework of Arabisation shows that there has been considerable direct state intervention to regulate and promote this language policy. As stated at the outset of this chapter, however, it is clear that the basic objectives of the policy, both explicit and implicit, have still not been achieved. French remains the *de facto* language for most of the higher education system, particularly in science and technology, as well as the working language of parts of the government administration and much of the private sector. It is estimated that there are more than 10 million Berber speakers, and their numbers are not in terminal decline. Far from disappearing, the two major groups in opposition to total Arabisation, those in favour of balanced French–Arabic bilingualism and the Berber cultural movement, are growing stronger. Arabisation appears to be failing in its attempt to unite the country linguistically and culturally.

Supporters of *Francophonie* tend not to criticise Arabisation outright, for fear of appearing 'unpatriotic' or favouring Western domination and neo-colonialism, but they do advocate bilingualism, claiming it is necessary for a more efficient education system. Critics of the present system would point out that since Arabisation was completed in schools in the late 1980s the number of private schools offering a bilingual education has multiplied rapidly. This highlights the fact that the provi-

31   Taarji, 'Et si on apprenait le dialecte'.
32   CIA, *The World Factbook* (http://www.odci.gov/cia/publications/factbook, 1998).

sion of an exclusively Arabic education is not producing good results, particularly in science and technology, where the resources are simply not available in Arabic. During the first two decades after Independence, when the education system – still bilingual – was opened up to all social classes, children of all backgrounds had access to all domains of professional activity. Since the completion of the Arabisation process in education, most children do not acquire a grounding in French adequate to enable them to compete for the best posts, which now go to those whose parents have the means to send them to a private bilingual school. There is therefore some evidence that Arabisation has led to the very opposite of what was claimed for it: lesser rather than greater equality of opportunity.

In contrast to the pro-French lobby, the Amazigh (Berber) cultural movement has become more open and acceptable in recent years. This movement seeks to restore value to languages that have historical legitimacy as the 'original' languages of Morocco, but that have been under attack for centuries, and aims to revive the written forms of these languages, and the folklore and oral culture that accompany them. The success of this movement can be judged by the setting up of a daily news bulletin in each of the major dialects, the creation of an Institute of Amazigh Studies,[33] and the speech in favour of the teaching of Berber languages in schools made by the late King in 1994. These successes may be mere tokens, but they indicate official recognition and are vital to the ultimate success of this movement, which will be discussed in greater depth below (pp. 378–84). The rest of this chapter will look in more detail at the two major counter-currents to Arabisation and the cultural antagonisms they represent.

To conclude this section, a brief mention must be made of the *Charte nationale d'éducation et de formation*, the most recent attempt at educational reform, which takes effect from the start of the school year in September 2000. At the time of writing it is too early to comment on its impact, but its implications for Moroccan language policy are far-reaching. According to Article 110 of the *Charte*, Morocco will now be adopting 'en matière d'enseignement, une politique linguistique claire,

---

33   Boukous, *Dominance et différence: essai sur les enjeux symboliques au Maroc*, p. 91.

cohérente et constante', which involves three major points: 'renforcement et perfectionnement de l'enseignement de la langue arabe', 'diversification des langues d'enseignement des sciences et des technologies' and 'ouverture sur le Tamazight'.

Significantly, the word 'Arabisation' appears nowhere in the whole document, a recognition of the negative connotations of the term. Berdouzi[34] acknowledges that systematic Arabisation of science teaching would consign millions of young Moroccans to a 'cultural and socioeconomic ghetto'. The *Charte* does announce the creation of an Arabic language Academy, which will oversee the modernisation of the language, but in the meantime it acknowledges that science and technology should be taught in schools in the language used for these subjects at university. At present, this means French, but this is not made explicit, and there is the implicit suggestion that it could equally well mean English. The *Charte* thus appears to acknowledge implicitly that Arabisation in state education has not been a total success, and heralds a temporary return to some degree of Arabic–French bilingualism.

The other new departure is the 'ouverture sur le Tamazight', the eventual recognition of the fact that not all Moroccans are Arabic-speakers. The *Charte* allows local authorities to use any local dialect 'dans le but de faciliter l'apprentissage de la langue officielle au préscolaire et au premier cycle de l'école primaire' (Article 115). It also provides for the creation of research and development projects in some universities, and support for teacher training and programme development in Tamazight. Such measures, though falling short of those demanded by some activists, nevertheless go a lot further than any other policy document to date.

This latest and most thorough reform of the education system appears to be making major steps towards acknowledging and seeking to rectify problems caused by national language policy since Independence, but it is as yet too early to know the extent to which it will have a real impact.

---

34   M. Berdouzi, *Rénover l'enseignement: de la charte aux actes* (Rabat: Renouveau, 2000), p. 21.

The Changing Role of French

This section will assess the changing view of French in Morocco on the basis of a number of sociolinguistic studies covering the last two decades. The salient findings of each study will be discussed, in chronological order, with the aim of indicating how language policy is viewed, and to what extent attitudes have changed in recent years.

Bentahila's study (1983) set out to assess language attitudes among Arabic–French bilinguals in Morocco and was based on a sample of Moroccans from various parts of the country, including both men and women from a variety of occupations. What all these informants had in common was what Bentahila called a 'balanced' bilingualism: they felt themselves to be equally fluent in both French and Arabic as a result of a bilingual education. These informants

> represent the majority of the reasonably educated younger generation, those who are under forty-five and have received a bilingual education at least to secondary school level,[35]

and are fairly unequivocal in their attitudes towards Arabisation and bilingualism: while they may support the ideals behind Arabisation, they do not wish to give up the advantages that knowledge of French brings, and they do not want their children to miss out on these advantages. Bentahila's conclusion is clear:

> Our study suggests that Moroccan bilinguals consider their knowledge of French to be a considerable asset, which offers them greater knowledge, wider experience, access to the Western world and to an endless supply of material which they would not otherwise be able to reach. The language planners who seek to impose a policy of Arabization should pay considerable attention to what they are offering to Moroccans as an alternative to the present bilingual situation, for they are unlikely to succeed in gaining the support of ordinary Moroccans unless they can offer an equally practical and adequate alternative.[36]

---

35   A. Bentahila, *Language Attitudes Among Arabic-French Bilinguals in Morocco* (Clevedon, Avon: Multilingual Matters, 1983), p. 153.

36   Bentahila, *Language Attitudes Among Arabic-French Bilinguals in Morocco*, p. 160.

In 1991 Elbiad reported on his study, which considered the role of professionals and students in the progress of Arabisation. His informants fell into two categories: professionals who were already working at a reasonably high level in 1985 and had therefore been educated in a bilingual system during the first decades after Independence; and students who had received a predominantly Arabised education, and would therefore be expected to have a more favourable attitude towards Arabisation than the older group. He wanted to establish the extent to which Arabisation affected and was affected by, these two groups.

Elbiad found that although French, like Classical Arabic, is restricted to the domain of work,

> French is so entrenched in Moroccan society that any program of Arabization would be in vain unless it affected all aspects of public life and all segments of the population.[37]

Although questions on language use indicated widespread use of French in the world of work, questions on attitudes indicated an ambivalence towards French attributed to its association with colonisation, and a positive view of Arabisation, which was seen as a viable option for the future of the country. It did not appear to be the case that the students were more favourably disposed towards Arabisation than the professionals, but both groups felt that there was a lack of political determination to enforce Arabisation and felt no motivation to improve their ability in Classical Arabic. Despite the ongoing Arabisation of the school system taking place by the mid-1980s, this study indicated that students were well aware that Arabic–French bilingualism was still the norm for most professional walks of life and valued their own command of French accordingly.

Mouhssine's study, conducted a few years later, also aimed to examine whether or not the Arabisation of education had changed attitudes towards the languages in contact in Morocco. Her study involved students at the University of Fez, whose responses revealed ambiguous attitudes, 'imprégnées d'une forte ambivalence'.[38] Attitudes towards French seemed

37 M. Elbiad, 'The Role of Some Population Sectors in the Progress of Arabization in Morocco', *International Journal of the Sociology of Language*, 87, 1991, p. 34.
38 Mouhssine, 'Ambivalence du discours sur l'arabisation', p. 53.

contradictory, and it was rejected as the symbol of an overbearing Western culture, yet also claimed as a 'second language':

> dans 26,5% des réponses, les étudiants estiment que l'arabisation doit éliminer la culture française, mais conserver le français comme instrument de communication. L'enquête révèle de manière générale le rejet du français quand il s'agit de question portant sur l'identité ou la culture.[39]

Attitudes towards Arabic were favourable, but so were attitudes towards a bilingualism that would provide access to the wider world (the West). Mouhssine concludes that the students in her study represent the younger generation of Moroccans, who want to conserve their identity while remaining open to outside cultural influences, and suggests that,

> l'arabisation ne pourra concrétiser ses objectifs que si elle intègre les autres composantes identitaires; celles du présent, par l'ouverture aux langues et cultures étrangères.[40]

Even more recently, Boukous has published a series of brief interviews with young people and their parents on their attitudes towards Moroccan language policy. These interviews indicate:

> un malaise profond qui perturbe les élèves et les étudiants et déconcerte les enseignants et les parents, malaise qui se nourrit des ambivalences d'une PL [politique linguistique] dont les incohérences apparaissent de plus en plus comme une stratégie de sélection sociale, une politique détournée au profit des groupes dominants.[41]

The overwhelming feeling to emerge from his interviews is one of resentment that people were led to believe in Arabisation as a means of creating equality of opportunity, whereas the reality is that French is the language needed for success. He concludes his analysis of Moroccan language policy with the following statement:

> l'arabisation est objectivement une stratégie idéologique conçue par les élites pour verrouiller l'accès à la formation qui produit les décideurs de demain; une telle

39   Mouhssine, 'Ambivalence du discours sur l'arabisation', p. 57.
40   Mouhssine, 'Ambivalence du discours sur l'arabisation', p. 60.
41   Boukous, *Dominance et différence: essai sur les enjeux symboliques au Maroc*, p. 99.

analyse est confortée par le fait que l'enseignement arabisé ne permet plus la mobilité sociale sur le plan vertical.[42]

To conclude this sociolinguistic assessment of how Moroccan language policy is working out in practice, the following section will look at the author's own study of language use and attitudes, conducted in 1997 in Settat.

The Settat study

This study, like the others, aimed to assess attitudes towards the languages in contact in Morocco and the extent to which French is used. Unlike the others (except perhaps Boukous), it includes among the informants not only Arabic–French bilinguals, but also people with little or no education. The sample included men and women from a wide age range and of varying educational background, as indicated in the Table 1.

Level of education	% of sample
None	47.3% (130)
Up to CM2*	10.5% (29)
CM2 to *baccalauréat*	32.4% (89)
Baccalauréat and above	9.5% (26)

*The end of primary education.

Table 1.

From the breakdown by educational level it might be expected that roughly half of the informants had no knowledge of French at all, but the self-evaluation on ability in French gave the, rather surprising, results presented in Table 2.

Although only 52.4% of the sample admitted to having any education, 58.5% claimed to understand at least 'a little' French, and virtually everyone who had been to school felt they could speak at least a little. Even the figures for reading and writing are surprisingly high; indeed,

42   Boukous, *Dominance et différence: essai sur les enjeux symboliques au Maroc*, p. 105.

Ability in French	% of sample		
	Well	A little	Total
Understand	18.9%	39.6%	58.5%
Speak	11.6%	40.7%	52.3%
Read	23.3%	26.2%	49.5%
Write	19.6%	29.1%	48.7%

Table 2.

more people claim to be able to read and write well than to speak and understand well. These figures indicate a predisposition towards using French: it is not untypical in sociolinguistic studies for informants to overestimate their ability in a language that confers prestige, or in which they would like to be fluent.[43] The categories 'well' and 'a little' are of course vague, and could include extremely limited ability, but it is none-theless significant that informants choose to claim this ability, and corrob-orates the conclusions of Boukous and Mouhssine, among others, that it is widely felt that French is needed for social and professional success, despite official discourse claiming that Arabisation is leading to equality of opportunity for all. The use of a 'self-report' study, rather than a study based on observation of actual linguistic behaviour is of particular value here. Responses reflect the symbolic importance of French in everyday situations, whereas actual use may be far less clear-cut.[44]

Questions on use of French

There were two questions in this part of the questionnaire, one relating to the informants' own use of French, the other relating to how they perceived the general use of French in Morocco. Informants were asked whether they used French in a variety of contexts, and then whether they thought Moroccans in general used French in these contexts. The contexts were chosen on the basis of previous studies, which had indicated that

43   See, for example, S. Romaine, *Language in Society* (Oxford: Oxford University Press, 1994), pp. 37–43.
44   Cf. Linguistic Minorities Project, *The Other Languages of England* (London: Routledge & Kegan Paul, 1985), p. 116.

people had learnt, or wished they had learnt, French for use in certain situations.[45] These contexts reflected the fact that French continues to pervade many aspects of everyday life, even for the most illiterate Moroccan citizen. Anyone who can read will constantly be aware of road signs, shop signs, postage stamps, receipts, doctors' prescriptions, bills and cheques, among other everyday items, labelled in both French and Arabic, often with French in first position. Those who cannot read will hear French daily on national radio stations and television channels. Tables 3 and 4 show the responses of the full sample to these two questions.

	% of sample	
Occasion	A lot	A little
When watching television	8.4%	37.1%
When reading newspapers	6.2%	34.9%
When going to the bank	7.6%	27.6%
When dealing with administration	6.5%	27.6%
When looking for a job	12.4%	24.0%
When socialising with friends (in cafés etc)	2.2%	33.1%
When writing letters	8.4%	37.1%

Table 3: Personal use of French.

The responses show a very clear pattern: on the whole, less than 10% of the sample claim to use French 'a lot' in any activity, which is to be expected, since only 11.6% claim to speak French 'well', and roughly one-third of the sample claim to use French 'a little' in all the activities. French is thus an everyday sociolinguistic reality for over one-third of the population sampled.

It is also immediately noticeable that the figures for perceived general use are almost universally higher than those for personal use, indicating an awareness on the part of those who do not use French much that it is widely used in Moroccan society. The perception is that in most domains well over 10% of Moroccans use French 'a lot', and in every

45   See D. Marley and Z. Ould-Dada, 'Attitudes envers les langues dans une ville de province au Maroc', in Jones, Miguet and Corcoran (eds), *Francophonie: mythes, masques et réalités* (Paris: Publisud, 1996), pp. 175–202.

	% of sample	
Occasion	A lot	A little
When watching television	12.0%	54.5%
When reading newspapers	11.6%	64.4%
When going to the bank	9.6%	56.0%
When dealing with administration	12.4%	53.5%
When looking for a job	20.0%	56.0%
When socialising with friends (in cafés etc)	2.5%	59.3%
When writing letters	5.1%	55.3%

Table 4:   General use of French in Morocco.

domain over 50% uses it 'a little'. This overestimation is particularly true of the items 'when reading newspapers', 'when going to the bank' and 'when finding a job', items that perhaps do not feature largely in the daily lives of a number of the informants, but that are perceived to involve the use of French for many people who engage in these activities. These responses thus corroborate results of previous studies and go further, since they concern even respondents who have no knowledge of French, and should, in an Arabised society, feel no need of it. In order to understand why informants should feel so strongly that French is an everyday part of the sociolinguistic reality of their lives, the next section will look at each domain under consideration in order to ascertain the extent to which French is used.

Situations where French may be used

Watching Television

The Moroccan national channel, RTM, broadcasts most of the time in Arabic, but French is not absent. The news is shown in French every day, albeit for ten minutes only. French 'variétés' are shown every Saturday evening, and French, or other foreign (e.g. American) films dubbed in French, are shown regularly, at least once a week. Furthermore, other programmes, such as documentaries and discussions, may include French if they feature speakers who are unable to speak, or express themselves fully, in Arabic, usually due to technological or scientific subject matter. The second national channel, 2Mi, originally a private channel but now available to all, broadcasts about 50% of its output in French. Moreover, most town-dwelling Moroccans have access to satellite TV and are able to watch French channels, thus increasing potential exposure to French.

It is therefore not surprising that almost half the sample say they use French at least a little when watching television. For most people, the only way they will ever see foreign films is by attempting to follow them in the French version, as they are rarely dubbed in Arabic. The second response indicates that a lot of people who cannot claim to use French at all for watching television think that other people do use it, which again is not surprising, since they are clearly aware of the quantity of exposure to the language for those who understand it.

Reading Newspapers

As with national television, there is plenty of French in Moroccan national newspapers, even without taking into account the fact that French newspapers are readily available in any Moroccan town (indeed, some French daily papers are printed simultaneously in Paris and Casablanca). In recent years the Moroccan press has expanded rapidly, in both French and Arabic: in the period from 1990 to 1992, 64 new publications appeared in Arabic and 31 in French.[46] New publications in French tend to be business or technical magazines, but the last five years have also seen the launching of a number of new weekly newspapers, which claim to be independent of political parties. In addition, a number of magazines aimed at a well-educated audience have appeared.

Fewer informants claim to use French when reading newspapers, perhaps simply because the television is easier, even for those who can read. Again they tend to assume that a higher proportion of the population read the French press than is the case according to their self-evaluation, reflecting the awareness that French is so prevalent in the press.

---

46   *État de la Francophonie* (La Documentation Française, 1993), pp. 445–6.

Going to the Bank

All Moroccan banks advertise themselves in French and Arabic, and dealings with the outside banking world, apart from other Arab countries, would be conducted in French. Nevertheless, the personnel in banks are Moroccan, and facilities are available in both languages. However, for a lot of Moroccans, including many of these informants, the bank is not an important part of their lives, as they are either unemployed or in such low-paid employment that a bank account is not a necessity. Thus, although the number who claim to use French 'a lot' in banks is similar to the figures for the previous two items, the number of those who claim to use it 'a little' is significantly lower. This suggests that a small percentage of the sample – those who are well-educated – watch and read French, and also use it in banks because it is easier for them than to use Arabic. The rest of the sample, who may sometimes watch a French film or read a French newspaper, are less likely to go into a bank, and if they did, would not speak in French. As with the previous items, however, they think that a lot of Moroccans do use French in banks, indicating that it is not seen as unusual behaviour.

Dealing with Administration

The administrative structures set up by the French have proved particularly difficult to Arabise. Even a document as basic as the identity card, which all Moroccans are required to have, is printed in Arabic and French, and previous studies have suggested that most people working in any administrative body are likely to operate at least partly in French.[47] Although a relatively low number of these informants claim to use French when dealing with administration, they think that about double that number in the general population use it for this purpose, indicating that for many people administration and the French language are synonymous.

---

47   Bentahila, *Language Attitudes Among Arabic–French Bilinguals*; A. Moatassime, *Arabisation et langue française au Maghreb* (Paris: Presses Universitaires de France, 1992).

Looking for a Job

This item gave the highest number of informants claiming to use French 'a lot' and the lowest number claiming to use it 'a little'. This is perhaps indicative of a widespread perception that competence in French is essential for anyone wishing to gain a good job, and therefore many people who do not claim to French much in any other sphere of life would feel it necessary here. They also assume that this is the case on a much wider scale than would appear to be true from their own responses, possibly because many of them are not in very good employment, and when they think about looking for a job they relate this to people applying for more prestigious and lucrative employment, which would require competence in French.

Socialising with Friends

This is the only item that does not show a significant difference in self-evaluation and general perceptions of those who use French 'a lot'. Although well-educated Moroccans are likely to use a high number of French words in any conversation with other well-educated people, they would think of themselves as speaking Moroccan Arabic, and so few would claim that they use 'a lot' of French when socialising. There is still a large gap between perception and reality for those who use French 'a little' when socialising – the perception is that it is used almost twice as much as it actually is – perhaps indicating that many people think they hear a lot of French about them when they are out, or that a significant number of our informants never go out (because they are women, and tend to socialise in each other's houses) and thus make false assumptions about those who do (men).

Writing Letters

This item was added because a previous study indicated that it was one of the prime uses of French for those who could write it. It is the only item where actual use (self-evaluation) is higher than perceived use for 'a lot' of French. Those who can write in French are likely to use it for letters rather than Arabic, as it lends itself more easily to colloquial expression in personal letters and is seen as the language of business, and thus the logical choice for work-related correspondence. Figures for using French 'a little' are similar to all the other items and possibly indicate that a large proportion of our informants do not write letters, and assume that if around half the population uses French in other contexts, it will do so in this one.

Attitudes towards French

In order to evaluate attitudes towards French, informants were presented with a list of statements on the French language and asked whether or not they agreed. Table 5 presents the statements and responses.

The responses detailed in the Table 5 are for the most part unambiguous, indicating that most ordinary Moroccans have a highly favourable attitude towards French. It is widely perceived as an important language for all Moroccans, now and in the future; it is considered a beautiful language, which is easier to learn than Arabic. It is perceived as bringing benefits to the individual – making it easier to get a good job – and to the nation as a whole – in terms of development. There is no doubt in the minds of most people that Moroccans now, and in the foreseeable future, should be learning French; they do not see French as the language of the colonial past, but very much as a language of the present and future. They do not, however, see it as a replacement for Arabic. This set of responses thus echoes an earlier small-scale study,[48] which found that French is widely appreciated as a useful language, but not as a marker of identity.

Breakdown by Age, Gender and Level of Education

In order to ascertain whether or not the variables of age, gender and level of education had any effect on responses, one-way ANOVAs (analysis of variance) were conducted on the data. In most cases neither age nor

48   D. Marley, 'French in Morocco: Not a Question of Identity?', in Marley, Hintze and Parker, *Linguistic Identities and Policies in France and the French-Speaking World.*

Statement	Agree strongly*	Agree	Disagree
1 French is an important language in Morocco	57.1%	23.6%	9.8%
2 All Moroccans should learn French	50.2%	32.0%	14.9%
3 French should replace Arabic in Morocco	5.1%	5.5%	80.4%
4 French is difficult to learn	21.5%	38.2%	27.6%
5 French is a beautiful language	59.3%	25.1%	9.1%
6 French helps you to get a good job	60.4%	24.4%	9.8%
7 French is easier than Arabic	34.2%	17.1%	30.5%
8 French should be abolished in Morocco	14.5%	9.1%	64.0%
9 Morocco needs French to develop	43.3%	20.0%	22.9%
10 Our children and grandchildren should learn French	69.1%	22.5%	6.5%

Table 5.

*In an attempt to obtain more precise data, informants were asked to agree strongly, or simply agree, but the distinction was felt to be meaningless by most informants. It is therefore perhaps unwise to read too much significance into the two categories.

gender had any significant effect either on use of French or on attitudes. In the series of questions on personal use of French the effect of age was significant at 99.9 % CI (confidence interval) in all cases. In every case it was the younger age groups, 14–19, 20–24 and 25–34, who consistently claimed to use French more than any of the other age groups, whereas the oldest groups, 55–64 and over 65, claimed to use French significantly less. This finding is of particular interest, as it indicates that French is actually more widely used among the post-Independence generations than among those born and brought up under French rule. This may simply reflect the fact that a higher percentage of younger people have been to school, and thus the majority of well-educated informants fall into the younger age groups. Nevertheless, it is significant that they should claim to use a language that they regard as 'foreign' in everyday situations. This corroborates Mouhssine's findings that young people are not convinced of the necessity of eliminating French from Moroccan society.

The effect of level of education was significant both for use and attitudes. Inevitably, those with a higher level of education claim to use French themselves far more than those with little or no education. There is also a clear tendency for the better-educated informants to assume that French is more widely used by all Moroccans than it apparently is, judging from the responses to the first series of questions. This indicates that those who use French fairly widely themselves believe that their own linguistic behaviour is more typical of all Moroccans than it really is. This is a reasonable assumption for them to make, given the prevalence of French in Moroccan everyday life: it would be easy for someone who does understand all the sights and sounds of French met with on a daily basis to assume that a majority of other people do too, at least to a certain extent. As far as attitudes are concerned, the differences are only minimal, but it is true that the better-educated informants are, on the whole, more favourably disposed towards French than those who are less well edu-cated. It must be stressed, however, that it is simply a matter of degree: even illiterate informants have favourable attitudes towards French.

This study then suggests that well over a third of a population of indifferent academic achievement consider that they regularly use French in a number of everyday situations, albeit only 'a little' in most cases. Moreover, there is a tendency to assume that more than half of all Moroccans regularly use French in these situations, indicating a general feeling that French is by no means a foreign language, but an everyday means of communication for most 'ordinary' people. The implication of this study is that French, far from fading from public life, is very much a part of it, not only in the offices of power or among the privileged few who deal in international business and finance, but also in the homes and workplaces of ordinary Moroccans in a provincial town. They see it as a normal part of their everyday life and assume that this is the case for most Moroccans. Obviously, the extent to which French is used varies widely, and this study reveals, not unsurprisingly, that those with a higher degree of education are likely to use French more than those with little schooling. Perhaps more surprising is the fact that younger people claim to use French more than older people, despite the fact that they have been brought up in an increasingly Arabised education system. This study, like all the others mentioned, confirms that while Moroccans may agree with the explicit ideological motivation behind Arabisation, they still accept the dominance of French in a number of domains of modern life. Moreover, the questions on attitude indicate that favourable attitudes towards French continue to permeate all classes of society: not only those who benefit from being bilingual, but also those who know little or no French have overwhelmingly favourable attitudes towards the language.

It is clear, then, that despite widespread support for the ideological basis of Arabisation, French is widely used and appreciated as the language of modernity in Morocco, although few Moroccans openly challenge the role of Arabic as official language, or seek a similar status for French. As these studies and others indicate, despite official lack of support, French remains a significant language of everyday use for many Moroccans, and there is no indication, at the time of writing, that the current ambiguity over the role of French is likely to change. For the moment, it needs no official recognition because its role as unofficial second language is still secure. The situation of Berber, however, is quite different: supporters of the Berber movement openly criticise official language policy and demand official recognition of their language and culture, which are in a historical sense more 'authentic' than Arabic as representative of Moroccan identity.

The Berber Cultural Movement

I have used the term 'Berber' until now, as this is the name by which the indigenous peoples and languages of Morocco are known to Europeans, and it is a blanket term covering a range of related languages. However, the growing cultural movement in support of these languages is known as *Amazigh*, meaning 'free man', so this term will be used henceforth in this chapter. The term *Tamazight* (the feminine form of Amazigh) is also used, more usually to refer to the language itself, and the plural form, *Imazighen*, is often used to refer to the Berber people.

Within the Berber community there is a keen awareness of the danger of language loss as a result of the assimilationist policy implicit within the official process of Arabisation, and a number of strategies to ensure language maintenance have been developed.[49] The Amazigh cultural movement, which has been growing within Morocco and outside since the 1960s, is a heterogeneous collection of associations who all share the basic aim of maintaining and protecting Tamazight, calling for its recognition as a national and/or official language, and for recognition of their language and culture as a historical component of Moroccan identity. As Boukous points out, there is no doubt that Amazigh language and culture have been a reality in Morocco for far longer than Arabic, and he claims, 'la culture amazighe structure l'inconscient collectif de l'être marocain et fonde la personnalité culturelle de base du pays.'[50] There is also a wider context to this issue, which is the fact that using one's own language is a basic human right, and that Arabisation may be seen as a means of depriving large parts of the Moroccan people of this right. The movement claims that the Amazigh dimension of Moroccan society is as important as the Arabic dimension, and that to deny the former is to impoverish the whole nation.

There is no clear political stance articulated by the Berber movement, but Boukous[51] suggests that there are two main tendencies. The

49   Boukous, 'La langue berbère: maintien et changement, pp. 12–15.
50   Boukous, 'La langue et la culture amazighes: entre la plénitude du fait et la vacuité du droit', p. 23.
51   Boukous, 'La langue et la culture amazighes: entre la plénitude du fait et la vacuité du droit', p. 28.

first sees the issue as a cultural and linguistic one, which involves giving Tamazight proper legal status and recognising the right of speakers to use it in education and the media, or even going as far as to recognise institutional bilingualism at national level, and the right to use Tamazight in every domain. The second approach sees the issue as one of identity, which could be resolved along the lines of Spanish regionalisation, or Swiss federalism. Either solution would be problematic, in that both would lead to further fragmentation of Tamazight, thus making any attempt at standardisation impossible, and they would ignore the fact that the rural exodus has created enclaves of Imazighen in urban areas far from their historic regions. In any case, it appears that there is no desire, as yet, to turn any of these cultural associations into political parties.[52]

The associative movement in Morocco can trace its roots as far back as 1929 (when the association *Les élèves d'Azrou* was founded), but has seen its greatest growth in the last 20 years or so, at the national, local and international level. The national movement began in 1967 with the establishment of the Association marocaine de la recherche et de l'échange culturel (A.M.R.E.C). This association was founded against the backdrop of the Pan-Arabism and Marxism of the 1960s, and offered a forum for all those who did not want to forget their own language and culture. A.M.R.E.C. has always been perceived as a moderate organisation, due to its emphasis on cultural activity and academic research, though it has also sought dialogue with political parties, with a view to creating a 'berberist lobby'.[53] Some members felt that such cultural activity was not enough and in 1978 founded the second important national association, the Association nouvelle pour la Culture et les Arts Populaires (A.N.C.A.P./Tamaynut), which has a far more political orientation. Article 4 of its 1995 statutes reads:

> L'association a pour objectifs de s'intéresser aux droits linguistiques, culturels, économiques, sociaux et à l'environnement du citoyen marocain et à les défendre conformément aux dispositions des conventions internationales.[54]

52 G. Kratochwil, 'Les associations culturelles amazighes au Maroc: bilan et perspectives', *Prologues*, 17, 1999, p. 42.

53 Kratochwil, 'Les associations culturelles amazighes au Maroc: bilan et perspectives', p. 39.

54 Quoted in Kratochwil, 'Les associations culturelles amazighes au Maroc: bilan et perspectives', p. 39.

A number of other associations were created in the 1970s and 1980s, but none of them have had the same national impact as the two already mentioned.

At local level, the movement first gained in importance during the early 1990s, following the *Charte d'Agadir relative aux droits linguistiques et culturels amazighs* of 1991, which was signed by six associations, some national, some regional. This charter encouraged co-ordination between the different regional groups and sought to unite them around some clearly defined objectives, as well as encouraging the creation of further associations. The movement became more organised in 1993 with the creation of the Conseil National de co-ordination, and saw greater growth in 1994 after the speech in which King Hassan II spoke of the need for recognition of 'dialects'. This speech (delivered on 20 August 1994) is seen as an important turning point in the history of the Amazigh cultural movement. Nevertheless, in 1996 the Conseil national de co-ordination found it necessary to address a letter to the king concerning its demands for recognition.

As is often the case in minority language movements, the people involved are for the most part well-educated, middle-class and urban. Boukous claims:

> force est de constater ici que le mouvement culturel n'a pas encore atteint la dimension d'un mouvement social; son assise est essentiellement constituée par la petite bourgeoisie intellectuelle et urbaine.[55]

According to Kratochwil,[56] however, while it is true that the executives of both national and local associations tend to be drawn from the middle class, and the membership in urban areas is predominantly professional and intellectual, in rural areas militants come from all social classes. In urban areas, it appears that people feel drawn to these associations because their education has led them to an awareness of the devaluation of their language and culture, and to the need to reassert their cultural identity within an institutional framework. In rural areas, however, people

---

55   Boukous, 'La langue et la culture amazighes: entre la plénitude du fait et la vacuité du droit', p. 26.
56   Kratochwil, 'Les associations culturelles amazighes au Maroc: bilan et perspectives', p. 41.

of all classes tend to feel excluded from power, and the movement is seen as a means of social or political protest. For many young people, unemployed and disillusioned with the corruption of the state system, this cultural movement gives a meaning to their lives.

The Amazigh Cultural Movement exists not only within Morocco, but around the world: at university level, research into Berber linguistics and literature is being undertaken in Morocco itself, and in France, the United States, Canada, Great Britain and Holland, in the form of numerous doctoral theses and post-doctoral projects. There is a Centre de Recherche Berbère at the Institut National des Langues et Civilisations Orientales (INALCO) in Paris and a Centre d'Études et de Recherche Amazigh, also in Paris. The movement receives national and international support through a large number of internet sites, which means that there is an educated, computer-literate global audience that is aware of the Amazigh situation.[57] Perhaps the most important associations worth mentioning here are the Amazigh World Congress, founded in 1995, and the Amazigh Cultural Association in America, founded in 1992.

The Amazigh World Congress is an international non-governmental organisation, whose principal aim is the defence and promotion of the cultural identity of the Amazigh nation. A communiqué from the first Amazigh World Congress held in 1997 proclaimed:

> AWC has set as its objectives, among others, the defense and the promotion of the cultural identity of the Amazigh Nation. It expresses the will of Imazighen (Berbers) to act in unity in order to reconcile North Africa (Tamazgha) with its history. Its struggle is based on the respect for universal values: human rights, democracy, tolerance and peace.

The AWC has issued declarations on a variety of situations, such as the marginalisation of Amazigh in the new Moroccan constitution (22 November 1996), and addressed an open letter to the late King Hassan II, to remind him of the promises he made about the teaching of Tamazight in 1994 (5 May 1996).

The Amazigh Cultural Association in America (ACAA) is described on its website as:

---

57   A list of some of the more useful websites can be found at the end of this article.

> a non-profit organization […] organized and operated exclusively for cultural,
> educational, and scientific purposes to contribute to saving, promoting, and enrich-
> ing the Amazigh (Berber) language and culture. […] ACAA participates globally
> in the revival of the Amazigh culture.

To this end, it is engaged in a number of projects, including the development of computer applications for Amazigh culture, publication of
newsletters, the organisation of seminars and conferences, and the development of language lessons.

This international support seems to indicate that the Amazigh cause
is assured of a future, while the movement is gaining in strength and
credibility within Morocco. In terms of language policy, however, recent
changes represent little more than token gestures; Boukous, in a recent
assessment of the Amazigh situation, concludes that:

> sans volonté politique effective, sans engagement réel de l'État et sans le consensus
> de toutes les parties engagées dans la problématique linguistique et culturelle, les
> initiatives de planification linguistique ne peuvent être que cautère sur jambe de
> bois ou slogans sans consistance.[58]

Although the Amazigh cultural movement was encouraged by the late
King's speech (20 August 1994), in which he recommended the teaching
of 'dialects' in primary schools, many claimed that it was simply unrealistic, given the lack of a commonly accepted script and competent teachers. Many saw his remarks as 'un "os à ronger" jeté aux berbéristes',[59]
and two years later (5 May 1996) the Amazigh World Congress addressed
an open letter to the King, reminding him that his promise to introduce
Tamazight into schools in Morocco had not yet been fulfilled. Nevertheless, others claimed that it was a significant turning point in national
language policy; as M. Laroussi, of the Ministère de l'Information commented: 'après le discours du souverain, personne n'osera se dire contre
l'enseignement du berbère.'[60] Since then optimists have seen the hesitant
beginnings of a language policy towards Tamazight in the form of daily
news bulletins on national television in the three main Berber varieties

---

58   Boukous, 'La langue et la culture amazighes: entre la plénitude du fait et la vacuité
       du droit', p. 28.
59   J. Donnet, 'Renaissance berbère au Maroc', *Le Monde Diplomatique*, 1995.
60   Donnet, 'Renaissance berbère au Maroc'.

and the creation of an institute of Berber studies. On the other hand, the adoption of the *Charte nationale de l'enseignement* in 1999 was seen as a further blow to the Amazigh cause in that it failed to recognise 'la dimension identitaire et culturelle amazighe en tant que support civilisationnel au Maroc'.[61] The Tamaynut association issued a communiqué calling on 'all democratic citizens' to write to those in power, protesting at this further instance of undemocratic treatment of Tamazight.

Amazigh organisations also reacted with outrage in November 1996 when a new law, referred to as *Dahir No. 1.96.97*, sought to regulate the choice of given names for Moroccan citizens within Morocco or living abroad. The law is accompanied by an official list of first names, which are 'original Moroccan' names, in other words, Arabic, and forbids the use of 'foreign' names, or names based on the name of a city, village or tribe. The primary effect of this law would be to prevent Amazigh families from giving their children Amazigh names. The Amazigh Cultural Association in America issued a press release in May 1998, denouncing this law as a breach of human rights, and called on all human rights groups to join in the protests against it. AZAmazigh, the association of Moroccan Berbers in France, also issued a communiqué in March 2000, following the visit of the new king, Mohammed VI, to Paris, reminding the government of their promises to rehabilitate Amazigh identity and protesting against this anti-democratic law. At the time of writing there is no sign that this law will be changed, but it is clear that the Amazigh people have international support for their cause.

One final instance of support overseas is in the possibility of Tamazight being recognised as a language of France.[62] Although the French government has still not signed the European Charter for Regional and Minority Languages, Berber now features on the list of 'languages of France'. When this possibility was first mooted in the 1980s, there was a strong negative reaction in the Assemblée nationale, but this time Berber was recognised, for three main reasons. Firstly, it is the language of hundreds of thousands of French citizens; secondly, it is a language spoken in former French territories; thirdly, it is not the official language of any state and is therefore in danger of disappearing if not protected by

61 *Communiqué de Tamaynut* (Rabat: November 1999).
62 H. Sadi, 'Le berbère, langue de France', *Le Monde*, 4 March 1999.

the European Union. In consequence, Tamazight speakers currently receive more protection and support if they live abroad than if they are in Morocco.

Despite this support at international level, and significant cultural activity at home and abroad, in sociolinguistic terms Tamazight must still be regarded as a language in danger of extinction. In common with thousands of obsolescent languages worldwide, the forces acting against it are still stronger than those supporting it, and the existence of a centre for Berber studies or a few minutes of Berber on national television will not make any difference. An analysis of Tamazight according to Fishman's theory of reversing language shift (1991), would indicate that Tamazight is at stage 6 on the Graded Intergenerational Disruption Scale,[63] since Tamazight is 'the normal language of informal, spoken interaction between and within all three generations of the family, with [Arabic] being reserved for matters of greater formality and technicality'.[64] Having been minoritised due to the presence of another, more powerful language, the only way for Tamazight to survive and go beyond this phase (i.e. become 'normalised') in modern society, is for a programme of literacy to be set up, and for greater institutional support to be made available. This would require a substantial change in Moroccan language policy, even if it only affected certain areas of the country. It would represent recognition of the fact that Morocco is not a monolingual nation and acknowledgement of the validity of languages other than Arabic as means of expressing cultural and national identity.

Conclusions

As this chapter has made clear, Moroccan language policy since Independence has struggled to reconcile ideology with reality; a monolingual uniform culture has been imposed on a culturally diverse, multilingual

63   J. A. Fishman, *Reversing Language Shift* (Clevedon, Avon: Multilingual Matters, 1991), p. 395.
64   Fishman, *Reversing Language Shift*, p. 92.

nation. Nationalist discourse has consistently argued that Arabisation is essential if Morocco is to regain and retain its 'authentic' Arabo-Islamic identity, and a legislative framework has been developed in order to pursue this aim. However, the process of Arabisation has been constantly hindered, not only by practical considerations (the fact that Arabic simply does not have the vocabulary to operate in certain domains, for example), but also, more importantly, by opposition from those who favour plurality or linguistic diversity.

Those who support Arabic–French bilingualism claim it makes practical sense to maintain French for business, science and other areas. They may also fear that total Arabisation would mean total identification with the Arab world and the loss of real advantages, both material and cultural, associated with French and the access it gives to the Western world. In many ways, exposure to French is actually growing, rather than declining, with the advent of satellite television and the Internet, in addition to the close contact with Morocco's large immigrant communities in France and Belgium, and so the advantages of knowing French are greater than ever before. Since the completion of Arabisation in state schools there has been an enormous growth in the number of private schools offering a bilingual French–Arabic education, indicating a widespread reluctance to abandon French, which is seen as a useful language for a wide number of reasons. This continuing attachment to French can be described as largely pragmatic and instrumental.

In contrast to this, opposition from the Amazigh movement has an integrative motivation: Amazigh activists claim that their language and culture are an integral part of Moroccan identity and should be recognised as such. They claim that Morocco cannot become a democratic nation that claims to respect human rights, while so many citizens are denied the basic right to their own language. The Amazigh movement appears to be gathering strength, leading to increasing demands for some kind of institutionalised bilingualism in Amazigh areas, and recognition of their language and culture as valid expressions of Moroccan identity.

It appears, therefore, that Moroccan language policy has failed to achieve either its explicit or implicit goals after more than four decades: neither French nor Tamazight have disappeared from the sociolinguistic landscape. Moreover, the fact that it is now four decades since Independence means that Arabisation can no longer have the ideological impact it had on generations who had lived through the colonial era. Young people today have no personal memory of that time and are more interested in the future, a future that looks bleak to the Arabised school leaver unable to offer French to a potential employer or the young Amazigh speaker who feels alienated by a system that consistently discriminates against him in his own country. Though studies show that most Moroccans are in favour of keeping Arabic as the national language, they also show an overwhelming desire to keep other languages, most notably French. At one level Morocco is now a fully Arabised country, where all state schooling is conducted in Arabic, and it is the first language of government, the administration and the media. At another level, however, Arabisation remains a myth, while the reality is a country of great linguistic and cultural diversity, where French and Tamazight, in their different ways, are as much part of Moroccan national identity as Arabic.

Amazigh websites

http://www.amazigh.co.uk
http://www.wordlynx.net/tamazgha
http://www.al-bab.com/maroc/soc/berber.htm
http://www.multimania.com/aza
http://www.encarta.msn.com/find/concise.asp?t=00210000
http://www.tamazgha.org/Home.htm
http://www.ens-fcl.fr/%7Echabane/amizour/berber_3.htm

FARID AITSISELMI

Language Planning in Algeria: Linguistic and Cultural Conflicts

This chapter analyses the linguistic situation in present-day Algeria and assesses the future of the French language as a result of the language policies implemented since the country gained independence from France in 1962. Despite the numerous Arabisation laws introduced with the aim of imposing Arabic as the sole national language, Algeria is still a multilingual country where at least three languages are in competition.[1]

The first language is Berber or Tamazight, which is the language of the indigenous people of North Africa. Although this language is mentioned in none of the country's constitutions, it has succeeded in achieving a certain degree of official recognition as a result of social pressure – including strikes, riots and demonstrations – from the Tamazight-speaking populations. The second language is Arabic, a diglossic language whose High variety has been declared constitutionally the national and official language of the country. It is used in all key domains, such as religion, government, education, the mass media, law, etc. The Low variety is viewed as a degraded form of pure Arabic and therefore has no official status. Like Tamazight, it is classed in the derogatory category 'dialect'. The objective of all governmental linguistic laws has been to eliminate all dialects and replace them with High Arabic. The third language is French, which is the country's linguistic inheritance from the colonial period. It has also been under attack, and its status as the main foreign language is under threat. Today it is competing not only with Arabic but also with English as the language of access to science, technology and international business. The language policy implemented by Algeria ignores the other languages used by Algerians on the grounds that they are either a threat to national unity (Tamazight) or a legacy of a colonial past that needs to be eliminated (French).

1   'Arabic' here refers to several language varieties.

Historical Survey

In order to understand current language policy in Algeria, it is important to examine the historical events that led to the present linguistic situation. Sociolinguists recognise the importance of taking a historical perspective in order to understand the language-planning policies of a country. 'La politique linguistique d'un état (et les conflits qu'elle suscite ou cherche à résoudre) n'est compréhensible que dans une perspective historique.'[2]

Historically, the first inhabitants of Algeria are referred to as Berbers. Originally, this term meant foreigners, uncivilised or non-Greek/Latin speakers. It has therefore been felt to have pejorative connotations because it derives from a Greek/Latin root related to Barbarian. Berber-speaking people use regional names[3] or tribal names[4] to refer to themselves. They do not describe themselves as Berbers. This is nowadays perceived as 'a foreign label given to the indigenous population by various invaders of North Africa'.[5]

Amazigh (in which 'gh' represents a voiced uvular fricative), meaning noble or free man, is the term that is considered to designate Berbers in general. Its plural is *Imazighen* (formed by the addition of plural affixes), and its feminine form, *Tamazight* (formed by addition of feminine affixes), refers to the language. All scholars as well as the 40 associations gathered under the umbrella of the Amazigh World Congress, which was founded in France in 1995, now accept it as a generic term. It is also accepted by the younger generation, and can be found in many recent poems and songs as the signal of a sense of belonging to a larger cultural community beyond the tribe or region, a feeling that was lacking among the older generation.

Tamazight is classed in the same group as Semitic languages, either as a sub-branch of a Hamito-Semitic or Chamito-Semitic family in the

---

2 Jean William Lapierre, *Le pouvoir politique et les langues: Babel et Léviathan* (Paris: PUF, 1988), p. 254.
3 E.g. the Aqbayli from Kabylia in North West Algeria.
4 E.g. the Ashawi who live in the Saharan Atlas Mountains.
5 Amazigh World Congress (AWC), speech at the Geneva meeting of the UN Decade for the Rights of Indigenous People, 1996.

French tradition,[6] or next to Semitic in the Afro-Asiatic group.[7] Although the language is still spoken in North Africa, very few written documents exist in ancient Berber, with the exception of inscriptions on tombstones, to show that it was used more extensively for writing. In the official Algerian terminology, it used to be referred to as a dialect, because it does not have a recognised standardised form. This label changed with the creation of the Haut Commissariat à l'Amazighité (HCA) in 1995.

With the destruction of Carthage in AD 40, Algeria became a province of the Roman Empire, and Latin became the language of written communication. The Roman dominion lasted for five centuries and was followed by brief invasions by Germanic tribes, the Vandals in AD 455 and the Byzantines, who ruled the area from AD 541 to 642.

Linguistically, the most important historical event was the invasion of the country by the Arabs in the seventh century. They introduced their language – Arabic, and their new religion – Islam. This event is of special importance from a cultural and linguistic point of view because it marks the beginning of a language shift from Tamazight to Arabic. Tamazight-speakers intermingled with Arabic speakers in the plains and the plateaux, gradually abandoning their language and becoming Islamised as well as Arabised. 'In North Africa the islamization of the Maghreb preceded arabization and the latter was never completed.'[8] Indeed, the population living in mountainous or Saharan regions escaped this transformation on account of the inaccessibility of these areas. However, the Tamazight-speaking areas receded before the advance of Arabic, and this process is still going on as a result of present-day language policies.

> Berber is in constant regression, given its official status as a 'dialect' (i.e. a local variety that is neither codified nor standardised), and given that the social domains in which it is used are becoming more and more restricted.[9]

6   Salem Chaker, 'Langue et culture en Algérie depuis 1988: rupture ou continuité?', *Cahier de Linguistique sociale*, 22, 1993, p. 16.
7   J. H. Greenberg, *Studies in African Linguistic Classification* (New Haven: Compass, 1955), p. 42.
8   Robert Wardhaugh, *Languages in Competition: Dominance, Diversity and Decline* (London: Blackwell, 1987), p. 174.
9   Moha Ennaji, 'The Sociology of Berber: Change and Continuity', *International Journal of the Sociology of Language*, 123, 1997, p. 25.

Statistics concerning the number of Tamazight-speakers vary, because Algerian censuses do not take linguistic factors into consideration. They are estimated to make up between 20% and 25% of the total population.[10] In North Africa Tamazight is spoken by 30 million people[11] spread between ten states from Morocco and Egypt to Niger, Mali and Mauritania.

The new conquerors introduced two main varieties of spoken Arabic into Algeria: an urban variety used by the Arab armies who settled in the cities in the seventh century, and a rural variety spoken by the nomadic tribes who settled in the countryside in the eleventh century. Classical Arabic was normally used for written communication, in which role it was supported by the Qur'an and a long pre-Islamic literary tradition. In 1517 Algeria became part of the Ottoman Empire, which reinforced the Islamisation of the country and the role of classical Arabic. The influence of the Turkish language was relatively minimal, since the Ottomans contented themselves with maintaining military garrisons in the main urban centres, such as Algiers, Constantine and Medéa.

The next historical event to have a major impact on the linguistic and educational situation in Algeria, as well as its economic and political life, was the colonisation of the country by France, which ruled there from 1830 to 1962.

The Colonial Period

As part of its policy of divide and rule, the French administration quickly established a distinction between Tamazight and Arabic-speaking populations. Algeria was treated as a mosaic of hostile ethnic groups, emphasising the differences between the 'Berber and Arab races' on the one hand, and the similarities between the 'Berber and European races' on the other. Ageron[12] refers to this policy as the Kabyle myth, from the

---

10   Chaker, 'Langue et culture en Algérie depuis 1988: rupture ou continuité?', p. 16.
11   Amazigh World Congress (AWC), http://www.worldlynx. net/tamazgha/agraw3_ eng. html.
12   Charles Robert Ageron, *Modern Algeria: A History from 1830 to the Present* (London: Hurst, 1990).

name of the largest Tamazight-speaking group: 'The Kabyles were held
to be descendants of the Gauls, the Romans, Christian Berbers of the
Roman period or the German Vandals.'[13] This policy was supported by
the work of Christian missionaries who stressed the Christian history of
the Tamazight-speaking people (under the Roman Empire), implying
that they should unite with the French against their common enemy,
represented by Islam, the Arab invaders and their language.

> The Berbers were considered to be more assimilable than Arabic speakers because
> it was said that they were superficially islamised and hereditary enemies of the
> Arabs.[14]

As far as Arabic was concerned, when the French invaded Algeria
they found a well-structured social system, with education in Arabic
widely available in religious institutions such as *zawiyas*. Estimates put
the Algerian literacy rate in Arabic in 1830 at between 40% and 50% of
the population.[15] Turin observes that some French army leaders, such as
General De Lamoricière, were amazed at the number of schools existing
in the regions under their responsibility. He reported that in the Tlemcen
area, education was available for all:

> L'instruction était donnée à tout le monde. 2000 élèves recevaient l'instruction
> secondaire, 6000 faisaient leurs hautes études. Chaque établissement avait sa
> bibliothèque.'[16]

In religious institutions, education consisted of teaching the students to
read and write in order to be able to memorise the Qur'an, as well as
Islamic law and theology. They also received formal instruction in subjects such as 'geography, history, mathematics, astronomy, and perhaps
some natural science and medicine'.[17]

13 Ageron, *Modern Algeria: A History from 1830 to the Present*, p. 72.
14 Ageron, *Modern Algeria: A History from 1830 to the Present*, p. 73.
15 Wardhaugh, *Languages in Competition: Dominance, Diversity and Decline*, p.
184.
16 Quoted in Yvonne Turin, *Affrontements culturels dans l'Algérie coloniale: écoles,
médecines, religions, 1830–1880* (Paris: Maspero. 1971), p. 130.
17 Wardhaugh, *Languages in Competition: Dominance, Diversity and Decline*, p.
187.

As a colony, Algeria came to be regarded as a territorial extension and an integral part of France. The French administration undertook a policy of European settlement with a view to eliminating the Arabic language and Islamic culture from the country. From the very beginning, the French insisted that their language would be used as the sole language of administration as it was considered to be the most efficient means to help the progress of French domination in Algeria. This position was made clear by the declaration of the first governor of Algeria (1830–1832), the Duke of Rovigo: 'Je regarde la propagation de l'instruction et de notre langue comme le moyen le plus efficace de faire des progrès à notre domination dans ce pays.'[18]

As part of their policy of assimilation and their administrative tradition of standardisation, the French destroyed the existing system and imposed their own educational norms, using French as the sole medium of instruction. The majority of the Algerian population refused to send their children to French schools, which they saw as instrumental in the transformation of their society on the basis of a model that was not only French but also Christian. Their fears were confirmed by the important role that the Jesuit missionaries were allowed to play in education (the Pères Blancs ran boys' schools, and Soeurs Blanches girls' schools). 'Le traumatisme causé par les conquérants français pousse les Algériens à se retrancher dans une sorte d'opposition contre le modèle colonial qui se présente comme une menace à leurs propres valeurs. Cette 'rigidité culturelle' se traduit par le refus des parents d'envoyer leurs enfants à l'école française.'[19]

18   Mohammed Benrabah, *Langue et pouvoir en Algérie: histoire d'un traumatisme linguistique* (Paris: Séguier, 1999), p. 44.
19   Benrabah, *Langue et pouvoir en Algérie: histoire d'un traumatisme linguistique*, p. 49.

Algerian Nationalism

It is not surprising then that the rise of the nationalist movement at the beginning of the twentieth century was based on appeals to revive the Arabic language and the cultural identity of the Algerian people. Islam as a political phenomenon has developed as part of the nationalist movement. Religious groups organised under the Association of Oulémas (religious scholars) led by Ben Badis saw Algerian identity as rooted in Islamic values. In conformity with the ideals of the reform Islamic movement known as the *Nahda* (or Arab Renaissance), which spread all over the Arab world in the 1930s, 'the oulémas undertook to restore the faith to its original purity while reasserting the Arabic character of a country menaced by the French language and culture.'[20]

In 1954 the leaders of the various nationalist movements (except the MNA, the Algerian National Movement of Messali Hadj) announced the founding of the FLN (National Liberation Front), whose objective was to obtain total independence. The Front was a grouping that encompassed a wide range of different tendencies, including members of the religious group, Tamazight native speakers and the moderates of the UDMA (Union Démocratique du Manifeste Algérien), which was 'the party of westernised professionals and the francophile Muslim élite'.[21]

One of the main objectives of the nationalist movement was to maintain and preserve national cohesion by insisting on the unity of the nation, of its people and its language. Their motto was: Islam is our religion, Algeria is our fatherland, Arabic is our language. Fishman points out that, together with culture, religion and history, language is a major component of nationalism. 'It serves as a link with the glorious past and authenticity.'[22] With its prestigious historical past, only Classical Arabic could be considered a serious competitor to the French language.

20 Ageron, *Modern Algeria: A History from 1830 to the Present*, p. 94.
21 Ageron, *Modern Algeria: A History from 1830 to the Present*, p. 106.
22 Joshua Fishman, *Language and Ethnicity in Minority Language Perspective* (London: Multilingual Matters, 1989), p. 47.

The Arabic Language

Arabic is a diglossic language, i.e. the term Arabic refers to several language varieties, which exist side by side throughout the community, each with a definite functional distribution. They can be divided into three main categories. The first is Classical Arabic, the most prestigious variety. It has a long literary tradition and, as the language in which the Qur'an is written, it is considered to be a model of linguistic excellence. It is called the High variety by sociolinguists. The second is Modern Standard Arabic or literary Arabic, the form that has evolved from efforts to modernise the High variety and make it better able to meet the demands of modern life. It is the official language of government, the courts, education, science and the media. It is also the medium of oral communication used by educated Arab people across nations with different spoken varieties. Its prestige also stems from the fact that it is recognised as an official language of various international organisations and used in all the Arab countries stretching from the Persian Gulf in the east to the Atlantic Ocean in the west. The third is the Low variety, which is also known as Dialectal, Colloquial or Algerian Arabic. It is spoken by the majority of the population, for whom it is the mother tongue (except for Tamazight speakers). It consists of a number of regional varieties, including rural and urban forms, which are not normally used for written communication.

For the purpose of this article, unless Arabic is qualified (for example, 'Algerian Arabic') the term refers to the written varieties, and more specifically to literary or Modern Standard Arabic, which is recognised as the sole national and official language of the country.

The Policy of Arabisation

When the French were expelled from Algeria in 1962 they left behind a situation in which the French language was very well entrenched, particularly in the school system, where French was the language of instruction and Arabic was taught as a minor language. There was some recognition given to Arabic during 'the last few bitter years of French occupation: it could be taught as a foreign language.'[23]

Immediately after achieving Independence, Algeria launched a series of measures to re-Arabise a country that was considered to have been 'de-personalised' by colonisation. Owing to the high rate of illiteracy, in 1962 education became the most important means of claiming membership of the new élite. This policy of Arabisation, which was largely a reaction against the cultural and linguistic domination of France, had three principal objectives. Firstly, to reverse the dominance of the French language and expand the use of Arabic to all the sectors that were then the exclusive domain of French. Secondly, to replace a foreign language (French) by what was seen as the national language (Arabic). These measures are referred to as the policy of 'de-Galicization'[24] or 'défrancisation'.[25] Thirdly, the policy aimed to replace all vernaculars, i.e. spoken varieties of Arabic and Tamazight, to ensure national unity around a central government whose working language would be Arabic.

The Arab and Islamic heritage of the Algerian nation is protected by the country's constitution. Algeria's various constitutions have been based on the principle that a nation should have one language only, and that linguistic diversity is a threat to national unity. In spite of the fact that most states are composed of several national or ethnic groups, the equation of nation and state does persist, and according to Wardhaugh

> nearly everywhere language is regarded as a potent unifying and integrating force within the bounds of the modern state, which is seen as the natural domain of a particular language.[26]

All the Algerian constitutions (1963, 1976, 1989 and 1996) reject multiculturalism and multilingualism, stating that Arabic is the sole official and national language. Although an Amazigh component in the national

23 Wardhaugh, *Languages in Competition: Dominance, Diversity and Decline*, p. 185.
24 James Ciment, *Algeria: The Fundamentalist Challenge* (New York: Facts on Files, 1997), p. 120.
25 'De la défrancisation à l'Algérianisation', *El Watan*, 21 November 1999, p. 6.
26 Wardhaugh, *Languages in Competition: Dominance, Diversity and Decline*, p. 3.

identity is mentioned in the preamble of the latest constitution, Tamazight as a language is ignored. The preamble to the constitution stipulates that the fundamental components of the Algerian people's identity are Islam, Arabism and Amazighity: 'Les composantes fondamentales de son [the Algerian people's] identité [...] sont l'Islamité, l'Arabité et l'Amazighité.'[27]

Recent laws have confirmed Tamazight's place as a marginal language in the life of the country. For instance, on 22 July 1998 the National Assembly voted a set of rules imposing Arabic as the sole language to be used in the Assembly. This law requires all government offices, educational institutions and political parties to conduct their business exclusively in Arabic. Thus it would be an offence for any politician to address a crowd in Tamazight in a Tamazight-speaking area of Algeria.

As far as French is concerned, it is never mentioned as such in the official terminology. French is always referred to as 'the foreign language', stressing its alien character as opposed to Arabic, which is always referred to as 'the national language'. After Article 1, which states that Algeria is a Republic 'une et indivisible', Articles 2 and 3 of the 1996 Constitution stipulate: 'L'islam est la religion de l'État. L'Arabe est la langue nationale et officielle.'[28]

The policy of recovering Algerian identity began in 1965 with the Arabisation of the crucial field of education, i.e. the replacement of French with Arabic as the sole language of instruction. This policy was implemented gradually, with Arabisation extended to another year group each year, beginning with primary school and ending with higher education while, at the same time, certain subjects were Arabised throughout the system, starting with the social sciences and ending with technological and scientific subjects. Parallel courses were run together in what were labelled 'bilingual sections', where French could still be used as the language of tuition for science and technology. In 1970 a decree was issued requiring all civil servants to pass an oral and written exam in Arabic. A certificate of proficiency in Arabic was to become necessary for the promotion of existing personnel and the recruitment of new staff.

27   'Algerian Constitution' of 28 November 1996, p. 1.
28   'Algerian Constitution' of 28 November 1996, p. 2.

In the same year the only Tamazight professorship in the country was abolished at the University of Algiers.

The Arabisation plan proceeded steadily over the years, and the Arabisation of primary and secondary education had been completed by the late 1980s. The last bilingual *baccalauréat* was taken in 1988. Bilingual students who had failed the exam that year had to retake it in Arabic the following year. In the same year a decree forbade Algerian nationals from enrolling in the few remaining French *lycées*, which were to become international schools reserved exclusively for the children of diplomats and other foreigners working temporarily in Algeria. This policy culminated in the law passed in December 1996 stipulating that all education in all disciplines, including medicine, science and technology, should be in Arabic by 2000. All public institutions and administrative bodies have had to use Arabic as their language of business and sole language of communication since 5 July 1998. The fifth of July is a highly symbolic date, as it is the official Day of Independence from France. This law provides for the imposition of substantial fines on offenders.[29]

Language Conflict and Social Promotion: French vs Arabic

A national language is more than just the language of government or education. It is also a symbol of the people's identity as citizens of that nation. In a multilingual setting the choice of a language is fraught with emotions, ideals and loyalties, i.e. questions related to language as a marker of ethnic identity, but also with issues related to language as a medium of social advancement and mobility. As a marker of identity, the policy of Arabisation met with resistance from the Tamazight-speaking populations, who saw it as a negation of their national cultural heritage. Socially, language is seen as a 'key to a desired (re)distribution of resources and power.'[30] According to Fishman, there is little reason to adopt a language if it does not

29 'Arabisation: le retour en force', *Liberté*, 7 October 1996. p. 3.
30 Fishman, *Language and Ethnicity in Minority Language Perspective*, p. 241.

provide (or promise to provide) entrée to scarce power and resources [...] to better positions, to useful specialised knowledge, to more effective tools, to more influential contacts (and thereby to control over human and material resources), to more consumable goods.[31]

Although Arabic has come to be more widely used in Algeria, French is still a working tool in the industrial sector. This situation has created a conflict between the French-educated Algerians already occupying high positions and the Arabic-educated graduates who have come onto the job market more recently. Three main tendencies can be identified among the Algerian population as far as attitudes towards the language policy are concerned. Firstly, there is a 'bilingual group', who hold that Arabisation, as a slow, progressive process, should be completed later rather than sooner. In the meantime a situation of bilingualism in Arabic and French must be maintained, as this is essential in order to gain access to modern technology. Secondly, there is a 'multilingual group', who call for the recognition and promotion on an equal footing of the full range of the Algerian cultural heritage embodied in all the languages used by Algerians, i.e. Algerian Arabic, Tamazight and French. Thirdly, there is a 'total Arabisation group', who stress that the country's major priority should be to re-establish Arabic, the sole national and official language, as the expression of the Arabic and Islamic identity of the Algerian people.

The third group sees the first two positions as a disguised way of maintaining the predominance of the French language and culture in Algeria. At the root of the issue lies a difference of perspective in terms of the model of society that Algerians want for their country. On the one hand, some regard the modernisation of the country as a priority, with the maintenance of the French language as an essential part of the process. On the other hand, some advocate a return to a glorious Arab-Islamic past that would be incompatible with Western norms and would involve a cleansing of Western (particularly French) cultural influence from Algeria.

The group that favours total Arabisation sees no reason whatsoever to maintain a bilingual situation, since both Classical and Modern Standard Arabic can replace French in all domains immediately. They illustrate

31   Fishman, *Language and Ethnicity in Minority Language Perspective*, p. 241.

their claims with examples of language planning in countries such as Japan or Israel, which have been successful developing economically and technologically while promoting their classical languages.[32] Concerning the promotion of Algerian Arabic, they claim that it cannot be done rapidly since this language has no recognised standard variety. Its codification and elaboration is bound to take a long time, during which French will consolidate its position in Algeria. The threat is all the more serious in that Algeria has undertaken a policy of industrialisation that relies heavily on western technology and therefore on foreign languages.

> This strategy favors French-educated experts, technicians and administrators, and disadvantages the Arabic-educated elements in important jobs and/or reaching high positions in the growing industrial state enterprises.[33]

Mansouri[34] is a good representative of the total Arabisation group. He represents the view that French-educated Algerians or 'the francophones' are opposed to the Arabisation of the public administration because 'they practically control the affairs of this sector and are anxious to preserve their dominant position.'[35] He sees the maintenance of the French language in Algeria as 'imposed by a privileged minority over the majority of the people in order to safeguard the interests and power of the Francophones.'[36] For him, the total Arabisation of the country is being hindered by the Francophones, who insist on maintaining bilingualism. They do everything they can in order to 'make the educational reforms favoring Arabization ineffective and inconsistent.'[37] Mansouri describes the Algerian Francophones as 'a small but economically powerful group of executives, managers and administrative experts', whom he refers to as technocrats.[38] These, according to him, are 'French-educated élites created by the French policy of assimilation'[39] entirely devoted

32 Abdelhamid Mansouri, *Algeria between Tradition and Modernity: The Question of Language*, unpublished PhD thesis (Albany: State University of New York, 1991), p. 74.
33 Mansouri, *Algeria between Tradition and Modernity*, p. 9.
34 Mansouri, *Algeria between Tradition and Modernity*, p. 10.
35 Mansouri, *Algeria between Tradition and Modernity*, p. 76.
36 Mansouri, *Algeria between Tradition and Modernity*, p. 77.
37 Mansouri, *Algeria between Tradition and Modernity*, p. 70.
38 Mansouri, *Algeria between Tradition and Modernity*, p. 95.
39 Mansouri, *Algeria between Tradition and Modernity*, p. 77.

to the maintenance and expansion of the French language in Algeria, especially in higher education, by means of discrimination against Arabic-educated citizens. According to him, what is interesting about the Algerian technocrats is that they possess, in addition to economic wealth,

> a French cultural 'capital' that enables them to further their control to include the cultural and linguistic spheres. One area in which this cultural capital has been effective is the educational system in terms of access to higher education, reproduction of French-educated technocrats, and the discrimination against Arabic-educated cadres in the industrial job market.[40]

Similarly, Assous[41] blames the slow pace of the Arabisation process and the fact that French is still used in Algeria on the Francophone Algerians, who refuse to comply with government policies that favour Arabic-educated Algerians. He believes that total Arabisation will not be achieved for at least another 15 to 20 years:

> This time frame is postulated to take into account the production of a new Arabized generation, educated in the new school system. From these students will come the Arabized cadres whose competency in Arabic will provide the necessary trained personnel to implement government decrees in all sectors of Algerian life.[42]

The conflict between French-educated and Arabic-educated Algerians is exacerbated by the fact that each group sees the other as occupying better professional positions and doing their utmost to increase or at least maintain their privileges while trying to prevent the other group from gaining access to the same positions. Benrabah[43] reports that some inspectors in the Ministry of Education refuse to appoint teachers of French to certain schools in order to prevent their pupils from receiving tuition in this language.

At the other end of the spectrum, as far as language is concerned, Benrabah claims that neither Classical nor Modern Arabic represents Algerian national identity, which can only be expressed by all the lan-

40   Mansouri, *Algeria between Tradition and Modernity: The Question of Language*, p. 122.
41   Omar Assous, *Arabization and Cultural Conflicts*, unpublished PhD thesis (Boston, Massachusetts: Northeastern University, 1985).
42   Assous, *Arabization and Cultural Conflicts*, p. 221.
43   Benrabah, *Langue et pouvoir Algérie*, p. 108.

guages used by Algerians, i.e. Algerian Arabic – the mother tongue of the majority, Tamazight – the indigenous language, and French – the colonial inheritance and the key to technology:

> C'est notre proposition de solution à la question de la langue arabe en Algérie où berbère, arabe algérien et français pourront bien évidemment exister côte à côte dans une situation d'égalité et de convivialité.'[44]

According to Benrabah, the language policy implemented in Algeria since Independence has been aimed at favouring Arabic-educated Algerians and eliminating the French-educated élite from all prestigious positions: 'La politique d'arabisation a, dès le départ été conçue sur le mode de l'exclusion.'[45] To those who claim that speaking a language means expressing a certain nationality, Benrabah presents examples of countries such as the Republic of Ireland, where both English, the old colonial language, and Gaelic, the nationalist language, were declared official languages without there having been any loss of Irish identity. He goes on to argue that multilingualism has proved to be a positive factor in the cultural and economic development of countries like Switzerland and Belgium. He advocates 'unity in plurality': 'Le pluralisme linguistique est une bénédiction, un bienfait insoupçonné, et non une malédiction.'[46]

It is generally accepted that language differences alone do not lead to conflict. It is the presence of, or perceived, inequality of social status and unequal access to economic positions or political power that produce social conflict. According to Lapierre, linguistic policies are related to issues of political and economic domination that may lead to violent confrontation.

> Il n'y a pas de conflits 'purement' linguistiques [...] l'enjeu de la langue est en général, lié à des rapports de domination économiques et politiques [...]. Si la classe dirigeante de la communauté dirigeante adopte une stratégie d'exclusion absolue [...] 'l'élite' de la communauté dominée finit par se poser en *pouvoir concurrent*. La stratégie du mouvement qu'elle anime et encadre devient *offensive*: non plus médiation, bons offices et compromis, mais compétition, affrontement, conflits éventuellement violents.[47]

44 Benrabah, *Langue et pouvoir Algérie*, p. 327.
45 Benrabah, *Langue et pouvoir Algérie*, p. 25.
46 Benrabah, *Langue et pouvoir Algérie*, p. 272.
47 Lapierre, *Le pouvoir politique et les langues. Babel et Léviathan*, pp. 261, 264.

Language Conflict and Culture: The East vs The West

Linguistic choices in Algeria also reflect the expression of a model of society turned either towards France and the Western world as a necessity for modernisation and technological development or towards the Middle East as the source of national religious and cultural identity. Each group believes that the other wants to impose an alien model on already existing Algerian cultural values, which they ignore, reject or despise. Thus, for Benrabah, the total Arabisation group suffers from an inferiority complex in relation to the Middle East and the Arabic peninsula where Islam originated:

> Ce besoin maladif d'homogénéiser l'ensemble provient d'un profond sentiment d'insécurité linguistique doublé d'un complexe d'infériorité. Lorsque les deux se conjuguent chez un individu, ils tendent à dévaloriser chez ce dernier sa propre langue tout en glorifiant un idiome non usité.[48]

He claims that the policy of Arabisation has produced Algerians who are totally fascinated by Middle Eastern cultural norms, which they want to impose on Algerians:

> La politique d'arabisation permet l'émergence de cadres vouant une admiration béate envers les Moyen Orientaux, leur empruntant même des idéologies sectaires qui ne font que creuser davantage le fossé séparant les francophones et les arabisants.[49]

As far as Benrabah is concerned, this policy has succeeded in transforming the Algerians so much that he can no longer identify with them:

> En l'espace d'une quinzaine d'années, l'Algérien est devenu méconnaissable. Au vu des seuls accoutrements (tenues afghanes, foulards islamiques etc.), la société algérienne a subi en peu de temps une véritable orientalisation.'[50]

---

48 Benrabah, *Langue et pouvoir en Algérie*, p. 242.
49 Benrabah, *Langue et pouvoir en Algérie*, p. 115.
50 Benrabah, *Langue et pouvoir en Algérie*, p. 132.

This transformation can be seen not only in the appearance of individuals, but also in their immediate environment. For instance, by law all street signs and shop signs must be exclusively written in Arabic.

At the other extreme, Mansouri claims that French-educated Algerians suffer from 'a psychological complex of inferiority toward the ex-colonizer'.[51] He does not identify with them because

> by imitating the ex-colonizers in clothing, manners and way of life [...] the western-educated element try to prove [...] that they are not underdeveloped, traditional, backward people, but they are like them and also speak their language.'[52]

Mansouri claims that,

> some push this 'exaggerated' tendency further, to the point where they prefer to communicate in the language of the ex-colonizers for no other reason than to feel 'superior' to the rest of the population who choose to speak its own language, so they can meanwhile compensate psychologically for their inferiority complex.[53]

In Algerian Arabic, these people are referred to as *hizb frança*, which translates as 'the Party of France'.[54] This label is not as innocent as it may sound. In a country that fought a seven-year war of liberation against France during which 1.5 million people died (according to Algerian official statistics), this label is synonymous with *harki*, a term for a traitor to the Algerian cause guilty of collaboration with the enemy. This may explain why French-educated intellectuals were the first targets of the fundamentalist groups:

> En Algérie, ce sont surtout ceux qu'on appelle les 'arabisants monolingues' qui nient aux Algériens bilingues le droit d'exister [...] ils ont en quelque sorte montré le chemin aux illuminés qui entament en 1993 l'élimination physique des intellectuels. La majorité du pôle républicain moderniste comprend des francophones parmi lesquels on compte le plus grand nombre de ces victimes.[55]

51 Mansouri, *Algeria between Tradition and Modernity*, p. 76.
52 Mansouri, *Algeria between Tradition and Modernity*, p. 76.
53 Mansouri, *Algeria between Tradition and Modernity*, p. 76.
54 Martin Stone, *The Agony of Algeria* (London: Hurst, 1997), p. 20.
55 Benrabah, *Langue et pouvoir en Algérie: histoire d'un traumatisme linguistique*, p. 131.

Language Conflict and National Unity: Arabic vs Tamazight

When Algeria gained its Independence, the liberal Tamazight-speaking minority opposed the new government's tendencies towards authoritarianism and resigned from the FLN in 1965 in order to establish an illegal opposition political organisation: the FFS (Front des Forces Socialistes). 1968 saw the emergence of the MCB (Mouvement Culturel Berbère), a cultural organisation affiliated to the FFS.[56] Its objective was to place an emphasis on cultural and linguistic concerns, rather than political issues. In the early 1970s, with the closure of the sole Amazigh language course at the University of Algiers, research into Amazigh language or culture became a subversive activity viewed as threatening national unity. Students caught with copies of the ancient alphabetic transcription system (*Tifinagh*) were liable to be arrested and tortured, actions designed to repress Amazigh aspirations: 'Des lycéens arrêtés en possession de l'alphabet Tifinagh sont arrêtés, d'autres torturés.'[57]

In April 1980 Mouloud Mammeri, a well-known Tamazight scholar and writer, was prevented from giving a lecture on Tamazight poetry at the university of Tizi Ouzou, the capital of Kabylia, one of the main Tamazight-speaking areas in the north of Algeria. The students went on strike to protest against the authoritarian nature of this measure, and the action quickly spread to schools and the population at large when a general strike was called in mid-April. This led to a harsh crackdown by the army, and more than 30 people were killed and 200 injured in the weeks of unrest that followed. These events have become an important landmark for the Amazigh movement in Algeria, where it is referred to as the Amazigh Spring[58] by analogy with the Soviet crackdown following the Prague Spring of 1968.

The introduction of political pluralism after the October 1988 riots saw the end of the single-party system. It became possible to found independent political and cultural associations committed to the promo-

---

56   Stone, *The Agony of Algeria*, p. 206.
57   'La révolte kabyle', *Le Point*, 1346, 4 July 1998, pp. 20–21.
58   For a day-by-day account of these events, see 'Amazigh Spring' on http://www.tamurt.imazighen.com/tamzgh/tafsut-eng.html.

tion of the Tamazight language and culture. Between 1989 and 1990 no less than 44 political parties were formed. The Amazigh movement split into two main wings led by two political parties: the FFS and the RCD (Rassemblement pour la Culture et la Démocratie), as well as the more culturally oriented MCB. Both the FFS and RCD developed national political manifestos and remain committed to changing the Arabisation law. However, the FFS favours a policy of dialogue with the fundamentalists, while RCD, on the basis of its secular ideals, refuses to support any negotiation with Islamist groups.

In 1995 the MCB split into two factions when the government agreed to investigate the possibility of introducing Tamazight into the state education system in response to a school boycott between September 1994 and April 1995 organised by parents and students who demanded the introduction of Tamazight teaching: the group who supported the RCD argued that the boycott should be ended, while those who supported the FFS favoured its continuation. However, as a result of their combined actions, including demonstrations and strikes, the government appointed an advisory Haut Commissariat à l'Amazighité (HCA), whose objective is the promotion and development of Tamazight with a view to introducing it in the educational system. It can be said that some level of official recognition has been achieved in the 1990s with the appointment of the HCA, as well as the broadcast of a news summary on national television and the opening of undergraduate and postgraduate courses in Tamazight linguistics, literature and culture at the universities of Tizi-Ouzou and Bejaia in the Kabylia region.

However, the use of Tamazight as a language of education requires a process of codification and transcription, since the language has no established written form. The question of which alphabet to use is not only a technical issue. Three possible options can be considered. The first option is the *Tifinagh* alphabet, which is an ancient writing system preserved in the Sahara. It can still be found on stone inscriptions and certain types of implements, such as shields or pottery. Being specific to Tamazight, these symbols, which can now be found written on signposts and shops in Kabylia, have an important symbolic value because they represent an independent Amazigh culture and identity. They refer to a mythical past civilisation when the language was written. However, nowadays they are not used and, for the purpose of printing, they represent the least economical system. The second option is the Arabic Alphabet. Since Arabic is the medium of instruction in Algeria, the whole population is familiar with this script, particularly the younger generation who receive their education in Arabic. Moreover, it enjoys great prestige, as it is the alphabet used to transcribe the words of God in the Qu'ran. As such, these characters establish a clear link with Algeria's oriental, Arab, Islamic past. However, this is one of the reasons why some scholars who reject this system favour a third option: the Latin alphabet, which is seen as the key to accessing universal culture through modern information technology. In addition to this, there is a long tradition of writing Tamazight in Latin script in Algeria.[59] The HCA has now resolved this issue by announcing that their last meeting, with linguists and historians, agreed that the Latin alphabet should be used to write Tamazight.[60]

According to Quandt, there are no separatist movements in Algeria and 'Algerians share a sense of common identity.'[61] In spite of being accused of being a threat to national unity, separatism was never a dominant element in the Amazigh movement. Their slogans invariably state that they are not Arabs, but Algerians, and that Arabic is not their language. Their primary goal is to change the status of Tamazight and to obtain its recognition alongside Arabic as an official and national language that expresses their cultural identity:

> Nous sommes Algériens mais nous ne sommes pas arabes; nous sommes Algériens mais l'arabe n'est pas notre langue! Le berbère est notre langue et nous voulons préserver notre culture et notre identité propres!'[62]

The final declaration of the Amazigh World Congress, issued at the end of its second congress in Brussels in August 2000, includes no mention of the word 'separatism'. The congress decided to make Tamazight its

59   Salem Chaker, 'La Kabylie: un processus de développement linguistique auto-
     nome', *International Journal of the Sociology of Language*, 123, 1997, p. 90.
60   'L'enseignement de la langue Amazighe: une affaire d'état', *El Watan*, 12 Novem-
     ber 2000, p. 13.
61   W. B. Quandt, *Between Ballots and Bullets* (Washington DC: Brookings Institu-
     tions Press, 1998), p. 97.
62   Salem Chaker, 'Pour l'autonomie linguistique de la Kabylie', *Le Monde*, 11 July
     1998, p. 12.

official language, but it 'reaffirms its determination to continue to fight for the official and national recognition of Tamazight.'[63]

However, recent events such as the killing of Matoub Lounes, one of the most popular singers in Kabylia, in June 1998 have strengthened the urgency of the demands made by the Amazigh movement and pushed some of its members into more radical positions.

> La vague de colère qui a secoué la Kabylie après l'assassinat de Matoub Lounes constitue un symbole révélateur: la revendication identitaire Kabyle est plus vivace que jamais.[64]

Similarly, a statement made by the President fuelled the general sense of frustration and anger of Tamazight speakers. In September 1999, while campaigning in Tizi Ouzou, the city where the Amazigh Spring began, the President declared that, 'Tamazight ne sera jamais une langue officielle et si elle devait devenir langue nationale, c'est tout le peuple qui devrait se prononcer par voix référendaire.'[65] In a country where Arabic-speakers constitute a large majority, the result of a country-wide referendum would inevitably go against Tamazight. This statement angered the Tamazight-speaking community, and the AWC and other organisations sent a message to the President expressing their 'consternation at his statement' and reminding him that 'dictators have passed but Tamazight is always here.'[66]

Since the institutional framework is biased against Tamazight, Chaker has recently argued for a change of strategy. He claims that the future of Tamazight should be decided by Tamazight-speakers and the population who live in Tamazight-speaking areas. These, he goes on, should be recognised as separate entities with specific linguistic and cultural rights. Comparing the situation with that of Catalonia or the Basque Country in Spain, he argues that the only solution for regions like Kabylia is linguistic and cultural autonomy:

---

63 Amazigh World Congress, Final Declaration of the 2nd Amazigh World Congress, Brussels, 7–9 August 2000, http://www.tamurt.imazighen.com/tamazgha/index-eng.html.
64 'La révolte Kabyle'.
65 *El Watan*, 9 September 1999, p. 3.
66 World Algerian Action Coalition, 11 September 1999.

Défendre la langue et la culture Berbères, vouloir assurer leur survie passe nécessairement par la reconnaissance des groupes Berbérophones en tant qu'entité
spécifique, dont les droits culturels et linguistiques doivent être reconnus et proté-
gés dans les faits. D'une façon ou d'une autre, l'autonomie linguistique et culturelle
des régions berbérophones qui le souhaitent – et c'est à l'évidence le cas de la
Kabylie – doit être assurée.[67]

The organisation of a referendum to decide the status of Tamazight might,
in fact, prove to be more divisive than any other measures taken so far,
since it would pit Arabic-speaking and Tamazight-speaking Algerians
against each other. At the moment, Tamazight is not institutionally recognised and is not protected by an article of the constitution. Unless this
situation changes, its future will depend on unilateral decisions taken by
whoever happens to be in power at any given time.

Language Conflict and Educational Bilingualism

It is necessary to take account of language planning, in the sense of
deliberate government intervention to promote or eliminate a particular
language or languages, in any attempt to understand how languages gain
or lose speakers. In multilingual countries political and economic power
plays an important role in the choice of national language as the expression of identity, group membership and nationhood. The language that
offers the greater possibilities of social promotion will eventually relegate
the other languages to domestic and private domains.

In these settings in which either the myth or the reality of social mobility is
widespread, bilingualism is repeatedly skewed in favor of the more powerful,
with the language of greater power being acquired and used much more than that
of lesser power.[68]

---

67 Chaker, 'Pour l'autonomie linguistique de la Kabylie', p. 12. See also Chaker,
    'La Kabylie: un processus de développement linguistique autonome', pp. 81–99.
68 Fishman, *Language and Ethnicity in Minority Language Perspective*, p. 241.

As far as French is concerned, the language planning process in Algeria has resulted in a language shift, with Arabic replacing French more or less completely in the various areas of social life. However, the influence of the French language was so widespread that this shift inevitably produced tension and conflict between different social and cultural groups. According to Grandguillaume, this is true of all three of France's former colonies in the Maghreb:

> La profondeur de l'implication du français dans la société maghrébine était telle que le changement de langue ne se réduisait pas à une opération linguistique, mais entraînait des conséquences sociales, politiques, culturelles, qui ont contribué à faire de cette question un problème conflictuel.[69]

In Algeria a number of factors seem to point to the success, at least in quantitative terms, of the policy of Arabisation. According to Grandguillaume, 'L'Algérie de 1962 était totalement francisée. Celle de 1996 est largement arabisée. La loi récente la veut totalement arabisée.'[70] The number of readers of Algerian newspapers is a good indicator of the importance of Arabic. In 1993 there were 220,000 readers for the press in Arabic, as compared with 625,000 for newspapers printed in French.[71] In 2000 *El Khabar*, the main newspaper published in Arabic, sold 400,000 copies a day, while the figures for the main newspapers in French were as follows: *Liberté*: 160,000; *Le Matin*: 140,000; *Le Quotidien*: 120,000; *El Watan*: 100,000. [72]

Although it will take some time to implement in higher education, Arabic has officially been the sole medium of instruction for all subjects at all levels since 2000. As the influence of the growing numbers of graduates educated in Arabic increases, there will be more pressure on the government to take action aimed at ensuring that all sectors of society

---

69 Gilbert Grandguillaume, *Arabisation et politique linguistique au Maghreb* (Paris: Maisonneuve et Larose, 1983), p. 9.
70 Gilbert Grandguillaume, 'Arabisation et démagogie en Algérie', *Le Monde Diplomatique*, February 1997, p. 5.
71 Benrabah, *Langue et pouvoir en Algérie: histoire d'un traumatisme linguistique*, p. 271.
72 'Un journalisme d'investigation', *Jeune Afrique/L'Intelligent*, 19–25 December 2000, p. 34.

effectively substitute the use of Arabic for French, both orally and in writing, in all their official proceedings. In that case, French will be relegated to the position of a foreign language taught in schools on the same footing as other foreign languages, such as English, German or Spanish.

Indeed, nowadays French is taught as a foreign language in schools, but paradoxically, owing to the policy of compulsory education for all, more people have a working knowledge of French today than during the colonial period. A survey of the languages spoken or understood in the homes of the capital city published by an Algerian newspaper[73] reported the following results, which seem to show that French is still widely used in Algiers: Arabic: 95%; French: 79%; Berber: 44.5%; English: 35.8%. Although French maintains a respectable position, the survey found that male informants (particularly professionals) expressed a strong desire to learn English:

> Cela s'explique par le fait que l'anglais, la langue la plus parlée dans le monde commence à gagner les foyers algérois longtemps renfermés sur le français (colonisation et héritage culturel obligent).[74]

These figures concern a relatively small number (1,697) of inhabitants of the capital city, where French has always had the strongest influence. Obviously, the results would be different if another city was surveyed.

It is worth noting that, while French was mastered as a native language or second language with near native proficiency by previous generations, large numbers of Algerians now possess French as a foreign language. This difference in the level of competence is acknowledged by Benrabah as 'une régression qualitative dans la compétence linguistique'.[75] Among the factors that signal the decline of a language, Wardhaugh mentions the fact that it is spoken by fewer and fewer monolinguals, and that French-speakers represent an ageing group in the population. In this situation the dominant language intrudes into ever more domains of life, while the dominated language is used less and

---

73   'Pratiques linguistiques', *El Watan*, 21 July 1999, p. 9.
74   'Pratiques linguistiques', p. 9.
75   Benrabah, *Langue et pouvoir en Algérie: histoire d'un traumatisme linguistique*, p. 269.

less.[76] This seems to be the case in Algeria, where Arabic, now the dominant language, benefits from enormous governmental support and is spreading in all the spheres of society. French, now the dominated language is used in a diminishing number of domains and spoken as a native language by an ageing population. The editor of a magazine notes that 'many young people do not speak French or speak it very badly' and that if a Francophone reader dies 'he will not be replaced.'[77]

At the same time, it is necessary to remember that in the current educational system some pupils start French later than the previous generation, thus reducing further their competence in the language. This concerns a large proportion of the population. Out of a total population of 30 million in 2000,[78] about 20 million, all educated in the Arabised educational system, are under 30 years of age. Algeria has a fast increasing population with an annual growth rate of 2.5%. In the same year 7 million pupils enrolled in primary and secondary schools.[79] These will form the future 'arabised generations' that Assous predicted (see note 43).

However, President Bouteflika has ordered a review of the educational system by a national committee (Commission Nationale pour la Refonte du Système Éducatif) established in May 2000. School education is divided into a compulsory foundation stage (École fondamentale) from the age of 6 to 15 and a secondary stage from 15 to 18. Concerning language teaching, the committee recommends the introduction of French as early as the second year of primary education. It also recommends that French should be the first foreign language taught in secondary schools, and that sciences and technological subjects should be taught in French at university level.[80] The Ministry of Education has recognised that the teaching of foreign languages has been a failure:

---

76   Wardhaugh, *Languages in Competition: Dominance, Diversity and Decline*, p. 19.

77   Quoted in Stone, *The Agony of Algeria*, p. 22.

78   'L'Office National des Statistiques annonce que la population atteint 30 millions d'habitants en 2000', *El Watan*, 27 March 2000, p. 2.

79   Office National des Statistiques, 1999.

80   'Refonte du système éducatif: le français à partir de la 2ème année fondamentale', *Liberté*, 15 January 2001, p. 4.

more than 50% of schools do not have foreign language teachers, particularly in rural areas where the teachers of French and English have
abandoned their posts after receiving threats from Islamist terrorists.
'Des dizaines d'enseignants d'anglais mais surtout de français menacés
jusqu'au seuil de leurs salles de cours ont été contraints à abandonner
leurs postes et à fuir.'[81] Moreover, the ministry has recognised that the
problem is more complex, since it also affects the teaching of Arabic,
which has been far from being satisfactory, to judge by the poor results
obtained in Arabic in the last *baccalauréat* exam.

Language Conflict and International Communication: French vs English

There are two possible ways forward for French, depending on the language policies implemented by future governments. If the pro-Arab-
isation lobby maintains its influence, reinforced by the rise of Muslim
fundamentalism in Algeria, more stringent Arabisation measures will be
taken to speed up the elimination of French from the country, even as the
key to technology. Indeed, the total Arabisation group calls for the replacement of French by English as the language of access to modern
science. This group is supported by the fundamentalists, who call for the
use of English as an alternative to French. Since 1993 pupils beginning
their fourth year of compulsory education have been offered a choice of
either French or English as their first foreign language. Until then French
was introduced as a compulsory subject in year 4 and English or another
foreign language in year 7. The argument presented to support this decision is that since a foreign language is necessary for the modernisation
of their country, Algerians would be better off with English, since it is
the language universally recognised as the key to modern science and
technology.

---

81   'L'école fondamentale au pique', *Liberté*, 28 January 2001, p. 3.

A report on the debates of the 1998 Conférence Nationale de l'Éducation shows that the anti-French lobby is still quite powerful in educational circles:

> Le courant anti-français est bien implanté au sein de cette structure. Sinon com-
> ment expliquer son acharnement à proposer la langue anglaise tout en sachant
> l'inadéquation de son enseignement en Algérie.'[82]

Indeed, the introduction of English as an alternative to French seems to
have been a 'total fiasco'. The number of pupils choosing English as
their first foreign language has decreased each year from 48,000 when
the measure was first introduced in 1993 to 11,000 in 1999.[83] On the
global scene, the country has so far refused to associate itself with the
campaigns to promote the use of French internationally: Algeria has never
been a member of the Francophone movement and only attended a Francophone summit for the first time in 1999 with observer status. This has
to be interpreted in the framework of the revival of Algerian–French
relations and the overall change of policy towards the old colonial power.
Similarly, Algeria attended the 21st Franco-African meeting in Cameroon
this year, the first time it has taken part in these events.[84]

　　If the current trend initiated by President Bouteflika continues,
French will go on playing a major role in the life of Algerians. A number
of factors reinforce the presence of French in Algerian society. Firstly, a
large community of Algerian immigrants (600,000, excluding citizens
with dual nationality, and 2 million, counting those with French nationality and members of the second and third generations) live in France,[85]
maintaining strong links with their families and friends in Algeria. As a
result of these socio-cultural links, France is the most popular destination
for Algerian tourists. In the early 1990s the French consulates granted
800,000 entry visas to Algerians every year.[86]

82　'Quel avenir pour le français?', *El Watan*, 21 November 2000, p. 4.
83　'L'enseignement de l'anglais à l'école fondamentale: un fiasco', *Liberté*, 5 Sep-
　　tember 2000, p. 3.
84　'L'Algérie au Sommet France-Afrique: le tabou et les interrogations', *Liberté*, 29
　　January 2001, p. 3.
85　'France-Algérie, la réconciliation en marche', *Le Monde*, 2 August 1999, p. 2.
86　'Bouteflika parie sur la France', *Jeune Afrique*, 10–16 August 1999, p. 24.

Furthermore, improved telecommunications and the ready availability of satellite dishes have introduced all the French television channels into Algerian homes. According to Mostefaoui, three main factors contributed to the importance of French television in the Maghreb; history, geography and economy:

> l'histoire nourrie d'échanges et de conflits millénaires entre les deux rives de la Méditerranée, la géographie physique qui offre des conditions favorables à la communication et la géographie économique et humaine, post-indépendance dont les caractéristiques continuent de marquer d'une forte extraversion les anciennes colonies envers la métropole.[87]

Satellite television has brought about an internationalisation of the audio-visual media in Algeria, with viewers now being able to watch Arabic channels from the Middle East, but also programmes from France and other European countries. This has meant exposure to images of material wealth and modernity, but also to the moral degradation of the West, i.e. the prevalence of sex, drugs and violence on Western television. Satellite television is seen as a threat to national identity and is regularly attacked[88] by the fundamentalists as an instrument of western influence or 'westoxification'.[89]

Language Conflict and Reconciliation

The election in May 1999 of a new president, Abdelaziz Bouteflika, seems to have put the Arabisation programme on hold for a while. The President does not hesitate to address his audiences in French,[90] effectively ignoring the 1996 law that makes it a punishable offence for politicians to use any other language apart from Arabic in their public speeches or

---

87 B. Mostefaoui, *La télévision française au Maghreb: structure, stratégie et enjeux* (Paris: L'Harmattan, 1995), p. 26.
88 'La revanche de Bouteflika', *L'Express*, 5 August 1999, p. 33.
89 Ciment, *Algeria the fundamentalist challenge*, p. 142.
90 'La revanche de Bouteflika', p. 33.

declarations. In the past the French connections of some Algerian politicians or top generals who had served in the French army have been 'used
by the fundamentalists to discredit them' and to prove their abandonment
of Algerian ideals.[91] The often-strained relations between the two countries are undergoing a strong revival. Bouteflika stresses the need to renew
Franco-Algerian cultural co-operation and he has not hesitated to respond
to challenges from the fundamentalists, saying that Algeria does not have
an irreversible position concerning the French language.

As part of its attempts to bring the country back onto the international scene, the new government has decided to develop its links with
all the regions of the world, including a preferential relationship with
France. The French minister of foreign affairs described the new situation
as a new foundation for Franco-Algerian relations adding that 'l'alchimie
franco-algérienne est de nouveau à l'oeuvre.'[92] France has seized this
opportunity to reinforce its presence in Algeria by announcing the re-
opening of the French cultural centres that were closed in 1994 following
a bomb attack.[93]

However, it is necessary to note that President Bouteflika was elected unopposed amid complaints of vote-rigging, and that six other candidates withdrew from the election on the grounds that widespread fraud
meant that Bouteflika's victory was a foregone conclusion. Ahmed Taleb
Ibrahimi was one of the candidates who called for an Islamic state in
Algeria. He is well known as the former minister of education who
launched the total Arabisation plan in the sixties. Benrabah refers to him
as 'l'artisan de l'arabisation à tout prix'[94] because he went ahead with
the Arabisation plan believing that it would not be feasible. He is quoted
as saying, 'Cela ne marchera pas mais il faut le faire.'[95]

The President succeeded in creating a new optimism in Algeria. In
the first few months after he took office he announced a peace plan to
end the Islamic insurgency. It offered an amnesty to Islamist militants

91 Quandt, *Between Ballots and Bullets*, p. 96.
92 'France-Algérie, la réconciliation en marche', p. 2.
93 'France-Algérie, la réconciliation en marche', p. 2.
94 Benrabah, *Langue et pouvoir en Algérie: histoire d'un traumatisme linguistique*,
    p. 112.
95 Gilbert Grandguillaume, 'Comment a-t-on pu en arriver là?', *Esprit*, 208, January
    1995, p. 18.

who were not guilty of murder, bombing or rape. Bouteflika promised that this plan, which became the 'Loi sur la Concorde civile', would bring about peace and reconciliation. A year later he was able to claim partial success, saying that

> 90% des terroristes sont neutralisés ou ralliés. Dans les 10% restants, 5% sont des criminels de droit commun. Il ne reste que 5% qui constituent une dangereuse minorité agissante.'[96]

However, brutal killings are still reported in the press almost daily, and violence is threatening to derail the President's attempts to end the conflict and his campaign for national reconciliation. On the social and the economic front, the situation has not changed a lot either, and more and more voices can be heard blaming Bouteflika for failing to meet the population's expectations: 'Pas un jour ne passe sans que la presse privée ne le rende responsable de la recrudescence actuelle de la violence.'[97] At the same time, rumours about attempts on the President's life have been widely publicised, adding to the atmosphere of instability and fear.[98]

Everything seems to suggest that once more an Algerian president may be forced to resign. According to Addi, a sociologist, 'Il est de plus en plus probable que Bouteflika va partir. Les généraux n'ont plus confiance en lui.'[99] The government has failed to bring about the social and cultural changes that the population expected. 'Face aux conflits sociaux qui se multiplient, le pouvoir semble paralysé. À Alger on se demande si le président finira son mandat.'[100]

If Algeria is to achieve long-term stability, it must have a constitution drawn up freely by means of a democratic process. Any such constitution must guarantee the linguistic and cultural rights of all Algerians, incorporating all the dimensions of the Algerian identity rather than excluding some of them. This is not the case at present, since languages

---

96 'Entretien de Jean Daniel avec le président Bouteflika', *Le Nouvel Observateur*, 22–8 June 2000, p. 28.
97 'Dix ans de cauchemar et plus de 100 000 morts', *Le Monde*, 22 December 2000, p. 8.
98 'Rumeurs sur l'attentat contre le président', *Le Monde*, 22 December 2000, p. 3.
99 'Le procès de la violence reste à faire', *L'Express*, 8–14 June 2000, p. 56.
100 'L'Algérie en panne', *L'Express*, 8–14 June 2000, p. 52.

other than Arabic have been ignored in all the country's constitutions. 'L'arabisation est le socle invariant de la politique algérienne.'[101] The constant goal of linguistic planning in Algeria has been the Arabisation of Tamazight and French-speaking Algerians. However, the pace at which the Arabisation of Algeria will proceed is hard to predict, given that the political situation in the country is far from stable. The tensions between the various lobbies are due to a dead-end reached by Algeria's political system, a system in which it is impossible to resolve problems and decisions are taken unilaterally without consensus.

Conclusion

The underlying reason for Algeria's linguistic, cultural and social conflicts is a struggle for power between groups with competing visions of how the country should be ruled. This is a struggle between Muslim fundamentalists and supporters of secular rule, but also a struggle between the military establishment, who regard themselves as the guardians of national unity, and those who believe it is time to put a democratic system in place.

In the past decade Algeria has had nine prime ministers and five Presidents (Bouteflika, Zeroual, Kafi, Boudiaf and Chadli). In August 2000, yet again, the Prime Minister resigned, accusing the President of violating the constitution.[102] This political instability does not seem to have come to an end. According to Quandt, 'the struggle over Algeria's basic institutions is likely to remain unsettled for some time.'[103] Addi argues that the only solution to the Algerian situation is for the government to call a truly free and democratic general election. Nobody can predict the results of such an election. The last one was cancelled in 1992 when the fundamentalists looked certain to win.

101   Chaker, 'Pour l'autonomie linguistique de la Kabylie', p. 12.
102   Lakhdar Benchiba and Ellyas Akram, 'Rentrée scolaire, crise sociale', *Le Monde Diplomatique*, October 2000, p. 14.
103   Quandt, *Between Ballots and Bullets*, p. 138.

Language planning in Algeria is extremely controversial, representing as it does an attempt to reconcile authenticity, national identity and
modernisation, and eliminate any legacy of the country's colonial past.
The Arabisation programme has been disputed since its inception, setting
social groups against one another on the basis of emotional loyalties,
social issues and practical realities. It has been proceeding steadily in
spite of strong resistance to its implementation and temporary periods of
slow progress, for example, in 1992 under the short presidency of Mohammed Boudiaf (from January to June 1992, when he was assassinated)
and now under Bouteflika.

The actual process may appear to be too slow for the advocates of
total Arabisation or too quick for those who believe in bilingualism or
multilingualism, but the overall long-term goal remains unchanged, i.e.
the complete replacement of French and Tamazight with Arabic, as the
sole language of the Algerian people also used by all Muslim people in
the world. Lapierre claims that, 'Un État dont les citoyens sont musul-
mans ne peut être légitime aux yeux de croyants que si sa langue officielle
est la langue sacrée.'[104] Similarly, according to Wardhaugh, in the Maghreb countries, 'the only politically acceptable position for leaders to take
is to arabize.'[105] If this is true, the French language is bound to have less
and less importance in the life of Algerians. It might eventually disappear
from the country in the same way as the languages of other conquerors
have disappeared, leaving behind them Arabic, the sacred language and
Tamazight, the language of an indigenous linguistic minority.

Concerning Tamazight, it appears that Algeria is trapped in the logic
of its nationalist movement. The Arabic and Islamic character of the
Algerian nation has been preserved through constitutional provisions as
a tool for ensuring national sovereignty. Having decided to opt for a
single official and national language, Algeria is obliged to deny any status
to the indigenous language, pushing members of the Tamazight-speaking community into more radical positions, including calls for regional
autonomy.

104   Lapierre, *Le pouvoir politique et les langues: Babel et Léviathan*, p. 242.
105   Wardhaugh, *Languages in Competition: Dominance, Diversity and Decline*, p.
      187.

Concerning the future role of the French language in Algeria, Mansouri notes with optimism 'the rise of Islamic fundamentalism and its religious stand against French education',[106] while Benrabah sees it as a disaster, 'une catastrophe imprévue comme la prise de pouvoir par les islamistes.'[107] Although French still maintains its position as the most important foreign language for Algerians, it has lost a great deal of the prestige that once attached to it. French still plays a major role on the Algerian scene, but a number of elements seem to indicate that, despite recent attempts by the President to reverse the situation, in the long term its privileged position is threatened for two main reasons: on the one hand, the increasing use of Arabic as the constitutionally instituted national and official language, and, on the other, the rise of English as the language of international communication.

The President's recent statements in favour of French and his public use of the language have been heralded as a revolution: 'C'est le Président lui même qui a fait le premier pas en cassant le tabou linguistique. Personne avant lui n'avait osé s'exprimer dans la langue de Voltaire.'[108] However, it can be argued that the president is in fact ignoring a law that was passed by an Algerian assembly. He should set an example by upholding the law until it is abrogated. This seems to confirm that legislation can be ignored at will by those who are supposed to enforce it.

Grandguillaume argues that the only solution for Algeria would be for the government to promote free debate and democracy by allowing the citizens to express themselves freely. A beginning should be made with the abrogation of the Arabisation laws, which constitute an obstacle to the development of democracy.

> La seule manière de faire reconnaître sa légitimité, ce serait, pour les dirigeants algériens, de développer la démocratie, à commencer par la libre expression de la population. Or la loi sur l'arabisation constitue, au contraire, un obstacle à cette évolution.'[109]

106 Mansouri, *Algeria between Tradition and Modernity: The Question of Language*, p. 127.
107 Benrabah, *Langue et pouvoir en Algérie: histoire d'un traumatisme linguistique*, p. 269.
108 'La grande famille francophone. Alger doit intégrer', *Liberté*, 22 June 2000, p. 4.
109 Grandguillaume, 'Arabisation et démagogie en Algérie', p. 5.

MANSOUR SAYAH
TRANSLATED BY KAMAL SALHI AND ANNE JUDGE

Linguistic Issues and Policies in Tunisia

With a population of almost eight million people,[1] Tunisia is a country of complex sociolinguistic patterns characterised by Arabic–French bilingualism, closely linked to a diglossic situation where Arabic is concerned. The Berber language, having survived competition from Phoenician, Latin, Arabic, Turkish and French, is now only spoken by 1% of the population in the extreme south of the country. There are still some traces of Turkish in the form of prefixes and suffixes, but only in colloquial Arabic. As for French, it made its appearance in the country long before the 1881 French Protectorate and has survived Tunisian Independence. It is Arabic however, in its various forms, that remains the real language of the country. This makes for a very complex situation that, added to various political problems linked in particular with Independence, has led to various and often conflicting linguistic policies on the part of the state.

This chapter will examine the different forms of Arabic in use in Tunisia, the traditional role of French and the Arabisation of Tunisia, the coexistence of monolingualism, bilingualism and diglossia, the educational problems resulting from the linguistic situation and the extent of present-day use of French in Tunisia. Politics naturally play a part under all of these headings.

---

1   This is the official government figure, but there has been no recent census in
    Tunisia.

The Different Forms of Arabic used in Tunisia

Classical Literary Arabic

This language is mostly used nowadays in traditional poetry, which tends to repeat old themes and old clichés. It is also used in some novels aiming at a particularly high register. It tends to be associated with the archaic, particularly in the context of the sermon delivered during Friday prayers – though there has more recently been a tendency for commentaries to be added in colloquial Arabic.

Standard Arabic

Standard Arabic is a prototype language that has been heavily influenced by French, both lexically and syntactically. It is mainly used by the media, but its impact has been so strong that it is also used as a literary form. In order to adapt to the modern world, it either borrows terms which are then 'Arabised', often by adding *ijja* (e.g. *dîmûqrâtijja* for democracy), or else new words are created from Arabic roots.

Colloquial Arabic

This is the language of the majority of Tunisians. There are regional variations at the level of both phonology and lexicology, but they do not present an obstacle to communication and mutual understanding. Originally only a spoken language, it is now also written, and there are plays and novels in Colloquial Tunisian Arabic. Whereas Classical Arabic belongs to a high register, Colloquial Arabic is a popular and familiar language for everyday communication. It is used conversationally by the educated classes and for most formal discourse on radio and television programmes. It functions, therefore, at both a familiar and an intellectualised level.

Intermediary Arabic

'Intermediary Arabic' is situated between the written and colloquial forms of Arabic. It is also known as the 'third language'. It is defined by some as a 'simplified form of Classical Arabic' and by others as a 'polite form of spoken Arabic'. This 'third language' has never, to our knowledge, been systematically studied to identify its specific structures, probably because it seems initially a language difficult to define since it ranges from a simplified literary form (notably with the suppression of casual terminology) to a sophisticated dialectal form enriched with abstract notions drawn mostly from Standard Arabic, but retaining a dialectal structure.

Even though most Arab scholars see this intermediary form of expression as a single linguistic form, the author believes that it is in fact a mixture of two varieties of language, Classical and Colloquial Arabic, with mutual interference and borrowings. Its undisputed advantage is to reduce the gap between the literary and dialectal forms, whose structures – morphological and grammatical particularly – make them distinct languages belonging to different but closely related types. The author believes, therefore, that each of these language varieties needs to be systematically described, starting from different corpora, which should in turn be compared statistically with the 'third language' in order to understand how these linguistic varieties have combined. This is important, since it would seem that this variety is fundamental to the development of modern Arabic as a whole. Indeed, it is likely that it will become more widely used by the press, as it reflects a local reality that Standard Arabic, which is seen as a language for 'purists', does not. It is also already noticeable that dialectal expressions and constructions are infiltrating all other forms of Arabic, even Standard Arabic.

Franco-Arabic[2]

This is a mixture of dialectal Tunisian Arabic and French. It is a complex language in that it goes beyond the lexical interference of French to encompass a curious mixture of syntactic forms. These 'interfering struc-

---

2   This term has been coined by analogy with Étiemble's 'franglais'.

tures', however, are not fixed, but vary from person to person. It seems to have originated with French people living in Tunisia, who only knew the dialectal form of Arabic and filled in any gaps in their Arabic with French borrowings. The ever-increasing prestige of French meant that most bilingual Tunisian speakers, spreading particularly among professional people and students, adopted this variety. There was also a desire to 'Tunisianise' French by diluting it with Arabic words and dialectal expressions, plus a tendency on the part of bilinguals to use the first word that came to mind, whatever the source. The use of a foreign word may demand changes to phrase and even sentence construction, thus introducing French constructions into Arabic syntax.

Rather surprisingly, this language became even more popular after independence, but historically it is a variety that will logically disappear sooner or later, once the education system and the civil service have become completely Arabised, which is the policy for the present and for the foreseeable future. It is nonetheless of considerable interest both from a historical and psycholinguistic point of view.

The Traditional Role of French and the Arabisation of Tunisia

The introduction of French education in Tunisia started 40 years before the French Protectorate was established in 1881 with the foundation of the Bardo Military School. French was the vehicle for the dissemination of European scientific and technological knowledge. A few years before the Protectorate, the great reformer Kheireddine also introduced French as an important part of the programmes taught at the Sadiki College, for the same reason. The Bardo Military School played a crucial role under the Protectorate, training a new bilingual élite, and similar colleges were later established along the same model. These institutions also gave rise to a sense of national identity, which led, ultimately, to Independence.

The success of the education received by the chosen few explains later policy, especially in the area of education. Thus, following Independence on 20 March 1956, Arabic became the official language of the country according to Article 1 of the Constitution. The 1958 Messadi 'reform'[3] established a policy of bilingualism that remains officially in place to this day, despite pressures from influential monolingual Arabic-speakers, most of whom had been educated at Zitouna.[4]

Although generally seen as an important and legitimate objective, teaching in Arabic was never properly implemented, for lack of good teachers. At one stage, an experimental stream known as '*Section A*' was introduced, which used Arabic for teaching, but it ended in complete failure. Arabic as the language of education was mainly perceived as a long-term goal. Its introduction was initially postponed and then only implemented at primary level. This hesitation was also due to a fear on the part of many people that the introduction of Arabic could lead, as elsewhere, to a rejection of the modern world.

Two other important objectives pushed Arabisation down the list of priorities. The first priority was to develop a body of professionals to take over from the French in every economic sector of society. Instead of importing teachers from the Middle East, as had been tried in Algeria with a complete lack of success, Tunisia relied mainly on Tunisians trained previously in the old 'Sadikian'[5] fashion. During the 1970s, these were replaced by newly trained local staff. The other important goal was the fundamental democratisation of the educational system, which completely transformed Tunisian society and also had an impact on the language issue.

This postponement of Arabisation did not please monolingual Arabic-speakers, who were, in fact, totally marginalised. They were restricted to traditional sectors, such as justice, religious instruction or teaching Arabic at primary level. It did not please the monolingual Francophones either. These were Arabs who had not studied Arabic and had

3   This was the first educational programme set up after the end of the French Protectorate. It aimed at 'Tunisifying' the educational system. This did not mean, however, eliminating French, because the Francophone President Bourguiba maintained that it was possible 'to build new buildings with foreign materials'.

4   A long-established traditional educational institution in Tunisia attended by most of North Africa's scholars. It specialises in Arab philosophy and literature.

5   A social and intellectual élite. Bilingual, this élite was educated at the *Collège Sadiki* in Tunis. The college was successful and its bilingual programmes followed a secular approach to education. Most educated Tunisians of post-independence Tunisia attended the Sadiki College which constituted the basis of Tunisia's present-day education.

been given a French education in the few schools that had survived the country's accession to Independence. While fitting easily into the economic sector, these people did not have any political muscle. It was for their benefit that a purely Francophone stream was created in the national educational system, in which only a minimum level of Arabic had to be achieved. This special stream, '*Section C*', failed for the same reasons as the Arabic '*Section A*', since neither stream entirely fulfilled the needs of the country.

This was the general position until the 1973 reform, which aimed at introducing a progressive, gentle Arabisation programme. This reform, although it never expressly questioned the principle of bilingualism, nevertheless resulted in a move in the opposite direction. An ideological struggle, although rarely made explicit during that period, therefore continued to set bilinguals against monolinguals, with some people clinging on to French in a way rendered pointless by the new realities born out of the democratisation of the educational system, while others, seizing on these new realities as an excuse, wished to work towards the realisation of the ideal of a monolingual Arab-speaking country.

This situation led to the teaching of French being entrusted to unqualified local teachers, recruited solely on the basis that they had studied other subjects in French. Since they replaced French teachers of French sent over from France under co-operation agreements, this obviously brought about a fall in the standards of French spoken and written in Tunisia. French as a compulsory subject for the *baccalauréat* was also discontinued briefly on the pretext that philosophy was being taught in French. However, this decision was reversed after the subject of philosophy was 'Arabised'. (This Arabisation, which took place in the space of one year, merely removed the content and the methodology from the subject.) But when the teaching of French was reinstated, there was a sudden transition to new methods for the teaching of French inspired by the FLE streams in French universities (FLE stands for *Français Langue Étrangère*, i.e. French as a foreign language). It included structural exercises, and a functional and communicative approach, which excluded grammar as such. Literature was also replaced by documentary and popular-science texts. The Francophone, Francophile President Bourguiba, for his part, imposed a return to the teaching of French at an early stage, for the period of one year, during the second year of schooling.

Thus, Tunisia's policies on French have been marked by contradictions, but on the whole the measures taken suggest that the politicians wanted to achieve an irreversible change that would eliminate French as a language for the transmission of culture, but keep it as a vehicle for international communication although, as such, it was faced with increased competition from other languages.

These and subsequent years were mainly marked by a struggle between Arabic-speakers and Francophile bilingual Francophones, though this conflict was rarely made explicit. It also went way beyond the linguistic issue. In this context, the terms 'Francophile' and 'Francophone' refer exclusively to French language and culture, and not to France as a country. It was not an issue of one side being less patriotic than the other. It was simply a matter of two differing visions of the future of an independent Tunisia, a struggle between different ideologies. At first official policies seemed to favour Tunisian Francophiles, since they saw a return to a French cultural dimension in language learning with an increasing return to literary texts, the express teaching of grammar, and the rejection of the notion of French purely as a tool for the teaching of science and technology. Once again, French became a compulsory subject for the *baccalauréat*. But these pro-French measures went hand in hand with a progressive and planned Arabisation of the country. This was to extend beyond primary education, which had long since been Arabised, to include all subjects during the first four years of secondary education (*premier cycle*[6]), the aim being that the dynamic energy of the programme would carry it into the last three years (*deuxième cycle*). This meant strengthening the national language, while, at the same time, according French a privileged status different from other foreign languages. (English was also a compulsory language, but only during the last three years of study (*deuxième cycle*), while German, Italian and Spanish remained optional languages, though again only during the last years of education.)

This was the theory, but matters were very different in practice, since the democratisation of the educational system and some measures

6   The 'first cycle' corresponds in Tunisia to the first three years of secondary education, whereas the 'second cycle' corresponds to the last four years (whereas in France the *premier cycle* corresponds to the first four years and the *deuxième cycle* to the last three.

which undermined the teaching of French led to a situation in which French no longer enjoyed its special status. French, which was initially a language that transmitted a culture, became a vehicle for access to the world scene, and today it is seeking a new role. Indeed, statements issued by the Ministère de l'Éducation et des Sciences now describe French as Tunisia's 'first foreign language'. As such, it seems to have become a 'second language' with the same status as other foreign languages. In other words, the recognition of the special status accorded to a language does not guarantee that this will become a permanent state of affairs.

As things stand, there are now theoretically two possibilities for the future: the acceptance of a national language as a major pillar of the state, with other smaller pillars alongside, or the recognition of two linguistic pillars. The former would lead to the gradual deterioration of the status of French, since the choice is between monolingualism and bilingualism. Whether to choose in favour of a 'second language' or a 'first foreign language', and how to assign the specific roles of the national language and the 'second', or 'foreign', language are matters for debate. Monolingualism, however, cannot be a pathway to progress.

Forty years after Independence, Tunisia is still trying to resolve the fundamental debate between traditionalism and modernism. The traditionalists are associated with a return to the concept of Arab nationhood illuminated by the teachings of Islam. This approach makes religion an absolute term of reference: the tenets of Islam are to be generally applied, because Islam is seen as an absolute and eternal truth relating to every human problem. They are often seen as preserving the nation from 'foreign interference'. Having lost their influence under Francophone President Bourguiba, the traditionalists were determined to regain a position of power as soon as possible.

But it is not only traditionalists who call for Arabisation. Others have also, for varying reasons, at different times, pushed for the Arabisation of the country. For example, when the French courts found the brother of President Ben Ali, Moncef Ben Ali, guilty of drug trafficking and sentenced him to ten years in prison, the Tunisian government passed a law in July 1993, which came into force in April 1994 and considerably accelerated the process of Arabisation. It made it mandatory for all civil servants to make Arabic the only language of the Civil Service and of 'life in general'. But once diplomatic relations were re-established with

Paris, this law was quietly dropped. The prohibition against watching the French-speaking TV channel, Antenne 2 (now France 2), remained in force, however, and the French press was banned for a while for having led an investigation into what was called the *couscous connection*. In particular, *Le Monde* was banned for a year. This shows how the French language has become a weapon to be used against France whenever the French government or media criticise the Tunisian government.

And yet Tunisia remains a Francophone country. French remains a prestigious language that is used on an everyday basis and enjoys a status different and above that of a second language reserved for international communication only. It has, indeed, through generations of use, become more entrenched. The hostility felt by pre-Independence Tunisians towards the language of the occupier has disappeared, along with the memory of being 'colonised'. The very fact of the merging of French and Arabic into 'Franco-Arabic' is evidence of a high degree of bilingualism. Moreover, when the intelligentsia wishes to know what is happening either in their own country, or abroad, they turn to the French media, which has become a symbol of democracy and therefore developed a new prestige.

Colloquial Tunisian Arabic has naturally spread everywhere, having almost entirely replaced Berber, the language spoken prior to the Arab invasion. It derives status from its association with the language of the Qur'an and a sense of solidarity with Arabo-Islamic civilisation. It is therefore heard everywhere, and is the real mother tongue of the whole population, though this same population uses Standard Arabic for writing and French in specific domains.

It has been said that teaching a foreign language bestows a kind of 'bilingualism on people'.[7] Over the years Tunisia seems to have opted for a form of French-Arabic bilingualism. French, already predominant under the Protectorate in the most important sectors of modern society, where it progressively ousted Classical Arabic, has continued to dominate even after Independence. Themselves educated in the French tradition, the country's leaders have found themselves embracing French rather

---

7   See J. A. Fishman, *Language Loyalty in the United States* (Mouton), which refers to 'producers of bilinguals'.

than having it imposed upon them.[8] They readily identify themselves as bilinguals, or even as Francophones. French is the rule rather than the exception in most public services, apart from the Ministère de la Justice, the Ministère de l'Intérieur and the Ministère de la Défense Nationale. The same is true in the economic sector, in commerce and any technological context. Applications for employment in the Civil Service are generally in French, and spelling mistakes can rule out a candidate.

The coexistence of French and Arabic in Tunisia has been marked by humour, passion and mutual praise. Indeed, there is a rich repertory of witty comments, turns of phrase and jokes involving both languages. Unfortunately, however, French is associated with the upper classes and the ruling political power, whose legitimacy is currently the subject of heavy attacks. There is a danger that the French language could become identified with a political power base, which could put its special status at risk.

The Coexistence of Monolingualism, Bilingualism and Diglossia in Tunisia

French is now a compulsory language taught in primary schools from the third year on. At secondary school, French is used for teaching basic subjects like mathematics, physics, chemistry, natural science, technical skills, technology, accountancy, etc. At university, all courses are in French apart from law. In the commercial world, French is still the commonly used language, rather than English, except that Arabic is used in negotiations with Libya and monolingual Arab-speakers. Medicine is taught in French, but for medical visits the language used is Colloquial Arabic.

Thus, French is a necessary tool for social advancement because it is still the language of the privileged, the class from which the political and economic leaders of the country are selected. And yet these are precisely the people responsible for the creation of a sense of national

8   See J. Berque, quoted by S. Garmadi, *RTSS*, 13, March 1968.

identity, implying linguistic and political Arabisation. Indeed, for them Arabisation is a kind of '*second independence*' and a matter of principle.[9] It is, moreover, a necessary position for them to adopt in order to fight Muslim Fundamentalism.

In other words, French is more than either a 'foreign language' or even a 'second language'. Furthermore, if a Saussurian definition of language is adopted (i.e. as a 'group of conventions adopted by a social body which allow individuals to exercise their language faculties'), the current linguistic situation seems neither static nor simple. There are individuals and small groups of people who 'exercise their language faculties' mainly, and even exclusively, in French; while some educated people willingly declare their mother tongue to be Standard Arabic, even though they hardly use it in their private lives, with their children or friends. The one language corresponding to Saussure's definition is, paradoxically, the one never mentioned when discussing bilingualism. It is the language that constitutes the normal means of communication among the great majority of the population, the 'daily' language, 'Colloquial' Arabic (*al-luga-darija*), or 'lower' 'communal' language (*al-'ammijja*), as opposed to the 'purest and the most expressive' language, that of the Qur'an (al-fusha) or even Standard Arabic (*al-'arbi*) by opposition with Intermediary Arabic (*al-'arabijja*).

Apart from a small minority of people who are completely Francophone, the majority of Tunisians use mostly Colloquial Arabic (CA), French (F) and Standard Arabic (SA). Tunisia's 'linguistic possibilities' are shown in Table 1 in declining order of the number of speakers.

Table 1 gives an initial idea of the country's linguistic diversity and helps to define what is called 'Tunisian bilinguism' as 'the norm in all situations that demand the use of a written language and, in some cases, the spoken form too, as well as other languages besides the Colloquial Tunisian Arabic language.'[10]

---

9   P. Marthelot, *Revue Culture Française*, 4, 1968. See also J. Chatenier, *Bulletin Pédagogique*, 27, Tunis, 1967.

10   I.e. 'le fait général de toutes les situations qui entraînent la nécessité de l'usage écrit et, dans certains cas, parlé, d'autres langues que l'arabe parlé tunisien'. This definition is adapted from A. Tabouret-Keller's definition of bilingualism in general (cf. *La linguistique. Guide alphabétique*, Paris: 1969).

Possible linguistic situations	Language(s) used
1 Bilingualism	CA + F
2 Diglossia	CA + SA
3 Bilingualism and Diglossia	CA + F + SA
4 Monolingualism	CA

Table 1:   Linguistic diversity.

The situation is not without its conflicts. There are conflicts between French and Standard Arabic (used during the War of Independence as a means of political communication and as a weapon against the French presence). There is also conflict between Standard Arabic and Colloquial Arabic. The former, because of its links with religion, is used mainly by the traditional intelligentsia, who speak both forms, whereas the underprivileged usually only speak Colloquial Arabic. There are, in other words, 'common tensions'[11] in such diglossic situations. The degree of tension depends on levels of illiteracy since the gap is between a language that has been codified, and thereby acquired prestige, and one that is seen as no more than a 'degenerate' version of the former.

The degree of tension is, however, diminishing thanks to improvements in education which have led to an ever-increasing proportion of the population having access to Standard Arabic, and the appearance of a kind of compromise between Standard Arabic and local Colloquial Arabic, known either as 'polite daily language' (*addariza-Imuhaddaba*) or as 'simplified' Standard Arabic (*al-'arabijja-ilmubassata*), i.e. the 'intermediary' language previously referred to. It is quite unstable and difficult to describe from a synchronic point of view. Ferguson has defined it as 'a kind of spoken Arabic much used in certain semi-formal or cross-dialectal situations, [which] has a highly classical vocabulary form, with few or no inflectional endings, having certain features of classical syntax but with a fundamental colloquial base in its morphology and syntax and a generous admixture of colloquial vocabulary.'[12]

---

11   To use A. Ferguson's terminology. Cf. A. Ferguson, 'Diglossia', in *Word*, vol. 15, 1959, pp. 325–40. Reprinted in D. Hymes (ed.), *Language in Culture and Society* (New York: Harper & Row; London: Evanston, 1964), pp. 429–39.

12   A. Ferguson, p. 433.

In Tunisia, the linguistic situation is, therefore, complex and changing, and characterised by the competitive coexistence of a number of languages or language varieties that interact with each other, sometimes in the same discourse. This clearly favours the phenomenon of linguistic interference, which has already had a lasting impact on the existing languages. This is why it is possible to speak of a North African variety of French, and why Standard Arabic shows signs of a kind of 'Indo-Europeanisation' at all levels, syntactic or lexical (borrowings and calques, etc.). There seems to be a tendency for the different languages or language varieties to function either in complementary distribution or to supplement one another. As regards different forms of Arabic, the situation is one of diglossia, the two forms being Standard Arabic and Intermediary Arabic. Standard Arabic ensures cohesion throughout the Arab world and functions as a *lingua franca*. Intermediary Arabic is the means of communication throughout the country. Thus, all educated Arabs will speak three varieties of Arabic: Standard, Intermediary and Colloquial.

As far as French is concerned in relation to the various forms of Arabic, the situation may be described as one of 'diglossic bilingualism'. But Intermediary Arabic is gradually replacing French in all semi-formal situations. It remains, however, the language of professional intercourse and all technical activities, and still enjoys a dominant position. The problem is that, since there is no longer an accepted consensus as to which language should be used in any particular context, bilinguals have to make a choice. This dilemma is exacerbated by the fact that bilingualism is related to problems of cultural identity. If some Tunisian intellectuals are to be believed, this leads to a double blockage, which is both linguistic and cultural. Bilingual Tunisians, with both an Arabo-Muslim and Franco-Western education, seem to see themselves as different and 'more complicated' than other Tunisians. This creates in them a certain unease, but it does give them an insight into the country's linguistic position. Some of them, particularly writers, try to overcome their mental blockage, and find answers to their own linguistic and cultural contradictions. A. Ben Cheikh, a teacher and novelist writes that

Je me refuse à dire que j'écris en arabe classique ou en arabe dialectal ou en français. Je serais tenté de dire que j'écris en une seule langue, mais une langue composée et complexe qui puise, et d'une manière dynamique dans trois univers linguistiques et culturels à la fois.[13]

The Educational Problems Resulting from the Linguistic Situation

Some sort of practical compromise seems to have been reached in respect of the conflicts and tensions arising from bilingualism and diglossia by Tunisian society generally, and to a lesser extent within the context of the educated classes. They pose, however, a more serious problem in schools, where education is provided in French and Standard Arabic while everyday life is lived in Colloquial Arabic. This creates major psychological problems and counterbalances some of the benefits of the educational experience: the fact that a Tunisian pupil is faced with two foreign languages every day can be profoundly traumatic, especially for children from disadvantaged socio-economic and cultural backgrounds.

Education is in fact affected by another anomaly, the ambiguous position of Standard Arabic. The teachers ignore the fact that this is not a real 'mother tongue'. They act as if all they have to do is teach the children how to transcribe and decipher a language they already know, when in reality it is something with which they are completely unfamiliar, since there is no pre-school education to prepare the ground. For many, Standard Arabic will be no more than 'the language used only for exams.' Because of this

> [the pupil] is absolutely not aware that it is an important language [...] he may make mistakes but they do not matter because 'we' do not speak this language [...] and because its position in the country is not seen as important [... while] for the élite, the intelligentsia or the bureaucracy, it does not play a role in either daily life or in obtaining employment.[14]

---

13   A. Ben Cheikh is the author of *Wa nasibi minal'ufuq* (*My Share of the Horizon*), (Tunis: STD, 1970).
14   Cf. S. Garmadi, in 'Discussion de la communication de A. El Ayed', TTRTSS, 13, 1968.

And yet Standard Arabic is taught both as an independent subject and as a means of access to basic mathematics and general knowledge during the first few years at school.

As regards French, the poor quality of teacher training, the breadth of the educational programmes and the ignorance of the children's linguistic ability are such that, in spite of many declarations of principle and many practical efforts to improve matters, there does not seem to have been any noticeable improvement. Nonetheless, it remains both an independent subject and the medium for teaching a number of basic subjects.

As for the everyday language actually used by children, it is banned from the classroom and totally ignored by the world of education. This is, not surprisingly, the source of many failures and inhibitions. And while teachers often wonder why children experience such difficulties in the course of their education, the answer, that it is because it is forbidden to take Colloquial Arabic into account in the classroom, remains taboo. This is because Colloquial Arabic is still considered a vulgar and degenerate form of Arabic. And yet, although it may not be desirable actually to teach in Colloquial Arabic, recognising its existence linguistically and psychologically would certainly be a pedagogical improvement. The whole problem is summed up by A. Ben Cheikh:

> Quel rôle pédagogique pouvait jouer la langue maternelle dans l'acquisition linguistique ou la formation intellectuelle de l'élève, quelle place devait occuper l'arabe dialectal, etc? Ces questions pouvaient se poser, mais la réponse semblait impossible. Des contraintes extérieures et des résistances profondes freinaient et freinent encore la réflexion de l'enseignant. On dirait que nous sommes aveuglés par un certain contenu historico-linguistique. Autrement, comment expliquer la négation d'un bagage linguistique que l'enfant de six ans doit déposer au vestibule de l'école primaire, bagage qu'il n'utilisera jamais en classe, qui ne peut même pas lui servir de point de départ ou de supplément de sa formation intellectuelle?'[15]

In reality, whether the teacher likes it or not, children do not leave their 'linguistic inheritance' at the door of their primary school; they use it not only as a starting point but also as a permanent point of reference when learning Standard Arabic and French. Nowadays, moreover, the principles of positive linguistic transference and negative interference

15   Ben Cheikh, p. 45.

are largely recognised in Tunisia, at least as far as the learning of French is concerned. What is needed is a scientific study of the psychological and linguistic impact of Colloquial Arabic that will make it possible to rethink both educational programmes and language-teaching methods. To achieve this, it is necessary to look at the problems involved, not only from the teacher's perspective, but also from the pupil's point of view. There cannot be any permanent solution to the educational problems in Tunisia today without an understanding of the learning strategies used or the role played by the pupil's 'linguistic leanings', i.e. their specific realisation in the pupil's *langue maternelle et naturelle* (Rabelais), the *parlar materno* and its *vulgari eloquentia* (Dante). This would help children perceive, understand and eventually use, albeit on a purely academic level, the two language systems of Standard Arabic and French, since both of these languages are equally secondary to the pupil, in the sense that they are both learned simultaneously after having learned Colloquial Tunisian Arabic. However, Standard Arabic inhabits more or less the same cultural space as Colloquial Arabic, and when it is perceived by the whole community as being a national language, it will become 'the second 'first' language' (or 2nd L1 in French terminology), and at that point French will become simply 'the second language' (or L2).

It is worth noting that a number of studies of the interference in L2 caused by L1 have been carried out, not only in Tunisia but also in the other countries that share a virtually identical linguistic heritage, namely Algeria and Morocco. Most of these studies have, however, been undertaken by teachers who were not specialist linguists, which means that they are rarely systematic, especially in areas other than phonetics and phonology. It is this area that is badly in need of research.

The Extent to which French is used in Tunisia

According to the parameters established by Robert Chaudenson, it would seem difficult to be able to assess the degree to which French is used in Tunisia without proper research. All that can be said is that in a country where school attendance has become compulsory and 90% of school-age children now receive an education, it can be expected that French will be widely known, at least at a *francophonoid* level.[16] This is indeed the case, since it is impossible for Francophones, wherever they are in the country, not to find somebody with whom they can converse in French. The level of expertise is very variable, and the degree of variation is determined by easily identifiable factors, such as the contrasts rural/ urban, affluent/poor, more educated/less educated, young/old, men/women, etc. The fact remains that some French is spoken throughout the whole country.

As regards the media, the most widely read daily newspaper continues to be *La Presse*, a Francophone newspaper subsidised by the Tunisian state and distributed to its civil servants. It is, however, closely followed by the Arabic *Essabah*, and a number of Arabic newspapers and magazines have been founded recently. All French newspapers are supposedly available in Tunisia, though some have sometimes been banned by the government of the day. This happened, as was previously mentioned, in 1993, then in 1999 after the French press criticised the way the presidential elections were conducted (President Ben Ali was re-elected with 99% of the vote). At the time of writing (January 2001), the French press is still generally banned. *Le Monde* was allowed back into the country in December 2000, but banned again on 2 January 2001 on account of the publication of an article about Moncef Marzouki, the President of the Tunisian League of Human Rights, which displeased the government. *Le Figaro*, which is not so critical of the regime, is banned less frequently.

The weeklies with the widest circulation are written in Arabic, but among non-specialist, general-interest publications, the bilingual magazines are more popular. There are very few literary magazines and all are published in Arabic, but scientific publications are Francophone, and those relating to the social sciences are bilingual, though with the majority of articles in Arabic.

On the book market, French publications sell less well than those in Arabic, although both sectors are in difficulties. As far as the audio-visual media are concerned, there are a number of Arabic radio stations with a wide audience, one national and the others regional. There is also

16   In Chaudenson's terminology.

an international station that broadcasts in French, apart from three hours of daily broadcasts in Italian, German and, more recently, in English. This station is quite popular among the urban young, including those in Eastern Algeria. One reason for its popularity is possibly the fact that it plays listeners' requests for songs in English. Television is in Arabic and the language of publicity is Standard Arabic. French essentially dominates the cinema: all international films are dubbed in French apart from Tunisian or Egyptian films. The same applies to foreign films shown by the two national television channels, which otherwise show 100% of their material in Arabic.

Until the last presidential elections in October 1999 the Tunisian people were able to tune in to France 2, which was twinned with Tunisian television. They were also able to receive RAI 1, which broadcasts the French programmes of TV5, a French cultural channel, as the result of an agreement reached with France. Following criticism of the elections, these channels were all subject to a ban. Now the only Tunisian Francophone TV production is the news programmes that replace those normally on France 2, and related interviews and court reports. The ban is, however, impossible to enforce, since wealthy Tunisians have satellite dishes and can access these and other foreign channels. The fact that they have been banned only makes them more attractive.

As in the past, business continues to be carried out nearly exclusively in French. Arabic and English are sometimes used, but this is rare. This situation is a consequence of complex agreements made with foreign countries. In the civil service, however, an attempt has been made to move towards Arabisation, but there is a tendency to revert to French when the subject matter is technical. Official documents are written in Arabic because the army and the courts have been Arabised for a long time. Until 1986 legal texts were written in both languages. The Arabisation of computer software was supposed to be complete by the end of 2000, but this target was not met. In the meantime, the civil service has to ask permission to use non-Arabic software, which it does. Students and researchers do not bother to request permission to do this. In effect, then, the State cannot enforce its linguistic policies in many areas.

As previously mentioned, French is taught in school alongside Arabic from the third year of primary education, when children are aged nine. As far as the present generation is concerned, French will be the medium for science and technology during the last four years of schooling (*le second cycle*) for a number of years to come. Standard Arabic has already become the language of science, technology and the social sciences during the first three years (*le premier cycle*), as these subjects have been completely Arabised. At university, however, apart from being taught in French language departments, French is still used to teach science and technology. Nearly all departments also provide classes both on French and in French. This includes the departments of Arabic, since the students who have the best command of Arabic are also good French-speakers.

Thus the use of French, which has suffered a slide in status, remains dominant in certain sectors. Any further loss of influence on the part of French will be to the advantage of Arabic. Other languages, such as English, do not seem to be a threat at present: even if a rapid development in information technology has resulted in some dozens of specialists being trained in Anglophone countries, they still wish to function in the language in which they feel most at ease. This may change, however, for a new danger facing the French language is a noticeable decline in the psychological investment Tunisians are prepared to put into learning it. There are various reasons for this. One is the ideal of solidarity with the Arab world. Another is the attraction of America, which symbolises modernity, and scientific and technological superiority. The USA has the added advantage that English is a more 'neutral' language without links with colonial Tunisia.

It is, therefore, not at all certain that Tunisians will retain their intimate relations with, and understanding of, the French language. The best Francophone Tunisian writers are now aged 40 or more, and few young ones seem to be emerging. On the other hand, Tunisia is a keen member of the Organisation Mondiale de la Francophonie, which a previous Tunisian president, Bourguiba, was instrumental in establishing in its original form. It now comprises 53 countries in which French is far more than just a foreign language, but a language for work and development, a language that expresses communal values and ambitions, and a real sense of solidarity. In consequence, without threatening the national language or excluding English as a foreign language, many Tunisians see French as the language for progressive global advancement within this organisation. The question is not whether or not a foreign language should be taught, but how to extend its teaching to a greater number of people in order to make Tunisians citizens of the world.

On the cultural and ideological level, French–Arabic bilingualism helps the country to avoid the dangers that monolingualism poses to an under-developed country, even if this underdevelopment is relative. In other words, it plays a balancing role that creates for more freedom of thought; in whichever language this may be taking place. It is true that French is no longer a vernacular language in Tunisia, but neither is it limited to a scientific and technological context. It is still not a foreign language in the didactic sense. It is acknowledged in the official texts and described by the country's political leaders either as a *lingua franca* or as a language for specialist purposes, and sometimes as a foreign language with a particular and a privileged status. It is easy to see why the subject of the French language has always been approached with great prudence, with a terminology more characterised by political aspirations than linguistic accuracy. All these labels, at once multiple and changing, reflect the complexity of the situation. The problems that have ensued in the educational system are merely the outward signs of a deeper problem.

Conclusions

French occupies a special position for many Tunisians. They do not feel that it has been imposed on them or that it is a 'foreign' language. They have given it a special place in their hearts, and this explains the ever-growing presence of the French language and culture in Tunisia. They agree with the Algerian writer, Kateb Yacine, who claimed that French was the Algerians' *'butin de guerre'*. To this it could be added, echoing a well-known Arabic expression, that this booty of war should be kept 'like an old family jewel'. On the other hand, Arabisation is increasing and is inevitable in terms of national identity. This creates a real ideological dilemma.

On the public stage, the language issue is a political football with internal and external dimensions. Internally it is used to pacify the fundamentalists and externally to punish France for any criticism of Tunisia. It is a matter of one step forward, and one step back. This has given French a new prestige, at least with many of the opposition parties, which are both Francophone and Francophile. But the claims of Arab solidarity and the attraction of the USA are ever-present and competing options.

There should be research into what Tunisians really want with the aim of developing sensible policies, and the taboos about Colloquial Arabic in the field of education need to be overcome. The possible future of Intermediary Arabic should also be examined. As for the position of French, it is important to clarify how its role will change as it moves from being a language of instruction to becoming a taught language, which is the necessary outcome of Arabisation. If it is to retain a special status in Tunisia, this must be clearly defined in order to avoid the current confusion, with its serious consequences for the educational system and public life in general.

It is clear that introducing a 'foreign language' or 'second language' in a context where there are already two 'first languages', Standard Arabic and Colloquial Arabic, places an added burden on students. Nevertheless, pedagogical and linguistic research has shown conclusively that the acquisition of a second or even a third foreign language is not only an enriching experience, but also necessary to development and international communication.

MALAK BADRAWI*

French in Egypt, Syria and Lebanon: Attitudes and Policies

France's preoccupation with the promotion of her language has been a long-standing concern of French politicians. Nowadays it is evident in the existence of the Haut Conseil de la Francophonie, which is chaired by the President of the French Republic, and in the creation of the international Agence de la Francophonie. Both organisations strive to encourage the spread of the French language globally, and their aims and motives seem benign, especially when compared to the not-so-distant past, when the French sought to impose their language on the nations they controlled. The underlying purpose continues to be the need to propagate the French language as a means of promoting French interests and influence, but current attitudes are radically different from those of a century ago. The French can no longer impose themselves through their military power and claim that it is their moral duty to 'civilise' 'backward' countries, nor can they force their language and culture on peoples as they once did.

It is, however, true that colonial ambitions were not confined to the French, nor was France the only nation to impose her authority with cannons and bayonets. Moreover, French policies were not immutable; they depended on various factors: the public mood in France, the dispositions of different political parties, the tendencies of the cabinet in power, the vagaries of the international situation and the personalities of those responsible for implementing French policy abroad.

Furthermore, France's attitudes and policies towards the teaching of French in Egypt and the Levant, i.e. Syria and Lebanon, seemed inextricably linked with, and conditioned by historical factors. First, there was the idea of the religious Protectorate, through which France, as a

*   The author gratefully acknowledges the help of Dr Mona Younès in researching this article.

Catholic power, sought to gain a measure of influence in the predominantly Muslim Orient by establishing colonies there. Subsequently, after
several centuries during which France exerted its influence and gained
considerable advantages in the region, circumstances changed, and the
French were forced to concede some of their privileges. As a result France
attempted to impose its language and culture in the hope of gaining new
advantages. Consequently, it is relevant to examine the role played by
history in these developments.

Historical Links with the Region

French diplomats and politicians writing about the region early in the
twentieth century observed that France had been engaged in lucrative
trade with these countries since the reign of Charlemagne, and that it
could be said that political relations between France and the region were
established during the Crusades.[1] Thus, in the thirteenth century the
French King Louis IX, who was regarded by the French as a personifica-
tion of religious fervour and chivalrous valour, was captured and held to
ransom in an Egyptian city.[2] The following year, after his release in May
1250, Louis expressed his conviction that the Maronites of Lebanon, a
community united by their faith in the teachings of St Maron, were part
of the French nation, because the good will they had shown towards the
French people was akin to the friendly feelings the French felt towards
one another. Louis IX promised to give the Maronites and their people
the same protection afforded to the French themselves, and to do whatever was necessary for their happiness.[3] The idea of a religious protector-

---

1   F. Charles-Roux, 'L'Échelle française d'Égypte', in *Égypte France, Exposition
     Française au Caire* (Comité français des expositions et comité national des exposi-
     tions coloniales, 1929), pp. 65–6.
2   Gaston Wiet, 'Le rôle de la France en Égypte', *Bulletin de la Société des Amis de
     l'Université de Lyon*, 1912–1913, Fasc. I. 26th year, January–February 1913, pp.
     265–7.
3   René Pinon, 'Le protectorat français en Orient', *Questions diplomatiques et colo-
     niales*, vol. XXV, 1908, p. 395.

ate dated from this time, but it was another four centuries before it came into being. Meanwhile, the Crusades also brought about a resurgence of commerce between France, Syria and Egypt; Frenchmen engaged in trade and also went to the Holy Land as pilgrims.

After Syria and Egypt fell to the Ottoman Empire early in the sixteenth century, French trade gained greatly from the privileges, or Capitulations, granted in 1535 by the Ottoman Sultan, Sulayman the Magnificent, to Francis I, King of France.[4] French traders, mainly based in Marseilles, gained exclusive rights to trade within the Ottoman Empire. The various *Échelles*, the *Échelles du Levant* and the *Échelles de l'Égypte* came into being at this time. Initially, these were docks where ships loaded or unloaded their merchandise, but the *Échelles* soon became permanent establishments, incorporating a large group of residents who were regarded as a separate nation. Their leaders subsequently became the Consuls who protected merchants' rights and privileges, and dealt with local authorities.[5] French merchants thus gained extra-territorial privileges that shielded them from the jurisdiction of local authorities. France was the first great Christian power to obtain such privileges from the Turks, but this regime was very rapidly extended to other nations.

These privileges were renewed under successive Ottoman Sultans and Kings of France. In 1649, and then in 1740, the Maronites invoked the promise made by Louis IX, and it was due to Anne of Austria, and then to Louis XV,[6] that the Capitulations of 1673 and 1740 included clauses pertaining to the French political and religious protectorate that were found nowhere else. These provisions stipulated that non-Muslims who came from a territory that had not submitted to Islam and who did not have a representative in Constantinople could trade within the Empire and go on a pilgrimage to the Holy Land, but only under the protection

4   According to some historians, the Capitulations only became effective in 1569. See Antoine Hokayem, *Les Provinces arabes de l'Empire Ottoman aux archives du Ministère des Affaires Étrangères de France: 1793–1918* (Beirut: Les Éditions Universitaires du Liban, 1988), p. XVI.

5   Charles-Roux, 'L'Échelle française d'Égypte', pp. 67–8; *Comité de défense des intérêts français en Orient*, Maurice Pernot, *Rapport sur le voyage d'étude à Constantinople en Égypte et en Turquie d'Asie (Janv.–Août 1912)* (Paris: Firmin Didot, 1914), pp. VIII, X.

6   Pinon, 'Le protectorat français en Orient', p. 395.

of France. They were not allowed to travel under any other banner. Furthermore, bishops and priests, whatever their nationality, could claim French protection. In addition to this, France's status as most favoured nation was enhanced even further in 1740, when the Ottoman Sultan asserted that the Capitulatory privileges would continue throughout his reign and the reigns of his successors.[7] It was not long before the protection given to French Christians was extended to include indigenous Catholics as well. Not surprisingly, the French, who guarded their special privileges most jealously and were extremely keen to maintain them, eventually came to feel

> that their Protectorate in the Orient was neither the work of one day nor of one man; it was the result of a long history. Each century of [their] national existence had added a stone to the edifice of [their] influence; each phase of [their] political existence had increased [their] clientèle.[8]

Moreover, there were those who pointed out that

> apart from the privileges and rights spelled out in the treaties recognised by the governments, there were also the facts, there was the effort pursued patiently and generously for centuries, there was the civilising and charitable work France had accomplished in the Orient and which she extended and improved on daily. Our institutes, schools, asylums, hospitals have gathered an immense clientèle. It is not only our official protégés who receive from us the benefits of education or assistance; the Catholics, Christians from diverse Oriental rites, attracted by our early reputation, and assured of our generosity, have come to us in large numbers. The Muslims themselves have sent their children to our schools and their suffering to our hospitals. Today [in 1912] French schools [in the Middle East] are attended by more than a hundred thousand pupils.[9]

Relations between France and the Ottoman Empire broke down during Napoléon Bonaparte's expedition to Egypt (1798–1801), but they were promptly restored in 1802. The ease with which the French had taken Egypt from the Ottomans demonstrated the Turks' growing weak-

7 Hokayem, p. XX. See Article 43 and new Article 16 of the Capitulations of 1673, and Articles 32–34 of 1740. Christian and Jewish subjects of the Ottoman Empire were allowed to keep their faith, laws and traditions, but foreigners travelling within the empire did not fall within the same category.
8 Pinon, 'Le protectorat français en Orient', p. 389.
9 Pernot, p. XI.

ness to the European powers. This was confirmed when Bonaparte sent one of his generals to assist the Ottomans against a military threat from the Russians in 1802.

Later, French scholars and diplomats who referred to the French expedition praised it, and pointed out how it had benefited Egypt. They listed the numerous initiatives undertaken by their compatriots, such as the foundation of the Institut d'Égypte, the *Description de l'Égypte*, a monumental work that remained one of the most comprehensive studies of that country for well over a century, and the academic studies that formed the foundations of Egyptology. Brief mention was also made of a mission of Egyptian students sent by Bonaparte to France and then distributed among various schools in the French capital.[10]

Egypt remained an Ottoman province after the departure of the French, but in contrast with Syria and Lebanon, it gained a measure of autonomy under its new Viceroy, Muhammad 'Ali (1805–48). This Viceroy, who was a military man, focused on establishing a modern army and was heavily dependent on Europeans for assistance. In 1825, a French general who headed a military mission in Egypt indignantly reported that the only language taught in Muhammad 'Ali's military schools was Italian, and that French was only the second language. He added that the books used were translated from the Italian and were too elementary, and that the mathematics and language teachers were Italian. Boyer also complained that the administration of Egyptian affairs was largely in Italian hands.[11]

The French gradually gained ground, however, and the military mission headed by Boyer worked hard to introduce French officers into Egypt and thus weaken the position of the Italians.[12] One of the Viceroy's principal aides was a Frenchman, Colonel Sève, who took the name of Sulayman Pasha. Clot Bey, another Frenchman was responsible for the School of Medicine. Furthermore, the Staff College founded in the 1830s was established on French lines, with French as the main language of

10 Wiet, pp. 268–9.
11 G. Douin, *Une mission militaire auprès de M. Ali*, p. 40. Boyer to Jomard, 20 May 1825, cited in Ahmad 'Izzat 'Abd al-Karim, *Ta'rikh al-ta'lim fi 'asr Muhammad 'Ali* (Cairo, 1938), p. 91.
12 J. Heyworth-Dunne, *An Introduction to the History of Education in Modern Egypt* (London: Frank Cass, 1968), p. 116.

instruction. French officers who applied for positions in Egypt were required to bring elementary textbooks with them. Moreover, the Viceroy insisted that students sent on educational missions abroad had to translate as many textbooks as possible to compensate for the lack of suitable materials in Egypt.[13] This partly explained the preponderance of French technical, scientific and literary books translated into Arabic in Egypt during the 1830s and 1840s. These works included treatises on hygiene, anatomy, medicine, mineralogy, elementary engineering, history, memoirs and biographies, and books that dealt with the mores and customs of various nations.[14]

French influence was also evident in Egypt with the presence of the Saint-Simonians, who initiated many projects, and pledged themselves to contribute to the country's industrial and cultural development. Some headed educational establishments, such as the colleges of engineering and mineralogy.

Muhammad 'Ali was the first ruler to send Egyptian missions to France and other European countries, while making sure that a system of public education – modelled on European lines – was established in the country. The last mission sent during his reign was dispatched to France in 1844. It consisted of 70 students and included members of the Viceroy's family.[15] In the same year the leader of the growing French community protested to Muhammad 'Ali about the lack of European schools in Egypt. The Viceroy, who was a practical man with no prejudices against denominational establishments of any kind, probably saw them as an inexpensive way of spreading education in the country, and he subsequently gave the Sisters of St Vincent de Paul and the Lazarist Fathers a large piece of land on which to build a school.

Syria and Lebanon were taken over by Egypt between 1832 and 1838. As a result, American and English missionaries were allowed to settle in these countries, and there was a revival of the Old Catholic missions, which were extended throughout Syria.[16] However, many Syri-

---

13   Heyworth-Dunne, p. 177.
14   Gamal al-Din al-Shayyal, *Ta'rikh al-tarjamah wa al-harakah al-thaqafiyyah fi 'asr Muhammad 'Ali* (Cairo: 1951), Appendix 1, nos. 1–127.
15   Wiet, p. 269.
16   A. L. Tibawi, *A Modern History of Syria including Lebanon and Palestine* (London: Macmillan, 1969), p. 88.

ans, including the Christians among them, strongly disapproved of the religious, even sectarian, nature of these schools.[17]

French Educational Achievements in the Region

Following the resumption of Ottoman rule in Syria and Lebanon, a conflict broke out between the Maronites and the Druzes of Lebanon in 1840. This lasted for almost 20 years until the Maronites appealed to the French Emperor Napoleon III in 1859. A French expeditionary force was sent to Lebanon the following year to assist them. The French military presence ended the war, in which as many as 11,000 Christians, including Jesuits and members of the Catholic missions, were believed to have been killed. Once order had been restored, Lebanon gained autonomous status as a province of the Ottoman Empire, under a Christian governor. Credit for this was justifiably given to the French, and it greatly enhanced their reputation and popularity. This partly explains why, after 1860, French Catholic priests and missionaries travelled in droves to the Levant, where they established schools, hospitals, hospices and orphanages. They were given subsidies and assistance by the French government. However, the French did not hold an exclusive position. Although their influence was strong among Levantine Catholics and other Christians, Russia supported Orthodox Christians. Moreover, Germany and Italy were eventually to challenge France's position in the Levant.[18]

In Egypt, the Crimean war and the construction of the Suez Canal brought a very large number of French nationals, as well as clerics, into the country. At this time, foreigners were estimated to make up half the population of Alexandria, and one-eighth of that of Cairo.[19] This was the

---

17 Tibawi, p. 141.
18 William I. Shorrock, *French Imperialism in the Middle East: The Failure of Policy in Syria and Lebanon* (Wisconsin: University of Wisconsin Press, 1976), pp. 16–17.
19 Édouard Dor, *L'Instruction Publique en Égypte* (Paris: Lacroix & Verboeck Hoeven et Cie, 1872), p. 31.

turning point in the history of European schools in Egypt, and successive viceroys offered different religious orders, irrespective of nationality, grants of land and buildings in order to enable them to establish schools. Some schools, which accepted needy pupils free of charge, received a yearly allowance from the viceroys to help them maintain their services.[20] The Francophile tendencies of one viceroy, Sa'id Pasha (1854–63), as well as the educational demands of the growing Christian community and the political opportunism of the French, guaranteed France's dominance in this area.[21]

In 1872, Édouard Dor, the Swiss-born Inspector General of Education, completed a substantial report on schools in Egypt. Dor had been appointed to develop education in Egypt by the new Viceroy, Isma'il Pasha (1863-79).[22] The principal language taught in most foreign schools at this time appears to have been Italian. The Inspector General, who was very critical of most of the denominational schools he visited, judged that their methods had not changed in two centuries. Instruction was mechanical and based on memorisation rather than on understanding of the texts, which were either inappropriate or boring.[23] Dor's views are relevant, as they corresponded with similar opinions expressed in 1906 by another inspector, Marcel Charlot.[24] However, the Inspector General was very impressed by the education offered by the Lazarist Fathers. The Fathers, who had established themselves in 1852, followed the same programme as the Lycées of France. Also, the great majority of their clientele appears to have been drawn from the French colony at Alexandria.[25] While French was taught in some government schools,[26] Dor's report was not always clear as to which languages were taught in the foreign schools, or about the enrolment of Egyptians – or indeed Syrians

20 Dor, pp. 267, 269, 277–8, 279, 280, 290, 291, 295.
21 Heyworth-Dunne, pp. 330, 331.
22 Yacoub Artin, *L'Instruction Publique en Égypte* (Paris: Ernest Leroux, 1890), p. 97.
23 Dor, p. 271.
24 Marcel Charlot, 'Rapport au Ministre des Affaires Étrangères sur la situation des écoles françaises d'Orient', *Journal Officiel de la République Française*, 26 October 1906, p. 7240. Charlot's views will be examined later.
25 Dor, pp. 274–75.
26 Heyworth-Dunne, pp. 384–5.

and Lebanese pupils – in these institutions. Dor did note, however, that the British and American Missions, whose educational methods he deplored, were popular.[27] The Inspector General recommended the teaching of two foreign languages, French and English, in all Egyptian state schools.[28]

The Impact of the Dispute about Secularism in France on the Region

Meanwhile, France's defeat at Prussian hands in the war of 1870–71 and the uprisings of the Commune enabled the Republicans to regain power. By 1878, they had political control of France, and were able to set about the implementation of a programme that would republicanise the country and liberalise existing institutions. One plan was to reform the educational system, offering free, compulsory, non-denominational education. State schools staffed by lay teachers now replaced existing state and denominational schools in France, which had previously been largely controlled by members of the religious orders.[29]

Consequently, the following year, large groups of priests, including Jesuits who had been expelled from their places of residence in France, travelled to Ottoman Turkey, where they established schools, hospitals and orphanages. Their efforts were largely responsible for the spread of the French language, and French culture and influence. Indeed, one of them said that, had it not been for their presence, the British flag would have been fluttering over all Oriental establishments.[30] Not to be outdone by the American missionaries who had founded the Syrian Protestant College in Beirut in 1871, the Jesuits, whose college was at al-Ghasir, moved to Beirut, where they established the Jesuit College, which even-

27   Dor, p. 270.
28   Artin, p. 99.
29   Thomas F. Power Jr., *Jules Ferry and the Renaissance of French Imperialism* (New York, Octagon Books, 1966), p. 18. The French attributed the disasters of the war to the authoritarian regimes of the monarchists and the clerics.
30   Shorrock, pp. 16–17.

tually became the Université St Joseph. It was Gambetta who effectively helped the Jesuits to create their college in Beirut, and he foresaw a great future for France in the Eastern Mediterranean.[31] This college had a strongly missionary character; all subjects were taught in French, but gradually an excellent programme of Arabic studies was added.[32] Furthermore, in 1883, with support from the French government, the college developed a department of medicine.[33] By then, France was offering many more scholarships, and helping both French and native Catholic schools. The Ottomans subsequently built a military school in Damascus in 1904 to counteract French influence and to attract students who would otherwise have gone to the Jesuit College or the Syrian Protestant College.[34]

The Jesuits also founded several colleges in different parts of Egypt, starting in the 1880s.[35] There was the Collège de la Sainte Famille, founded in 1888, and a subsidiary college was established in Upper Egypt, with a girls' school, the *Filles de la Sainte Famille*, in 1896.[36] From that decade on, French was taught in all denominational schools, irrespective of nationality.[37] In contrast with denominational schools in the Levant – which were funded by the French Ministry of Foreign Affairs – those in Egypt appear to have been helped with grants from the viceroys, as well as receiving assistance from the Office of Propaganda in Rome.[38]

The church schools did not teach Arabic and were therefore avoided by young Egyptian Muslims. More importantly, however, Muslims stayed away from these schools because of the proselytising spirit that pervaded them. At this time, three lay schools, in Cairo, Alexandria and Port Said,

---

31 René Pinon, 'Les Écoles d'Orient et le Rapport de M. Marcel Charlot', *Questions Diplomatiques et Coloniales – Revue de Politique Extérieure*, vol. XXIV, 1907, p. 415.
32 Tibawi, p. 143.
33 Tibawi, p. 169.
34 Tibawi, p. 195.
35 Artin, p. 105.
36 Norbert Carnoy, *La Colonie Française du Caire* (Paris: Les Presses Universitaires de France, 1927), p. 116.
37 Artin, p. 106.
38 Heyworth-Dunne, p. 308.

the *Écoles libres gratuites et universelles*, also received large subsidies from princes of the Egyptian Royal family. The popularity of these schools was reflected not only in the large numbers of pupils attending them, but also by the fact that two-thirds of these pupils were Muslims.[39] However, the pupil numbers quoted for these schools were not reliable. Yacoub Artin, who succeeded Dor, reported the foundation of new lay schools by the Alliance Française that were attended by only a small number of Muslims. Artin added that the mass of Egyptians in the towns had become convinced of the need for education, which they understood as learning languages, French or English.[40]

It was at this time that the French colony in Egypt took the initiative that led to the foundation of the School of Law in Cairo. This was a useful step, as the legal system in Egypt, which had been elaborated earlier, was based on the French *Code Napoléon*. In 1891 13 candidates were enrolled in the new school, and the following year the French government sent a well-known scholar, G. Pelissié du Raussas, to act as its director.[41] The French were proud to point out that the Egyptian School of Law, better known as the Khedivial School, further 'demonstrated the French intellectual influence in Egypt.'[42]

Notwithstanding all the French efforts, France did lose both diplomatic and political influence after the Franco-Prussian war. For instance, the Ottomans, who had relied on a French military mission to reform their army since 1850, replaced them with Prussians after the Franco-Prussian war. Then, although France was able to retain the sympathy of the people of Syria and Lebanon, where the events of 1860 had not been forgotten, the French also failed to react appropriately after the Armenian massacre of 1894 – because they did not want to antagonise Russia. Furthermore, while France had continued to receive strong support from the Pope, who issued papal decrees reiterating the exclusive French rights to the Catholic Protectorate, French diplomatic relations with the Holy See broke down after France affirmed its continued support for Italy,

---

39   Artin, pp. 106–7.
40   Artin, p. 110.
41   Carnoy, pp. 145–6.
42   Léon Polier, 'La France en Égypte', *Revue des Deux Mondes*, 1 August 1914, p. 659.

which had annexed Rome. The French position weakened further as first Germany, and then Italy, claimed the right to protect their own nationals in the Ottoman Empire. Following an amicable agreement concluded with Italy in August 1905, France had to abandon its exclusive rights to protect Christian institutions in the Ottoman Empire, as Italy announced it would consider favourably any requests made to her for protection by 'Italian religious communities' in the Ottoman empire.[43] Thus, there were instances later of Franciscans in Egypt telling the French authorities that they no longer considered themselves to be under French protection.[44]

The anticlerical dispute continued to rage, and there was a certain ambivalence about the debate. This was reflected in Léon Gambetta's statement, 'Le cléricalisme, voilà l'ennemi', which the French prime minister tempered by saying, 'L'anticléricalisme n'est pas un article d'exportation.' This meant that many, including senior officials at the Quai d'Orsay, were very reluctant to allow anticlericalism to affect France's Protectorate. Indeed, many believed that the Protectorate was a privilege that belonged to France and one that no one could either remove or contest. It was regarded as

> an important instrument of our policy, an efficient tool for our action, and France should not renounce its use. [Consequently,] when one speaks of defending French interests in the Orient, the question is not only that of the Protectorate, it is much greater and more important. The beneficial and civilising work undertaken for more than three centuries by France in the Levant [was] begun by French Catholics. France has continued this work at the price of admirable efforts, and all her future action rests on it; [indeed] today the French of all creeds and parties collaborate together to uphold this work.[45]

Other voices were raised, and a certain René Pinon remonstrated with those who had spoken in Parliament demanding that France abandon her

---

43   Shorrock, p. 43.
44   *M.A.É. Correspondance diplomatique N. S. 1897–1914 sous-série Saint-Siège,*
       vols. 74 and 74 bis. Sister Alphonsina, who was a Franciscan, declared that she
       had quit the French Protectorate (14 April 1906, pp. 325–7). There was a great
       deal of correspondence relating to this matter, including a letter from a representa-
       tive of the Vatican who claimed not to understand, but nevertheless appeared
       delighted with the news.
45   Pernot, pp. XII–XIII.

Catholic Protectorate in the Orient and cancel the subsidies allocated every year by the French state to denominational schools in the Levant. Pinon insisted that, even if the Protectorate disappeared, it was in France's interests to protect French schools and missions. Pinon recalled that when Léon Bourgeois came to power, the radicals in his party had insisted on replacing religious schools in the Orient with non-denominational institutions.

Those who took an anticlerical stand in the debate in the *Chambre des Députés* disapproved of the religious character of the French schools, and some opposed the government subsidies allocated to them, suggesting that these grants be given to the non-denominational schools. They pointed out that the vast majority of the population in the Levant was Muslim, and secular institutions would create Francophile sympathies among the Muslims.

Yet a third faction concluded that the present shape of the French Protectorate no longer conformed with the needs of French politics and threatened to become a fruitless endeavour. This group therefore proposed that it should be reinforced and enlarged. They argued that it was necessary to continue to subsidise Catholic schools, as educated native Catholics would eventually themselves become a clerical élite directing the affairs of their nation. Just as the Russians continued to support the Orthodox community, and the English the Protestants, it was essential for the French to preserve their patronage of the Catholics, and continue to offer the Roman congregations both moral and financial support. This faction wished to call on Rome to ensure that all Roman Catholics sent to the Orient should be French nationals, though others pointed out that, since diplomatic relations with the Holy See had been broken off, it was not possible to demand anything of Rome.[46]

46 Pinon, 'Le protectorat français en Orient', p. 406.

Spheres and Extent of Influence

The *Entente Cordiale* signed in 1904 with Great Britain stipulated that, in exchange for a protectorate in Morocco, France would not obstruct in any way the actions of Great Britain in Egypt. Two concessions were made to France: firstly, a French savant would continue to occupy the position of Inspector General of Antiquities, and secondly, French schools would enjoy the same liberties as they had in the past.[47] French deputies saw the agreement as a grave defeat for France in the Orient, because ceasing to demand that Great Britain end her occupation of Egypt meant that France was abandoning the Nile Valley to the British. It also suggested that France was amiably yielding all her assets in that country,[48] and that the French would soon pack their bags and leave.[49] Some foresaw that soon English would replace French as the language most commonly used in Egyptian towns,[50] and that all that remained was for the French schools to disappear.[51] For example, French was slowly being replaced by English at the French School of Law in Cairo, and the importance of the French faculty of law diminished every year. Moreover, the medical school in Cairo, founded by a Frenchman during the reign of Muhammad 'Ali, was now under British control. There were also those who pointed out that Egyptian nationalists felt they had been let down by France, their traditional ally, and were therefore turning to Germany.[52]

French diplomats in Egypt, who seemed fully aware of the consequences of France's controversial policies, nevertheless recommended that special attention be paid to the school establishments destined for

---

47   British Government Sessional papers, 1904, vol. cx, 313. France, No. 1, 1904. Cd. 1952. *Agreement between Great Britain and France of April 8, 1904. Declaration respecting Egypt and Morocco.*

48   M. F. Deloncle, Chambre des Députés, 3 November 1904, cited in Emmanuel Brunet, 'Les intérêts français en Orient', *Questions Diplomatiques et Coloniales – Revue de Politique Extérieure*, vol. XXVI, 1908, p. 753.

49   M. Léon Daudet, Chambre des Députés, 3 November 1904, cited in Brunet, p. 753.

50   M. Archdeacon, Chambre des Députés, 3 November 1904, cited in Brunet, p. 753.

51   M. Deschanel, Chambre des Députés, 3 November 1904, cited in Brunet, p. 753.

52   Brunet, p. 755.

the children of the élite, because it was they who would become the future administrators of the country.[53]

The importance attached to the teaching of French was also reflected in a number of articles. The author of one pointed out that while France had built bridges, canals and railways in order to develop her commercial activities, the French also needed to extend their intellectual influence by propagating their language. 'The role of French schools is vital amid these far-flung populations that we wish to civilise, or simply to befriend. By erasing language differences, [the schools] remove the greatest obstacle to the diffusion of our ideas. This education does more than popularise our language and spread the French idea, it creates in the personality of every student who has risen to the rank of lawyer, physician, professor or priest a site of influence, an auxiliary of propaganda, an instrument of action.'[54]

One of the consequences of the ongoing debate was French premier Léon Bourgeois's decision to send Marcel Charlot, the Inspector General of French Public Education to Egypt and the Ottoman Empire to visit French secular and denominational schools there.[55] As Charlot left in the summer of 1906, shortly before the summer holidays, he was only able to visit 116 schools in Egypt, Palestine, Syria, Lebanon and Turkey.[56]

According to some, Charlot's trip was too brief for him to 'penetrate the moral and intellectual atmosphere that characterised the countries he had visited.'[57] Nevertheless, the inspector praised the work done by the religious schools, which, in his view, had served France well in the past. However, he wondered whether they would continue to do so in future, as there was great rivalry with other nations.[58] Charlot subsequently made several recommendations, namely: that the French state stop subsidising

53   *M.A.É. Nouvelle Série 1897–1914 K – Afrique Égypte*, vols. 101 – '*enseignement français*' (1907 – Jan.–Sept.) – 102, '*enseignement français*' (1907 Oct.–July 1913). Letter from Chevalier de Valdrome to French Minister of Foreign Affairs, dated 24 September 1907, *A.S. des établissements scolaires et hospitaliers à Alexandrie*, pp. 199–200.
54   Gaston Bordat, 'L'Influence française en Orient', *Questions Diplomatiques et Coloniales – Revue de Politique Extérieure*, vol. XXI, 1906, p. 472.
55   Pinon, 'Les Écoles d'Orient', p. 418.
56   Charlot, p. 7240.
57   Pinon, 'Les Écoles d'Orient', p. 419.
58   Charlot, p. 7243.

schools which, by proselytising and showing a lack of tolerance, had harmed France's reputation; that it continue to subsidise other denominational establishments and offer assistance to secular schools hampered by a lack of funds; and finally that it should found new secular establishments, especially in areas where there were none, or where circumstances were favourable.[59]

Charlot's report did not end the uncertainty. In 1909 the Comité des Intérêts Français en Orient was founded in Paris. It informed the press that the men who made up this committee had a single objective in mind, 'that of working, irrespective of partisanship and in the broadest possible sense, to maintain and develop [France's] moral, political and economic situation in the Orient.' The committee stressed that despite France's good fortune in expanding her empire to include the Western basin of the Mediterranean, she could not afford to forget that she had 'first-rate interests in the Orient, and that the privileges [she] still had there were tantamount to duties that could not be abandoned.' The committee

> proposed to call on [public] opinion and to back French policy by using its resources and propaganda to support all the efforts that contributed to France's honourable standing in the Oriental countries, and that helped extend her influence there.[60]

The importance of this committee was underlined by the prominence of its 48 members, who included Raymond Poincaré, then President of the French Republic, and a few former premiers, among them Léon Bourgeois, who chaired the committee. Senators, deputies, cabinet ministers, bankers, financiers, academics and important journalists, many of whom were members of the Académie Française or the Académie des Sciences, joined it as well. The involvement of so many prominent personalities undoubtedly helped to raise the funds it needed, which comprised grants from the Paris Chamber of Commerce, Crédit Lyonnais and the Ottoman Bank. Also, a large and generous gift had been made by a group of Armenians residing in Paris. The funds were allocated for subsidies, and then to send a representative on a mission to Constantinople, Egypt and the neighbouring Ottoman provinces. This was Maurice

---

59   Charlot, p. 7242.
60   Pernot, p. I.

Pernot, a journalist employed by the *Journal des Débats* who was to inspect all the religious and secular schools under France's protection in that region, and then report impartially and comprehensively to the committee.[61]

Pernot's mission was one of the outcomes of the debate carried out by France's *parlementaires* on the subject of French education in Egypt and the Levant, which may have been instigated by the *Entente*. This debate certainly showed the importance attached to the issue of French schools, and it may have been one of the motives for the establishment of the Comité des Intérêts Français en Orient.

Pernot judged that France's position in the Orient was not threatened or compromised; indeed, it remained predominant. However, it was important to defend, and even consolidate it, if the French did not want it to dwindle away and slowly disappear. 'We have certain advantages over our rivals which we need to use. We arrived in the Orient before them, and we have not stopped extending our civilising influence and our beneficial action.' During his trip Pernot had often been told by the natives, 'Foreigners from other nations come here to pursue their own interests, whereas you French are here for us.'[62]

Referring to Egypt, Pernot said that secular and denominational schools complemented each other and were not competing with one another. However, it was important to note that the results obtained by secular establishments created and supported at a great cost to France were very inferior to those obtained by the religious schools, and particularly those obtained by the Frères de la Doctrine Chrétienne. Their programmes attached importance to the sciences, modern languages, commerce and accounting, all of which were subjects that corresponded exactly to the aptitudes and needs of the clientele to which they were addressed. This was in contrast with the programmes of the French *lycées* and colleges. The upper classes of all the secondary education establishments were almost empty, and they would have been completely empty if some young people attracted by the prestige of a *diplôme* had not decided to prepare for the *baccalauréat*. Moreover, Pernot warned that it was not by multiplying the *lycées* and colleges that the French would

---

61   Pernot, p. I.
62   Pernot, p. XIV.

develop their influence, but rather by encouraging the creation of technical, commercial, agricultural and industrial institutes, and by improving primary schools that would prepare these pupils for these institutes. Indeed, Pernot insisted that primary and professional schools in Egypt would find an unlimited clientele.[63] As for the French School of Law in Cairo, Pernot observed that it had actually benefited from the failure of the French section at the Khedivial School of Law after the abrupt and regrettable departure of Édouard Lambert, the former French director, in 1907. The British had taken advantage of this and replaced Lambert with an English director. The French section was still directed by French professors, but the number of pupils attending it was falling steadily. The statutes required that the section be closed when the number of pupils in each of the three years of courses reached ten, and at present there were 12 pupils in each year. Pernot stressed that it would be in the French interest to maintain the French section, as it constituted a sort of buffer between the French School and the English administration. The latter exerted its control over the French section of the Khedivial School of Law, but it had no authority to exert any control over the French School. However, on the day the French section of the Khedivial School of Law ceased to exist, the English administration could use any excuse to interfere in the direction of the French School of Law. This school had a great many students (403); indeed, if one was to believe some authorities, there were far too many. Former students rarely became government officials: most became businessmen, although some went on to be lawyers. In fact, business was an increasingly popular career, while industry and agriculture were less attractive to young Egyptians. Pernot recalled reading a speech by Lord Kitchener, the British Agent in Egypt, warning young Egyptians not to acquire an education that was too theoretical, and the Frenchman therefore suggested that France establish a higher school of commerce, an *Institut des Arts et Métiers* or a school of Agriculture. He also cited senior administrators and bank directors who deplored the absence of a school in Egypt that could prepare efficient officials, suggesting that a school of commerce would compensate for this lack.[64] According to Pernot, French schools existed in all the large

63   Pernot, pp. 75–6.
64   Pernot, p. 77.

towns, and French was taught even in the schools of the Alliance Israélite. He estimated that, in all, 20,369 pupils (13,114 boys, and 7,255 girls) were learning French in Egypt at this time.[65] Meanwhile, Egyptian intellectuals had expressed concern that the Egyptian education system was a confused amalgam of French and English principles that showed neither direction nor national character.[66]

As for French educational provision in Lebanon, the journalist mentioned that the Faculty of Medicine, which was founded in 1883, had 243 students, 20 of whom were Muslims. Only Orientals or Europeans born and residing in the Orient were admitted, and candidates either had to hold the French *bachot* or else sit an entrance exam before a jury nominated and chaired by the French Consul-General. Thanks to the Comité de l'Asie Française and the Parisian press syndicate, a subscription had been launched with the aim of giving the Faculty of Medicine a proper building. This would make it possible for the faculty to hold its own against the competition presented by the American Faculty of Medicine. This building was inaugurated late in 1912.[67]

The Université St Joseph, which was praised by Pernot, had 459 students. Its secondary education programme included classical and modern subjects. Pupils learned English, German, Italian and a very little Turkish. French was the language used in classes, and the diploma given was equivalent to a university bachelor's degree. The Oriental seminary of the Jesuit Fathers, which was established in 1902, prepared priests and missionaries for missions in Oriental countries, and had 45 students. Seminarists studied there for 10–12 years and followed the classical secondary school programme of the Université St Joseph. All the pupils spoke French and were taught to prepare their sermons in French. Only philosophy and theology were taught in Latin.[68] The Collège des Frères de la Doctrine Chrétienne, founded in 1894, had more than 500 pupils. The college had acquired land in 1908, and this had allowed the Fathers to establish themselves on a larger scale. The college included a *section*

65   Pernot, pp. 312–17.
66   Ahmed Loutfi el Sayed, 'La jeunesse égyptienne et l'avenir de l'Égypte', *La Revue Egyptienne*, 5 October 1912, first year, nos. 10–11. p. 295.
67   Pernot, p. 177.
68   Pernot, p. 179.

d'enseignement secondaire moderne, which was popular with the pupils, a number of whom were preparing to take the French *baccalauréat* examination in Egypt (sciences and modern languages). However, most pupils aspired to receive the diploma for commercial studies awarded by the establishment.

There was much competition from foreign schools, some of which were quite important. Thus, Russia subsidised the Greek Orthodox schools, as well as a reputed girls' school; and the Italians had both a boys' and a girls' school, where French was taught as well as Italian. Yet it was the Americans who were considered the most redoubtable opponents, because the Syrian Protestant College had been enlarged and improved since its foundation in 1871 and now had 895 students.

Whereas some centres were very active and admirably organised, such as for example, those in Beirut and the Lazarist college at Antoura, which had 300 pupils, the predominance of the French language and French prestige were far from being equally well assured in all parts of Syria. There were some excellent higher and secondary education establishments, but the primary schools, which were particularly important, were not all equally useful. Even taking into account the idea that the mountain population of Syria was generally less receptive and less keen on education than that of the plains, the inferior results obtained in Syria could nevertheless be attributed to the fact that the French teaching staff in Syria had been concentrated on the higher schools, where the subjects taught were often too difficult and unsuited to pupils' needs. Elementary schools were usually the most effective way of promoting French influence, but they were neglected in Syria. Although there were innumerable elementary schools, they were neglected and thus the quality of French attained was not as might be expected.

Pernot was further struck by the mediocrity of most of the French schools in Lebanon, especially publicly funded schools and those that were free of charge in Beirut, Damascus and Aleppo. He frequently wished that it was possible to find as widespread and practical a knowledge of the French language in Lebanon as in the Iraqi provinces. English was certainly better known than French in certain parts of Lebanon, and Italian was rapidly gaining ground in some regions on the coast.[69]

69   Pernot, p. 224.

The total number of pupils enrolled in French schools in Syria and Lebanon was 40,099, with 25,801 boys and 15,198 girls.[70]

What Pernot's report did not say was that the French had designs on Syria and Lebanon, and that the French lobby was aware of this at the time of Pernot's mission. According to a French diplomat, although France had promised to maintain the integrity of the Ottoman Empire, the French President, Raymond Poincaré, had publicly pledged himself to listen to the wishes of some subject populations in the empire. He had therefore pressed the Ottoman government to adopt a reformist project that would favour the Lebanese. It was also understood that if the empire suffered any losses in Asia, France would not abandon her traditions, and would neither repudiate the sympathies it had won nor sacrifice its interests there. Consequently, after the First World War, having gained official assurances that Britain had no intentions with regard to Syria, the French took the opportunity to signal their interests in Syria and Lebanon, making it clear that France would refuse to yield to anyone in these areas of the Levant.[71] The diplomat added that France could not continue to play the role it had played earlier during its 20-year presence in Syria. Its approach had to be different, and the work of penetration in Syria needed to be intensified.[72]

In the meantime, Arab nationalists had endorsed Faysal, the son of the Hashimite clan leader, as ruler of Syria. Faysal's decision to replace Turkish with Arabic as the official language of Syria and have school textbooks translated into Arabic met with popular approval. In July 1919 he convened the General Syrian Congress, which declared Syria sovereign and free. Then, in March 1920, the congress proclaimed Faysal King of Syria. However, Syrian hopes for independence and an Arab revival were short-lived, as the French took Damascus in July 1920.

The French military men responsible for implementing the mandate in Syria were eventually to claim that they had given the Arabic language its due status. Indeed, the terms of the mandate stipulated that classes had to be given in Arabic. Nevertheless, at the same time, the study of

---

70   Pernot, pp. 324–9.
71   F. Charles-Roux, *France et Chrétiens d'Orient* (Paris: Flammarion, 1939), pp. 277–8.
72   Charles-Roux, *France et Chrétiens d'Orient*, p. 306.

French was made compulsory in all schools.[73] The commander of French forces in Syria subsequently reported that French, although badly spoken, was now in use everywhere.[74] Yet the decision to force state primary schools to teach French and the emphasis on the French influence in school programmes prompted a very strong reaction, as the Syrians did not want the French to repeat what they had been doing in Algeria since 1830, namely gallicising the country. Consequently, since government-run schools, where French influence was less preponderant, were slow to grow and develop on the French model, they became more popular under the mandate than private foreign schools, most of which were French.[75] In 1934, a year after primary school education became free of charge, there were 37,786 primary and secondary school pupils enrolled in government-run schools, representing 50% of the region's young people.[76] A French official was also forced to admit that those who did not follow the French system were discriminated against. For instance, the school of medicine in Damascus only accepted students who had taken the *bachot*.[77]

In 1938 there were 71 French schools in Syria, with 11,493 pupils equally divided between boys and girls. In higher education, 330 Syrian students had joined the schools of law and medicine in Damascus, while 152 Syrians had enrolled in educational institutions in France.[78]

Reaction against the French in Syria and Lebanon began in the cultural sphere. In 1944 the Syrian Chamber of Deputies passed a law prohibiting the teaching of French in primary schools. Subsequently, in May 1945, demonstrations and serious fighting broke out in the towns. The fighting went on until February 1946, when the French bombed

73   Lt. Colonel Catroux, 'Le mandat français en Syrie – son application à l'État de Damas', *Revue politique et parlementaire*, Paris, 1922, p. 26.
74   Catroux, p. 27.
75   Philip S. Khoury, *Syria and the French Mandate* (London: I.B. Taurus, 1987), p. 409; Tibawi, p. 345
76   In 1930 a Norwegian lady appointed by the League of Nations to report on France's 'civilising' influence in Syria noted that male illiteracy was 66%, and that female illiteracy was 80%. 'Only 39% of the boys and 17% of the girls of school age were actually at school.' Tibawi, p. 361.
77   Tibawi, p. 361.
78   Tibawi, p. 357.

Damascus. Two months later, a United Nations' resolution forced the French to leave Syria, but their reluctance to withdraw and the fighting that ensued left the Syrians feeling very bitter.

In Egypt, the French managed to secure their privileges after the First World War. Indeed, one French author subsequently reassured his compatriots that French was as frequently used in Egypt as Arabic. Thus, tramway itineraries, postage stamps, and train tickets were in French as well as Arabic. Moreover, French continued to be the language used in the administration, for business transactions and by the élite. He added that although four languages were used in the courts, nine-tenths of court procedures, including the speeches by counsel, were conducted in French.[79] French educational establishments were so popular that in 1921–2 the Lycée Français at Alexandria, which depended on the non-denominational missions, had 1381 pupils, including girls. The Collège St Catherine and the non-fee-paying school attached to it had 1300 pupils, 139 of whom were taking its commercial course. The École de la Sainte Famille des Frères d'Alexandrie had 325 pupils. In Cairo, the Lycée Français had 772 pupils, while the Jesuits had 550 pupils, and the Collège des Frères had 500. He added that there were 27,600 pupils enrolled in primary schools, several of which were first-class establishments in which French was taught exclusively. Pupil numbers in the French schools had increased significantly each year since 1919. Moreover, despite attempts by certain British officials to obtain the closure of the French School of Law, or at least its fusion with the Egyptian School of Law, the French had been successful in securing their privileges. The school's 477 students were preparing either for the *licence* or for a *doctorat*. The state acknowledged the diplomas awarded by this school, and its graduates were able to work in the mixed courts. Most students were Egyptian Muslims, and they constituted the intellectual élite of the country.[80]

Egypt was granted partial independence in 1922, and a fierce struggle for influence ensued between the French and the British. The Egyptians, however, had their own views. For instance, Egypt's King Fuad

79   English, Arabic, French and Italian.
80   Raymond Recouly, 'L'Égypte et les Intérêts français', *Revue de France*, 4, 1 July 1922, pp. 143–4.

demonstrated his Gallic sympathies and insisted on recruiting Frenchmen for the Egyptian University.[81] He added that if Frenchmen were unavailable, Italians or Belgians would do just as well. The Minister of Education irritated the British by agreeing to hire northern Europeans to teach in English at the university, vaguely promising to give preference to English professors, but actually recruiting French-speaking staff. As for the nationalists, they had two demands, firstly that the university employ Egyptian professors, and secondly that Arabic should be the language of instruction there. However, the need to maintain Western academic standards and retain an international community of scholars induced many professors, especially those in the Faculties of Medicine and Science, to choose English as the language of instruction.[82]

By the mid-1920s English, rather than French, was the language taught at Egyptian state schools, and their Egyptian students now spoke very little French.[83] Furthermore, by the end of the 1920s more Englishmen had been recruited to teach at the Faculty of Arts. One of these English academics later described his embarrassment when told by British officials at the Egyptian Ministry of Education that he had to keep the British flag flying at the Faculty of Arts. Accordingly, although he did not consider himself an ambassador of Empire, he was determined not to allow the French to 'indulge in semi-political activities at [his] expense.'[84]

A former British High Commissioner in Egypt later admitted that in its first 20 years the British occupation had done nothing to remould education in Egypt, but had simply taken the already existing Egyptian government schools and turned them into 'factories of government officials'. He observed that the French, who were traditionally hostile to the occupation, had noted Britain's failure to introduce a system calculated to spread English ideals and English culture. They had consequently taken advantage of this, and of the Egyptians' dissatisfaction with British educational policies in Egypt, to give young Egyptians 'an education in an anti-British point of view'. As a result, he believed that

81   Founded in 1908.
82   Donald Malcolm Reid, *Cairo University and the Making of Modern Egypt* (Cambridge: Cambridge University Press, 1990), p. 87.
83   Reid, p. 96.
84   Robert Graves, *Goodbye to All That*, cited in Reid, pp. 91–2.

the very many young Egyptians who had received a French education either in Egypt or in France could hardly be expected to emerge from their studies entirely convinced of the sincerity of Britain's political professions or of the disinterestedness of British motives.[85]

Competition between the French and the British lasted throughout the 1930s, 1940s and early 1950s; English continued to be the first language taught in government schools, and students who had not been to private French schools chose to stick to English in university if they could not do Arabic.[86] This suggested that the concerns regarding Egyptian national identity expressed by Egyptian intellectuals before the First World War were partly justified. Thus, university students exhibited pro-Nationalist and anti-British feelings, but they were nevertheless keen to understand Wordsworth, Byron and Shakespeare.[87] Meanwhile, French continued to be the language in general use, and French schools continued to stress French concerns. Indeed, Egyptians who attended French schools between the 1930s and early 1950s recalled having to learn all about *Nos Ancêtres les Gaulois* and the confluents of the Loire and Rhône rivers. Also, actors in Egyptian films produced before the mid-1950s frequently used French on the screen to show their ability to make polite conversation. A British lecturer explained that this was because English only had its sordid uses in business and in sport, and it was therefore 'not considered quite the thing in high Egyptian society.'[88] This, of course, was in contrast with the 1970s, 1980s and 1990s, when English became the first foreign language.

It was the Anglo-French attack on Suez in 1956 that brought about a denunciation of Western imperialism. In retaliation to France's 'aggression', French *lycées* in Egypt were renamed *Lycée La Liberté*, or the Arabic equivalent *al-Hurriyyah*, to indicate that Egypt was liberating itself from French cultural influence. Similarly, the names of all the British schools were altered to correspond with the country's anti-Western, anti-imperialist mood. In Syria the aggression against Egypt revived

85   Lord Lloyd, *Egypt since Cromer* (London: Macmillan, 1933), vol. 1, p. 166.
86   Reid, p. 96.
87   Reid, p. 98.
88   D. J. Enright, *Academic Year*, cited in Reid, p. 96.

anti-Western sentiments. As a result, Syria broke off diplomatic relations with France and Great Britain.[89]

Present Statistics on French Speaking in the Region

Although education in Egypt has veered more towards the English language,[90] a study conducted by the Agence de la Francophonie in 1997–8 showed that 2,500,000 of the country's people were learning the French language; 2,200,000 of whom were currently engaged in the second part of their secondary education, in which 85% of the pupils learned French. Also, because it was one of the languages in use in law, tourism and international trade, 100,000 students were learning French outside the French departments.[91] Moreover, many Egyptians continued to consider French to be the 'language of the élite'. Indeed, rather contradictory tendencies had been observed: on the one hand, English was the language used by nearly all professionals, as well as French firms established locally; on the other, the demand from families for a French school education remained stable, and may even have increased. The report concluded that the existence of private or publicly funded foreign language schools nevertheless continued to present the best possible guarantee for the use of French.[92] Thus in Egypt, where the population had once been very cosmopolitan, Egyptians had not been forced to learn French but still did so, partly in reaction to the British presence in the country, and mainly because the French system of education was generally viewed as excellent.

In Lebanon, where French had a dominant position as the first foreign language, English is now an important contender, especially in

89   Elisabeth Picard, 'La Syrie de 1946 à 1979', in André Raymond, *La Syrie d'aujourd'hui* (Paris: CNRS, 1980), p. 150.
90   Haut Conseil de la Francophonie, *État de la Francophonie dans le Monde en Données 1997–1998 et 6 études inédites*, p. 180.
91   Haut Conseil de la Francophonie, pp. 65–6.
92   Haut Conseil de la Francophonie, p. 180.

billposting, signs and the media. However, the Council of Ministers' adoption, in May 1997, of new school programmes allowing simultaneous training in two languages was expected to promote the choice of French, as well as English, as a foreign language.[93] In 1998 the number of French-speakers in Lebanon was estimated at 780,000 out of a population of 4,210,000. This represented 75% of the school population, and 12% of higher education students. Although some educational establishments considered English as the only language necessary, the Mission Laïque Française nevertheless had 13,000 pupils. Lebanon was also a member of the Agence intergouvernementale de la Francophonie – as opposed to Egypt, which was only an associate member.[94]

Syria had less than 300,000 students learning French. Also, though it was taught in the last two years of primary education, only 19% of primary pupils and 12.5% of secondary school pupils chose to study it. Press reviews there, as in Algeria, showed very conflicting perceptions of the French-speaking presence, and historical constraints continued to prevent Syria from joining the French-speaking community. Despite this, a Syrian ambassador to France expressed the hope that, with French encouragement, the country's French-speakers would constitute an effective international bloc that would help to break down prejudices about Syria, which was anxious to encourage as much resistance as possible to 'America's hegemony in a unipolar world'.[95]

93   Haut Conseil de la Francophonie, p. 29
94   Internet, http://www.francophonie.org.Liban.
95   Haut Conseil de la Francophonie, p. 410.

Selected Bibliography

Abou, S. and Haddad, K. (eds), *Une Francophonie différentielle* (Paris: L'Harmattan, 1994).

Aitsiselmi, F. (ed.), *Black, blanc, beur. Youth Language and Identity in France* (Bradford: Interface, 2000).

André, P., *La Suisse française, terre alémanique?* (Montreux: Éditions Transjuranes, 1946).

Antoine, G. and Martin, R. (eds), *Histoire de la langue française 1880–1914* (Paris: Éditions du CNRS, 1985).

Antoine, G. and Martin, R. (eds), *Histoire de la langue française 1914–1945* (Paris: CNRS Éditions, 1995).

Artin, Y., *L'Instruction Publique en Égypte* (Paris: Ernest Leroux, 1890).

Bach, D., *La France et l'Afrique du Sud, Histoire, mythes et enjeux contemporains* (Paris: Karthala, 1990).

Bachmann, C. and Basier, L., *Mise en image d'une banlieue ordinaire* (Paris: Syros, 1989).

Baetens Beardsmore, H. (ed.), *European Models of Bilingual Education* (Clevedon: Multilingual Matters, 1993).

Bakhtin, M., *Esthétique et théorie du roman* (Paris: Gallimard, 1978).

Bakhtin, M., *Le principe dialogique* (Paris: Seuil, 1981).

Barko, I., *Seventy Years of the McCaughey Chair of French* (Sydney: University of Sydney, 1991).

Bazin, H., *La culture hip-hop* (Paris: Desclée de Brouwer, 1995).

Bentahila, A., *Language Attitudes among Arabic-French Bilinguals in Morocco* (Clevedon: Multilingual Matters, 1983).

Benveniste, E., *Problèmes de linguistique générale I* (Paris: Gallimard, 1966).

Benveniste, E., *Problèmes de linguistique générale II* (Paris: Gallimard, 1974).

Berdouzi, M., *Rénover l'enseignement: de la charte aux actes* (Rabat: Renouveau, 2000).

Berthold, M. (ed.), *Rising to the Bilingual Challenge* (Canberra: NLLIA, 1995).

Bevan, D., *Écrivains d'aujourd'hui. La littérature romande en vingt entretiens* (Lausanne: Éditions 24 Heures, 1986).

Bhabha, H., *The Location of Culture* (London/New York: Routledge, 1994).

Blampain, D. *et al.* (eds), *Le français en Belgique* (Louvain-la-Neuve: Duculot and Ministère de la Communauté française de Belgique, Service de la langue française, 1997).

Boak, D. (ed.), *Essays in French Literature* (Perth: University of Western Australia, 1964).

Borgomano, M., *Ahmadou Kourouma: Le 'guerrier' griot* (Paris: L'Harmattan, 1998).

Borgomano, M., *Des Hommes ou des bêtes* (Paris: L'Harmattan, 2000).

Bouchard, C., *La langue et le nombril. Histoire d'une obsession québécoise* (Québec: Fides, 1998).

Bouchard, P. et al., *La féminisation des noms de métier, fonctions, grades ou titres, au Québec, en Suisse romande, en France et en Communauté française de Belgique* (Belgique: Éditions Duculot, 1999).

Boukous, A., *Société, langues et cultures au Maroc. Enjeux symboliques* (Rabat: Faculté des Lettres et des Sciences Humaines, 1995).

Boukous, A., *Dominance et différence: essai sur les enjeux symboliques au Maroc* (Casablanca: Éditions Le Fennec, 1999).

Bourdieu, P., *Ce que parler veut dire* (Paris: Fayard, 1982).

Bright, W. (ed.), *International Encyclopedia of Linguistics*, vol. 3 (New York/Oxford: Oxford University Press, 1992).

Calvet, L.-J., *Linguistique et colonialisme: petit traité de glottophagie* (Paris: Payot, 1974).

Carnoy, N., *La Colonie Française du Caire* (Paris: PUF, 1927).

Centlivres, P., *Identité régionale. Approche ethnologique. Suisse romande et Tessin* (Neuchâtel: Institut d'Ethnologie, 1981).

Chambers, A. and Ó Baoill, D. P. (eds), *Intercultural Communication and Language Learning* (Dublin: RIA/IAAL, 1999).

Chambers, J. K. and Trudgill, P., *Dialectology*, 2nd edn (Cambridge: Cambridge University Press, 1998).

Charles-Roux, F., *France et Chrétiens d'Orient* (Paris: Flammarion, 1939).

Charles-Roux, F., *Souvenirs diplomatiques d'un âge révolu* (Paris: Arthème Fayard, 1956).

Cholette, G., *L'action internationale du Québec en matière linguistique: coopération avec la France et la francophonie de 1961 à 1995* (Québec: Les Presses de l'Université Laval, 1997).

Churchill, S., *Official Languages in Canada: Changing the Linguistic Landscape* (Canada: Canadian Heritage, 1998).

Conac, G., Dreyfus, F. and Maziau, N. (eds), *La République d'Afrique du Sud. Nouvel État, Nouvelle Société* (Paris: ECONOMICA, 1999).

Conrick, M., *Womanspeak* (Dublin: Marino Books/Mercier Press, 1999).

Conwell, M. J. and Juilland, A., *Louisiana French Grammar* (The Hague: Mouton, 1963).

Cooper, R. L., *Language Planning and Social Change* (Cambridge: Cambridge University Press, 1989).

Cortes, J. et al., *Une introduction à la recherche scientifique en didactique des langues* (Paris: Didier-Crédif, 1981).

Cosnier, J. and Kerbrat-Orecchioni, C., *Décrire la conversation* (Lyon: Presses universitaires de Lyon, 1987).

Coupland, N. and Jaworski, A. (eds), *Sociolinguistics: A Reader and Coursebook* (Basingstoke: Macmillan, 1997).

Courtés, J., *Sémantique de l'énoncé: applications pratique* (Paris: Hachette, 1989).
Coveney, A., *Variability in Spoken French. A Sociolinguistic Study of Interrogation and Negation* (Exeter: Elm Bank, 1996).
Cryle, P., Freadman, A. and Hanna, B., *Unlocking Australia's Language Potential. Profiles of 9 Key Languages in Australia: French* (Canberra: NLLIA, 1993).
Crystal, D., *The Cambridge Encyclopedia of Language* (Cambridge: Cambridge University Press, 1991).
Cuendet, J-P., *Parlons vaudois* (Chavannes-de-Bogis: Slatkine, 1991).
Culioli, A., *Opérateurs énonciatifs* (Paris: Ophrys, 1991).
Dabène, L., *Repères linguistiques pour l'enseignement des langues* (Paris: Hachette, 1994).
Damé, F., *Nouveau Dictionnaire roumain-français*, 4 vols (Bucharest: Imprimerie de l'État, 1873).
Dannequin, C., *Les Enfants bâillonnés* (Paris: CEDIL, 1977).
de Certeau, M., Julia, D. and Revel, J., *Une politique de la langue, la Révolution française et les patois* (Paris: Gallimard, 1975).
De Vriendt, S. and Van de Craen, P., 'Bilingualism in Belgium: A History and an Appraisal', *CLCS Occasional Paper*, 23 (Dublin: Trinity College, 1990).
Dixon, M. and McCorquodale, R., *Cases and Materials on International Law*, 3rd edn (London: Blackstone Press, 2000).
Dollot, L., *La France dans le monde actuel* (Paris: PUF, 1986).
Dor, É., *L'Instruction Publique en Égypte* (Paris: Lacroix & Verboeck Hoeven, 1872).
Du Bois, P., *Alémaniques et Romands entre unité et discorde: histoire et actualité* (Lausanne: Favre, 1999).
Du Bois, P. (ed.), *Union et division des Suisses. Les relations entre Alémaniques, Romands et Tessinois aux XIXe et XXe siècles* (Lausanne: Aire, 1983).
Ducrot, O., *Dire et ne pas dire, principes de sémantiques linguistiques* (Paris: Hermann, 1972).
Ducrot, O., *Le structuralisme en linguistique* (Paris: Seuil, 1973).
Dumont, G-H., *Histoire de la Belgique* (Brussels: Le Cri, 1997).
Duneton, C., *A Hurler le soir au fond des collèges* (Paris: Seuil, 1984).
Duverger, J., *Mission Report – Telopea Park School, French-Australian Bi-lingual School* (Canberra: The French Embassy, 1998).
Eco, U., 'Lumi mici' ['Small Worlds'], in *Limitele interpretarii* [*Limits of Interpretation*]. Translated into Romanian by Stefania Mincu and Daniela Bucsa (Constanta: Editura Pontica, 1996).
Eloy, J. M. (ed.), *Variétés d'oil et autres langues, Actes du Colloque international, 29–30 November 1996* (Amiens: Centre d'Études Picardes XLVII, 1998).
Erfurt, J. (ed.), *De la polyphonie à la symphonie, méthodes, théories et faits de la recherche pluridisciplinaire sur le français au Canada* (Leipzig: Leipziger Universitätsverlag, 1996).

Favre, É., *François Coillard au Lessouto* vol. II; *François Coillard, missionnaire au Lessouto (1861–1882)* vol. III; *François Coillard, missionnaire au Zambèze (1882–1904)* (Paris: Société des Missions Évangéliques, 1908).

Fishman, J. A., *Language Loyalty in the United States* (Paris: Mouton 1966).

Fishman, J. A., *Sociolinguistics: A Brief Introduction* (Rowley: Newbury House, 1971).

Fishman, J. A., *Reversing Language Shift* (Clevedon: Multilingual Matters, 1991).

Fitouri, C., *Biculturalisme, bilingualisme et éducation* (Paris/Neuchâtel: Delachaux et Niestlé, 1983).

Fleisch, H., *L'Arabe classique, esquisse d'une structure linguistique* (Beyrouth: Dar El Machreq, 1968).

Fondation Marc Bloch, collective (Paris: Albin Michel, 1999).

Foulkes, P. and Docherty, G. (eds), *Urban Voices: Accent Studies in the British Isles* (London: Arnold, 1999).

Francillon, R. (ed.), *Histoire de la littérature suisse romande*, vol. 4 (Lausanne: Payot, 1999).

Gadet, F., *Le Français ordinaire* (Paris: Armand Collin, 1989).

Gallet, D., *Pour une ambition francophone. Le désir et l'indifférence* (Paris: L'Harmattan, 1995).

Garmadi, S., 'Les problèmes du bilinguisme en Tunisie', *Renaissance du monde arabe* (Gembloux: Duculot, 1972).

Gassama, M., *La Langue d'Ahmadou Kourouma* (Paris: ACCT/Karthala, 1995).

Gauchat, L., Jeanjaquet, J. and Tappolet, E., *Glossaire des patois de la Suisse romande* (Neuchâtel: Attinger, 1924).

Gay, J., Gill D. and Hall, D. (eds), *Lesotho's Long Journey. Hard Choices at the Crossroads* (Lesotho: Sechaba Consultants, 1995).

Gorceix, P. (ed.), *L'identité culturelle de la Belgique et de la Suisse francophones* (Paris: Champion, 1997).

Gougenheim, G. *et al.*, *L'élaboration du français fondamental* (Paris: Didier, 1964).

Grandguillaume, G., *Arabisation et politique linguistique au Maghreb* (Paris: Maisonneuve et Larose, 1983).

Gsteiger, M., *La nouvelle littérature romande* (Vevey: Galland, 1978).

Guindon, R. and Poulin, P., *Francophones in Canada: A Community of Interests* (Canada: Canadian Heritage, 1996).

Hagège, C., *Le souffle de la langue* (Paris: Odile Jacob, 1992).

Hammel, E. and Gardy, P., *L'Occitan en Languedoc Roussillon* (Perpignan: Éditorial Trabucaire, 1994).

Hansen, A. B., *Les Voyelles nasales du français parisien moderne. Aspects linguistiques, sociolinguistiques et perceptuels des changements en cours* (Copenhagen: Museum Tusculanum, 1998).

Hargreaves, A. and McKinney, M. (eds), *Post-Colonial Cultures in France* (London: Routledge, 1997).

Harris, D. J., Boyle, M. and Warbrick, H., *Law of the European Convention on Human Rights* (London: Butterworths, 1995).

Henry, P., *Le parler jurassien et l'amour des mots*. 2 vols (Porrentruy, 1990, 1992).

Herriman, M. and Burnaby, B. (eds), *Language Policy in English-Dominant Countries: Six Case Studies* (Clevedon: Multilingual Matters, 1996).

Heyworth-Dunne, J. *An Introduction to the History of Education in Modern Egypt* (London: Frank Cass, 1968).

Hoffman, C. (ed.), *Language, Culture and Communication in Contemporary Europe* (Clevedon: Multilingual Matters, 1996).

Hoffmann, C. (ed.), *Language, Culture and Communication in Contemporary Europe* (Clevedon/Philadelphia/Adelaide: Multilingual Matters, 1996).

Hokayem, A., *Les provinces arabes de l'Empire ottoman aux archives des Affaires Étrangères de France: 1793–1918* (Beyrouth: Les Éditions Universitaires du Liban, 1988).

Ibnelfassi, L. and Hitchcott, N. (eds), *African Francophone Writing* (Oxford: Berg, 1996).

Istrati, P., *Les Chardons du Baragan* (Paris: Bernard Grasset, 1928).

Janis, M., Kay, R. and Bradley, A., *European Human Rights Law* (Oxford: Clarendon Press, 1995).

Jones, B., Miguet, A. and Corcoran, P. (eds), *Francophonie: mythes, masques et réalités* (Paris: Publisud, 1996).

Jousse, T., *La Mission française évangélique au sud de l'Afrique, son origine et son développement jusqu'à nos jours* (Paris: Librairie Fischbacher, 1889).

Knüsel, R., *Les minorités ethnolinguistiques autochtones à territoire: l'exemple du cas helvétique* (Lausanne: Payot, 1994).

Kohler, P. *La littérature d'aujourd'hui dans la Suisse romande* (Lausanne: Payot, 1923).

Kourouma, A., *Les Soleils des Indépendances* (Paris: Seuil, 1970).

Kourouma, A., *Monnè, outrages et défis* (Paris: Seuil, 1990).

Kourouma, A., *En attendant le vote des bêtes sauvages* (Paris: Seuil, 1998).

Kourouma, A., *Allah n'est pas obligé* (Paris: Seuil, 2000).

Kremer, D. and Monjour, A. (eds), *Studia ex Hilaritate, Mélanges de linguistique et d'onomastique sardes et romanes offerts à Heinz Jürgen Wolf* (Paris: Klincksieck, 1995–6).

Labeau, E. (ed.), *France-Belgique: des frères ennemis de la langue de chez nous?* (Québec: Centre International de Recherche en Aménagement Linguistique, 2000).

Labov, W., *Sociolinguistic patterns* (Philadelphia: University of Pennsylvania Press, 1972).

Labrie, N., *La construction linguistique de la Communauté européenne* (Paris: Champion, 1993).

Labrosse, C., *«Soit dites en passant» chronique sur le sexisme dans la langue* (Québec, Université Laval: Le GREMF édite, 1990).

Labrosse, C., *Pour une grammaire non sexiste* (Montréal: Les Éditions du remueménage, 1996).

Lane, P. and West-Sooby, J., *Traditions and Mutations in French Studies. The Australian Scene* (Mount Nebo, Queensland: Boombana Publications, 1997).

Lanly, A., *Le parler 'pied noir' des Français d'Algérie* (Paris: Bordas, 1970).

Latraverse, F., *La pragmatique: histoire et critique* (Brussels: Mardaga, 1986).

La variation et la norme (Neuchâtel: University of Neuchâtel Press, 1998).

Le Gleau, J-P. and Castaing, D., *Le recensement de la population à Saint-Pierre-et-Miquelon* (Paris: INSEE, 2000).

Leal, R. B., *Widening our Horizons: Report of the Review of the Teaching of Modern Languages in Higher Education* (Canberra: Australian Government Publishing Service, 1991).

Lemaire, J. (ed.), *Le français et les Belges* (Brussels: University of Brussels Press, 1989).

Léon, P., *Précis de phonostylistique* (Paris: Nathan, 1993).

Lepoutre, D., *Coeur de banlieue: codes, rites et langages* (Paris: Odile Jacob, 1997).

Liddicoat, A. J. (ed.), *Bilingualism and Bilingual Education* (Melbourne: NLLIA, 1991).

Liddicoat, A. J. (ed.), *Language Planning and Language Policy in Australia* (Melbourne: Applied Linguistics Association of Australia, 1991).

Lloyd, Lord, *Egypt since Cromer*, vol. 1 (London: Macmillan, 1933).

Lo Bianco, J., *National Policy on Languages* (Canberra: Australian Government Publishing Service, 1987).

Lo Bianco, J. and Monteil, A., *French in Australia: New Prospects* (Canberra: CNP Publications, 1990).

Lodge, R. A., *French: From Dialect to Standard* (London: Routledge, 1993).

Lucci, V., *Phonologie de l'Acadien* (Montréal: Didier, 1973).

Lüdi, G. *et al.*, *Le paysage linguistique de la Suisse* (Berne: Office fédéral de la Statistique, 1997).

Lugon, C., *Quand la Suisse française s'éveillera* (Genève: Perret-Gentil, 1983).

Maingueneau, D., *Sémantique de la polémique* (Lausanne: L'âge d'homme, 1983).

Maingueneau, D., *Genèse du discours* (Liège: Mardaga, 1984).

Maingueneau, D., *Nouvelles tendances en analyse du discours* (Paris: Hachette, 1987).

Maingueneau, D., *L'analyse du discours* (Paris: Hachette, 1991).

Marchand, B., *Paris, histoire d'une ville: XIXe–XXe siècle* (Paris: Seuil, 1993).

Marley, D., *Parler Catalan à Perpignan* (Paris: L'Harmattan, 1995).

Marley, D., Hintze, M-A. and Parker, G. (eds), *Linguistic Identities and Policies in France and the French-speaking World* (London: AFLS & CILT, 1998).

Marlin, J., *Rapport: Les Relations entre la France et la République d'Afrique du Sud* (Paris: Conseil Économique et social, 1995).

Marmen, L. and J-P. Corbeil, *Languages in Canada: 1996 Census* (Canada: Canadian Heritage and Statistics, 1999).

Marriott, H., Neustupny, V. J. and Spence-Brown, R., *Unlocking Australia's Language Potential: Profiles of 9 Key Languages in Australia: Japanese* (Melbourne: National Languages and Literacy Institute of Australia, 1992).

Martin, J-P., *Description lexicale du français parlé en vallée d'Aoste* (Mons: Musumeci Éditeurs, 1984).

Martinet, A., *La grammaire fonctionnelle du français* (Paris: Didier, 1979).

McKean, W., *Equality and Discrimination under International Law* (Oxford: Clarendon Press, 1993).

McRae, K. D., *Conflict and Compromise in Multilingual Societies: Switzerland* (Waterloo: Wilfred Laurier University Press, 1983).

Meienberg, N., *Le délire général. L'armée suisse sous influence.* Trans. M. Picard (Carouge-Genève: Zoé, 1988).

Meizoz, J., *Le droit de 'mal écrire'. Quand les auteurs romands déjouent le français de Paris* (Carouge-Genève: Zoé, 1998).

Menanteau, J. (ed.), *Les Banlieues* (Paris: Le Monde/Marabout, 1994).

Merle, P., *Argot, verlan et tchatches* (Toulouse: Éditions Milan, 1997).

Miller, C., *Theories of Africans* (Chicago: The University of Chicago Press, 1990).

Milroy, L., *Language and Social Networks,* 2nd edn (Oxford: Blackwell, 1987a).

Milroy, L., *Observing and Analysing Natural Language* (Oxford: Blackwell, 1987b).

Moatassime, A., *Arabisation et langue française au Maghreb* (Paris: PUF, 1992).

Monteil, V., *Études et Documents III L'Arabe Moderne* (Paris: Librairie C. Klinksieck, 1960).

Moreau, T., *Dictionnaire féminin-masculin des professions, des titres et des fonctions* (Genève: Métropolis, 1991/1999).

Morelli, A. (ed.), *Les grands mythes de l'histoire de Belgique, de Flandre et de Wallonie* (Brussels: Éditions Vie Ouvrière, 1995).

Moura, J-M., *Littératures francophones et théorie postcoloniale* (Paris: PUF, 1999).

Murray, K. (ed.), *The Judgement of Paris* (Sydney: Allen & Unwin, 1992).

Nash, S. and Furse, M. (eds), *Essential Human Rights Cases* (London: Jordans, 1999).

Nerlich, B., *La pragmatique* (Frankfurt: Peter Lang, 1986).

Ngugi, W. T., *Decolonising the Mind* (London: James Currey/Nairobi: Heinemann, 1981).

Nicolas, J-C., *'Les Soleils des Indépendances' d'Ahmadou Kourouma* (Issy-les Moulineaux: Éditions Saint-Paul, 1985).

Niedzwiecki, P., *Au féminin! Code de féminisation à l'usage de la francophonie* (Paris: Éditions A.-G. Nizet, 1994).

O'Keefe, M., *Francophone Minorities: Assimilation and Community Vitality* (Canada: Canadian Heritage, 1998).

Perelman, C. and Olbrechts-Tyteca, L., *Traité de l'argumentation, la nouvelle rhétorique* (Brussels: BUP, 1976).

Pernot, M., *Comité de défense des intérêts français en Orient, Rapport sur le voyage d'études à Constantinople en Égypte et en Turquie d'Asie (Janvier–Août 1912)* (Paris: Firmin Didot, 1912).

Perrot, J. (ed.), *Polyphonie pour Iván Fónagy: mélanges offerts en hommage à Iván Fónagy par un groupe de disciples, collègues et admirateurs* (Paris: L'Harmattan, 1997).

Pichard, A., *La Romandie n'existe pas* (Lausanne: Éditions 24 Heures, 1978).

Pinson, D., *Des Banlieues et des villes: dérive et eurocompétition* (Paris: Éditions Ouvrières, 1992).

Piron, M., *Aspects et Profil de la Culture Romane en Belgique* (Lille: Sciences et Lettres, 1978).

Poirier, C. (ed.), *Langue, espace, société. Les variétés du français en Amérique du Nord* (Québec: Les Presses de l'Université Laval, 1994).

Pottier, B., *Sémantique générale* (Paris: PUF, 1992).

Power, T. F., *Jules Ferry and the Renaissance of French Imperialism* (New York: Octagon Books, 1966).

Price, G., *The French Language* (London: Grant & Cutler, 1984).

Reymond, J. and Bossard, M., *Le patois vaudois. Grammaire et vocabulaire* (Lausanne: Payot, 1979).

Robertson, A. H. and Merrills, G., *Human Rights in Europe*, 3rd edn (Manchester/New York: Manchester University Press, 1993).

Roman, A., *Que sais-je?: Grammaire de l'arabe* (Paris: PUF, 1990).

Romaine, S., *The Language of Children and Adolescents* (Oxford: Blackwell, 1984).

Romaine, S., *Language in Society* (Oxford: Oxford University Press, 1994).

Rosseel, E. (ed.), *La langue française dans les pays du Bénélux: besoins et exigences.* (Brussels: AIMAV, 1982).

Rosset, T., *Les origines de la prononciation moderne étudiées au XVIIe siècle: d'après les remarques des grammairiens et les textes en patois de la banlieue parisienne* (Paris: Armand Colin, 1911).

Rossillon, P. (ed.), *Atlas de la langue française* (Paris: Bordas, 1995).

Saeed, J. I., *Semantics* (Oxford/Cambridge/Massachusetts: Blackwell, 1997).

Salhi, K. (ed.), *Francophone Voices* (Exeter: Elm Bank, 1999).

Salhi, K. (ed.), *Francophone Studies: Discourse and Identity* (Exeter: Elm Bank, 2000).

Sanders, C. (ed.), *French Today. Language in its Social Context* (Cambridge: Cambridge University Press, 1993).

Saussure, F. de, *Cours de linguistique générale* (Paris: Payot, 1972).

Sayah, M., *Bilinguisme et enseignement du français en Tunisie* (Toulouse: AMAM, 1997).

Sayah, M., *Le Nouvel État: l'héritage des siècles* vol. 1 (Tunis: Dar El Amal, 1982).

Sayah, M., *Le Nouvel État: l'héritage des siècles* vol. 2 (Tunis: Dar El Amal, 1983).

Schläpfer, R., *La Suisse aux quatre langues* (Carouge-Genève: Zoé, 1985).

Searle, J-R., *Les Actes de langage* (Paris: Hermann, 1972).

Seiler, D-L. and Knüsel, R. (eds), *Vous avez dit 'Suisse romande'? Une identité contestée: 29 personnalités s'interrogent*, 2nd edn (Lausanne: Éditions 24 Heures, 1989).

Senghor, L. S., *Ce que je crois* (Paris: Grasset, 1988).

Shaw, M. N., *International Law*, 4th edn (Cambridge: Cambridge University Press, 1997).

Shorrock, W. I., *French Imperialism in the Middle East. The Failure of Policy in Syria and Lebanon 1900–1914* (Wisconsin: Wisconsin University Press, 1976).

Singy, P., *L'image du français en Suisse romande. Une enquête sociolinguistique en Pays de Vaud* (Paris: L'Harmattan, 1996).

Spitteler, C., *Notre point de vue suisse*. Trans. C. Guilland (Carouge-Genève: Zoé, 1995).

Stanley, J., Ingram, D. and Chittick, G., *The Relationship between International Trade and Linguistic Competence* (Canberra: Australian Government Publishing Service, 1990).

Steinberg, J., *Why Switzerland?* 2nd edn (Cambridge: Cambridge University Press, 1996).

Swing, E. S., *Bilingualism and Linguistic Segregation in the Schools of Brussels* (Québec: CIRB/IRCB, 1980).

Thibault, A., *Dictionnaire suisse romand: particularités lexicales du français contemporain: une contribution au trésor des vocabulaires francophones* (Carouge-Genève: Zoé, 1997).

Tibawi, A. L., *A Modern History of Syria including Lebanon and Palestine* (London: Macmillan, 1969).

Trudgill, P., *Sociolinguistics*, 3rd edn (Harmondsworth: Penguin, 1995).

Tschoumy, J-A., *Les langues dites nationales hors de leur territoire* (Neuchâtel: Institut romand de recherches et de documentation, 1995).

Tutescu, M., *Précis de sémantique française* (Bucharest: Editura pedagogica, 1979).

Tutescu, M., *Du mot au texte* (Bucharest: Cavallioti, 1996).

Valdman, A. (ed.), *Le français hors de France* (Paris: Champion, 1979).

Veillard-Baron, H., *Les Banlieues* (Paris: Flammarion, 1996).

Vigner, G., *Lire: du texte au sens, éléments pour un apprentissage et un enseignement de la lecture* (Paris: Clé international, 1979).

Vouga, J-P. and Hodel, M. E. (eds), *La Suisse face à ses langues* (Aarau: Sauerländer, 1990).

Wagner, R-L. and Pinchon, J., *Grammaire du français classique et moderne* (Paris: Hachette, 1962).

Wakely, R. et al. (eds), *Profils d'enseignants, d'étudiants et d'institutions d'enseignement des langues vivantes de 1850 à 1950. Documents pour l'histoire du français langue étrangère ou seconde*, 15 (Paris: SIHFLES, 1995).

Walter, H., *Le Français dans tous les sens* (Paris: Robert Laffont, 1988).

Walter, H., *Le français d'ici, de là, de là-bas* (Paris: JC Lattès, 1998).

Wardhaugh, R., *Languages in Competition. Dominance, Diversity and Decline* (Oxford: Blackwell, 1987).

Weiss, F., *Jeux et activités communicatives dans la classe de langue* (Paris: Hachette, 1983).

Windisch, U., *Le Prêt-à-penser* (Lausanne: L'âge d'homme, 1990).

Windisch, U., *Les relations quotidiennes entre Romands et Suisses allemands: les cantons bilingues de Fribourg et du Valais*. 2 vols (Lausanne: Payot, 1992).

Wykes, O. and King, M. G., *Teaching Foreign Languages in Australia* (Melbourne: ACER, 1968).

Wyndham, H. S., Report of the Committee Appointed to Survey Education in New South Wales (Sydney: Government Printer, 1957).

Yacine, K., *Nedjma* (Paris: Seuil, 1970).

Yaguello, M., 'Madame la Ministre', *Petits faits de langue*, collective (Paris: Éditions du Seuil, 1998).

Yaguello, M., *Les mots et les femmes* (Paris: Payot, 1978).

Yaguello, M., *En écoutant parler la langue* (Paris: Éditions du Seuil, 1991).

Zarate, G., *Enseigner une culture étrangère* (Paris: Hachette, 1986).

Contributors

Farid Aitsiselmi is Lecturer in French Studies at the University of Bradford where he teaches French language and linguistics. His research interests include sociolinguistics and language in contemporary France with special reference to the North African migrant population. He has edited : *Black Blanc Beur: Youth Language and Identity in France* (Interface: Bradford Studies in Language, Culture and Society, Issue 5, 2000).

Nigel Armstrong teaches French and sociolinguistics in the Department of French at the University of Leeds. All current research projects focus on variation in the spoken French of the Hexagon. He has recently authored *Social and Stylistic Variation in Spoken French: A Comparative Approach* (John Benjamins, 2001) and co-edited with Kate Beeching and Cécile Bauvois, *La langue française au féminin. Le sexe et le genre affectent-ils la variation linguistique?* (l'Harmattan, 2001).

Malak Badrawi is part-time Lecturer of Middle East history at the Institute of Arabic and Islamic Studies at the University of Exeter. Her field of specialisation is modern Egypt. She has authored, *Ismail Sidqi 1875-1950: Pragmatism and Vision in Twentieth Century Egypt* (Curzon, 1996) and *Political Violence in Egypt in 1910–1925* (Curzon, 2000).

Peter Brown is Senior Lecturer in French at the Australian National University, Canberra. His research interests are in French literature and *la francophonie*, particularly concerning the Pacific. For the past decade he has been the Australian correspondent for *L'Année Francophone Internationale* and is currently a member of the *Asia–Pacific Observatoire du Français*, a project of the *Agence Universitaire de la Francophonie*.

Joy Charnley is Lecturer in French at the University of Strathclyde (Glasgow). She has published on Pierre Bayle, c17 travel literature and women writers in *Suisse romande* and is currently co-editor of the series 'Occasional Papers in Swiss Studies', Department of Modern Languages, University of Strathclyde.

Maeve Conrick is Senior Lecturer in the Department of French at the University College Cork, Ireland. Her research interests are in sociolinguistics (French in Canada, language and gender), applied linguistics (acquisition of French as L2) and Canadian studies. She has published widely in these areas in international refereed journals and in a book, *Womanspeak* (Marino Books, 1999).

Patrick Corcoran is Principal Lecturer in French at the University of Surrey Roehampton where he is Director of the Centre for Research in Francophone Studies. He is currently President of the Society for Francophone Postcolonial Studies (formerly ASCALF) and has published widely on francophone African literature. His most recent book is a critical study of Henri Lopes' *Le Pleurer-Rire* (Glasgow Introductory Guides, 2002)

Chantal Crozet is Language Educator and Applied Linguist who has worked for many years as a lecturer, researcher and consultant in language education. She is presently completing her PhD at the Australian National University in language acquisition and cross-cultural communication. Her other interests are in the areas of language teaching policy, the training of language teachers and intercultural competence.

Mikaël Jamin is completing a PhD in sociolinguistics at the University of Kent, on the phonology of *le français des cités*. He is interested in language change in progress in contemporary French, the influence of youth culture on language and social network theory. He has taught at the universities of Newcastle upon Tyne and Sunderland and has written on French slang and verlan, on: http:www.sunderland.ac.uk/-os0tmc/teci/verlan.htm/

Henri Jeanjean is Senior Lecturer in the Modern languages programme at the University of Wollongong (NSW, Australia) and teaches in various areas of French studies. His research interests are multidisciplinary and include various aspects of French society, minorities in France and their relationship with the state and other minorities in Europe. His publications include, *De l'utopie au pragmatisme?*(1992) and 'Nationalisme et Romantisme' in C. Torreilles (ed.), *L'Occitanie romantique* (C.E.L.O, Bordes, 1997), 'Les Occitanistes et l'Europe' in G. Tautil (ed.), *Camins d'Occitania: chemins d'Occitanie* (Paris, L'Harmattan, 1997).

Anne Judge is Professor of French at the University of Surrey. She has lectured and published extensively in the field of French grammar, including co-authorship of Judge & Healey, *A Reference Grammar of French* (Longman). She is also recognised and has established herself as an authority on French language policy and the institutions of the Francophone world.

Stephen Judge is Senior Lecturer in law at London Metropolitan University. He has published on English business law and is a specialist on French and English comparative company law. His research interests are in the influence of community law and the Council of Europe's Conventions on European linguistic policy particularly in respect of minority or regional languages.

Tony Liddicoat is Associate Professor in the School of Languages and Linguistics at Griffith University. His research interests include language planning and policy language issues in education, and conversation analysis. In recent years his research has focused in particular on the place of intercultural awareness in language teaching. He has published widely in these areas.

Dawn Marley is Lecturer in French at the University of Surrey. Her research interests focus on language attitudes and language and identity in France and North Africa. She has published mainly on French in Morocco, and has co-edited a volume on linguistic identities and policies in France and the French-speaking world.

Louise Maurer is Lecturer in French at the Australian National University. Her research interests are in the area of cross-cultural studies, as well as in the relationship between image and language. She is currently working on projects on the use of computer technology in the teaching of French and on the teaching of culture in the language class.

Gabrielle Parker is Professor and Dean of the School of Arts at the University of Middlesex. Her research is focused on French language policies and the politics of language. Her recent publications include 'Language Planning and language management: the case of French', in *International Journal of Francophone Studies* (2000); 'The Politics of French', in *Linguistic Identities and Policies in France and the French-speaking World*, in *AFLS/CILT* (1998) and 'French language policy in sub-Saharan Africa', M&CF *Review* (1996). She is the founder member (1992) and joint editor of the *AFLS/CILT* series: *'Current Issues in University Language Teaching'*.

Kamal Salhi is Director of the Centre for Francophone Studies at the University of Leeds. His research interests are on the politics and aesthetics of the cultural production of North and Sub-Saharan Africa and their post-colonial cultural/language policies. He has authored *The Politics and Aesthetics of Kateb Yacine* (Mellen, 1999) and edited *African Theatre for Development* (Intellect, 1997); *Francophone Voices* (Elm Bank, 1999); *Francophone Studies: Discourse and Identity* (Elm Bank, 2000). He is the founder and editor of the *International Journal of Francophone Studies*.

Mansour Sayah is *Chargé des enseignements et de recherches* at the University of Toulouse Le Mirail and pursues his research in the *Centre Interdisciplinaire des Sciences du Langage*. A specialist in French linguistics and the didactics of French as a foreign language he has particular interest in Tunisian Arabic and literary Arabic. He has authored *Bilinguisme et Enseignement du Français en Tunisie* (ANAM Toulouse, 1998), and co-edited, *Mélanges* (ANAM, 1998).

Richard Wakely is currently Head of the French Section of the School of European Languages and Cultures of the University of Edinburgh. He teaches a course on French as a national and international language, and French in Belgium has been of particular interest to him since Edinburgh became the home of its *Centre de recherches belges francophones*. He is preparing for publication a volume of proceedings from the conference *Les Belges : enregistreurs de tous les usages* held at the Centre in 2000.

Index